Organizational Change and Innovation Processes

Organizational Change and Innovation Processes

 Theory and Methods for Research

Marshall Scott Poole

Andrew H. Van de Ven

Kevin Dooley

Michael E. Holmes

OXFORD

UNIVERSITY PRESS

2000

OXFORD
UNIVERSITY PRESS

Oxford   New York
Athens   Auckland   Bangkok   Bogotá   Buenos Aires   Calcutta
Cape Town   Chennai   Dar es Salaam   Delhi   Florence   Hong Kong   Istanbul
Karachi   Kuala Lumpur   Madrid   Melbourne   Mexico City   Mumbai
Nairobi   Paris   São Paulo   Shanghai   Singapore   Taipei   Tokyo   Toronto   Warsaw

and associated companies in
Berlin   Ibadan

Copyright © 2000 by Oxford University Press

Published by Oxford University Press, Inc.
198 Madison Avenue, New York, New York 10016

Oxford is a registered trademark of Oxford University Press

Library of Congress Cataloging-in-Publication Data
Organizational change and innovation processes :
theory and methods for research /
by Marshall Scott Poole . . . [et al.].
p.   cm.
Includes bibliographical references and index.
ISBN 0-19-513198-3
1. Organizational change—Research—Methodology.
2. Industrial management—Research—Methodology.
I. Poole, Marshall Scott, 1951–
HD58.8 .O72898   2000
658.4'06'072—dc21   00-056677

1 3 5 7 9 8 6 4 2
Printed in the United States of America
on acid-free paper

Preface

THIS BOOK WAS BORN in the challenges that confronted the Minnesota Innovation Research Program, which began in 1983 with the objective of developing a process theory of innovation in organizations. Fourteen research teams, involving more than 30 faculty and doctoral students at the University of Minnesota, conducted longitudinal studies that tracked a variety of new technologies, products, services, and programs as they developed from concept to implementation in their natural field settings. Initial findings were published in *Research on the Management of Innovation: The Minnesota Studies,* edited by Andrew Van de Ven, Harold Angle, and Marshall Scott Poole (Ballinger/Harper & Row, 1989 and reissued by Oxford University Press, 2000). By documenting the historical and real-time events in the development of a wide variety of innovations, this first MIRP book provided a rich empirical database for subsequent analysis and grounded theory building.

At the time of the MIRP studies, two major tasks lay before us. First, how were we to theorize change processes? Most current theories of change did not address *how* change occurred, but rather focused on identifying *causes* of change. As we pursued our research, we became convinced that such theories were unsatisfactory because they did not take into account important characteristics of change processes, including their path dependence, the powerful influence that a single critical event often had on the direction and impacts of change, and the role of human agency in molding change according to plans or implicit models. The few theories that explicitly focused on change were also unsatisfactory because they oversimplified, typically positing relatively simple stage models of change. While such models captured some aspects of change, our studies and personal experience suggested that change processes were much more irregular and complicated than the models allowed. We became convinced that a fundamentally different explanatory framework was needed to capture change.

We found a solution in the process approach to explanation, first defined by Lawrence Mohr. The process approach attempts to account for how changes unfold over time and incorporates path dependence and the impact of critical events. Mohr's early conceptualization can be broadened by recognizing that a more general concept—a theoretical narrative—underlies process explanations, an insight we owe to the seminal work of Andrew Abbott. As we attempted to spell out the characteristics of narrative explanation, we realized that it constitutes a complementary alternative to causally based variance explanations. Another piece of the puzzle was provided by our work on process theories and motors of change, first published in a chapter of *Research on the Management of Innovation*, and elaborated in a 1995 article in *Academy of Management Review*. The multiple motors provided a range of theoretical narratives, and our analysis suggested that in many cases, more than one motor was in operation. The complexity observed in organizational processes could be explained in terms of switching from one motor to another as conditions changed or by complex, recursive interaction of two or more motors. We believe that the process approach, narrative explanation, and multiple motors of change offer a general theoretical framework that can provide new insights into change and innovation processes. We hope that this will ultimately translate into better understanding and improved practice.

The second challenge was to link these theoretical narratives to historical narratives, that is, to the actual unfolding of observed change processes. It is the task of research methodology to determine how to do this. At the outset we decided that it was important to go beyond single case studies and historical methods. While these approaches have produced profound insights, we believe that a comparative approach is more likely to help us identify the variables and processes that make a difference. We also wanted to design studies that include as many cases as possible, so that we can be confident that results generalize and are not artifacts of the cases at hand.

Turning to quantitative methods, we found that the most common and popular methods were framed around testing causal hypotheses and are not well-suited for the study of processes. These methods were designed to support the testing of hypotheses about relationships among well-defined variables, and most are not designed for important tasks required for process research, including identification of key events in an unfolding process, recognition and categorization of patterns in long series of events, evaluation of hypotheses about sequences and patterns of events or behaviors over time, linkage of multiple types of data, and evaluating hypotheses about narratives.

In the end, it became apparent that we needed methods that enable the deep, sensitive attention to details of the particular context that is traditionally associated with qualitative case studies or ethnographies, and also allowed testing specific narrative explanations on the larger samples needed to support generalization. This was a tall order, and it posed an intriguing challenge. This challenge was met by methods developed in a range of fields concerned with processes—child development, group communication, industrial engineering, occupational sociology, demography, biology, computer science, history. Methods like Markov analysis, phase mapping, and time series analysis, used properly, enable researchers to identify characteristics of event series that afford systematic specification and testing of narrative explanations. We experimented with these methods to determine how to use them in ways that retained some of the sensitivity of the narrative method, yet enabled us to systematically deal with larger and longer event sequence data in order to analyze complex processes and derive testable generalizations. We found it necessary both to extend traditional quantitative methods and to introduce some new approaches for diagnosing nonlinear dynamic patterns in our event sequence data on innovations.

While developing these methods we conducted research workshops in 1993, 1995, and 1997 at the University of Minnesota, each attended by 50–70 researchers interested in process research methods from universities throughout the United States and Europe. These workshops made us aware of a much larger community of researchers commonly interested in studying processes of organizational change but searching for methods to do so. Workshop participants encouraged us to document and distribute the process research methods we were developing. The result was this volume.

While this book is grounded in the study of organizational innovation and change processes, we believe that the theory and methods discussed here apply to all types of processes, not just those in organizations. So we hope to repay the scholars we have learned from in fields such as human development, group communication, and industrial engineering by advancing an informed view of processes that can clarify and inspire their research.

We are indebted to a number of people and organizations who supported this work. The Office of Naval Research supported the Minnesota Innovation Research Project with a grant from 1983 to 1986. The Decision, Risk and Management Science program of the National Science

Foundation, and in particular its director Arie Lewin, provided encouragement and support for the first conference that introduced these methods. The second and third conferences were sponsored by the Consortium of Centers for Organizational Research and the Strategic Management Research Center of the University of Minnesota.

Several individuals have exerted important influences on this project. Most significant was Andrew Abbott of the University of Chicago. His many articles on narrative positivism were inspirational, and this book owes a great debt to him. To Larry Mohr we owe the genesis of this project. His seminal and insightful book of twenty years ago set the stage for whatever contribution this volume holds. Dean Hewes of the University of Minnesota was an important part of two workshops, and his thinking on retroduction and mastery of Markov analysis helped us to understand their importance to our endeavors. Ken Koput contributed important insights about nonlinear modeling in our third workshop, and his thinking on this subject certainly informed our analysis of this matter. Joe McGrath of the University of Illinois read the first draft of the manuscript and provided very useful suggestions.

In preparing the book we were ably assisted by the superb professional editing of MaryBeth Branigan. Her patient review of the entire manuscript improved the clarity and style of presentation tremendously. We are truly grateful that Herbert Addison and Oxford University Press has agreed to publish our book. Herb provided us with wonderful encouragement, guidance and support in preparing this work. In his distinguished career as Oxford's executive editor of business books, Herb has made major contributions to management and organization science. He has truly made a difference.

We dedicate this book to our families and significant others. They are what make us what we are, and whatever insights there may be in this book depend on their support and inspiration.

Contents

PART I ∭ THEORY

1 Perspectives on Change and Development in Organizations

EXPLAINING ORGANIZATIONAL CHANGE has been an enduring quest of scholars in many disciplines. Change and development processes are central to such organizational phenomena as careers, group decision-making, organizational strategy formation, innovation, and interorganizational networks. Contemporary intellectual currents, exhibited in the rising interest in such topics as individual and organizational life cycles, structuration theory, and nonlinear systems thinking, echo Heraclitus's claim that "nothing is permanent save change." These positions view even seemingly stable phenomena such as industry structures, which appear to change slowly if at all, in terms of continuous processes that maintain stability under current conditions, but are capable of effecting broad, rapid change if circumstances change. They are consistent with Hernes's (1976) stricture that an adequate theory should explain stability and change in terms of a common process theory.

To understand how organizational changes unfold, researchers have borrowed many concepts, metaphors, and theories from other disciplines, ranging from child development to evolutionary biology. These include punctuated equilibrium, stage models of growth and decline, population ecology, and chaos theory. The resulting theoretical pluralism has produced intriguing insights into organizational change and developmental processes.

However, without a suitable infrastructure of research strategies and methods, such borrowing is more likely to generate metaphors than testable propositions. Testable propositions require the combination of well-defined theory with methodology appropriate to the theory. No matter how fertile their theoretical ideas, only with methods in mind can researchers generate precise, meaningful models and hypotheses.

Most current social scientific methods are not particularly well suited for research on change and development processes. Both quantitative and case methods have shortcomings. Most quantitative methods, including classical and modern measurement theories (e.g., Crocker & Algina, 1986; Cronbach, 1990) and statistical analysis using the general linear model, are designed for analysis of static patterns rather than the dynamics of change (Abbott, 1988). Case methods are more sensitive to the many nuances of change, but their major drawback is small sample size, which renders them vulnerable to sampling error and limits generalizability. While several promising approaches to multiple case analysis (e.g., Leonard-Barton, 1990; Miles & Huberman, 1984, 1994) have been developed, none afford the definitive, clear tests of hypotheses that are the hallmark of the quantitative methods.

This book provides an introduction to research methods specifically designed to support the development and evaluation of organizational process theories. Some of the ideas and methods we cover are emerging from the struggles of various researchers to make sense of mountains of process data. Others represent novel adaptations of traditional methods. In trying to place these methods in the proper context, we defined four criteria that adequate research on change and development processes should satisfy. The book is organized around these criteria.

First, *explanations of change and development should incorporate all types of forces that influence these processes.* The predominant research strategy and its methods, which Mohr (1982) called the *variance approach,* are well suited for continuous change driven by deterministic causation. However, this conceptualization of change is limited. Change and development processes are also influenced by critical incidents that may suddenly alter the course of a given case, by the particular historical context of the case, and by general formative patterns that give overall direction to development, yet do not entirely determine what happens at the microlevel. The *process approach,* first described by Mohr (1982) and enlarged here in our account of narrative explanation, is a complement to the variance approach. It offers an explanation of development and change that encompasses continuous and discontinuous causation, critical incidents, contextual effects, and effects of formative patterns. The process approach promises new and more satisfactory theories that enable researchers to express the narratives underlying organizational change processes.

However, we must address two shortcomings in most previous research on narrative in such fields as history, literature, and psychology. Most narrative studies focus on specific individuals or cases, and narrative research has tended to emphasize the idiographic over the nomothetic (Polking-horne, 1988). What is required in our case is a conception of narrative explanation that emphasizes generalizability and abstract narratives. We will explicate a process perspective that supports the discovery and testing of general theories of development and change.

A second shortcoming is the lack of processual models suitable for the study of organizations. This leads to our second criterion: *Explanations of change and development should incorporate generative mechanisms suitable for organizational contexts.* Based on Van de Ven and Poole (1995), we will delineate four fundamental motors that drive organizational change and development. These motors, and combinations of them, define general narratives that explain specific organizational processes. The typology of change motors also provides a unifying scheme to clarify similarities and differences among theories. It enables researchers to discern common points and to achieve theoretical integration that leads to a more comprehensive understanding of organizations and related phenomena.

In the long run, the best theory is only as good as its evidence. This implies a third criterion: *Research designs should capture data directly from the process through which development and change occurs.* Process theories of development and change can be adequately evaluated only if research is focused where the "action" is. In most process theories the appropriate unit of analysis is the event, the smallest meaningful unit in which change can be detected. Hence, development and change can be studied in the sequence of events an entity participates in or experiences. Events often consist of individual or collective actions, but they may also bring about changes in context that influence the developing entity. Through events the various forces that influence development and change, continuous and discontinuous, local and general, come into play. Taking the event as the basic unit of analysis requires special methods and raises problems somewhat different from those addressed by classical and modern measurement techniques, as we will see.

Along with a different type of data comes a need for different approaches to analysis, suggesting a final criterion: *Analytical methods should be able (a) to discover patterns in complex process data and (b) to evaluate process explanations.* Both discovery and evaluation are important phases of process studies. Studies of event sequences typically generate long data series which offer the opportunity to discover variations among cases. Methods are needed to help researchers work out typologies that reflect different development sequences. Event sequence data is also typically rich and volumi-nous. Methods are needed to help researchers discover patterns in complex datasets. Both typological and pattern recognition analyses afford the op-portunity for discovering new relationships and models. Testing process hy-potheses also requires specialized methods. Process theories generate pre-dictions that require the analysis of lengthy series of event data. In some cases, these predictions pertain to event-to-event (act-to-act) relationships, either causal or sequential. In other cases, the predictions may be about the series of steps or phases development follows. In still other cases, predic-tions about long-term properties of the event sequence, such as the shape of the developmental curve, are of interest. These and other predictions require methods adapted to the study of dynamics rather than statics.

These four criteria suggest the need for new methods and a revised con-ception of theory and method. This book attempts to explicate the foun-dations of a growing body of process-oriented research on organizational change and development. In so doing, we hope to encourage more re-searchers to venture into this area. The theory and methods discussed in this book are fairly abstract and at times quite difficult, so it will help to have a concrete example to follow throughout. To illustrate the different ap-proaches research on organizational processes can follow, let us now turn to an example.

CONTRASTING RESEARCH STRATEGIES

Let's take a not-so-hypothetical case of researchers interested in the role of the planning and implementation process in new business startups (Van de Ven, 1980a, b, & c). They decide to study the startup of state-funded child-care programs and are successful in gaining access and funding to support their research. They consider two different explanations for the effective-ness of new business startups. First, they hypothesize that startups that con-form to a normative model of the startup process will be more effective than those that do not. The normative model of program planning they are test-ing posits a five-step planning process:

1. *Planning Prerequisites:* Build community support; form a cohesive planning team; establish a planning policy board to ensure the pro-gram meets community needs; identify and counteract possible foes.
2. *Problem Analysis:* Conduct broad and careful assessment of commu-nity needs, with input from planning policy board, community, clients, and state and local officials.

3. *Knowledge Exploration:* Identify priority problems and alternative ways to solve them by surveying perceptions of experts in the problem area; planning board should review expert recommendations; distribute report of expert opinions to community, clients, and state and local officials.
4. *Program Design:* Design a program that realistically responds to problems identified in Phases 2 and 3; conduct workshops and problem-solving meetings with community, clients, and other agencies who have to coordinate with the program; conduct review of program by planning policy board and state and local officials; modify plan to satifsy diverse constituents.
5. *Program Implementation, Evaluation, and Operation:* Implement proposed program on a pilot basis; evaluate and fine-tune program; initiate broader scale implementation; operation and continuous evaluation and adjustment of program. (Delbecq & Van de Ven, 1971)

This model is designed to improve planning by ensuring participation of stakeholders and resource controllers, separating ideation from evaluation, retarding speedy convergence on less-effective alternatives, providing for critical review of ideas and alternatives, and ensuring an open and participatory process. The researchers hypothesize that startups that follow this sequence of phases will be more effective than those that do not because they will avoid problems that often arise and impede nascent community organizations.

The second hypothesis is that organizational characteristics of the startups will influence their effectiveness. Greiner (1972) comments that a common characteristic of unsuccessful innovations is that attempts are made to implement new programs on a large-scale and global basis. Hence, we might expect that programs that start small and gradually increase in size, number of service sites, and service provision would be more effective than those that attempt full-scale, broad implementation from the outset. A second characteristic of effective social service startups should be increasing formalization over time. Documentation of effective procedures and good record keeping are critical to certification and interorganizational relationships for public agencies, and these will gradually be built into procedure manuals. Third, a high level of staff participation should help decrease employee resistance to innovation and build employee "ownership" of the endeavor. Finally, highly qualified and talented staff would be expected to enhance startup effectiveness.

How could the researchers test these hypotheses? Three research strategies can be distinguished.

Cross-Sectional Survey

A common approach would be to conduct a single-shot survey of a large sample of state-funded childcare programs. The researchers might conduct survey interviews with directors of 300 childcare programs in several states. The interviews would gather data to indicate whether the program followed the tenets of the planning model and to gauge organizational structure. Indicators of planning include questions or indices that assess participation level, nature of board (if any) which oversees the effort, nature of the planning team (if any), degree of technical assistance for the programs, and steps taken to put the program into action. Indicators of structure include measures of size, participation, formalization, and staff characteristics. In addition, data on the effectiveness of the programs could be gathered by assessing variables such as number of units of service provided, financial independence, perceived effectiveness by peer organizations, efficiency, and number of implementation barriers or obstacles encountered.

The large sample size would ensure the inclusion of programs at a variety of stages of development. Classifying these by age and level of development would enable researchers to generate cross-sectional descriptions of programs at various stages of development. In essence, this would generate "pseudo-longitudinal" data. Process hypotheses could be tested by examining patterns across cases of different ages and at different levels of development. For example, we would expect the formalization-by-age interaction to predict effectiveness. We might also expect that effectiveness would be positively associated with amount of time devoted to problem identification/analysis behavior in young programs, and to have a weaker association in older programs.

A major strength of the single-shot cross-sectional approach is large sample size. The large sample and quantitative measurement employed in the single-shot case study enable researchers to use a whole array of statistical techniques that have been developed for parametric analysis. Careful validation of measurement instruments (e.g., Van de Ven & Ferry, 1980) and survey design ensures that data from many disparate cases is captured so that all observations are comparable and can be aggregated into a single dataset with many datapoints. This supports the clear, definitive tests of hypotheses that are a major strength of cross-sectional surveys. This design also controls for sensitization effects, since only a single questionnaire is distributed. The information this design yields about organizational change and development processes stems from a comparative analysis of cases at a single point in time, but if the general patterns conform to expectations, this type of study can provide useful evidence for a process model.

However, cross-sectional studies of change and development processes have three shortcomings. First, researchers must infer much of what has happened in the startups, because the variables used to assess processes are surrogate or summary indicators. Knowing the level of formalization of the startups and their age gives researchers an indication of whether formalization increases as startups mature, but it reveals little about how startups introduce formal structure or about the course that formalization takes. Knowing that startups which formed policy boards are more effective after one year than those which did not indicates that boards help, but it reveals little about the process by which boards were set up or about how boards interact with startups over the course of time. In general, single-shot cross-sectional data gives researchers little knowledge of the actual process that startups go through, the particular course of critical events or stages startups follow. On the basis of this design, researchers would be warranted to claim that their results are consistent with the process model, but they would not be warranted to claim that they had tested the model directly.

A second problem relates to measurement. Survey respondents must recall events which may have occurred months before. Hence, the data are subject to all the biases associated with recall. Respondents may fall prey to the tendency to remember what fits well-known patterns better than what deviates from them. They are more likely to recall events that relate to the planning model, which follows prescriptions of rational procedure, than to recall things that do not fit any larger pattern. Respondents may also supply missing parts of the pattern. Additional biases may be introduced by respondents' self-presentation efforts, or by their attempts to reconstruct events to fit their own theories about what "went right" or "went wrong."

Third, because there are no longitudinal data, inferences about causality are necessarily weak. One of the canons of causal inference is that the cause must be shown to precede the effect, and it is impossible to determine whether this is the case from single-shot data. The only temporal inferences that can be drawn are based on the comparison among programs of different ages. These causal claims, however, are weakened by cohort effects. It is possible that the four-year-old programs experienced very different economic and social historical situation than did the one-year-old programs in the sample. As a result, the two sets of programs are subject to a very different constellation of causal forces, and any inferences about causality are challenged by alternative explanations.

Because it does not give researchers direct access to the process, the single-shot cross-sectional design affords limited insight into change processes. Relationships are explained with stories which describe the processes that *should be occurring* to generate the relationships. However, the stories themselves cannot be evaluated without direct research on the process itself. They are speculative, and the only evidence researchers can provide for these stories is to measure surrogate variables which tap static results of the stories. To illuminate the stories that articulate the change process, a longitudinal design must be employed.

Panel Survey

This longitudinal survey design avoids some of the limitations of the single-shot survey. As Van de Ven (1980a) did in his study of Texas child care organizations, this design gathers data at three or more points in time using the same survey interview described above. Respondents are asked only to recall events for the period between survey administrations. The sample size for this design might have to be somewhat smaller than the ambitious 300 envisioned for the single-shot study, because it would take extensive resources to garner such a large sample three times (Van de Ven's panel study examined 14 organizations). Even if the researchers started with 300 organizations, by the third wave they would have a good deal fewer because some organizations would go out of existence and others would decide that participation was no longer in their best interest.

The longitudinal panel survey supports stronger causal claims than the single-shot cross-sectional survey, because longitudinal data enables investigators to establish temporal precedence, a requirement of causal analysis. It also gives researchers better insight into the nature of the processes involved in startups. This design yields three or more cross-sectional "snapshots" of the process, so researchers can directly track changes in organizations during startup. Theories about the nature of the process can be evaluated against longitudinal patterns. For example, to determine whether the startups followed the five-step planning process, researchers could assess whether successive waves of data showed progress through the steps. If the planning process was followed from initiation, wave one data would reflect problem definition and diagnosis activity, wave two solution development and testing activity, and wave three implementation activity.

By tracking the same cases across time, researchers become aware of changes they might not notice in the single-shot design. For example, researchers might find two or more different stage patterns: one pattern might follow the hypothesized sequence, another might start with solution development and implementation and then diagnose the situation only as problems arose, while a third might skip the stage setting and problem diagnosis stages and commence from knowledge exploration (Nutt's [1984b] research uncovered a pattern quite similar to the second one in strategic decision making, which he labeled the "off-the-shelf" approach).

This design shares with the single-shot cross-sectional study the advantages of large sample size and standardized, controlled measurement of variables. Statistical methods for testing causal relationships over longitudinal data are well developed. Provided they have chosen the intervals between observations judiciously, researchers have a good chance of identifying important temporal patterns.

However, longitudinal panel designs are still subject to some important limitations. While gathering data at three or more points in time does get researchers closer to processes, they must still infer what occurred between measurements. As is the case for single shot, cross-sectional designs, process explanations of change and development rely on stories which explicate *what should happen if the hypothesized relationships held*. In this instance, the stories concern the processes that should be occurring between time A and time B if certain relationships are found. These stories are still speculative, even if all the evidence is consistent with them, because the researcher has no way to unpack the "black box" of events that are occurring to move the organization from time A to time B.

As we have noted, an important advantage of the longitudinal design over the cross-sectional design is that it yields a more differentiated account of development or change that is not subject to cohort effects. However, both designs may miss important aspects of the process that their instruments are not designed to measure. Researchers employing either design must be to some extent clairvoyants, in that they must anticipate which variables are important enough to measure. The good news in this is that theory must guide the selection of variables. The bad news is that most information not anticipated by the researchers' theory is lost, because no provision is made for gathering it. Important information about the process may also be lost if the researcher has not chosen the proper temporal interval between measurements. It is possible that a conclusion of "no change" based on measurements six months apart might instead be interpreted as "moderate change," if the interval were set at eight months. Since most theories do not give much guidance as to what interval should transpire between measurements, this is a thorny problem for longitudinal surveys.

The only way to overcome these limitations is to get much closer to the changing phenomena and to measure at shorter intervals. If researchers' observations occur on the same metric as the change process unfolds, that is, through significant events, then the researchers are likely to have much more direct access to the "story" of the change process. To do this researchers must employ a third research strategy.

PROCESS STUDY

In this research strategy, investigators gather data that indicate how the process unfolds over time. Some of this data could be in the form of quantitative measurements of key variables, but other data would consist of detailed descriptions of the events that constituted change and development of the entity under study. Based on these descriptions, researchers construct a timeline of events that were significant in the development and change process. Each case will have a unique timeline, and real or apparent differences among cases are a major focus of the study. Instead of treating unique features of a case as sampling error, a process study attempts to identify the circumstances that created the particular twists and turns in each case. The flow of events and the conjunctions of causal forces that move the developing entity through its sequence are captured in a narrative that explains the case.

Of course, it is important to go beyond explaining a single case. A process study aims to find a general narrative that offers a common explanation for a range of cases. Finding such a general narrative requires matching specific cases to the general pattern. Cases that follow the same pattern may differ, however, in a number of respects. The same type of event may have a different duration in different cases; for example, one startup may consult with an expert for only one day, while another may consult with experts for a period of months as it attempts to define a workable program. Events that perform no function relevant to the startup may occur in one case, but not in another; these "nuisance" events, which neither help nor hinder the startup, make the two cases look different, but are unlikely to introduce substantive differences between cases. One case may have many more events than another, but the two may display similar overall patterns after they are normalized to the same length. Methods of analysis that can identify or test for common patterns are important tools in process research.

Process analysis takes the history of each case seriously. One of its guiding assumptions is path-dependence, that an entity's current state can be understood only in terms of the history of events that preceded it. Path dependence implies that each case may have a somewhat different set of forces acting on it, depending on the specific events that occur during its development. Hence, explanation in process theories does not rely only on causal diagrams, but rather on the narrative that explains what led to what. The narrative captures the particular causal factors that influenced the case, the order in which they occurred, and how long they operated.

For example, if the social service startups unfold according to the narrative implied in the five-stage implementation model, community conflict is likely to have a strong effect on the startup in stages one and two because it will interfere with development of a clear picture of community needs and with the formation of a board. The influence of community conflict will wane once the startup reaches stage three, because the change unit will be consulting outside experts and focusing on locating a plausible solution. Community conflict will wax strong in stage four, since community constituencies must be involved in design and testing of the program. And, in the final stage, community conflict will move into the "background" as a less important causal force, but it might once again loom larger, given the proper conjunction of events.

The narrative provides a larger frame that lends coherency to the event sequence and to the causal forces that come to bear through these events. Narratives give a sense of the whole, the "big picture" that gives individual events and causes their significance. Narratives tell in abstracted form how the entity got from point a to point b to point c on the timeline. To the extent that researchers can find narrative patterns which transcend individual cases, they move to the level of scientific explanation, which depends on generality.

A process study not only supports causal inferences, but also has the additional advantage of enabling researchers to trace the mediating steps through which causes act. In principle, researchers can track how forces or influences initiated in one event are transmitted or dissipated in subsequent events. They can also trace how conjunctions of events produce interactions among causal factors that build momentum or lead to decay in the developmental process. These moves can greatly enhance the precision of tests of developmental models.

Another advantage of the process strategy is that in some cases there is sufficient information to determine the weights that should be accorded to various events and the causes embedded in them. Researchers can use the rich information gathered by this design to identify critical events—"turning points"—in the process under study, and subsequent analysis can establish the forces or influences that these events set into motion. Hence, rather than according all events and causes equal status or sorting them out statistically into rough precedence orders, researchers can make much finer discriminations concerning the importance of specific events and their associated causal factors.

The rich data afforded by process analysis opens the door to unexpected or unplanned-for findings. Unanticipated factors or issues may be uncovered, and these may lead to the identification of novel developmental patterns. The level of detail in event sequence data is much greater than that provided by cross-sectional or panel survey data. As a result, the possibility of surprise is much stronger in process research. Further, different variants and deviations from expected patterns can be identified, facilitating the creation of typologies of development and change patterns.

In process research sample size is determined by *the number of events observed over time* on a relatively small number of cases, whereas in cross-sectional and panel studies sample size is determined by *the number of cases observed*. Process studies emphasize temporal development, while cross-sectional studies emphasize comparisons at a given time. The intensive longitudinal data collection efforts required to sample and observe numerous events over time constrains a researcher's ability to examine many cases. As a result, studies of temporal processes do not enable researchers to track as many cases as commonly observed in cross-sectional and longitudinal panel surveys. Depth of analysis takes the place of large samples in process research.

A second issue in the process strategy pertains to how to cope with the massive amounts of data it generates. In principle, this data allows greater discrimination and enhances discovery of new patterns, but in practice, it is a challenge to find the forest in the huge stand of trees. Rich data makes a wide variety of patterns possible, and researchers must find ways to sort out the significant from the incidental. Development of suitable methods for process research is just beginning and forms the main subject of this book.

How do the three research strategies relate to each other? Is one preferable to another? Can they coexist? We now turn to these complicated questions.

RELATIONSHIPS AMONG THE THREE STRATEGIES

Rather than advocating the process strategy over the other two, we believe that the three approaches can be complementary. As Table 1.1 shows, each strategy has strengths that compensate for weaknesses in the others, but no strategy has an across-the-board advantage.

Table 1.1   Comparison of Research Designs for the Study of Change and Development Processes

DESIGN	STRENGTHS	WEAKNESSES
Cross-Sectional	Large sample size No history effects Limited sensitization effects Systematic, valid measurement Measurement facilitates quantitative analysis	No direct access to process Reliance on recall Weak causal inference
Panel	Large sample size Systematic, valid measurement Measurement facilitates quantitative analysis Stronger causal inference	History effects possible Sensitization effects possible Only sporadic observation of process Reliance on recall Time interval between measurements usually arbitrary
Process	Strong causal inference Access to detail of process Ability to weight individual causal factors Possibility of unexpected discoveries	History effects possible Small sample size Must transform event data into format suitable for quantitative analysis Massive data analysis task

Any well-specified theory of change or development can generate predictions which can be tested in cross-sectional or longitudinal research. For example, the program startup model posited that programs with citizen boards would be more effective and survive longer than those without boards. Further, if the implementation model holds, then we should expect that respondents would report more problem definition and diagnosis activity at the beginning of a startup than later on, more design and expert consultation at the midpoint than in the beginning or ending phases of the startup, and more testing and implementation activity in the ending phase than in the first two. Cross-sectional and longitudinal survey strategies are well suited for testing these types of predictions. In general terms, the first two research strategies can test predictions about (a) conditions that are necessary for a process to occur, (b) social or organizational structures generated by a process, (c) global descriptions or perceptions of the process, and (d) accumulating outcomes of the process.

Cross-sectional and longitudinal studies yield only indirect evidence for process models, but they have an important place in process research because they offer a reliable, "first-cut" evaluation of whether a given model is worth pursuing. Strengths of the two survey designs, including large sample size, control through design, and the ability to assess measurement adequacy eliminate a number of confounds and competing explanations. In view of the extensive time and effort involved in a process study and the difficulty in coping with the large quantities of data generated by process research, it is very useful to have strong preliminary evidence that rules out some models and supports others. Our judgment is that if a process theory has sufficient explanatory power to be of interest to us, its operation will probably be reflected in surrogate variables that can be gauged in surveys.

However, evidence from cross-sectional or longitudinal studies is not sufficient. To understand development and change processes it is necessary to study directly the actions and events that enact the process as it unfolds. The process strategy tests the stories created to support the conclusions of cross-sectional and longitudinal studies. Process studies also enable researchers to discover novel patterns and influences, leading to improved theories. Direct observation and analysis of change and development processes must be the final arbiter in process research.

At the pragmatic level, then, it is evident that the three research strategies may be complementary and have synergistic potential. However, the three strategies imply very different modes of thinking about process. It is useful to consider different conceptualizations of process and their connections to the three strategies.

THREE CONCEPTIONS OF PROCESS

We can distinguish three ways in which "process" has been used in organizational research (Van de Ven & Poole, 1995): (a) as a logic that explains a causal relationship between independent and dependent variables, (b) as a category of concepts or variables that refer to actions of individuals or organizations, and (c) as a sequence of events that describe how things change over time. The three research strategies have affinities to different conceptions of process.

PROCESS AS EXPLANATION FOR A VARIANCE THEORY

In terms of an input-process-output model, the first definition uses a process logic to explain a causal relationship between observed inputs (independent variables) and outcomes (dependent variables) in a variance theory, as discussed by Mohr (1982). In this usage, a process story or logic is used to explain why an independent (input) variable exerts a causal influence on a dependent (outcome) variable, but there is no direct observation of the process. For example, to explain why an increase in organization size increases structural differentiation at a decreasing rate, Blau and Schoenherr (1971) invoked a process story that describes the sequence of events in which labor is progressively divided as additional personnel are hired with different skills in an organization.

In general, process explanations are commonly used to explain causation between independent and dependent variables. But, as Van de Ven and Huber (1990) discuss, such process explanations typically entail highly restrictive and unrealistic assumptions about the actual nature of events in organizations. One way to improve the robustness of process explanations in variance theories is to explicitly observe the process argument that is assumed to explain why an independent variable causes a dependent variable. To do so requires opening the proverbial "black box" between inputs and outcomes, and conducting direct observation of process. This involves a transition to the second view of process.

PROCESS AS A CATEGORY OF CONCEPTS

The second and most frequently used meaning of process is as a category of concepts of individual and organizational actions, such as communication frequency, work flows, decision making techniques, as well as strategy formulation, implementation, and corporate venturing. In this usage, process refers to a category of concepts that can be distinguished from other categories of concepts, such as organizational environment, structure, and performance. Like these other categories, process concepts are operationalized as constructs and measured as fixed entities (variables), the attributes of which can vary along numerical scales from low to high.

Studies that adopt this definition of process typically examine research questions dealing with the antecedents or consequences of organizational changes. These questions call for a variance theory explanation of the causal factors (independent variables) that statistically explain variations in some outcome criteria (dependent variables). Process variables are assumed to mediate or to moderate the causal relationships between input and outcome variables. Special tests for mediating and moderating relationships are conducted to clarify the role of process variables in the theory (e.g., Baron & Kenny, 1986; James & Brett, 1984). For example, a typical formulation of the research question might be: "Does having a citizen advisory board to oversee a startup social service program (an antecedent factor) increase participation of stakeholders and boundary spanning (mediating process factors), which increase organizational effectiveness and likelihood of survival (the consequent outcomes)? To answer this question, existence of a board, stakeholder participation, and program effectiveness are operationalized as exogenous independent, endogenous independent (mediating), and dependent variables, respectively, which are measured on numerical scales at different points in time. Changes in states of these variables can be calculated as the differences between scores obtained at various points in time on each variable. The researcher can then use statistical techniques to determine how board activity precedes changes in stakeholder participation, which in turn precede corresponding changes in a lagged program effectiveness variable.

Such studies of the mediating relationship of participation level between advisory board and startup effectiveness imply at a conceptual level that a sequence of activities or events go on in establishing and engaging an advisory board and in definition, design, and implementation of social program startups. However, these activities or events are not directly examined (as they are in the third definition of process, below). Instead, these process constructs are operationalized as variables. Abbott (1988) argues that this transforms the constructs into attributes of fixed entities that interact, in causal or actual time, to create outcomes, themselves measurable as attributes of the fixed entities. The variable attributes have only one causal meaning (one pattern of effects) in a given study. As a consequence, when process constructs are represented into this entities/attributes model of reality, one can only measure *if,* not *how,* a change occurred in a variable measured at different points in time. To understand how a change occurred requires a story that narrates the sequence of events that unfold over time.

In response, researchers wedded to defining process as a category of concepts may argue that one can decompose the innovation process into a series of input-process-output analyses by viewing each event as a change in a variable (i.e., as the difference between nonexistence at the beginning state and existence at the ending state of each event) and then determining whether state transitions are explained by some other variables (such as stakeholder participation or board activity). From this perspective, events represent changes in process and output variables in an input-process-output model and the essential influence can be captured through measuring these variables.

However, if the research question is *how*, not *if*, a change occurred, we will need a narrative that encapsulates the sequence of events that unfolded as an innovation emerged. Once the sequence or pattern of events in a developmental process is found to exist, one can turn to questions about the causes or consequences of events within the process pattern. Thus, to understand how an organizational change occurs, researchers should alter their typical methods of analysis. Rather than first generalize in terms of variables, researchers should first generalize in terms of a narrative history or a story. Only in this way will the key properties of order and sequence of events be preserved in making theoretical generalizations about processes of organizational change.

PROCESS AS A DEVELOPMENTAL EVENT SEQUENCE

The third, and least understood, meaning of process is a coherent sequence of events or activities that describe how things change over time. This sequence of events can represent any process, from a cognitive train of thought or an underlying pattern of psychological transitions in individuals as they deal with an issue, to a series of actions and decisions taken in a strategic planning group, to the events occurring during an organizational reengineering effort. Whereas the second definition of process examines changes in variables over time, the third definition of process takes a historical developmental perspective, and focuses on the sequences of incidents, activities, or stages that unfold over the duration of a central subject's existence. Table 1.2 exemplifies this third meaning of process by outlining a sample of well-known developmental process models pertaining to strategic decision making (Cohen, March, & Olsen, 1972; Mintzberg Raisinghani, & Theoret, 1976; Quinn, 1980), strategic planning (Gluck, Kaufman, & Walleck, 1980; Lorange, 1980), and organization development (Greiner, 1972; Scott, 1971).

While the process models in Table 1.2 are concerned with the development of very different things, they are strikingly similar in form. In contrast with the second meaning of process as a category of variables, variables are not the centerpiece of the process models in Table 1.2. Instead, the central focus of developmental process models is on progressions (i.e., the nature, sequence, and order) of activities or events that an organizational entity undergoes as it changes over time. As the table exemplifies, a linear sequence of stages or phases of development is a common form of progression in these process models. For example, a rational process of decision making is typically viewed as a sequence of separable stages (e.g., need recognition,

Table 1.2 Stage Models of Development in Organizational Studies

AUTHORS AND SUMMARIES	BEGINNING ▶	ACTIVITY PHASES OR STAGES ▶	END ▶
STRATEGIC DECISION MODELS			
Mintzberg et al. (1976) Field study of 25 strategic, unstructured decision process	1. Identification phase *Decision recognition routine* *Diagnosis routine*	2. Development phase *Search routine* *Design routine*	3. Selection phase *Screen routine* *Evaluation-choice routine* *Authorization routine*
Cohen, March, and Olsen (1972) Garbage can model of decision making		Decisions are probabilistic intersections of relatively independent streams within organizations of: *choices* ⋯⋯ *problems* ⋯⋯ *solutions* ⋯⋯ *energy of participant* ⋯⋯	▲ ▲ ▲ ▲
Quinn (1980) Case studies of nine major corporations	Fourteen process stages beginning with need sensing and leading to commitment to control systems. Flow is generally in sequence but may not be orderly or discrete. Some of the process stages are the following: 1. Sense need 2. Develop awareness and understanding	3. Develop partial solutions 4. Increase support 5. Build consensus	6. Formal Commitment

Strategic Planning Models

Gluck, Kaufman and Walleck (1980)
Study of formal planning systems in 120 companies

1. Basic financial planning
   meet budget
2. Forecast-based planning
   predict the future
3. Externally oriented planning
   think strategically
4. Strategic management
   create the future

Lorange (1980)
Normative model of corporate strategic planning

1. Objective setting
   identify relevant strategic alternatives
2. Strategic programming
   develop programs for achieving chosen objectives
3. Budgeting
   establish detailed action program for near term
4. Monitoring
   measure progress towards achieving strategies
5. Rewards
   establish incentives to motivate goal achievement

Organization Development Models

Scott (1971)
Stages of corporate development

1. Single product, channel, and entrepreneurial
2. Single product, channel, and functional structure
3. Multiple products, channels, and divisionalized structure

Greiner (1972)
Stages of organizational growth through evolution and revolution

1. Growth through creativity
   Leadership crisis
2. Growth through direction
   Autonomy crisis
3. Growth through delegation
   Control crisis
4. Growth through coordination
   Red tape crisis
5. Growth through collaboration
   Crisis of ??

search, screen, and choice activities) ordered in time and with transition routines to make adjustments between stages (March & Simon, 1958).

A second characteristic of most models in Table 1.2 underscores the need to develop methods for the study of process. With the exception of Cohen, March, and Olsen's (1972) garbage can, all the other process models were developed inductively based on cross-sectional observations or retrospective case histories in a variety of companies. The stages or phases of activities in each model were inferred either from company historical self-reports or by categorizing cohorts of companies into the stages or phases. In no instance was any one company or organizational unit actually observed over time to go through all the stages or phases of a model. Thus, there is a great need for systematic longitudinal research to substantiate and elaborate these process models of development.

DEFINITIONS OF PROCESS AND RESEARCH STRATEGY

It should be clear that the first two definitions of process are most compatible with the cross-sectional and longitudinal survey strategies, while the third definition is most compatible with the process strategy. Hence, if research guided by the third definition is most likely to yield meaningful insights into development and change—and we believe it is—then the process research strategy is an essential part of any program of research in this area.

However, the other two definitions also have their own parts to play in process research. To understand their contribution, it is useful to map the three definitions into each other. The third definition of process can be mapped into the second (which regards process as a category of concepts and variables referring to individual or organizational actions) by defining variables that describe attributes of the event sequence. For example, event sequences can be described in terms of the property of cyclicity, which refers to the degree to which sequences of events repeat over time. On the second view of process, cyclicity would be a variable describing the process occurring between inputs and outputs. To illustrate, we might predict that the greater the political opposition to a social service startup (an independent input variable), the greater the cycling through the stages of the planning model (a mediating process variable). In turn, we might predict that the number of cycles through the planning model is negatively related to the time taken for the startup to achieve financial independence (an outcome variable). These predictions encapsulate global descriptions of the process that can be tested with traditional variable-analytic methodologies.

The third definition can also be mapped into the first one (which views process as a logic explaining causal relationships between independent and dependent variables) by distilling the general narrative from the event sequence to create a "story" that accounts for the impact of a variable earlier in the sequence on subsequent dependent variables. For example, one general narrative that would serve as a good story posits that creating a citizen's advisory board enhances the effectiveness of startup programs by increasing boundary spanning. Members of an effective advisory board would circulate through the community, collecting intelligence about problems and opportunities, which they would then bring to the board and use to ground policy mandates for the program. This circulation would also "stir up" those interested in the program, and they would interact with development team and offer feedback and suggestions. Elements of this interested audience would also form the first clientele for the program, ensuring robust usage and possibly even the critical mass of clients needed to get the program to "takeoff" phase.

Mapping from the third to the first and second views of process involves "simplification" of the event sequence either by summarizing it into variables or by translating it into a general story. However, mapping in the "opposite" direction, from the first and second to the third views, is indeterminate, because there is less information in the first and second descriptions of process than in the third. In principle, a very large number of specific event sequences are consistent with any general process description derived under the first or second definitions of process. With only the resources of theory, there is no way to move directly from a process description cast in either the first or second views to a description consistent with the third definition. At best, the information in the first or second definitions can be used as parameters to guide the direct contact with process data that is necessary to create an event-level description.

One implication is that the process research strategy is not just desirable, but *essential* to develop adequate theories of process. As we concluded in discussing research pragmatics, direct study of the process must be the final arbiter of process theories. A second implication is that the first and second views of process contribute by suggesting parameters or boundaries for the process research strategy. They indicate the most promising subset of all possible process descriptions, thereby greatly reducing the work involved in direct study of the process.

A more sobering implication derives from tendencies currently at work in the organizational research community. Methods for conducting research driven by the first two definitions of process are much more accessible and much better disseminated than are methods for conducting event-level process research. As currently conceived, courses in theory construction, research design, and statistics emphasize methods best-suited for analyzing correlational and causal relationships among variables. They have much less to say about the analysis of event sequences or narrative models. With no straightforward alternatives, the dominant tendency is to frame process questions in terms of the first or second definitions rather than the third. This reduction of processes to variables or speculative stories so dominates thinking on the subject that researchers have generally been satisfied with what current methods and research strategies afford, and relatively few venture to attempt direct study of processes.

This tendency is understandable given the general dearth of process methods in the social sciences. However, several specialized areas of study, including quantitative history, developmental sociology, child development, group communication, and organizational innovation, have worked out methods applicable to process research. This book is dedicated to laying a theoretical groundwork for these methods and to describing how they might be used in the study of organizational change and development processes.

WHY DO PROCESS RESEARCH?

It is evident from our description that a process study is quite demanding. Researchers must gather masses of data over extended periods of time, derive an event sequence from this data, code events, analyze complicated data structures, and employ a very different mode of explanation. Why should we do this when traditional, widely accepted approaches require less time and effort?

This entire chapter, in a sense, makes an argument for the process approach, and it is useful to put some of the benefits noted here into perspective by organizing them under three general advantages of the process approach. *First, the process approach offers a flexible mode of inquiry that is ideally suited to explore critical features of change and development.* When undertaking a process study, researchers focus directly on the details of the change or development process, the stream of events through which the process unfolds. This fine-grained view affords researchers the ability to identify and explore the path the process follows, taking into account path-dependence. As succeeding chapters will show, multiple theories of the process can be compared using the rich event sequence data, and this enables researchers to work toward an adequate model by ruling out some theories in favor of others. It also encourages the development of "hybrid" theories that combine two or more explanations of development and change. The fine-grained view afforded by the process approach also opens up the possibility of discovering new patterns which have not been previously considered. The flexibility of the process approach is illustrated, finally, by the fact that variance-based analyses can be conducted on data derived in process studies (whereas process research cannot utilize data from variance studies). In view of the complexity of organizational change and development processes, the more flexible the approach taken, the more likely research will develop useful theories that are commensurate with the phenomenon.

A second advantage of the process approach is that it completes variance theories. Variance theories depend on stories or narratives that recount why variables are related to one another and how causal processes unfold. However, important aspects of these stories often remain untested and unexplored because the variance approach is not geared to study the essential components of stories, their narrative structure, and the uneven impact of causal factors on the narrative. Variance research strategies can be used to investigate such aspects of narratives as the assumptions underlying a story—for example, that planning policy boards are active in the initial period of program startup—and the consequences of a narrative—for example, that startups with active planning policy boards are more effective than those without. However, variance research is not suited for following the flow of the story or for identification of temporal structure in this flow—for example, the phase sequence through which the startup progresses. In contrast, the process strategy is designed to directly interrogate the structure and implications of stories. Its goal is to identify the form of narratives and their generative mechanisms and to test their plausibility and generality. And because it develops specific, systematic procedures for evaluating explanations against plausible alternatives, the process research approach does not sacrifice the rigor normally associated with variance research. As such, process research is an important complement to variance research. Indeed, insofar as we believe that the story is *the* most important aspect of a variance theory, process research is the most important and fundamental type of research endeavor.

A third advantage of the process approach is that it develops a social scientific explanation that acknowledges the human hand in development and change. Actors' decisions and plans play an important role in organizational change and development processes not only because they have immediate causal impact on what people do, but also because these plans and choices are premised on goals or visions of what the final product will be. Its ability to conceive of and bring into being actions and structures that conform to a preordained form or purpose distinguishes human action from the effects of inanimate or suprahuman forces. The process approach explicitly incorporates explanations based on form and purpose. It does not, however, presume that such explanations must be cast up in unique, idiographic accounts. The goal of the process approach is to develop general explanations, and it stresses systematic investigation and evaluation of narrative explanations.

Of course, no brief hymn to the benefits of any approach should be sufficient to win conversion. This book is intended to convince readers of the virtues of the process approach by elaborating its theoretical and methodological stance and to promote process research by introducing specific methods for collecting and analyzing process data.

PLAN OF THE BOOK

This book is divided into two parts. In the first, we develop theoretical underpinnings of process research. This chapter has compared three different approaches to research and the corresponding definitions of process. We have attempted to motivate the need for process research that is richer and more definitive than the most commonly used social scientific methods allow. Chapters 2 and 3 take this argument a step further and introduce a theoretical framework for process research.

Chapter 2 explicates the variance approach, the predominant theoretical paradigm in the social sciences, and contrasts it with the process approach. Following on the themes of this chapter, we believe that variance and process approaches are complementary and that each can illuminate organizational change and development. Ultimately, however, explanation of change and development processes will drive us to a narrative explanation, which can be mapped onto variance models for purposes of research.

Chapter 3 introduces an integrative framework that develops a number of options for process theories. Based on Van de Ven and Poole (1995), it explicates four basic types of process theories that explain how and why change unfolds in social or biological entities. These four types represent fundamentally different event sequences and generative mechanisms—we will call them "motors"—to explain how and why changes unfold. These four ideal type process theories form a typology if we distinguish the level and mode of change to which each theory applies. This typology is useful for understanding a variety of specific theories of change processes in organizations. Our contention is that specific theories of organizational change and development are built from one or more of the four basic types. While some theories express one of the four motors, in other cases they are predicated on the interplay of two or more motors. Narrative explanation and the four motors, respectively, describe the form and content of developmental and change theories. Together they suggest requirements for methods adequate to the task of process research.

The second, and longer, section of this book deals with how to do process research. Chapter 4 provides an overview of process research methods and introduces a dataset that will be used to illustrate process research applications. Chapter 5 is concerned with research design. We discuss alternative process research designs and issues that should be considered in the design phase. Chapter 5 also considers how to gather event data and the reliability and validity of such data.

Once the researcher has event sequence data, attention turns to analysis, and in chapters 6 through 9 we introduce four methods for the analysis of process data. These methods are presented in order of increasing scope of analysis.

Chapter 6 describes the use of Markov models and their relatives to model event-to-event relations. These models map event patterns at the microlevel, facilitating both descriptive and causal analysis. They help researchers uncover recurrent event sequences that describe larger dynamics; as these dynamics change, so too the patterns change, and Markov models can divulge significant changes. The description of event patterns can also be used to test hypotheses about narratives or the motors or other causal forces that drive them.

In chapter 7 we move to a more global level of analysis and consider the use of phase analysis. Phases are molar patterns of events that exhibit developmental progressions. Phase analysis allows description of developmental patterns and comparison of these patterns to those displayed by developmental motors or more complex theories. It also supports creation of typologies of developmental patterns that classify variants of ideal models.

Chapter 8 describes event time series models, which enable researchers to describe and to test hypotheses about whole event sequences or major segments of them. Time series models can be used in process studies to describe long-term developmental patterns, to uncover causal and other types of relationships among developmental constructs, and to test the plausibility of individual generative mechanisms or motors.

Chapter 9 introduces and applies recent advances in the theory and methods of nonlinear dynamic systems to process research. It discusses how to identify whether an observed pattern in an event time series reflects either (a) an orderly periodic progression of stages or phases, (b) a random sequence of chance "blind" events, or (c) a seemingly random process of chaotic or colored noise events. The chapter introduces and exemplifies a number of new diagnostic methods to empirically distinguish periodic, chaotic, colored noise, and truly random patterns in event time series data. Knowing what pattern exists in an event time series is important for knowing what types of models are appropriate to explain the observed dynamics.

Chapter 10 develops a summary considering how the methods enable researchers to build process theories, to test generative motors, and to discover novel patterns that inform later theorizing. This chapter also considers some general properties that process methodologies must have.

The four methods discussed here clearly do not exhaust the repertoire. Although modest in scope, they provide a foundation for guiding researchers in studying processes of change and development in organizations. Undertaking such studies will, no doubt, stimulate the development and application of other methods.

In 1980 John Kimberly wrote:

> I am convinced that the generally moribund state of much current organizational theory and research is owing to the lack of appreciation of the role of history in, and the effects of context on, organizational life. And I believe that there is a tight coupling in science between content of understanding and method for understanding. (p. 13)

We believe that the process approach and the methods elaborated in this book address the malaise Kimberly describes. We hope this book will inspire others to take the challenging but rewarding path of process research.

2 Process Theories and Narrative Explanation

WHILE THE VARIANCE APPROACH offers good explanations of continuous change driven by deterministic causation, this is a limited way to conceptualize change and development. It overlooks many critical and interesting aspects of change processes. However, because most organizational scholars have been taught a version of social science that depends on variance methods and because methods for narrative research are not well developed, researchers tend to conceptualize process problems in variance terms. One can see the "law of the hammer" in operation here: Give a child a hammer, and everything seems made to be hit; give a social scientist variables and the general linear model, and everything seems made to be factored, regressed, and fit.

Consider some alternatives to the variance approach. History conceives of the past in terms of successions of events. Successions are explained by historical narratives that indicate the significance of the events and the forces—human and otherwise—which influenced them. While some causal forces operate continuously, others influence the sequence of events only at particular points in time. For example, it makes no sense to say that Peter the Great caused the cold war; he had been dead for centuries before it started, and any direct causal influence would be impossible. However, Peter the Great took actions that set into motion historical events that promoted the unification and modernization of Russia. Without Peter, it is possible that Russia would have developed differently and that the cold war would not have occurred. Peter's actions exerted an influence in this case, but it is not the type of direct, continuous causal influence that most variable-based social science theories rely on.

Biology explains human development partly in terms of chemical fields and physical processes that operate continuously to shape the embryo. But there is also a preexisting genetic blueprint in the fertilized egg. This blueprint does not cause the organism to emerge, but provides a form or code that is enacted through biological, chemical, and physical processes. Biological development is not captured by continuous changes only, but in a series of stages or phases that mark qualitative differences in the organism. As in history, the direction of development is shaped by the context in which the developing entity lives and the particular conjunctions of forces that come together at critical developmental junctures. Depending on the forces operating at a given nexus, one embryo is set on a course for a healthy birth, while another develops spinal bifida.

Developmental psychologists and historical sociologists, too, lean heavily on the concept of stages or phases in their depictions of psychic or societal development. Indeed, the problem of how quantitative change may result in qualitative change—or if indeed it can—has been central at least since the writings of Marx. Both disciplines also acknowledge the importance of "idiographic" cases that recount the life history of individuals or societies in order to grasp the variety of individuals and the impact of multiple influences on actual cases.

These alternative perspectives suggest that in addition to continuity and calculus, our theories of change and development must be able to encompass discrete events, qualitative difference, conjunctions, context, intermittent causality, and formative influences. The *process approach* employs narrative explanation that notes the contributions actions and events make to a particular outcome and then configures these parts into a whole episode (Polkinghorne, 1988). It enables us to address both qualitative and quantitative aspects of development and change. Narrative explanation involves different assumptions about the relationships among constructs and the nature of explanation than does variance explanation. This chapter will explicate the process approach and the theoretical and empirical requirements for employing narrative explanation in research. We will also contrast process and variance approaches in order to highlight the nature of narrative explanations.

VARIANCE AND PROCESS APPROACHES

Several scholars have elaborated a distinction between two very different approaches to social science. Mohr (1982) first distinguished variance and process theories in the explanation of organizational behavior. In developing a formalism for the representation of social action, Abell (1987) contrasted variance and narrative approaches. Abbott (1984, 1990) compared stochastic and narrative explanations in sociology. Polkinghorne (1988) presents a general introduction to theories of narrative in the human sciences, in which he highlights differences between narrative explanation and traditional social science. The common thread running through these works is the difference between scientific explanations cast in terms of independent variables causing changes in a dependent variable and explanations that tell a story about how a sequence of events unfolds to produce a given outcome. We will refer to these divergent explanations as variance and narrative explanations, respectively. They constitute the foundation of the variance and process approaches to the study of change and development. The following discussion, which draws extensively on Abbott's work, contrasts variance and process approaches to social scientific research.

THE VARIANCE APPROACH

This perspective explains outcomes as the product of independent variables acting on dependent variables. The underlying causal process that generates the outcomes is presumed to operate continuously over time. Variables are defined and carefully distinguished from one another both in theory and in the operations used to measure them, and the character of the variables themselves is assumed to remain constant over time. Any unexplained variance is assumed to result either from misspecification (the omission of important independent variables or improper specification of relationships among variables) or from random error.

To continue with our example of new program startups from chapter 1, a researcher using a variance approach might define one dependent variable as the number of clients served per month. The next step would be to define independent variables that influence number of clients served, for example, degree of stakeholder participation or client-orientation. These variables might be measured at one, two, three, or more points in time, depending on the design. Regardless of when the measurement occurred, the assumption would be that the *same* thing is being measured—for example, that client service meant the same thing at time 3 as it did at time 1. Moreover, while the action of the independent variables on the dependent variable may change in level or degree, there is an assumption that this does *not* change the character of the dependent variable. Once defined and measured, clients served is clients served regardless of how much it has been affected by the independent variable, regardless of which independent variable influenced it, and regardless of when it was influenced by the independent variable. This approach regards unexplained variance in clients served as the result of measurement unreliability, other random errors, and mistakes in the hypothesized causal model.

Generally, more than one independent variable is included in the causal explanation. Typically, the effects of multiple independent variables are aggregated by simple linear combination, sometimes including multiplicative interaction terms. More complex schemes use a configuration of variables to predict outcomes. For example, contingency theory uses a combination of structural and contingency variables to determine the degree of "fit," and then fit is used to predict outcomes (e.g., Venkatraman & Prescott, 1990). However, the logic remains the same in that the independent variables are assumed to combine to cause outcomes. Because most variance theories of social phenomena incorporate several independent variables, Peter Abell (1987) argues that their outcomes are overdetermined. This means that there is usually more than one set of conjoined independent variables sufficient to bring about the outcome.

Variance approaches to the study of change and development are characterized by several assumptions:

V1. *The world is made up of fixed entities with varying attributes.* In the variance approach, the basic units of analysis are entities that maintain a unitary identity through time. These entities possess a fixed set of variable attributes that are assumed to reflect any significant changes in the entity (Abbott, 1990). For example, in the study of new program startups, the program is taken as the basic entity. The focus of the research are characteristic attributes of the programs and the process of their initiation, such as whether they have a planning policy board, their structural complexity, and whether and how they involve experts in program design. Changes in these variables represent the essential changes in the programs, and the goal of research is a satisfactory theory representing relationships among these and other variables.

The question of whether the programs per se undergo a qualitative change over time is not important; the variance approach assumes that any significant changes are captured by the variables. The entities are, in effect, settings within which the variables act.

To form a proper explanation it is necessary to identify the variable attributes that are essential to the process under study. Variables constitute the primitive terms used in theories. Hence, both causes and outcomes of change and development must be framed as variables. Employing this mode of explanation requires one to "variabilize" the world, that is, to view the order underlying observed phenomena as comprised of variables standing in relationship to each other.

V2. *Explanation is based on establishing necessary and sufficient causality.* As Mohr (1982) argues, the ideal variance explanation identifies conditions necessary and sufficient for the outcome. The canonical form for such an explanation is a causal account of how the independent variables influence the dependent variable. In overdetermined cases—that is, when several sets of variables *sufficient* to bring about the effect can be identified—the ultimate goal of theory and research is to cut through this morass to the few critical factors that are *necessary and sufficient* conditions for the effect. Hence, parsimony is the final arbiter among competing theories.

V3. *Causal explanations utilize efficient causality.* Aristotle (1941) distinguished four types of causality: material, formal, efficient, and final. A variance approach emphasizes efficient causality. Mohr explains, "An efficient cause is a force that is conceived as *acting on* a unit of analysis (person, organization, and so on) to make it what it is in terms of the outcome variable (morale, effectiveness, and so on) or change it from what it was. It may be thought of as a *push-type* causality" (1982, p. 40). Each necessary and sufficient cause in variance theories is assumed to function in the manner of an efficient cause. Other types of causality, such as final causality that posits that phenomena are influenced by the ends to which they are tending, are not regarded as valid generative mechanisms.

V4. *The generality of explanations depends on their ability to apply uniformly across a broad range of contexts.* One criterion for evaluating variance explanations is their *generality*. In the variance view, the generality of a causal mechanism refers to the domain of cases and contexts in which it is able to operate *uniformly and consistently* at all levels of both independent and dependent variables. The broader this domain, the more general the explanation. Causes are assumed to operate "at equal speed" and in the same way across all cases (Abbott, 1990). The generative mechanism is also assumed to be continuously efficacious across time; independent variables are always operating on dependent variables in a continuous fashion as the process unfolds.

When causality from independent to dependent variable does not exhibit uniformity over cases or time, researchers attempt to define the variables in the context that account for the differences. These are then incorporated in the theory so that all relationships can be said to operate uniformly. This process of identifying additional variables continues until the remaining variability falls within the range acceptable for error variance in estimates of model parameters.

V5. *The temporal sequence in which independent variables trigger is immaterial.* When several independent variables are included in a model, the time order in which the variables come into operation makes no difference in the level of the outcome, so long as the theory employs a time frame in which they can all operate or trigger. The level of outcome variable Y is the same whether variable X occurs before variable Z or vice versa, so long as their influence is fully brought to bear on Y. This is consistent with the general linear model, which employs linear combinations of independent variables to predict dependent variables. This combinatorial process yields equivalent results no matter which independent variable operates first.

Variables that act in grossly different time frames are commonly separated into two different explanatory theories, distinguished as "macro" and "micro" levels. For instance, variables affecting program initiation might be partitioned into three sets on the basis of temporal duration—variables that influence individual creativity and innovation in programs, variables that influence program planning, and variables that influence initiation and diffusion of programs in society. Initially, the focus would be on developing a theory or model for each level and once this has been accomplished, the interrelationship of the levels is addressed.

A minimal time unit is also assumed. Since many variance models assume causation to operate continuously over time, the existence of variables which require time to be partioned into bits of definite length presents a thorny conceptual problem (Abbott, 1990; McGrath, 1988). For independent variables to be in continous operation on a dependent variable, all variables—independent and dependent, nominal or continuous—must be susceptible to measurement at the same point in time, and the temporal unit of measurement must be equal for all variables. Otherwise variables of different statuses are included in the same model, a logical error. As temporal units grow finer and finer, the model breaks down, because eventually the unit is so fine that at least one variable cannot be realized in the time frame, and measurement becomes impossible.

For example, consider a model that explains program startup effectiveness as a function of level of formalization, program size, and adherence to the implementation sequence described in chapter 1. Formalization and size can be assigned meaningful values for exceedingly small time intervals, since they represent the state of the program at a given instant. However, adhering to the sequence requires a more molar unit of measurement; since it takes a certain amount of time to go through the sequence, it is impossible to gauge adherence to the sequence at microsecond intervals. The minimal meaningful time frame for measuring adherence to the planning sequence is probably several months.

V6. *Explanations should emphasize immediate causation.* Causal relationships in variance models can be described as "shallow," because at each point in time the variables in the model contain all the information needed to estimate their values at the next point in time (Abbott, 1990). The variance approach reduces development and change to a sequential list of the results of a deterministic or stochastic model: "A set of initial values faces the model and produces new values that in turn face the model and so on; the immediate past is perpetually producing the future. . ." (Abbott, 1990, p. 146). The basic assumption is that extended narratives or accounts involving long sequences of actions are not required for a valid explanation. It is not necessary to know the particular twists and turns of an entity's history to explain it, because any effects of the past that matter in the present are represented in the immediate past state of the entity.

V7. *Attributes have one and only one causal meaning over the course of time.* Because variance models operate continuously and uniformly over time, they treat each variable as though it has the same status or meaning throughout the process. A variable such as task formalization is required to have the same meaning and place in the model at time 100 as it had at time 1 for the model to be "fittable." This assumption is a logical result of assumption V1, in that entities can only remain fixed if the attributes that make them up retain a unitary identity and meaning over the course of time.

THE PROCESS APPROACH

Given its prevalence, it is easy to presume that the variance approach represents the basic, objective approach of social science. However, variance research is based on a certain way of constructing the object of study, a certain way of cutting up the world into researchable pieces. Variance models and the associated general linear statistics work best for this reduction of the world.

The variance approach works perfectly well for examining research questions about comparisons among entities or relationships among variables. However, in the study of change and development, its assumptions prove too restrictive. An alternative scientific approach that has been articulated in recent years is much better for addressing process research questions.

The process approach offers a model of scientific explanation that differs in several ways from the variance model. The contrasting assumptions of the two models are displayed in Table 2.1. At the outset, however, several similarities between the two approaches should be mentioned. Like the variance approach, the process approach is interested in developing general explanations, though its criteria for generality differ. Unlike some other per-

Table 2.1 Comparison of Variance and Process Approaches

VARIANCE APPROACH	PROCESS APPROACH
Fixed entities with varying attributes	Entities participate in events and may change over time
Explanations based on necessary and sufficient causality	Explanations based on necessary causality
Explanations based on efficient causality	Explanations based on final, formal, and efficient causality
Generality depends on uniformity across contexts	Generality depends on versatility across cases
Time ordering among independent variables is immaterial	Time ordering of independent variables is critical
Emphasis on immediate causation	Explanations are layered and incorporate both immediate and distal causation
Attributes have a single meaning over time	Entities, attributes, events may change in meaning over time

spectives critical of variance research, the process approach does not reject quantitative methodology. It utilizes any methods that can help make sense of change and development processes. However, the form of narrative explanation places certain restrictions on the type of data that should be used and the nature of models that can be employed, and hence influences methodological choices. The process approach also assumes that explanation occurs by specifying generative mechanisms, but narrative generative mechanisms differ in form and operation from those employed by variance approaches.

The process approach conceptualizes development and change processes as sequences of events which have unity and coherence over time. It explains outcomes as the result of the order in which the events unfold and of particular conjunctions of events and contextual conditions. The generative mechanism for narrative explanations is a sequence or cycle of prototypical events that enact the developing entity's path through space and time. Unlike variance generative mechanisms, this motor cannot be reduced to a set of factors that operate consistently and uniformly over time to produce change. Process models locate the generative mechanism in the particular progression of events and their conjunctions with other events and conditions. The same type of event may have different effects on the process, depending on when it occurs and on its particular conjunction with other factors.

The importance of conjunction and order in narrative explanations and the uniqueness of each particular narrative requires researchers to be concerned with colligation, "the procedure of explaining an event by tracing its intrinsic relations to other events and locating it in its historical context" (Walsh, 1967, p. 59). Process approaches realize that each sequence of events has unique qualities; they take these into account in coding and preparation of data, in data analysis, and in the types of models and generalizations that they derive and test. The process perspective recognizes unique features of sequences as an important source of variation and does not consign all such variance to the "error" category. Ideally, a narrative explanation provides an account of how and why a sequence of events unfolds which is sufficiently flexible to encompass a range of observed cases, yet sufficiently powerful to help researchers discern the operation of the generative mechanism in a multitude of particularized sequences.

Chapter 1 discussed in general terms how a narrative study of the process of program startup would operate, and here we will put a little more flesh on the bones. A researcher taking the process approach would study startups by capturing their event sequences leading from initial program planning to implementation. The event sequences would be constructed based on interviews, observation, and archival analysis. Event sequence data can be historical in nature, pertaining to startups that have occurred in the past, or it can be collected during direct study of startups as they progress. The resulting database would be a chronological list of events from the time planning began to the time startup and implementation were completed for each program.

Events in the sequence database would be coded for changes pertaining to key dimensions of program planning and implementation, such as problem diagnosis and program development. Goals or motives are important aspects of narratives, so researchers would attempt to define the goal or final state toward which startups tend. For example, one goal of a startup social program is to achieve stable funding, and (assuming participants held such a goal) this would be considered one factor pulling the developing program along, an end toward which various actions are directed. Aspects of events relevant to goals or end states, both intermediate and long-term, would be coded as well. The particular circumstances of each event and the time it takes to unfold would be taken into account in coding and, later, in the analysis of the data.

While the variance approach would assume that variables such as formalization, size, and existence of a policy board always had definite values, a process approach assumes that events relevant to these dimensions of development may occur only intermittently. So there may be *no* events relevant to the program startup policy board for six months, and then a flurry of board activity which fundamentally restructures the program. Hence, there may be an absence of developmental effects due to a particular variable at various points in time. The importance of variables in explaining development and the nature of their effects on the process may also differ over time. For example, building a talented core team may be very important early in new program development, but later on become less important than other dimensions, such as finding stable funding sources.

From the initial set of sequences, one or more general sequences could be derived which represent observed narrative patterns. These could be used to test hypotheses about the generative mechanism driving development and change, since each generative mechanism implies that observed narratives should have certain properties. For example, researchers could assess the hypothesis that more effective program startups followed the five stages in the Program Planning Model (Delbecq & Van de Ven, 1971) rather than some other sequence. If this hypothesis is correct, for example, program design activities should be low in the initial phases of a startup, increase in the middle phases, and exhibit cycles in implementation phases, occurring only when the modifications in the program are indicated by feedback or problems. If a number of temporal patterns consistent with the model were found and no inconsistent patterns emerged, then the researcher would conclude that this model "fit" the process for the sample of sequences under study.

Alternatively, event sequence analysis could be used retroductively to derive plausible generative mechanisms (this will be described in more detail in chapter 7). Program effectiveness could be tracked throughout and related to other sequence characteristics under the assumption that development and change are dynamic processes that change in response to intermediate outcomes. Analysis would attempt to identify the generative mechanism that is consistent with these dynamics.

One could also look for conjunctions of events that commonly lead up to transition points. Such conjunctions may also give clues to the nature of the generative mechanism. For example, a sequence of events that indicate experimentation just prior to a major shift in direction might suggest that trial-and-error learning is one process driving program development.

These and other analyses would attempt to develop a "story" that accounts for the development of social programs. A process model would delineate typical phases or critical events in startups and give an account of temporal development that explains how some sequences produce takeoff while others lead to crashes.

Variance approaches, too, rely on "stories" to undergird their explanations. However, their stories are the "mininarratives" described in the first and second definitions of process, which give a more in-depth understanding of a causal process and justify links among variables, but do not form an integral part of the explanation itself. The explanatory work in variance theories is done by a continuously operating causal model. In contrast, the process approach explains in terms of the order in which things occur and the stage in the process at which they occur. The story itself is the generative mechanism.

Process approaches to the study of development and change can be characterized by several assumptions in contrast to those of variance theories:

P1. *The world is made up of entities which participate in events. These entities may change over time as a result.* The unit of analysis in the narrative approach is an evolving central subject that makes events happen and to which events occur (Abbott, 1988). While attributes of an entity (central subject) may change, the entity itself may also change through a number of processes: through transformation into a different type of entity, merger with another entity, division into two different entities, and death or dissolution. These processes cannot be represented adequately in a set of variables, because they have to do with qualitative change in the entity. "Entity processes" (Abbott, 1992) are enacted through sequences of events and can themselves be coded as macrolevel events, that is, as discontinuous occurrences that represent qualitative shifts.

To return to the example of social programs raised in assumption V1 of the variance perspective, programs not only change their attributes, but they also merge, split up, are founded, and go out of business during the course of study. Programs undergoing these qualitative changes should not be regarded as incomplete data or outliers, but rather as objects of explanation in their own right. Process explanations attempt to encompass not only changes in attributes of programs, but also qualitative changes.

While a discriminating choice of variables is important in forming variance models, process explanations hinge on discerning essential central subjects and the types of events and characteristics that mark qualitative changes in these subjects. *Central subjects* are individual entities (people, groups, organizations, machines and other material artifacts) around which the narrative is woven. It is important to note that the term "subject" does not refer

to human subjectivity, but rather to the subject(s) participating in the narrative. Hull explicates the idea of a coherent central subject as follows:

> At any one moment the parts of an historical entity must also be interre-
> lated in such a way that the entity exists continuously through time. But
> in any case, for an historical entity to remain the same entity, no degree of
> similarity between earlier and later stages in its development is required,
> as long as this development is spatio-temporally continuous. (1975,
> p. 256)

As Hull observes, central subjects may maintain the same form over time,
but they may also undergo qualitative changes. A merger or transformation
of a developing entity would not remove it from a process study; instead,
the entity would be redefined and the events that drove its transformation
would be of interest.

Events are the natural units of the social process; events are what central
subjects do or what happens to them. The process perspective explicitly
focuses on events rather than variables because of the inherent complexity
of developmental processes (Abbott, 1990). The variance approach would
regard events as a combination of particular values of many variables.
However, as Abbott puts it:

> To a narrativist, the justification for thinking directly in terms of these
> events, rather than in terms of dimensions or the uncrossed categories
> themselves, is the surprising empirical fact that once we consider a state-
> space [a space that defines all possible events in terms of all possible com-
> binations of variables] of any real complexity, most events are null. That
> is, most combinations of particular values of discrete variables are never
> observed and most neighborhoods of a continuous variable space are
> empty. If it is the case that the state-space is mostly empty—if most pos-
> sible events don't happen—why should we design models covering all
> possible events? . . . It is more parsimonious to define the actually ob-
> served locations as "events" and to investigate their narrative structure di-
> rectly without recourse to reified "causes." We usually justify the use of
> "variables" on the ground that reality is too complex to do otherwise.
> Maybe that isn't true. . . . (1990, pp. 141–142)

Abbott concludes, "The narrative analyst therefore views events as the natural way to simplify the social process. Rather than disassembling complex
particulars into combinations of supposedly independent variable properties . . . such an analyst views direct conceptualizing of the observed events
as the best way to simplify the complex flow of occurrences" (1990, p. 142).

We might add that the process approach also views events as the most valid representation of what occurs in development and change processes.

Central subjects must be identified independently of the events in which they figure, because they are primary and give the narrative its basic unity and continuity. However, this is not to say that identification of central subjects is a straightforward process. In the study of program startups, for instance, the researcher must define what constitutes the startup at the outset. Does the startup begin with the idea for the program, with the need for it in the community, or when two people get together and try to develop the idea, or when the program is first chartered in some form or some other criterion? What sort of entity exists if the startup combines with another program? Does it stop being the original entity or has it just changed forms? Should a new entity be introduced whenever existing ones combine? There are no definitive answers to these questions, but defining criteria for identification of central subjects is an important part of process research. It should be noted that variance research is not without this type of problem as well. Researchers working in this tradition must also decide what to do with subjects who change or merge, whether to include them in the sample or regard the data as incomplete.

P2. *Explanation is based on necessary causality.* Process theories focus on critical events and conjunctions of events to explain development and change, and hence they hinge on necessary causality. Each causal event imparts a particular direction and pushes the developing subject toward a certain outcome. This influence is necessary for development and change to proceed down a particular path. However, subsequent events, conjunctions, and confluences also influence the subject and may alter the direction imparted by earlier events. Because causal influences come to bear "eventwise"—through one or more events—rather than continuously, it is rare for a cause to be sufficient in narrative explanation. Only the entire set of forces that influence the developmental span, in the particular order and combinations in which they occur, are necessary and sufficient to explain a narrative.

P3. *Final and formal causality, supplemented by efficient causality, is the basis for explanation.* Narrative explanations employ efficient causality to explain the influence imparted by particular events and, often, to explain the mechanics of transitions between events and between more macrolevel units, such as phases. However, narrative explanation also admits other forms of causality, especially final causality and formal causality. While micro-moves from event to event and even some larger transitions are explicable in terms of efficient causes, to explain why larger patterns evolve requires a broader causal scheme. In Mohr's terminology, narrative explanation requires a "*pull-type causality:* X [the precursor] does not imply Y [the outcome], but rather Y implies X" (1982, p. 59).

Aristotle distinguished four causes—literally, *aitia,* "answers to the question" of why change occurs (Aristotle, 1941; Randall, 1960)—material, formal, efficient, and final. Respectively, they indicate that from which something was made (material cause), the pattern by which it is made (formal cause), "that from which comes the immediate origin of movement or rest" (efficient cause), and the end for which it is made (final cause) (Ross, 1949). The modern scientific enterprise is most explicitly concerned with efficient cause, tending to downplay other sources of change. However, by Aristotle's analysis the four causes were inseparably linked, though one may be more prominent than others in a given account. Both final and formal causes have the potential to account for the "pull-type" nature of narrative causality more satisfactorily than efficient causality can.

Final causality posits an end or goal that guides the unfolding of development and change. Many modern accounts equate ends or goals with agency (divine, human, or animal; cf. Mohr, 1982). However, Aristotle was clear that this need not be so. Final causality also includes natural ends and outcomes of natural processes. In its broadest sense, final causality is any end-state that attracts a developmental or change process to itself. As such, the final cause draws the central subject along the path it follows, within the constraints of particular events and conjunctures that occur along the way. Some of these events and conjunctures function to advance the final cause, while others are "accidents," in that they either do not serve or detract from attainment of the final cause. Together the efficacy of the central subject in moving toward the final cause and efficient causation in particular events determine the degree to which the final cause is realized.

Formal causation is a pattern that enforms change. The pattern must be applied to the developing entity somehow, either through plan or through some other governing mechanism. Form can be conceived as "an object of thought, rather than of sense, as the inner nature of a thing which is expressed in its definition, the plan of its structure" (Ross, 1964, p. 74). In the organizational arena, form may be materialized as a blueprint, an organizational chart, or a legal code specifying requirements of a merger. It may also be something conceptual rather than tangible, for example, an institutionalized interpretive scheme specifying the components and programs that make up a legitimate public school (Meyer & Rowan, 1977; Scott & Meyer,

1994). To the extent it is effectively applied, the plan shapes the course of development and change, independent of the final cause that is sought.

In Aristotle's analysis, final and formal causality are sometimes identical, especially in cases when the plan is the goal of development. In the organizational arena, goals or outcomes often have structures or plans strongly associated with them. However, this is not always the case. Organizations are often equifinal, and there are goals that do not imply a particular structure, sequence, or plan. The obverse is also true. Sometimes the structure or plan may remain constant, yet goals or outcomes change. Messinger's (1955) famous case study of the March of Dimes is a case in point. So, although final and formal causes are often isomorphic (with final cause granted presumption as the ultimate mover of development), there will be cases where formal causality has an independent or preeminent role.

P4. *The generality of explanations depends on their versatility.* Like variance theories, process theories are evaluated on the basis of their generality. The generality of a narrative explanation, however, stems not from its uniformity and consistency, but from its *versatility,* the degree to which it can encompass a broad domain of developmental patterns without modification of its essential character. The broader its domain—the greater the variety of cases, contexts, events, and patterns the theory can adapt to—the more general the explanation. A key difference between process and variance explanations hinges on the use of terms such as "encompass" and "adapt" as opposed to "uniform and consistent operation." These terms capture a basic quality of narrative explanation, which attempts to discern a common process in a range of complex and seemingly disparate events and sequences.

A defining feature of narratives is their inherent complexity. The events that comprise them are complicated. Narratives with the same "plot" often differ considerably in specific sequences due to the particular conjunctions of causes and contextual factors operating in specific cases. Narrative causality is "loose" in that it specifies only the pattern or form that arranges events in space and time; therefore, it does not exert the deterministic influence over events that efficient causes exert in variance theories. Moreover, in process theories efficient causation is event-centered and hence may be intermittent and uneven over time. As a result, narratives explainable in terms of the same theory may vary considerably in the nature and patterns of events that transpire.

The challenges for process researchers are to create theories versatile enough to discover common narrative forms and to elucidate generative mechanisms applicable to a broad range of complex and disparate cases. The narrative approach attempts to encompass the uniqueness of individual cases that share a common developmental process. It does not categorize all differences among cases as "error variance," but considers the uniqueness in individual cases as added nuance to the general explanation.

Meeting this challenge requires process researchers to pursue a strategy of simplification (Abbott, 1990). Typologies that categorize events and event sequences are a key element of this strategy. Typologies ground coding procedures that enable researchers to identify qualitatively similar events and sequences. Typologies must be sufficiently flexible to capture types from a wide variety of cases, yet clearly defined to ensure validity. A versatile explanation incorporates typologies that enable it to recognize family resemblance among a broad range of seemingly different events and sequences. This includes recognizing resemblance among events that differ in duration, have multiple particularizing features, and are enacted by diverse central subjects. Typologies of sequences should enable the researcher to recognize resemblance among patterns that differ in length, exhibit different degrees of overlap among contiguous events, and exhibit "noise" in the form of nonessential events which complicate the sequence.

Classifying an event or sequence into a type is fundamentally different from measuring its variable attributes. Typologies acknowledge that the entities being classified are too complex to decompose into variables. They are premised on the assumption that the character of an entity emerges from the entire configuration of its properties and their interrelationships. Reducing the entity to dimensions that reflect these properties misrepresents the entity's essential nature. Typologies preserve the entity's integrity and also recognize the categorical nature of the social world. As Weber (1949) noted, typological thinking highlights variations from the type as well as conformity to it. Such variations may lead the researcher to notice contextual features or external causes that should be incorporated into the theory; they may also suggest revisions in the typology; or they may turn out to be nonessential, so that the case at hand may be classified into an existing type.

A versatile process theory can see through idiosyncratic features to recognize family resemblance among events and sequences. To develop a complete theory, however, classification must be complemented by explanation. The second criterion by which versatility is judged is the degree to which the theory enables generative mechanisms to be uncovered in a broad range of cases.

As noted above, narrative explanations typically are comprised of a constellation of causes, combining the global influence of formal and final causes and the local influence of event causality. In narrative explanations causes do not operate "at equal speed" across all cases. Shaped by final or formal causes that organize the operation of intermittent efficient causes, narrative theories do not require that the forces pushing development be uniform or consistent across cases, contexts, or time. Causal factors important at one point in the developmental process may not be as important at another. Many narrative explanations posit that different factors come into play at different stages of the development or change process. In the organizational life cycle, for example, the founder's style and leadership may be critical in early stages, but once the firm has grown, other factors become more important. Abbott notes:

> Historians write their narratives to follow the causal action. If that action now seems to involve one or two principal causes and not other causes central just one or two events ago, then the historian simply ignores the presence of those prior causes. They are assumed to be bubbling along in the background and not really affecting much. Such a view directly contravenes the views of most social scientists. The physical science model on which social scientists try to operate makes no allowances for causes that appear and disappear. One can hardly imagine a sociologist who says that "race simply doesn't matter much except at a couple of conjunctures." Yet this kind of argument is clearly implicit in standard narrative procedures in history. (1990, p. 143)

Differential importance of causes is also a function of events unique to the case at hand. A particular conjunction of events may make cause X a particularly strong determinant in case A, whereas another conjunction may weaken its effect in case B, even though both cases can be subsumed under the same narrative explanation.

Explaining narratives hinges on seeing how templates provided by formal and final causes shape the *arrangement* of events in space and time. The movement of the process through time and space is affected and influenced by efficient causes operating through specific events. The combination of formative causation by final and formal causes with immediate pushes of efficient causation means that a wide variety of sequences may result from the same generative mechanism. To the extent this explanation can generate and account for a broad range of cases in different contexts, it can be said to be versatile.

P5. *The temporal sequence of independent variables is critical.* The implication of assumption P4 is that the order in which causal forces come to bear is crucial in narrative accounts. The order in which events occur in narratives determines when efficient causes come into play, while the duration of events and the continuity across events determines how long these causes operate. Differences in order can make large differences in outcomes. Stagewise models of development posit that differences in order can make large differences in outcomes. In group decision development, for example, if groups start with solutions, the solution orientation acts to narrow their frame of reference, and later attempts to define the problem will generally be constrained by the frames implied in the solutions first entertained. On the other hand, groups which start with a broad search for understanding the problem are not so constrained and therefore may consider a much wider range of solutions during subsequent solution phases. The order in which the "solution development" and "problem diagnosis" events occur brings different causal forces to bear. In the case of the solution-oriented group there is a strong framing effect, while the problem-oriented group is driven by forces enabling and constraining search behavior and only later experiences solution framing effects. The different temporal orderings result in quite different outcomes (Maier, 1970).

Whereas establishing a minimum time unit is crucial for variance theories, this is relatively unimportant for process theories. Process theories have to be able to expand and contract their windows for event recognition (this is called "time warping" in the sequence recognition literature). As noted in P4, this is accomplished through typologies.

P6. *Explanations should incorporate layers of explanation ranging from immediate to distal.* If variance theories are "causally shallow," process theories are "causally deep" (Abbott, 1988). They explain the state of development at any point in terms of the prior history of events and associated causal influences. In process theories, history cannot be encapsulated in the immediate past state of the entity (as it is in variance theories), because the ordering and context of previous events is critical to narrative explanation. Within the same narrative framework the particular histories of individual cases may lead them to take different paths to different outcomes. To subsume these differences under a common theory, it is necessary to show how the sequence of events for each case resulted in a unique causal history that caused the narrative to unfold in different ways.

This creates an interesting situation: Whereas a particular cause may operate for only a limited time in a narrative, in a sense it never ceases to influence the entity, because it forms part of the entity's history. A new product startup that is subject to a strict regulatory regime, such as a drug or safety device, bears the influence of this regime long after regulatory requirements have been satisfied. The particular characteristics of the product and its ultimate success or failure are shaped by its history and the measures taken in response to regulation.

The different durations of events are related to a second reason that process theories must allow for "deep" causal analysis. Efficient causal factors are associated with events, and to the extent that one event runs longer than another its causal influence is more enduring. In a childcare program startup the influence of the state licensing and regulatory process may stretch over months or years. However, the influence of a county board to turn down financing comes to bear in a short period of time. While duration per se has no relation to the importance of a cause, the possibility of causes with different time horizons forces process theories to look back much further than the previous state of the entity.

P7. *An entity, attribute, or event may change in meaning over time.* As noted in P1, the process approach presumes that the unit of analysis may undergo metamorphosis over time. So the entity, for example a new program, may be fundamentally transformed into a different type of unit, merge with another unit, or go out of existence over the course of the narrative. In the same vein, an attribute of the entity may change in essential meaning as the entity develops; strategic planning will be fundamentally different for a small startup than for the larger firm it grows into. Finally, events may also change in meaning for the narrative. The event, "denied funding," is likely to mean very different things to a nascent product development team than to the project team that has shepherded an innovation through several years. To the young program implementation team, denial of funding is likely to constitute a catastrophe which threatens the very life of the project; to the experienced team it represents an unfortunate but survivable event and sets in motion plans for obtaining interim funding from "soft" sources. This does not represent different interpretations of the same event, but rather fundamentally different meanings for the two events.

RELATIONSHIP OF PROCESS AND VARIANCE APPROACHES

The process and variance approaches emphasize different aspects of change and development. The variance approach captures the continuous variation in development and change with powerful mathematical representations, whereas the process approach includes the role of human projects and agency in change and development. Deriving a variance theory requires the researcher to construct the development and change process in a particular way. This construction emphasizes those aspects of the phenomenon amenable to variabilization at the expense of others. It may also require translation of concepts into variable forms, which changes or restricts their meaning. Finally, the variance approach portrays the process as driven by continuous efficient causality operating on and through stable entities. Deriving a process theory requires a different construction of development and change. The researcher must isolate meaningful elements that lead to the outcome and then derive a story that ties these elements into a coherent whole. Narrative explanation relies on formal or final influences that draw the entity along its path; as a result, narrative explanations can only be advanced once the process has been consummated. Final and formal causation must be supplemented with careful attention to context and to the particular confluence of forces that influences the developing entity; these exigencies influence the particularities of change and development.

As noted in chapter 1, at the empirical level the two approaches stand in an asymmetric relationship, in that information used to generate a process explanation can always be transformed into a format amenable to variance explanation, whereas the reverse is not the case. It is possible to identify variables within a series of events that enable the continuous analysis of that series. As we will see in Part II, this strategy can yield very important and definitive information about narrative processes. However, longitudinal datasets based on measurement of variables generally do not have enough information to recover events.

There are also advantages to the reduction of information that accompanies variance analysis. A clear, well-defined set of variables enables researchers to plan unambiguous tests of bounded hypotheses and models. The powerful statistical methods of variance research can handle large samples and protect against researcher bias in the evaluation of models.

Once a typology of narratives has been defined, variance methods can be used to test hypotheses about causes and effects of various sequence types. For example, a set of 30 event sequences for a program startup might be classified into three types—conforming, moderately conforming, nonconforming—based on their similarity to the Program Planning Model. Variance methods could then be used to determine whether there are differences among types in program effectiveness and also to explore the antecedent variables that cause typal variation.

In sum, process and variance approaches are complementary. The process approach offers a more complete picture of development, but lacks the power and protection from bias afforded by the variance approach. Each approach is richer for the other.

SCHEMES FOR NARRATIVE EXPLANATION

Most process research has been resolutely qualitative. It has emphasized the idiographic nature of narratives and has focused on deriving typologies based on the plot of the narrative or other aspects of the story (e.g. Polkinghorne, 1988). In this volume we are interested in a scientific approach to narrative analysis, which advances general theories that posit specific generative mechanisms for narratives. The process approach seeks to develop theories that can be put to a formal test versus alternative narrative possibilities. The logic of narrative explanation has not been worked out as well as that of variance explanation. However, at least three different schemes have been advanced, and to these we now turn.

PROBABILISTIC LAWS

In his seminal work on process explanations, Mohr (1982, ch. 2) advanced a view of narrative explanation based on probabilistic laws which govern the occurrence of forces that direct the process toward certain outcomes. For Mohr, process explanations posit that the outcome was produced by one or more sequences of precursor events. Events represent exposure of the entity (Mohr called it the "focal unit") to one or more necessary conditions for the outcome. Each event is necessary, but not sufficient to bring about the outcome, and it is only their combination in specific sequences which is sufficient. The occurrence of events (i.e., the combination of the entity and the necessary condition) is governed by laws of probability which represent the distribution of the event in the population of possible events and the rate at which the event is likely to occur. Particular sequences of events are thus the joint probabilities of the specific events that constitute them.

Mohr uses the example of malaria contagion as an illustration: A certain proportion of the people in a population harbors the malaria parasite. Female anopheles mosquitos are driven to bite people in order to get the blood necessary to lay their eggs, and they have a probability of biting someone with the malaria parasite that is determined by the proportion of the population which are carriers. There is also a certain probability that the mosquito will withdraw sufficient numbers of parasites to become a carrier of the disease; this is based on the number of parasites in the human host's blood. The mosquito is then driven to bite another person to get blood for more egg-laying. The probability of transmission from this bite depends on the probability that the person bitten does not have the disease already and on the probability that sufficient parasites will be injected into the potential host's bloodstream to sustain the infection (it is also influenced by the probability that the mosquito will not get eaten by a dragonfly in the meantime and other accidental events). So transmission of malaria depends on a sequence of events: mosquito bites infect human host; mosquito bites uninfect human host; parasite reproduces in sufficient numbers to infect new host. The occurrence of this sequence is not deterministic, but probabilistic, depending on the distributions detailed previously.

Mohr also presents the example of diffusion of innovations, which is closer to the concern of this volume. The process starts with a probability distribution of individuals who do and do not have knowledge of or use an innovation. As they go about their day-to-day lives, individuals come into contact with various others who either do or do not have the knowledge or innovation. The probability of a particular pair of individuals coming together is a function of their social class, social circles, work, and other factors. During this contact there is a probability that others who do have the knowledge or innovation will "transmit" it to someone who does not currently have it, and a second probability that having the knowledge or innovation will "take" and lead to adoption.

Mohr's vision of narrative explanation allows human agency to enter via its influence on some of the probability distributions and via external directional forces. However, Mohr gives a rather sere version of narrative; the outcome is generated by a set of probabilistic laws that are at one remove from the sphere of human action. Mohr's primary concern was to define process (narrative) explanations in terms equivalent to those used to describe variance (deterministic, variance) explanations, and to this end he spelled out an explanatory logic that has a mechanistic flavor.

HUMAN AGENCY: MODELS OF ACTION SEQUENCES

Sociologist Peter Abell (1987, 1993) has elaborated a different scheme of narrative explanation based on the theory of human action (Anscombe, 1957; Von Wright, 1971). For Abell narratives are constituted by sequences of actions (what people or collectives choose to do) and forebearances (what they choose not to do). Actions are situated in four senses: (a) a given action is the consequence of prior actions by this and other actors; (b) actions may be contingent on sets of circumstances which are not the consequences of prior actions (e.g. economic downturns, accidents); (c) beliefs, values, and effects which lead to the action are the products of prior social-ization of the actor; and (d) action is shaped by the actor's strategic calcu-lation about what others may do concurrently or subsequently. Abell de-fines narrative as a "structure of interconnected, socially situated actions (and forebearances) [that] account[s] for (or explain) the generation of specific outcomes" (1993, p. 94).

Abell is concerned with being able to generalize across narratives to iden-tify common generative mechanisms. To compare narrative sequences in order to find commonalities, Abell represents them as noncyclic digraphs in which one action leads to others along nonrecursive paths that may branch and converge. Abell then performs what he calls "semantic generalization" to reclassify specific sequences of actions in the graph into larger units of ac-tion and interaction. This yields a more abstract narrative that simplifies the original graph; each larger action or interaction unit replaces two or more individual actions. When a sufficient level of abstraction has been achieved, the abstracted narratives can be compared using formal and interpretive methods to identify relatively simple, basic narrative structures that gener-alize across specific cases (see Abell, 1993, for an extended example).

Abell (1987, 1993) argues that these narrative structures are generated by purposeful and strategic action along the lines of the model of human ac-tion advanced by Von Wright (1971). Von Wright argued that action must be understood in light of two understandings agents have: the understand-ing that they have of their ability to do something to interfere with the flow of natural events (i.e., their understanding that they can use laws of nature and the social world for their own purposes and even sometimes counter-vene them); and the understanding that agents have of their ability to do something so that something else happens (their understanding that actions can be intended to accomplish something). These understandings are in-corporated into "practical syllogisms" that actors use to reason through the best means to obtain their goals: the actor intends to bring about a result; she/he knows that this cannot be done unless he/she carries out a partic-ular action; therefore, the actor sets to the task of carrying out that partic-ular action. Abell (1993) asserted that strategic choice in interdependent activities could best be represented formally as a game in which two or more actors jointly employed rationality. The game maps the interdependence structure that actors refer to when producing the action sequence, and thus generates the narrative.

Abell's approach to narrative explanation leans strongly on the rational action model of human agency. The unfolding of the action is generated by actors' strategic choices, which are based on calculations of what others may or may not do in response. The role of agency is explicit in and central to Abell's version of narrative explanation. Other conditions also influence development and change, including physical and social constraints and socialization which shapes what actors want and consider acceptable to do; however, these represent constraints on choice rather than key drivers of the narrative.

ECLECTICISM: MULTIPLE INTERDEPENDENT NARRATIVES

Abbott (1993) argues that Abell's approach is too narrow and advocates a more flexible approach that allows for multiple narrative forms. He believes this is important because most social action cannot be reduced to a single narrative with a single central actor. Instead narratives typically intertwine so that the events in one narrative are influenced by other narratives. Each of these narratives may follow its own particular "storyline." While Abell's model of narrative may be very appropriate for explaining action and interaction of individuals, it may not be appropriate for explaining phenomena such as the rise of professions, the pattern of steps in traditional dances, or group decision making. Thus, Abbott "insists on the widest possible latitude for the actual mechanisms propelling a narrative" (1993, p. 206).

Abbott (1991) illustrates these concerns in his study of the development of professionalization in medicine. He identifies a variety of basic events in professionalization: control of work, development of schools, creation of professionally dominated work sites, associations, licensing, and scientific research formalization. He found different sequences of events operating at local, state, and national levels. At the local level, the sequence was control, practical knowledge, association, professionally dominated work sites, and scientific formalization. At the state level, which was constituted in part by local events, a different sequence emerged in which control and association at the state level emerge first and in the state's major city, with widespread local association and control coming only later. At the national level, a different sequence seemed to hold, but it, too, was constituted in part by state and local event sequences. The three interdependent sequences at local, state, and national levels each seemed to follow somewhat different narratives, though the common theme of power and control as the motive driving professionalization could be found in all three accounts.

DISCUSSION

The views of Mohr, Abell, and Abbott offer different schemes for narrative explanation and illustrate the diverse possibilities of this approach. Nor do these seem to be the only schemes possible. Heise's event-structure analysis (Griffin, 1993; Heise, 1989) advances another promising model. Choosing among the various perspectives on narrative explanation depends in part on the nature of the phenomenon studied. Abell's approach seems promising if a limited number of actors or units are involved in the process, while Abbott's is likely to yield better results for cases where different levels of social processes are involved. However, the choice also depends on "aesthetic" considerations. Researchers with strong commitments to classical social science may prefer Mohr's perspective, while those who lean toward qualitative accounts will probably find Abbott's eclectic approach preferable, and those with strong commitments to human agency and formal models will find Abell's formulation most persuasive. In chapter 3 we explore potential connections between different narrative schemes and four generative mechanisms for development and change. The final topic for this chapter is to consider the methodological challenges the process approach faces.

REQUIREMENTS FOR PROCESS METHODS

The process approach seeks to go beyond the idiographic accounts of literary or qualitative narrative analysis to generalizable results. To this end, methods for process research must be developed to accomplish five key tasks:

(1) *Identify events and event types:* Generalization is possible only if equivalent types of events can be identified across sequences. Therefore, it is important to develop typologies that classify events into meaningful types consistently and validly. One complication is that the significant elements of the development or change sequence are not always synonymous with observable, bounded occurrences. Often an event is extended over time; for example, the event of the development of professional schools might stretch over a number of years and give rise to a number of distinct occurrences. It is important to develop reliable and valid methods for mapping occurrences into event types.

(2) *Characterize event sequences and their properties:* Special methods are needed to compare and classify different types of event sequences. Since each particular narrative has unique qualities, identifying similar sequences is not a trivial operation. Methods are needed for finding similarities among sequences which differ in length, but not in essential qualities and which differ in terms of "nuisance" occurrences. In some cases, research starts with

hypotheses about the nature of the narrative, but in others it is useful to be able to approach sequence classification inductively, that is, to first identify similar sequences and then derive the narratives they imply.

In some cases methods associated with the variance approach are useful for identifying characteristics of event sequences. To do this, it is necessary to variabilize aspects of events or sequences in order to apply statistical methods that can help the researcher recognize properties of the development or change process. However, this variabilization is always a transformation away from the fundamental object of interest, the sequence of events that makes up the process, and the research must ultimately make reference back to the sequence. Traditional methods for analysis of continuous data must be modified to suit the concerns of process analysis.

(3) *Specify dependencies in temporal sequences:* To establish necessary causality requires establishing necessary linkages and enchainments of events in sequences. One type of evidence that such dependencies exist is cross-case regularities in event sequences. Such regularities suggest the existence of a generative mechanism or plotline that produces them. The same methods that enable comparison of event sequences can identify such regularities. A second type of evidence are longitudinal relationships among variables which measure characteristics of event sequences. If variable A is logically prior to variable B, and evidence can be found that A "causes" B in time series or other analyses, this constitutes evidence for timewise dependencies. A third type of temporal dependency is reflected in event-to-event chaining. Stochastic models can be used to identify such dependencies, which may provide evidence for claims of necessary connection.

(4) *Evaluate hypotheses of formal and final causality:* Formal and final causation can only be determined once the development and change process has come to its conclusion, and researchers can comprehend the whole event sequence in terms of its form or final outcome. Systematic assessment requires a test of the fit of event sequences and other characteristics of the development or change process to what would be expected if a formal or final cause were operating.

(5) *Recognize the coherent pattern that integrates the narrative:* Process methods must convert a heap of confusing data into a synthetic account in which readers can comprehend all the data in a single act of understanding. This requires the ability to recognize recurrent patterns in event sequences, to establish necessary connections, and to identify formal and final causation. But while these may be necessary components of a narrative explanation, they are not in themselves sufficient. A synthetic move that compre-

hends all the particular evidence as part of a larger pattern is required for a complete narrative explanation. While methods for measurement and analysis can supply the materials and evidence necessary for this comprehensive move, it must be taken by the researcher who writes the compelling narrative that encapsulates the explanation.

Subsequent chapters of this volume describe methods for mapping and analysis of event sequences that undertake one or more of these tasks. In each case, we will attempt to describe the particular aspects of the five tasks that each method helps us tackle, along with possible limitations and problems.

CONCLUSION

Jerome Bruner (1986) distinguished two basic types of human intelligence: the paradigmatic, logico-scientific mode of thought and the narrative mode of thought. He contrasts them as follows:

> There are two modes of cognitive functioning, two modes of thought, each providing distinctive ways of ordering experience, of constructing reality. The two (though complementary) are irreducible to one another. . . . Each of the ways of knowing, moreover, has operating principles of its own and its own criteria of well-formedness. They differ radically in their procedures for verification. (Bruner, 1986, p. 11)

Bruner notes that we have relatively little knowledge about how narrative understanding works compared to the vast literature on paradigmatic thinking and its methods. Certainly recent research in many fields is filling this void, but much remains to be done.

We believe that it is time to develop a process-based social science to complement the variance approach. It is time to exercise more fully and in a systematic manner the human ability to understand and to explain through narrative. The process approach has the potential to unlock a different, more fundamental level of understanding of temporal processes.

3 A Typology of Process Theories ⚌

ORGANIZATIONS CHANGE constantly on many different levels. The processes that we see unfolding in these changes—whether they pertain to transitions in individuals' jobs and careers, group formation and development, or organizational innovation, growth, reorganization, and decline—have been exceedingly difficult to explain or predict. Kurt Lewin reminds us that in this buzzing, booming, confusing world of organizational change, "nothing is so practical as a good theory" (1945). Good theory is practical precisely because it provides a systematic way to understand complex phenomena in the real world. Moreover, good theory guides research toward crucial questions and issues, and in deciding what specific process or variance methods to use in a study. Hence, before going into a variety of data collection and analysis methods in the remainder of this book, this chapter will discuss alternative theories of organizational change and development that can guide researchers in conducting their studies.

We will introduce four basic theories that represent "archetypal" explanations of change and development: life cycle, teleology, dialectics, and evolution.[1] The four types are composed of distinctive event sequences and generative mechanisms—we will call them "motors"—that explain how and why changes unfold. They provide general templates for the content of change and development theories. Each of the four theories applies under a specific set of conditions, which are distinctive to each theory.

We have chosen to define the four motors in abstract and general terms because we wish to open the field to a wide range of theories. Also, we wish to avoid the common assumption that all development represents progress from a lower, simpler state to a higher, more complex one. This is one possible path development may follow, but not the only one. Organizational

---

1. This chapter relies heavily on the theories and perspective presented in A. Van de Ven & M. S. Poole (1995). Explaining development and change in organizations. *Academy of Management Review, 20,* 510–540.

development can also follow a regressive path, as in the case of organizational decline (Kimberly & Miles, 1980), or a pathological path, as in Merton's (1968) vicious cycle of bureaucracy.

The four theories may be studied with either variance or process approaches. They are spelled out in process terms, which is the most natural form for expressing development and change processes. We describe the general narrative underlying each motor in terms of a sequence or cycle of events through which the motor operates. Along with each narrative comes a generative mechanism that moves the entity through the event sequence. As we have noted, the narrative can also be transformed into terms suitable for variance analysis. Variables that map the entity's development and indicate aspects of the process can be defined, and the resulting data is suitable for variance methods such as time series analysis. Variance approaches can also be used to test whether requisite conditions for a given model hold.

This chapter first introduces the four basic process theories. Then we arrange these four ideal type process theories into a typology by distinguishing the level and mode of change to which each theory applies. Following this, we consider how the typology is useful for understanding a variety of theories of change processes in organizations. Our contention is that all specific theories of organizational change and development are built from one or more of the four basic types. While some theories can be reduced to one of the four motors, in other cases theories are predicated on the interplay of two or more motors. We consider a scheme of sixteen logically possible explanations of organizational change and development based on various combinations of the four motors and some exemplars of the combinations. The fourth section of the chapter discusses the implications of this typology for empirical research. We will focus on testing and distinguishing the models, with particular attention to the requirements this sets for process research methods.

DEVELOPMENTAL THEORIES: FOUR IDEAL TYPES

An interdisciplinary literature review was conducted to identify the alternative theories that are used to explain processes of change in the social, biological, and physical sciences.[2] About twenty different process theories were

---

2. This review was assisted by a computerized literature search across disciplines using "change" and "development" as keywords. To our surprise, more than one million articles have been published on the subject in the disciplines of psychology, sociology, education, business and economics, as well as biology, medicine, meteorology, and geography. Of course, not

found which vary in substance or terminology across disciplines. Inductive examination of the substance and intellectual heritage of these theories suggested that most of them can be grouped into four basic schools of thought. Each of these four schools has a rich and long-standing intellectual tradition, although various disciplines use different terminology. We will refer to them as life cycle, teleology, dialectic, and evolution theories. Table 3.1 outlines the four types of process theories in terms of their members, pioneering scholars, event progressions, generative mechanisms, and conditions in which they are likely to operate. These theories provide fundamentally different accounts of the sequence of events that unfold to explain the process of change in an organizational entity.

In this section the four process theories will be described in their pure ideal-type forms. As discussed below, scholars often combine elements of these ideal types to explain observed processes of change in specific areas or contexts. However, in such cases it is easy for the conceptual basis of specific theories to become obscure. While the logic of each ideal type is internally consistent, unreflective borrowing of elements from different types of theories may result in confounded explanations for observed processes of organizational change and development.

LIFE CYCLE THEORY

Many scholars have adopted the metaphor of organic growth as an heuristic device to explain development in an organizational entity from its initiation to its termination. Witness, for example, often-used references to the life cycle of organizations, products, and ventures, as well as stages in the development of individual careers, groups, and organizations: startup birth, adolescent growth, maturity, and decline or death. Examples of life cycle theories include developmentalism (Nisbet, 1970), biogenesis (Featherman, 1986), ontogenesis (Baltes, Dittman-Kohli, & Dixon, 1986), and a number of stage theories of child development (Piaget, 1975), human development (Levinson, 1978), moral development (Kohlberg, 1969), organizational development (Kimberly & Miles, 1980), group decision making stages (Bales & Strodtbeck, 1951), and new venture development (Burgelman & Sayles, 1986).[3] The Program Planning Model used

---

all these articles addressed theories of change or development; the vast majority focused on other substantive issues and dealt with change processes in a cursory fashion. To cope with this prolific literature, we reviewed about 200,000 titles, perused about 2,000 abstracts, which led us to carefully read about 200 papers that were useful in identifying about 20 different process theories of development or change.

3. The classification of management and organization literature into the life cycle and other

Table 3.1 Families of Ideal-Type Theories of Social Change

FAMILY	LIFE CYCLE	EVOLUTION	DIALECTIC	TELEOLOGY
Members	Developmentalism Ontogenesis Metamorphosis Stage and Cyclical Models	Darwinian Evolution Mendelian Genetics Saltationism Punctuated Equilibrium	Conflict Theory Dialectical Materialism Pluralism Collective Action	Goal-Setting, Planning Functionalism Social Construction Symbolic Interaction
Pioneers	Comte (1798–1857) Spencer (1820–1903) Piaget (1896–1980)	Darwin (1809–1882) Mendel (1822–1884) Gould & Eldridge (1977)	Hegel (1770–1831) Marx (1818–1883) Freud (1856–1939)	Mead (1863–1931) Weber (1864–1920) Simon (1916–)
Key Metaphor	Organic Growth	Competitive Survival	Opposition, Conflict	Purposeful Cooperation
Logic	immanent program prefigured sequence compliant adaptation	natural selection among competitors in a population	contradictory forces thesis, antithesis, synthesis	envisioned end state social construction equifinality
Event Progression	Linear and irreversible sequence of prescribed stages in unfolding of immanent potentials present at the beginning	Recurrent, cumulative and probabilistic sequence of variation, selection, and retention events	Recurrent, discontinuous sequence of confrontation conflict, and synthesis between contradictory values or events	Recurrent, discontinuous sequence of goal setting, implementation, and adaptation of means to reach desired end state
Generating Force	Prefigured program/rule regulated by nature, logic, or institutions	Population scarcity Competition Commensalism	Conflict and confrontation between opposing forces, interests, or classes	Goal enactment Consensus on means Cooperation/symbiosis

as an example in chapter 1 incorporates a life cycle model; it lays out steps programs must follow to be effective, and the attainment of each step sets the stage for advancing to the next one. Next to teleology, life cycle is perhaps the most common explanation of development in the organizational literature.

Life cycle theory assumes that change is immanent: that is, the developing entity has within it an underlying form, logic, program, or code that regulates the process of change and moves the entity from a given point of departure toward a subsequent end which is already prefigured in the present state. What lies latent, rudimentary, or homogeneous in the embryo or primitive state becomes progressively more realized, mature, and differentiated. External environmental events and processes can influence how the immanent form expresses itself, but they are always mediated by the immanent logic, rules, or programs that govern development (Poole & Van de Ven, 1989).

The typical progression of change events in a life cycle model is a unitary sequence (it follows a single sequence of stages or phases), which is cumulative (characteristics acquired in earlier stages are retained in later stages) and conjunctive (the stages are related such that they derive from a common underlying process). This is because the trajectory to the final end state is prefigured and requires a specific historical sequence of events. Each of these events contributes a certain piece to the final product, and they must occur in a certain order, because each piece sets the stage for the next. Each stage of development can be seen as a necessary precursor of succeeding stages.

Life cycle theory parallels the approach of the gross anatomist in biology who observes a sequence of developing fetuses, concluding that each successive stage evolved from the previous one. Hence, Nisbet (1970) claimed that development is driven by some genetic code or prefigured program within the developing entity. Nisbet's interpretation has been expanded by Flavell (1982), who discusses a number of historically driven processes of cognitive development, in which each stage logically presupposes the prior stage, such as when the development of manipulative skills precedes writing. There is no reason to suppose organizational systems could not have such processes as well.

---

ideal types of theories in this paper is very loose and done for illustrative purposes only. Since very little attention has been given to underlying theories of change processes in the management and organization literature, it is difficult to know what specific theories of change the authors had in mind.

Life cycle theories of organizations often explain development in terms of institutional rules or programs that require developmental activities to progress in a prescribed sequence. For example, the U.S. Food and Drug Administration institutionally regulates an invariant sequence of steps which all firms must follow to develop and commercialize a new drug or biomedical product. Other life cycle theories rely on logical or natural properties of organizations. For example, Rogers' (1995) theory posits five stages of innovation: need recognition; research on problem; development of idea into useful form; commercialization; and diffusion and adoption. The order among these stages is necessitated both by logic and by the natural order of Western business practices.

TELEOLOGICAL THEORY

Another school of thought explains development by relying on teleology, or the philosophical doctrine that purpose or goal is the final cause for guiding movement of an entity. This approach underlies many organizational theories of change, including functionalism (Merton, 1968), decision making (March & Simon, 1958); epigenesis (Etzioni, 1963), voluntarism (Parsons, 1951), social construction (Berger & Luckmann, 1966), adaptive learning (March & Olsen, 1976), and most models of strategic planning and goal setting (Chakravarthy & Lorange, 1991). Our Program Planning Model example also incorporates some elements of the teleological model; the program has to make choices about whether it will execute the following step or skip to a later step and also about how it will carry out a given step.

A teleological theory is based on the assumption that development proceeds toward a goal or end state. It assumes that the entity is purposeful and adaptive; by itself or in interaction with others, it constructs an envisioned end state, takes action to reach it, and monitors its progress. Thus, this theory views development as a repetitive sequence of goal formulation, implementation, evaluation, and modification of goals based on what was learned or intended by the entity. The theory can operate in a single individual or among a group of cooperating individuals or organizations who are sufficiently like-minded to act as a single collective entity. Since the entity consisting of an individual or group has the freedom to enact whatever goals it likes, teleological theory inherently affords creativity.

Unlike life cycle theory, teleology does not prescribe a necessary sequence of events or specify which trajectory development will follow. However, it does imply a standard by which development can be judged:

development is that which moves the entity toward its final state. Some teleological models incorporate the systems theory assumption of equifinality; there are several equally effective ways to achieve a given goal. There is no prefigured rule, logically necessary direction, or set sequence of stages in a teleological process. Instead, these theories focus on the prerequisites for attaining the goal or end state: the functions that must be fulfilled, the accomplishments that must be achieved, or the components that must be built or obtained for the end state to be realized. These prerequisites can be used to assess when an entity is developing: it is growing more complex, or it is growing more integrated, or it is filling out a necessary set of functions. We are able to make this assessment because teleological theories posit an envisioned end state or design for an entity, and we are able to observe movement toward the end state vis-à-vis this standard.

While teleology stresses the purposiveness of the actor or unit as the motor for change, it also recognizes limits on action. The organization's environment and its resources of knowledge, time, money, etc. constrain what it can accomplish. Some of these constraints are embodied in the prerequisites, which are to some extent defined by institutions and other actors in the entity's environment. Individuals do not override natural laws or environmental constraints, but make use of them to accomplish their purposes (Commons, 1950; Gibson, 1988).

Once an entity attains its goals, it does not necessarily remain in permanent equilibrium. Goals are socially reconstructed and enacted based on past actions (Weick, 1979). Influences in the external environment or within the entity itself may create instabilities that push it to a new developmental path or trajectory. Theories that rely on a teleological process cannot specify what trajectory development will follow. They can at best list a set of possible paths and rely on norms of decision rationality or action rationality (Brunsson, 1982) to prescribe certain paths.

DIALECTICAL THEORY

A third school, dialectical theories, begins with the Hegelian assumption that the organizational entity exists in a pluralistic world of colliding events, forces, or contradictory values which compete with each other for domination and control. These oppositions may be internal to an organizational entity because it may have several conflicting goals or interest groups competing for priority. Oppositions may also arise external to the organizational entity as it pursues directions that collide with those of others. In any case, a dialectical theory requires two or more distinct entities that embody these oppositions to confront and engage one another in conflict.

Dialectical process theories explain stability and change by reference to the relative balance of power between opposing entities. Stability is produced through struggles and accommodations that maintain the status quo between oppositions. Change occurs when these opposing values, forces, or events gain sufficient power to confront and engage the status quo. The relative power or legitimacy of an antithesis may mobilize to a sufficient degree to challenge the current thesis or state of affairs and set the stage for producing a synthesis. So, for example, an entity subscribing to a thesis (A) may be challenged by an opposing entity with an antithesis (Not-A), and the resolution of the conflict produces a synthesis (which is Not Not-A). Over time, this synthesis can become the new thesis as the dialectical process recycles and continues. By its very nature, the synthesis is something new, discontinuous with thesis and antithesis.

However, creative syntheses to dialectical conflicts are often not assured. Sometimes an opposition group mobilizes sufficient power to simply overthrow and replace the status quo, just as many organizational regimes persist by maintaining sufficient power to suppress and prevent the mobilization of opposition groups. In the bargaining and conflict management literature, the desired creative synthesis is one that represents a win-win solution, while either the maintenance of the thesis or its replacement with an antithesis are often treated as win-lose outcomes of a conflict engagement (Neal & Northcraft, 1991). In terms of organizational change, maintenance of the status quo represents stability, while its replacement with either the antithesis or the synthesis represents a change, for better or worse.

EVOLUTIONARY THEORY

Although evolution is sometimes equated with change, we use evolution in a more restrictive sense to focus on cumulative changes in structural forms of populations of organizational entities across communities, industries, or society at large (Aldrich, 1979; Campbell, 1969; Hannan & Freeman, 1977). As in biological evolution, change proceeds through a continuous cycle of variation, selection, and retention. Variations, the creation of novel forms, are often viewed to emerge by blind or random chance; they just happen (Aldrich, 1979; Campbell, 1969). Selection occurs principally through the competition among forms for scarce resources. The environment selects those forms that optimize or are best suited to the resource base of an environmental niche (Hannan & Freeman, 1977). Retention involves the forces (including inertia and persistence) that perpetuate and maintain certain organizational forms. Retention serves to counteract the self-reinforcing loop between variations and selection. Weick (1979) and Pfeffer (1982) note that while variations stimulate the selection of new organizational forms, retention works to maintain those forms and practices that were selected in the past.

Thus, evolution explains change as a recurrent, cumulative, and probabilistic progression of variation, selection, and retention of organizational entities. This motor is prescribed in the sense that one can specify the actuarial probabilities of parameters in differential equations to explain reproduction processes or the changing demographic characteristics of the population of entities inhabiting a niche. While one cannot predict which individual entity survives or fails, the aggregate population persists and evolves through time according to the specified population dynamics.

In organization and management applications, evolutionary theory is often used to depict global changes in organizational populations (e.g., Carroll & Hannan, 1989), although Burgelman (1991) and Singh and Lumsden (1990) have adopted the evolutionary model to explain processes of strategy making within organizations, and Weick (1979) and Gersick (1991) have applied parts of evolutionary theory at an even more microlevel to explain social-psychological processes of organizing in populations of shared behaviors. Whatever the level at which organizational change is examined, an evolutionary model consistently focuses on processes of variation, selection, and retention between numerous organizational entities.

Alternative theories of organizational evolution can be distinguished in terms of how traits can be inherited, whether change proceeds gradually and incrementally or rapidly and radically, and whether the unit of analysis focuses on populations of organisms or species. Darwinists (such as Hannan & Freeman, 1977, 1989; McKelvey, 1982; Nelson & Winter, 1982) argue that traits can be inherited only through intergenerational processes, whereas Lamarkian and cultural evolutionary theorists (Boyd & Richerson, 1985; Burgelman, 1991; Singh & Lumsden, 1990; Weick, 1979) argue that traits can be acquired within a generation through learning and imitation. A Lamarkian view on the acquisition of traits appears more appropriate than strict Darwinism for organization and management applications. As McKelvey (1982) points out, strict Darwinists have developed no adequate solutions to identify operationally an organizational generation and an intergenerational transmission vehicle.

Darwinian theorists emphasize a continuous and gradual process of evolution. In *The Origin of Species,* Darwin wrote, "as natural selection acts solely by accumulating slight, successive, favorable variations, it can produce no great or sudden modifications; it can act only by short and slow steps" (1936, p. 361). Other evolutionists posit a saltational theory of evolution, such as punctuated equilibrium (Arnold & Firstrup, 1982; Gould & Eldridge, 1977). Whether an evolutionary change proceeds at gradual versus saltational rates is an empirical matter, for the rate of change does not fundamentally alter the theory of evolution—at least as it has been adopted thus far by organization and management scholars.

The paleontologist Gould (1989) argues that another basic distinction between Darwinian evolution and his punctuated equilibrium theory is hierarchical level. While Astley (1985) made this distinction, other organizational scholars have not.[4] Gould (1989) points out that classical Darwinism locates the sorting of evolutionary change at a single level of objects. This sorting is natural selection operating through the differential births and deaths of organisms, as exemplified in many studies on organizational birth and death rates by population ecologists (see reviews in Carroll & Hannan, 1989, and Hannan & Freeman, 1989). Gould's punctuated equilibrium model adds a hierarchical dimension to evolutionary theory by distinguishing this sorting (the growth or decline of organisms of a given species through differential birth and death rates) from speciation (the process by which new species or a subgenus is formed). "Speciation is a property of populations (organisms do not speciate), while extinction [a sorting process] is often a simple concatenation of deaths among organisms" (Gould, 1989, p. 122).

A TYPOLOGY OF PROCESS THEORIES

Life cycle, teleology, dialectical, and evolutionary theories provide four internally consistent accounts of change processes in organizational entities. Where and when might these ideal-type theories apply to explain an observed process of organizational change? To address this question it is use-

---

4. An anonymous reviewer constructively pointed out that Tushman and Romanelli's (1985) usage of "punctuated equilibria" misappropriates the label from evolutionary science. Punctuation is a problem in macroevolution; i.e., how species are created and become extinct, not a problem in microevolution. Thus, it is appropriate to borrow the term if we wish to talk about creation or extinction of populations, forms, technologies, etc., but not if we wish to talk about incremental versus quantum change.

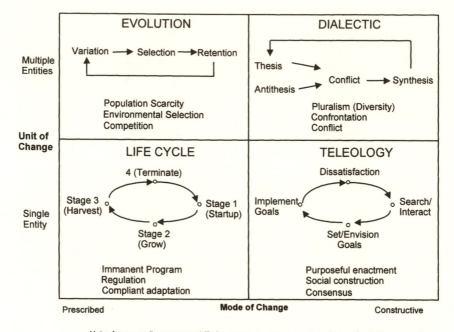

Note: Arrows on lines represent likely sequences among events, not causation between events.

Figure 3.1 Typology of organizational change and development theories

ful to emphasize four distinguishing characteristics in the preceding discussion of the four theories. Each theory (1) views process in terms of a different cycle or loop of change events, (2) which is governed by a different "motor" or generating mechanism that (3) operates on a different unit of analysis, and (4) represents a different mode of change. Figure 3.1 provides a metatheoretical scheme for illustrating and distinguishing the four ideal-type theories in terms of these four characteristics.

CYCLES AND MOTORS OF CHANGE

As the cells of Figure 3.1 illustrate, each theory views the process of development as unfolding in a fundamentally different progression of change events, and governed by a different generating mechanism or motor.

- A *life cycle model* depicts the process of change in an entity as progressing through a necessary sequence of stages or phases. The specific content of these stages or phases is prescribed and regulated by an institutional, natural, or logical program prefigured at the beginning of the cycle.
- A *teleological model* views development as a cycle of goal formulation,

implementation, evaluation, and modification of actions or goals based on what was learned or intended by the entity. This sequence emerges through the purposeful enactment or social construction of an envisioned end state among individuals within the entity.

- In *dialectical models* of development conflicts emerge between entities espousing an opposing thesis and antithesis that collide to produce a synthesis, which in time becomes the thesis for the next cycle of a dialectical progression. Confrontation and conflict between opposing entities generate this dialectical cycle.
- An *evolutionary model* of development consists of a repetitive sequence of variation, selection, and retention events among entities in a designated population. This evolutionary cycle is generated by competition for scarce environmental resources between entities inhabiting a population.

Figure 3.1 shows two analytical dimensions that are useful for classifying these developmental progressions in the four ideal-type process theories: the unit and mode of change.

Unit of Change

Change and developmental processes go on at many organizational levels, including the individual, group, organization, populations, or networks of organizations, and even larger communities or societies of organizations. Figure 3.1 collapses these different levels into whether the change in question is premised on the actions of a single entity or multiple entities.

Evolutionary and dialectical theories operate on *multiple entities*. Evolutionary forces are defined in terms of their impacts on populations and have no meaning at the level of the individual entity. Dialectical theories require at least two entities to fill the roles of thesis and antithesis. Even if we conceptualize the dialectic as occurring within a single person or organization, as does Riegel's (1975) dialectical theory of child development, the focus of the generative mechanism is on the interaction between two entities; the child and its environment. The explanatory model is thus taken down a level and entities are distinguished within the child's mind and the world. Notwithstanding level, the explanation must distinguish at least two (and in Riegel's case four) entities which engage in the dialectic.

Conversely, life cycle and teleological theories operate on a *single entity*. In the case of a life cycle model, development is explained as a function of potentials immanent within the entity. While environment and other entities may shape how this immanence manifests itself, they are strictly secondary to the immanent potentials. The real push to development comes from within the single, whole developing entity. Teleological theories, too, require only a single entity's goals, social construction, or envisioned end state to explain development. A teleological theory can operate among many members of an organization when there is sufficient consensus among the members to permit them to act as a single organizational entity. As in a life cycle theory, interactions between entities may influence the course of development, but this is subsidiary to the teleological generative mechanism that drives the entities' enactment toward an envisioned end state. Thus, an organizational entity in a nested hierarchy of organizational levels can be decomposed to examine its members or aggregated into its larger system without losing any of the theory's explanatory power, as long as the entity undergoing change has a singular, discrete identity. However, if we decide to examine processes of change between several distinct organizational entities, we move to either a dialectical or evolutionary theory, because we must specify laws, rules, or processes by which the entities interact.

MODE OF CHANGE

The generative mechanisms of the four process theories also differ in terms of whether the sequence of change events is prescribed a priori by either deterministic or probabilistic laws, or whether the progression is constructed and emerges as the change process unfolds. A *prescribed* mode of change channels the development of entities in a prespecified direction, typically of maintaining and incrementally adapting their forms in a definite, calculable way. A *constructive* mode of change generates unprecedented, novel forms that, in retrospect, are often discontinuous and unpredictable departures from the past. A prescribed motor evokes a sequence of change events in accord with a preestablished program or action routine. A constructive motor, on the other hand, produces new action routines that may (or may not) create an original (re)formulation of the entity. Life cycle and evolutionary theories operate in a prescribed modality, while teleological and dialectical theories operate in the constructive modality.

A prescribed motor tends to create what Watzlawick, Weakland, and Fisch (1974) termed first-order change: change within an existing framework that produces variations on a theme. The processes by which these variations are produced are prescribed and hence, predictable because they are patterned on the previous state. Over the longer term, small changes may cumulate to produce a larger change in degree or even in quality of the entity. The uncertainty experienced by those undergoing such changes is low, because there is sufficient continuity that the direction of change is discernible. Using a biological frame of reference, DeRosnay (1970) terms prescribed motors as concerned with ontogenesis, which involves the reproduction of entities similar to the original line.

Life cycle and evolutionary theories incorporate a prescribed motor. During the life cycle the immanent form realizes itself by steps. While some steps may seem like a radical morphogenic change, there is an underlying continuity due to the immanent form, logic, program, or code that drives development. Due to this immanent motor, seldom do frame-breaking changes or mutations arise in life cycle models. Evolutionary accounts rely on the statistical cumulation of small individual events to change gradually the nature of the larger population. The apparent exception to this statement, punctuated equilibrium, actually conforms to it on closer examination. In the punctuated equilibrium model of biological evolution posited by Gould and Eldridge (1977), species emergence at the microlevel is sudden, but the diffusion of species that ultimately alters the characteristics of populations occurs through many individual events spread over quite long periods of time (on the order of millions of years) (Gould, 1989). The application of punctuated equilibrium models to organizational change by Tushman and Romanelli (1985) departs from this account and, as we will show below, is actually a mixture of two of the theory types we have defined (see also Poole & Van de Ven, 1989).

Constructive motors tend to generate what Watzlawick termed second-order change, that is, change in basic assumptions or framework which represents a break with the past. The process is emergent as new goals or end states are enacted. It can produce highly novel features; the outcome is unpredictable because it is discontinuous with the past. Those undergoing such changes experience a high degree of uncertainty and they need to make sense of the changes. From a biological perspective, DeRosnay (1970) characterizes constructive motors as phylogenetic processes, which lead to the generation of originals and the emergence of new species.

Teleological and dialectical generative mechanisms incorporate a constructive motor. By their very nature, teleological processes seek to diverge from or to change the current order: a process that has as its goal to preserve or refine the status quo would not be a theory of development. Because goals can be changed at the will of the entity and because the prerequisites may be attained in many ways, teleological theories project a situation which is in principle unpredictable, may result in discontinuity, and may break current frames (Von Wright, 1971). As a result, teleological generative mechanisms project fundamental and novel changes in the entity.

However, there is an apparent problem: many theories in the literature that draw on teleology also explicate gradual processes by which the goals and end states are realized. For example, Chakravarthy and Lorange (1991) describe corporate strategic planning as a stagewise, incremental process. Such gradual accounts of how goals or end states are implemented actually combine two of the ideal types, teleological theory and life cycle theory, to form a composite model. The third section will discuss a number of such composites. In its pure form, however, the twin features of intentionality and the ability to change goals at will make teleological theories inherently emergent and creative.

Dialectical theory also incorporates a constructive motor. The sequence by which the thesis and antithesis confront and engage each other in conflict is highly uncertain; events leading to confrontation of opposites and resolutions may occur intermittently over the course of development. The result is a synthesis that breaks the current frame and represents second-order change. It produces a revolutionary change, resulting in a new entity that is an original rather than the reproduction of some prior state or entity.

SUMMARY

The two dimensions of unit and mode of change define generative mechanisms in terms of their action and process. They differ from other dimensions often used to classify theories of organizational change—including incremental versus radical change (e.g., Tushman & Romanelli, 1985), continuous versus discontinuous change (e.g., Meyer, Goes, & Brooks, 1993), first-order versus second-order change (Meyer, Goes, & Brooks, 1993) and competence-enhancing versus competence-destroying change (Abernathy & Clark, 1985)—which classify organizational changes based on their consequences or outcomes, rather than by their starting or process conditions. One advantage of the typology is that it is possible to identify the motor(s) of a change process before it has concluded.

Antecedent and outcome dimensions of change processes may be related in an actuarial or statistical sense, but not in a causal manner. Statistically, we should expect the vast majority of incremental, continuous, and competence-enhancing changes to follow the operations of a prescribed motor, just as radical, discontinuous, and competence-destroying changes are expected to follow the operation of a constructive motor. But these temporal relationships may not be causal. For example, the infrequent statistical occurrence of a discontinuous and radical mutation may be caused by a glitch in the operation of a prescribed life cycle motor of change. So also, the scale-up of a constructive motor designed to create a fundamental strategic reorientation of a company may fizzle, resulting only in incremental change.

Situating the four ideal theories on the two dimensions accentuates their differences and enables us to describe them in their pure forms. However, as our examples illustrate, the ideal types are not always encountered in pure form in actual theories of organizational change and development. To understand how the ideal types figure in theoretical "practice" and to appreciate their utility, we will now consider specific theories which focus on particular types of organizational change and development and particular contexts in which these occur. For the sake of clarity, we will refer to the ideal-type theories as *ideal types* or *motors* of change and reserve the term *theory* for the complex, specific theories that have been developed by various researchers.

THEORIES OF COMPLEX DEVELOPMENT AND CHANGE PROCESSES

SPECIFIC THEORIES AS COMPOSITES OF THE IDEAL TYPES

Most specific theories of organizational change and development are more complicated than the ideal types. This is so for two reasons. First, because the organizational context of development and change extends over space and time in any specific case, it is possible for more than one motor to come into play. Organizational development and change are influenced by diverse units and actors, both inside and outside the organization. Their spatial dispersion means that different influences may be acting simultaneously on different parts of the organization, each imparting its own particular momentum to the developmental process. In some cases more than one change motor may influence development and change. Development and change also take time to occur. As time passes, there is opportunity for different motors to come into play, especially given the dispersion of influences. The resulting observed process is multilayered and complex. Trying to account for this with a single motor runs the risk of oversimplification and selective attention to one aspect of the change process at the expense of others.

A study of the development of new business startups to produce cochlear implants (a hearing health innovation) by Van de Ven and Garud (1993) illustrates this. This innovation was shaped by change processes occurring on numerous fronts. A teleological process seemed to explain the course of development of the implant in the firm's R&D lab. In a different sphere, the actions of top managers in purposefully selecting and funding it were also consistent with a teleological model, but the decision premises and timing of managerial interventions moved at a different pace than efforts of the development team. At a certain point in its development, the product had to achieve FDA approval, which required a sequence of proposals, clinical trials, and regulatory reviews and approvals. This prescribed sequence, which embodied a life cycle motor, came into play later than the teleological motors, but it was so important that the other two centers of change had to rearrange their efforts to meet its requirements. A fourth influence operated on the larger field of researchers and clinicians concerned with hearing health: the firm's pioneering implant design was initially supported by the field, but evidence mounted that led most researchers and clinicians to switch allegiance to a competing firm's design. The complex interplay of these different motors, which operated in different times and places, created a complicated developmental sequence that was difficult to understand until these diverse influences were sorted out.

A second reason for the complexity of specific organizational change and development theories is the inherent incompleteness of any single motor. Each of the motors pictured in Figure 3.1 has one or more components whose values are determined exogenous to the model. For example, in the evolutionary model variations are assumed to arise randomly, but the process which gives rise to variation is left unspecified. In the dialectical model, the origin of thesis and antithesis is left obscure, as is the source of dissatisfaction in the teleological model and the processes that launch startup and conclude termination in the life cycle model. Other motors can be used to account for the origin of these terms. For instance, the selection process in the evolutionary model can be used to account for termination in the life cycle, the implementation step in the teleological cycle can trigger the startup step in the life cycle and the antithesis in the dialectic. The synthesis in the dialectic could be the source of variation in the evolutionary cycle. There are many other possible interrelations. In short, other models may need to be invoked to remedy the incompleteness of any single model of change.

We will argue that most specific theories of organizational development and change are actually composites of two or more ideal-type motors. This decomposition of complex theories into simpler ones has several precedents. In cognitive science Newell (1973) and Simon (1979), among others, have argued that complex behavior can be generated by the interplay of two or more simpler production mechanisms or motors. In organization science March (1981) and Masuch (1985) have shown that a few substitutions of one simple change sequence by another equally simple process can create exceedingly complicated and intractable action cycles. Poole (1983b, 1985; Poole & Roth, 1989a) has marshaled evidence that seemingly complex patterns of behavior in group decision making result from the interplay of life cycle and teleological motors. The Program Planning Model introduced in chapter 1 posits a teleological process whereby units decide to follow a life cycle or not; the degree to which they follow the life cycle and how effectively they enact its steps determines program effectiveness. All these approaches have in common the identification of simple mechanisms or motors whose interplay creates a complex phenomenon.

AN ARRAY OF COMPOSITE THEORIES OF DEVELOPMENT AND CHANGE

Each ideal-type theory describes a generative mechanism or motor of change. Combinations of these motors create, in effect, hybrid change theories. The simplest form of combination is to determine which of the generating mechanisms underlying the four ideal types are evident or in operation in a given applied theory of organizational change in the literature. By specifying the presence (operation) or absence (nonoperation) of the four motors in a given situation, an array of sixteen logically possible explanations of organizational change and development become apparent. This array, shown in Table 3.2, is analogous to examining the simple main and interaction effects of each of the four motors on alternative applied theories in the management literature.

The first four alternatives represent the "main effects" of the generating mechanisms underlying our four ideal-type theories: the immanent program of life cycle theory, purposeful enactment of teleological theory, conflict and synthesis of dialectical theory, and competitive selection of evolutionary theory. These "single-motor theories" apply to cases when only one of the four generating mechanisms or change motors is in operation.

The next twelve alternatives represent "interaction effects" of the interdependent operation of two or more of the four generative mechanisms. Alternatives 5 through 10 are called "dual-motor theories" because they represent cases when only two of the four change motors are in operation in a given organizational change process. Alternatives 11 through 14 represent four logically possible "tri-motor theories," when three of the four change motors operate interdependently. Alternative 15 is the "quad-motor theory," which represents the most complex situations when all four generating mechanisms operate interdependently in a given situation. Finally, alternative 16 represents the null set, when no motors are operating.

The left column of Table 3.2 lists exemplary theories for some of the six-

Table 3.2 Logically Possible Theories of Organizational Change and Development

	INTERPLAYS AMONG GENERATING MECHANISMS			
	PRESCRIBED MOTOR WITHIN ENTITY	CONSTRUCTIVE MOTOR WITHIN ENTITY	CONSTRUCTIVE MOTOR BETWEEN ENTITIES	PRESCRIBED MOTOR BETWEEN ENTITIES
	IMMANENT PROGRAM	*PURPOSEFUL ENACTMENT*	*CONFLICT AND SYNTHESIS*	*COMPETITIVE SELECTION*
1. Life Cycle (Cameron & Whetten, 1983)	yes	no	no	no
2. Teleology (March & Simon, 1958)	no	yes	no	no
3. Dialectics (Benson, 1977)	no	no	yes	no
4. Evolution (Hannan & Freeman, 1977)	no	no	no	yes
Dual Motor Theories				
5. Design Hierarchy Theory (Clark, 1985)	yes	yes	no	no
6. Group Conflict (Simmel, 1908; Coser, 1958)	no	yes	yes	no
7. Community Ecology (Astley, 1985)	no	no	yes	yes
8. Adaptation-Selection models (Aldrich, 1979)	yes	no	no	yes
9. Org. Growth & Crisis Stages (Greiner, 1972)	yes	no	yes	no
10. Org. Punctuated Equilibrium (Tushman & Romanelli, 1985)	no	yes	no	yes
Tri-Motor Theories				
11. Partisan Mutual Adjustment (Lindblom, 1965)	yes	yes	yes	no
12. ?	no	yes	yes	yes
13. ?	yes	no	yes	yes
14. Social Psychology of Organizing (Weick, 1979)	yes	yes	no	yes
Quad-Motor Theories				
15. Human Development Progressions (Riegel, 1976)	yes	yes	yes	yes
16. ? - Garbage Can (Cohen, March, & Olsen, 1972)	no	no	no	no

teen logically possible conditions in which an organizational change or developmental process may unfold. The rows with a "?" are conditions where we could not find an exemplary theory in the literature and represent opportunities for new theory building. Admittedly, the authors of these exemplary theories or models may not agree with our classification, since they did not have our framework in mind when they developed their theories. However, we contend that the framework provides a useful new way to understand and discriminate between alternative theories of organizational change and development. Specifically, we propose that what distinguishes these alternative theories is their incorporation of different combinations of generative mechanisms of organizational change and development.

Limitations of space prevent us from providing a systematic discussion of theories representing each of the sixteen logically possible combinations of the four generating mechanisms or motors of change. Instead, we will present several examples of how complex theories can be seen to be constructed from the interplay of a few simple motors of change.

Row 5. Interaction of Life Cycle and Teleological Motors. Clark (1985), building on the work of Utterback and Abernathy (1975), developed a theory of the gradual evolution of technologies. Abernathy and Utterback had proposed that the evolution of technological production proceeded from an early, "fluid" state to one that is highly "specific" and rigid. Product innovations predominate early in this evolution, but once the nature of the product begins to be determined and innovations decrease, process innovations increase and come to dominate until rigidity extinguishes innovation. The rise and fall of product innovations are succeeded by the rise and fall of process innovations because of the logic of the production, which pushes firms to try to optimize and standardize first the nature of a successful product, and, once the product is set, the procedures for producing it. The result is increasing rigidity through the life of the product.

To explain how changes in technologies come about, Clark discussed the interaction between designers and customers which establishes functional prerequisites for the product. This teleological process is in interplay with another life cycle motor, the technical design hierarchy. Clark argues that all technical design is hierarchical, because "there are choices in the development of a design that create precedents and are logically prior to other choices. These precedents create constraints that give rise to further search for alternative designs" (1985, p. 241). Once a certain technical path is taken it forecloses other paths and opens up a hierarchy of subproblems. Interaction between designers and customers influences progression through a hierarchy; the natural direction of movement is down the hierarchy until the technical agenda is fulfilled, but customer demands may encourage designers to move back up the hierarchy and pursue other paths or to jump to a different aspect of the design problem altogether. Hence, Clark's theory provides for the interplay of teleological and life cycle motors nested within the overall life cycle progression from product to process emphases.

Row 9. Interaction of Life Cycle and Dialectical Motors. In one of the earliest models of organizational development, Greiner (1972) proposed five stages to the life cycle of organizational growth: creativity, direction, delegation, coordination, and collaboration. Each of these stages culminates in a different dialectical crisis (of leadership, autonomy, control, red tape, and ?), which propels the organization into the next stage of growth. Thus, the model is grounded in temporal interactions between life cycle and dialectical theories of change. In the main, the model is rooted in a life cycle theory of change, in which "historical forces [organization age, size, growth rate, and stages of evolution and revolution] shape the future growth of organizations" (Greiner, 1972, p.166). Greiner uses dialectical theory to explain "as a company progresses through developmental phases, each evolutionary period creates its own revolution" (p. 166). Reflecting on his model, Greiner recently observed that,

> my model is a reasonably explicit attempt to combine unitary life cycle with dialectical theories—but not teleological. For me, life cycle explains the "form" of the unitary stages, while the dialectics explain the underlying dynamics of movement. For example, I put the "crises" in the model because I could not find data showing the stages as naturally and automatically evolving one after the other. Thus, it is not a model where a future life or end state is assured. . . . My reason for saying it is not teleological is that there is no envisioned end state that pulls the process—for me it is the current dynamics within the organization that are driving it forward—convergence around the thesis of each stage and then running into resistance (antithesis) and requiring reorientation for the conflict to be resolved. The model in fact has no ending and concludes with a question mark. . . . I also think it is the dialectics that added the power struggle reality and made the article so successful in managerial reaction. (Greiner, quoted in Van de Ven, 1992, p. 184)

Row 10. Interaction of Teleological and Evolutionary Motors. Tushman and Romanelli's (1985) punctuated equilibrium model of organizational metamorphosis can be viewed as a product of alternating cycles in the operation of an evolutionary reproductive motor of change at a population level of analysis for relatively long convergent periods, punctuated by relatively short and infrequent operations of a teleological constructive motor of change by top managers at the organizational level. During the convergence period an evolutionary process of competitive selection works to elaborate the structures, systems, controls, and resources of organizations toward increased environmental coalignment. Reorientations represent periods of discontinuous change where an organization's strategies, power, structure, and systems are fundamentally transformed by and realigned toward the purposive actions of executive leaders.

The punctuated equilibrium model uses time as the avenue for incorporating both evolutionary and teleological motors in a theory of organizational change. Purposeful enactment by top managers is used to explain the creative process of occasional organizational reorientations, while reproductive evolutionary processes explain long periods of organizational convergence with its environment. According to Tushman and Romanelli (1985), in no instance should we expect to find both motors of change operating at the same time in a given organization because they are mutually exclusive. Thus, time provides the vehicle for incorporating opposing change motors in a punctuated equilibrium model of organizational change.

Tushman and Romanelli's explication of the punctuated equilibrium model does not specify the interplay between the two motors in much detail. It is unclear what sparks the transition from the convergence to the transformational period and vice versa.

Row 14. Interaction of Life Cycle, Teleological, and Evolutionary Motors. Weick's (1979) theory of organizing is an ambitious attempt to explain organizations in dynamic fashion. Weick's well-known model for equivocality reduction has three stages, enactment, selection, and retention, which form a life cycle for the organizing process. This cycle may be repeated multiple times in the course of an organizing episode. As behavior cycles are selected and retained, there is considerable room for the initiative and creativity of individuals to influence the process, opening the way for the influence of a teleological motor. The assumptions of the teleological motor are reflected in Weick's definition of organizing as the development of a shared grammar. In addition to the life cycle and teleological motors, there is also an evolutionary process at work. While individual instances of equivocality reduction follow the three stages, over many repetitions an evolutionary motor operates which selects and retains certain organizational forms over others.

This evolutionary motor, strongly influenced by Campbell's (1969, 1974) theory of intellectual evolution, shapes the course of organizing over the longer term.

Again, time is a key mediator of different motors in Weick's theory. The immediate process of organizing is driven through a life cycle motor and influenced by the teleological motor describing participants' choices of adaptations and retentions. However, over the longer run, these short-term actions contribute to an evolutionary process through which different practices, structures, and ideas are selected and retained.

Row 15. Interaction of All Four Motors of Change. The most complex and sophisticated explanation of change and development in Table 3.2 is one that incorporates interactions from all four generating mechanisms. We have found no example of this composite in the organization and management literature. To illustrate how it might work, we will briefly discuss Riegel's (1975, 1976) theory of human development. Riegel distinguishes between four progressions of life events, which are analogous to our four generating mechanisms of organizational change: (a) an inner-biological progression of life cycle events as birth, illness, cell growth, and death, (b) an individual-personality progression in the psychological development of individuals, in terms of their wishes and duties, plans and skills, needs for belonging and identity, (c) a cultural-sociological progression of an individual's conformity or deviance with the culture, language, institutions, and customs of the social groups, organizations, and society in which the individual participates, and (d) an outer-physical progression of events, such as natural disasters, social demography, or economic cycles, that an individual may encounter. Riegel points out that events within and between these progressions are not always synchronized. Developmental crises occur whenever two sequences are out of step. These crises can produce either destructive outcomes or constructive leaps in development. Riegel goes on to state that

> once generated, these new developments can transform the previously contradictory interactions of conflicting events into a coordinated, synchronized pattern of interactions and change. As synchrony is reestablished, a form of individual and social progress is achieved. And yet with each successful new development, new questions and discrepancies emerge and, in this process, produce a continuous flux of contradictions and developmental change. (1975, p. 385)

Riegel's theory of human development provides a rich example of what a theory of organizational development might look like if it focused on the crises produced by asynchronies in the operation of life cycle, teleological, dialectical, and evolutionary motors of change.

EXTENSIONS OF THE FRAMEWORK

An important extension of the framework is to examine more fully the types of relationships that might hold between the four change motors. Several types warrant investigation. First, there is the degree of *nesting* of motors. In some instances motors may all operate on the same level of analysis, for example, the organizational level. However, one motor may be nested within the other, for example, when the first characterizes the development of the organization as a whole, while the second pertains to the actions of individuals within the organization, or when the first depicts the development of an industry and the second the development of individual organizations in that industry. When motors are all on the same level of analysis, relationships among them represent simple influences; however, when motors are nested, working out the relationships among them requires specifying macro-micro linkages. A second key relationship is the *timing* of the motors. Motors may operate simultaneously or may alternate at different times. If they operate simultaneously, the degrees of amplitude or influence of each motor on a change process over time should be examined. Third, we must consider the degree of *complementarity* among motors. Motors may reinforce or contradict one another.

As these types of relationships suggest, the *balance* between the constructive and prescribed motors operating at different levels of analysis is likely to play a major role in explaining patterns of stability and change in an organization. For example, when an institutionally prescribed motor dominates the development of an organization, it may suppress or dampen internally generated variety to the degree that the organization begins to act more rigidly and more predictably. When a constructive motor dominates through either teleological or dialectical processes, the organization may be unable to suppress rival subsystems that rise up from within, creating too much variety to integrate into one system. In other words, positive feedback between constructive and prescribed motors reinforces change and can produce exploding complexity, while negative feedback counteracts the effects of change events and is likely to produce a moving equilibrium in organizational development.

Temporal shifts in the relative balance between positive and negative feedback loops in the operation of different change motors can push an organization (a) to flow toward a stable, fixed-point equilibrium, (b) to oscillate in a periodic sequence between opposites, (c) to spontaneously create new structures, or (d) to behave in a random fashion. Let us discuss each of these cases in turn.

Organizational stability occurs when a negative feedback loop exists between the operation of prescribed and constructive motors of change. For example, the institutional routines or the established goals of the organization are sufficient to keep the creation of new programs, or conflicts between alternative programs, within limits so that the organization does not fly apart from too much novelty, and thereby produce incremental adaptations flowing toward a stable equilibrium.

Organizational oscillation, exhibited in phenomena such as cycles, fads, or pendulum swings, occurs when the relative influence of positive and negative feedback loops between change motors alternate in a periodic pattern and push the organization to oscillate somewhat farther from its stable equilibrium orbit. Such recurrent cycles are exemplified in some models of vicious circles in organizations (Masuch, 1985), group entrainment processes (McGrath & Kelly, 1986), and creative destruction (Schumpeter, 1942).

Spontaneous novel structures can be produced when strong imbalances occur between constructive and prescribed change motors. These may push the organization out of its equilibrium orbit and produce bifurcations (Prigogine & Stengers, 1984) or catastrophes (Zeeman, 1976) leading to chaotic patterns of organizational change.

Finally, the behavior of change motors in a developing organization may be so complicated and indeterminate as to render deterministic modeling infeasible; the best one can do is to stochastically model the behavior as a *random process.* Stochastic models based on the theory of random processes allow us to make better predictions than we could make with no model at all (Eubank & Farmer, 1990).

These latter two cases suggest a need to develop and study nonlinear dynamical systems models of organizational change and development. Nonlinearities may be produced by feedback loops between two or more simple motors of change. Organizational researchers have tended to focus on linear or cyclical models of organizational development, and to treat other seemingly random patterns as either truly stochastic processes (Tuma & Hannan, 1984) or as various forms of "error" distributions messing up their experiments (Abraham, Abraham, & Shaw, 1990). Advances in dynamical systems theory provide mathematical tools for examining chaos as an alternative explanation of organizational change and development processes. Recent work in this area in the management and organizational literature includes Cheng and Van de Ven (1996), Cottrell (1993), Koput (1992), and Polley (1993). In chapter 9 we discuss dynamic nonlinear models in more detail.

As Koput (1992) describes, a dynamic model is one where the variables (here the operation of the change motors) at a given time are a function (at least in part) of the same variables at an earlier time. Nonlinearity implies that there are feedback loops which vary in strength (loose or tight coupling) and direction (positive or negative) over time between opposing forces or demands. Depending on the nature of the feedback loops and relationships and on the states of key variables (parameters) which govern them, such systems are capable of exhibiting stable, oscillating, chaotic, or random patterns.

Such nonlinear dynamic models are often path dependent or sensitive to initial conditions. This means that small initial differences or fluctuations in trajectories of variables may grow into large differences over time, and as they move far from equilibrium they bifurcate or branch out into numerous possible pathways, resembling a complex decision tree in a chaotic fractal structure. In a chaotic state the pathways that are taken in the branching cannot be predicted; they represent spontaneously created new structures that emerge in a seemingly random order. What is impressive about such chaotic processes is that they have a hidden order that typically consists of a relatively simple nonlinear system of dynamic relationships between only a few variables (Eubank & Farmer, 1990). It seems entirely possible that underlying the indeterminate and seemingly random processes of development often observed in organizational entities there exists such a relatively simple system of nonlinear dynamic relationships between a few of the motors of change examined here.

RELATIONSHIP BETWEEN NARRATIVE EXPLANATORY SCHEMES AND THE FOUR MOTORS

The three different explanatory schemes for process theories defined in chapter 2 bear a strong relationship to the motors and frameworks defined in this chapter. Mohr's process model is quite similar to the evolutionary motor. Movement along the developmental path is dependent on probabilistic laws governing the occurrence of events and the likelihood that these events will result in certain outcomes, which in turn shape the probability of subsequent events. External forces influence the framework through shaping the probabilities that events will happen and lead to subsequent events in the developmental path. Interestingly, Mohr's description of process theories is cast at the level of the individual case, but as the evolutionary model suggests, we can only know the developmental process through study of populations of developing entities, because this is the only way to characterize the probabilistic laws.

Abell's narrative scheme is quite similar to the teleological model. It relies on the same cycle of voluntaristic choice that the teleological motor entails. The major difference between Abell's perspective and the teleological theory is that Abell's analysis only allows individual actors to be units of analysis, whereas the teleological motor is more general, allowing for individuals, groups, organizations, and even broader collectives to form and execute resolves.

Abbott's approach to process is more flexible, allowing for multiple intertwining narratives. This view is similar to the framework that shows combinations of more than one motor. Multiple intertwining motors produce complex developmental patterns; interacting motors from more than one level may form a hierarchical influence system such that microlevel activities constitute macrolevel patterns or macrolevel patterns determine microlevel possibilities.

The two motors not covered by process theorists suggest additional narrative patterns. The life cycle motor is certainly implicit in many narrative cycles in literature and individual psychology. There is no reason it could not also hold in social organizations. The dialectical process reflects the narrative process of conflict and emergence, exemplified by Kenneth Burke's (1969) dramatism. Organizational development has been addressed as a dialectical process, but it has not to our knowledge been theorized in narrative terms.

UTILITY OF THE FRAMEWORK FOR THEORY AND RESEARCH

The framework outlined here is useful in at least five respects. First, it describes in abstract terms the content of process theories. The life cycle, teleological sequence, evolutionary process, and dialectic each specify the steps of a process and the forces that drive it. These four motors serve as building blocks for more complex theories of change. Specific theories of organizational change and development are built by translating one or more of the four basic types into a particular problem context. While some theories are built around a single motor, others theories posit the interplay of two or more motors.

Second, the typology offers insights into the relationships among diverse explanations of organizational change and development. In recent years a wide variety of theories have been advanced, many borrowed from disciplines such as biology and human development. This theoretical pluralism has generated novel explanations of organizational change and developmental processes. However, the diversity of theories and concepts borrowed from different disciplines has often encouraged compartmentalization of perspectives that do not enrich each other and produce isolated lines of research (Gioia & Pitre, 1990).

Any single theoretical perspective invariably offers only a partial account of a complex phenomenon. It is the interplay between different perspectives that helps researchers gain a more comprehensive understanding. The typology can be used to uncover similarities in seemingly different theories and to highlight the "differences that make a difference" in explanations. The four ideal-type motors serve as theoretical primitives, and the complexities of the developmental process can be analyzed as interplays among these primitives. This makes it possible to discern commonality among a broad range of specific theories that might otherwise be overlooked. Some review articles, such as the Cameron and Whetten's (1983) discussion of organizational life cycle models, have attempted to do this for a limited range of developmental theories. The current framework extends this to the entire breadth of organization development and change.

Third, the framework also has normative applications. The four basic theories can be used as standards to evaluate the form, completeness, and tightness of specific developmental theories. When theories are developed for a specific context, such as new product innovation, one strength is that they are tailored to the phenomenon. However, theories built from the ground up sometimes have missing components which are not suggested by study of a particular phenomenon, but which are necessary for a well-formed, complete explanation.

For example, phase theories are often advanced to explain development or change in organizations; however, a surprising number of such theories do not specify what motivates or causes transitions from one phase to another. In specific cases the cause of transitions may either be obscure or may seem so obvious that it can simply be assumed (often this seems to be the case for phases that assume a logical order). However, a complete explanation of development must specify the mechanism or process that moves the organization from one phase to the next; phase changes do not occur automatically and must be explained. The four motors delineate the necessary parts of an adequate explanation, providing standards for constructing and evaluating theories of change and development.

Fourth, the typology suggests additional unexplored explanations of change and development in specific situations. In science, both natural and social, the reigning theory tends to push out alternative viewpoints, so that it becomes difficult to conceive of different ways of theorizing a phenomenon. The typology puts the four motors into tension with each other, promoting alternative perspectives as complements or corrections to any particular theory. Indeed, Table 3.2 has several rows with no entries. It is hoped that these may encourage novel applications of theories to different contexts.

Fifth, the framework supports inductive research by spelling out the characteristics of the four motors and the conditions under which they are likely to operate. Rather than relying on preconceptions of which theory is best, researchers can apply tests for the four motors in order to see which fit the complex phenomenon being examined. This helps to prevent the self-fulfilling prophecies that may occur when we expect a certain number of stages of development or a certain process; it is too easy to find evidence in complex processes for whatever we expect and ignore other motors (Poole, 1981).

IMPLICATIONS OF THE TYPOLOGY FOR PROCESS RESEARCH

As the example of cochlear implants showed, it is not always clear from the outset what forces are influencing a complex developmental process. Indeed, if it is true that the interplay of multiple forces often drives development, then conducting research with a simple a priori theory in mind may actually impede understanding. The researcher may look only for indicators of that particular theory, ignoring other possible explanations. In the best case, this leads to an incomplete account of development and change; in the worst case, the researcher may incorrectly reject his or her model because complexities introduced by other motors cover over evidence of its adequacy.

An alternative approach was suggested by the experience of the Minnesota Innovation Research Program (Van de Ven, Angle, & Poole, 1989): collect very rich data using the process design described in chapter 1 and elaborated in chapter 5 and canvass it for several alternative motors of change. To do this, the researcher must first determine which of the four types of motors could hold by testing whether the conditions required for

Table 3.3   Conditions for the Operation of Change Theories

For a Life Cycle Motor

A singular, discrete entity exists that undergoes change, yet maintains its identity throughout the process.

The entity passes through stages distinguishable in form or function.

A program, routine, rule, or code exists in nature, social institutions, or logic that determines the stages of development and governs progression through the stages

For a Teleological Motor

An individual or group exists that acts as a singular, discrete entity that engages in reflexively monitored action to construct and share a common end state or goal.

The entity may envision its end state before or after actions it may take, and goal(s) may be set explicitly or implicitly. However, the process of social construction or sensemaking, decision making, and goal setting much be identifiable.

A set of requirements and constraints exists to attain the goal, and the activities and developmental transitions undertaken by the entity contribute to meeting these requirements and constraints.

For a Dialectical Motor

At least two entities exist (each with its own discrete identity) that stand in opposition or contradiction to one another.

The opposing entities must confront each other and engage in a conflict or struggle through some physical or social venue in which the opposition plays itself out.

The outcome of the conflict must consist either of a new entity different from the previous two, or (in degenerate cases) in the defeat of one entity by the other, or a stalemate among the entities.

For an Evolutionary Motor

A population of entities exists in a commensalistic relationship (i.e., in a physical or social venue with limited resources that each entity needs for its survival.

Identifiable mechanisms exist for variation, selection, and retention of entities in the population.

Macropopulation characteristics set the parameters for microlevel variation, selection, and retention mechanisms.

---

the motor are present. This results in a set of one or more candidate motors. The second step is to analyze the data to determine which of the candidate motors actually hold, the concrete circumstances of their operation, and how they interrelate. This two-step approach, which we will call *template matching,* avoids the narrowness imparted by adherence to a simple developmental theory, while keeping a strong theoretical basis for research.

Each of the four ideal-type motors depends on a different set of conditions and results in different observable patterns, as depicted in Table 3.3.

Determining whether these conditions or patterns obtain enables re-searchers to make an initial judgment concerning whether a given type of motor could explain development in a particular situation. To test whether the conditions hold for all four models and to specify their mode of opera-tion in concrete terms requires a very rich and diverse dataset. Moreover, indicators for the conditions are likely to vary, depending on the nature and context of the change process being examined.

Template matching is sensitive to the context of organizational develop-ment and change. It promotes the development of explanations commen-surate with the complexity of a given process. Moreover, because explana-tions are cast in terms of the four ideal-type motors and their interplay, this approach promotes the development of more general theories of develop-ment and change.

At the end of chapter 2 we defined five tasks for process research meth-ods:

- event identification
- characterize event sequences and their properties
- test for temporal dependencies in event sequences
- evaluate hypotheses of formal and final causality
- uncover the overall pattern of a narrative.

As Table 3.3 indicates, these tasks are important for evaluating the opera-tion of the four motors as well. The conditions in the table indicate several other types of empirical evidence that must be supplied relevant to the con-tent of each particular motor. For example, to support the existence of a teleological motor requires evidence of reflexively monitored action by a person or group and of social construction, decision making, and goal set-ting. Both variance and process research approaches may be used to ground inquiry to establish the tenability of these conditions.

CONCLUSION

This chapter introduced a typology of four ideal-type theories of organiza-tional development and change: life cycle, teleological, dialectical, and evo-lutionary. These four theories have rich intellectual traditions and offer fun-damentally different explanations of change and development processes. Each theory relies on a different generating mechanism, or motor, which can be mapped as a distinct action cycle. However, observed change and de-velopment processes in organizations are often more complex than any one of these theories suggest, because conditions may exist to trigger interplay among several change motors and produce interdependent cycles of change. While each of these types has its own internal logic or generating mechanism, complexity arises from the interplay among different motors.

Based on the presence or absence of the generating mechanisms underlying the four ideal-type theories, we developed a framework of sixteen logical possible explanations of organizational change and development. As the examples illustrate, this framework provides a systematic way to compare and contrast alternative theories of organizational change in the literature, as well as a means to identify combinations which have not been heretofore applied in organizational research. In terms of theory construction, this involves, first, decomposing theories into constituent types, and then spelling out the interplay among the types. Recognizing what basic theories apply hinges on identifying necessary conditions and discerning the motors embodied in any specific theory.

The four motors offer a unifying scheme to clarify similarities and differences among theories of development and change without trying to impose one master theory that integrates everything. Some integration is desirable, but it must be an integration that preserves the distinctiveness of alternative theories of organizational change and development. We contend that such integration is possible if it is recognized that different perspectives can present quite different pictures of the same organizational processes without nullifying each other. This can be achieved by identifying the viewpoints from which each theory applies and the circumstances when they are interrelated. This approach preserves the authenticity of distinct theories, but at the same time, advances theory building by highlighting circumstances when relationships among the theories may provide stronger and broader explanatory power of organizational change and development processes (Van de Ven & Poole, 1988; Poole & Van de Ven, 1989).

In closing, we should note that while much can be said in favor of the analytical, heuristic, and research potential of this framework, one common objection will probably be that it seems overly reductionistic. Can all models of development be reduced to four relatively simple motors and their interactions? The typology is based on an extensive search through hundreds of works, and the four motors emerged as the "least common denominators" of the change theories reflected in those works, reflecting essential differences among these theories. Certainly, the ultimate determinant will be experience with the typology, using it to analyze existing theories and determining what, if anything, is left out.

This first part of the book has defined a need and laid theoretical groundwork for addressing it. In the second part, we describe methods for process research that tackle one or more of the five basic tasks we have defined. The first chapter of Part II lays out principles of research design for process studies. Successive chapters discuss various methods for analysis of process data.

PART II /// Methods

4 Overview: Methods for Process Research

W‍E HAVE MADE SOME PROGRESS on our journey to understanding change and development processes. The first part of our itinerary has been devoted to exploring the conceptual and theoretical grounding of organizational processes. The remainder of the excursion will be devoted to methods that put the concepts of Part I to work.

In Part I we established that both process and variance approaches have important roles in the study of organizational change and development. Part II will cover methods appropriate to both process and variance research. We will not attempt to describe every possible method that could be used in research on development and change. Instead, we identify novel and emerging approaches that seem well suited for the particular problems encountered in the study of organizational processes. We hope that our elaboration of these methods will demonstrate how researchers can modify existing approaches to meet the special demands of process research.

The following chapters introduce methodologies in generally accessible terms as they can be applied to process questions. Most of the methods in this volume are covered in other books and there is no need to discuss them in great detail here. Instead, we focus on potential applications and on the steps and choices that must be taken in tailoring the methods to particular questions about development and change. In addition, we provide numerous references to good original sources for readers who find the methods useful for their own research. Our discussions assume familiarity with traditional statistical techniques, but beyond this we have attempted to give readers an account of these methods in common language.

PROCESS RESEARCH METHODS

Perhaps the most stringent requirement for process research methods is that they must work with event sequence data. Analysis of event sequence

91

data enables researchers to evaluate process theories on their own terms or, alternatively, to derive narrative models inductively. This data can also be transformed into formats suitable for variance analyses. Variance methods can be used to test hypotheses regarding characteristics of the sequence and process-outcome relationships that are suggested by one or more plausible narrative models.

As developed in Part I, methods are needed that enable researchers (1) to identify events; (2) to characterize event sequences and their properties; (3) to test for temporal dependencies in event sequences; (4) to evaluate hypotheses of formal and final causality; (5) to recognize coherent patterns that integrate narratives; and (6) to evaluate developmental models. Achieving these tasks is in part a function of how researchers gather and record their data and in part a function of analytical methods.

EVENT IDENTIFICATION

Identification of events provides the substance for process analysis. Events are generally not simply "there"; the researcher must engage in the interpretation of raw data such as interviews or historical records to recognize relevant events. Identification of events requires that researchers have a clear definition of the central subject of the narrative (i.e., who or what the events are relevant to) and a sense of what is relevant to the change process under study. Event identification occurs through iterative analysis, moving from raw data to a set of incidents (meaningful occurrences) which serve as indicators for events, and then back again in circular fashion. This is facilitated by development of systematic coding rules that make the process transparent to other researchers; systematic procedures also enable an assessment of reliability and validity of classifications. Chapter 5 discusses methods for distilling event data from a record of the process.

In some cases events are layered. As chapter 2 indicates, events in the same process may have different duration and differ in the range of actors and contexts they span. In such cases, higher-order (more macro) events can be coded from lower-order (more micro) events. Chapter 5 discusses coding procedures that can be applied for this purpose. Chapter 7 covers phasic analysis methodology, which identifies coherent phases (macro events) from sequences of shorter (micro) events.

CHARACTERIZING EVENT SEQUENCES

Once we have identified one or more event sequences, the next step is to describe their properties. Several different kinds of properties may be captured:

1. *Type of sequence.* Does the sequence follow a certain path? This may be determined deductively, by comparing a model that implies a specific ordering of events to the sequence, or retroductively, by exploring the data with several models in mind. The result is a classification of sequences into types. These nominal types can then be related to contingency factors that produce them and to outcome variables.

2. Events may also function as indicators of *event variables,* such as the level of idea development in an event or the degree to which an event indicates interventions in the innovation process by outside resource controllers. Coding procedures may be used to generate values of the variable for each event, such as whether the event indicates resource controller intervention (a nominal variable), or the degree to which the event contributes to positive morale on the innovation team (an interval variable). Once individual events have been coded for the variable, researchers may also calculate the value of the variable for longer segments or subsequences (e.g., the total number of resource controller intervention events in a one-month period; the average level of morale across all events in a segment). Coding events for variables transforms the events into a time series of values that can be analyzed with various statistical methods.

3. *Summary properties of a sequence,* such as how long it is, the degree to which it matches a particular ideal-type sequence, or the amount of idea development in the sequence. This results in one or more variables, in which the sequence itself is the unit of analysis, allowing for comparison of different event sequences.

4. Another option is to identify the occurrence of *specific subsequences of events,* such as periods of interaction with outside regulatory agencies or sets of transactions to form joint ventures. These can be extracted and studied in their own right, as independent sequences.

Chapter 7 discusses methods for phasic analysis which are suitable for the analysis of entire sequences. These methods can also support the identification of subsequences and comparison of different sequences. Chapters 8 and 9, on event time series analysis and nonlinear event time series analysis respectively, describe procedures for analyzing time series of variables which characterize event sequences. They can also generate summary indices to describe event sequence properties.

Specifying Temporal Dependencies

To trace enchainments and linkages, it is useful to identify event-to-event dependencies. The simplest such dependency is sequential contingency, such that one or more events increase the probability of the occurrence of a succeeding event. For example, creating a citizen review board may be necessary for a social service program to build the community support required to garner government funding. One-step contingencies among a series of successive events could indicate that this particular sequence occurs regularly, suggesting a developmental type. Contingencies may also indicate causal linkages, such that event 1 leads to event 2 (efficient causality) or, alternatively, that event 2 is the purpose for which event 1 occurs (final causality).

There are two approaches to evaluating claims concerning dependencies and enchainments among events. The first retains the nominal categorizations of events and identifies dependencies among events. Stochastic modeling techniques, discussed in chapter 6, support this type of analysis. The critical incident technique offers a qualitative approach to the same question. It is also possible to generate time series event variables, as described above. Methods described in chapter 8, including time series regression and cross lag time series analysis, can then be used to analyze the event series or summary event indices for segments of the timeline.

EVALUATING HYPOTHESES OF FORMAL AND FINAL CAUSALITY

Hypotheses of formal and final causality are assessed (a) by comparison of the overall pattern in the event sequence to the pattern implied by the formal or final cause and (b) by tests for additional conditions or factors that must operate for a given formal or final cause to operate. For example, assume researchers wish to evaluate the hypothesis that the model of social program startups from chapter 1 described a set of cases. They would (a) determine whether the phases of the observed programs matched those in the Program Planning Model, and (b) search for evidence for the operation or application of this pattern (e.g., evidence that key actors explicitly thought in terms of this rational, stepwise model, or that resource controllers required satisfaction of the steps in the model to qualify for funding).

The stochastic modeling methods of chapter 6 and the phase analysis methods of chapter 7 are both well suited to determine fit between hypothesized and actual patterns of development and change for events classified at the nominal level. Time series methods described in chapters 8 and 9 can be used to detect patterns in continuous data based on event variables.

RECOGNIZING PATTERNS THAT INTEGRATE NARRATIVE EXPLANATIONS

Information gained from carrying out the first four requirements of process research is an invaluable support for pattern recognition. The hermeneutic circle, with its part-whole cycling, is the key to discovering integrative patterns, and ultimately, this depends on a critical insight on the part of the researcher. However, checking the validity of this insight and refining the narrative explanation is greatly facilitated by the application of systematic methods for pattern evaluation and characterization of sequences and their interdependencies. Systematic methods may also help researchers cut through the undergrowth of details to discern consistent and striking patterns in event sequences; this clears the way for the ultimately creative insights on which narrative coherence depends.

DISTINGUISHING AMONG ALTERNATIVE GENERATIVE MECHANISMS

In chapter 3 we described four basic models of development and change which incorporated different generative mechanisms. As we noted, any particular change or development process may be explained in terms of a single model or in terms of a combination of interrelated models. The question immediately arises as to how we might empirically assess whether one or more of these models operate in a given process. Several methods are available to test the plausibility of process theories and to determine which motor(s) are operating.

Table 3.3 listed the conditions necessary for the operation of each generative mechanism. These conditions imply that the following tests might be performed to determine which of the generative mechanisms operate for a given case or sample:

(a) *Does the process exhibit a unitary sequence of stages which is the same across cases?* Life cycle models posit a definite sequence of stages. Teleological models may exhibit stages, but the stages do not have to occur in a particular order; stages must occur and cumulate to satisfy the final goal or form of the process, but the order in which they are satisfied is not particularly important. Evolutionary and dialectical models do not have to exhibit distinguishable stages (though they may). The steps in the activity cycles for each generative mechanism may overlap so much that clear stages are not definable.

The methods for phase analysis introduced in chapter 7 can be used to identify phases that may correspond to developmental stages, if any exist. Phase methods also enable researchers to evaluate sequences to determine whether they display a unitary ordering and to cluster sequences into types. Stochastic modeling (chapter 6) and time series methods (chapter 8) can also support the identification of stages.

(b) *Is there a patterning device, such as a program, routine, code, or rule system that determines the nature of the change sequence?* As noted in chapter 3, life cycle models of organizational processes require a program or code either immanent within the developing entity or enforced by some external agency. Teleological models do not require such governing patterns; though the central subject may be oriented to such patterns, its activity is a result of willful choices and is not forced to follow a set sequence by internal or external patterns. Dialectical models, by definition, do not adhere to patterns, because they rely on emergence for resolution of conflicts. Evolutionary models are governed by patterns that drive enactment, selection, and retention.

Evidence for programs, routines, codes, or rule systems must be garnered from sources outside the event sequence. The event sequence may contain evidence of these patterning forces, but the patterns themselves will be found in factors influencing the sequence. For example, in medical innovations, one powerful patterning force is the testing sequence mandated by the FDA for new medical devices. The role of the FDA in various events and participants' actions and testimony vis-à-vis the FDA provide clues to its importance, but the FDA's procedures themselves must be investigated and described as an adjunct to the event sequence.

The same is true for patterning forces internal to the developing entity. Some evidence of the existence of a "blueprint" (Pondy & Mitroff, 1979) is required. It may be a logical scheme that defines why stages must logically unfold in a particular way. For example, it is necessary to generate an idea before it can be debated and modified. Alternatively, the process may be organized by an explicit patterning device, such as a strategic plan organized along the lines of the rational process discussed in chapter 1. Evidence of this plan and its use can be garnered from event data.

(c) *Is there a goal-setting process?* The teleological model requires a goal-setting process. It is the means by which purposes are set and is the first step in orchestrating unified action. Life cycles may include goal setting as one stage. Evolutionary and dialectical models do not exhibit goal setting; though goal setting may be undertaken by individual units within the process, it is not part of the generative mechanism in which the units interact.

Goal setting can usually be identified as part of the event sequence, but some adjunct evidence may be utilized as well. Coding and phase analysis methods, described in chapters 5 and 7, are useful for the identification of goal-setting activities. Adjunct evidence, such as a mission or goal statement or outsiders' reportage of goals, may also be useful to establish goal setting.

(d) *Is (are) the central subject(s) an individual entity or a set of interacting entities?* One of the critical steps in process analysis is defining who the central subject(s) are. This is necessary in order to define events that are relevant to the process. This step, discussed in chapter 5, requires interpretive analysis of the process. The model and general theoretical assumptions favored by the researcher usually imply a certain type of central subject and a choice of one versus several subjects. In addition, the process data itself conveys important information on which reading of the situation is most plausible. A researcher determined to find two interacting central subjects in a dialectic may find that his or her data clearly indicate the presence of only a single significant agent. In this case, the researcher should abandon the dialectical model in favor of either the life cycle or teleological models.

Interpreting raw data to derive events and larger narrative patterns is a cyclical process that follows the hermeneutic circle, tacking between particular facts and larger interpretive constructs and patterns. Cycling between raw data and narrative models provides the researcher with numerous opportunities to identify candidate subjects and to evaluate her or his choice. Chapter 5 addresses issues of design and coding that can support researchers in their quest to define the proper central subject.

(e) *Are individual cases to some extent unpredictable, so that the best level of analysis is the total population of cases?* For some change phenomena, it is not possible to predict accurately the behavior of individual cases. This may be because each case is influenced by "internal" factors or dynamics that are difficult to measure or access, such as individual decision-making processes based on private preference distributions. There may also be a truly unique, unpredictable element in the case. While individuals may be difficult to explain or predict, the behavior of a population of individuals may exhibit more regularity and allow the construction of theories of the population. In such cases, the evolutionary model is most appropriate. It explicitly deals with population-level dynamics, providing a theory of how the population of cases will evolve over time.

This test requires multiple cases in order to assess regularity at the individual case level. Stochastic modeling, discussed in chapter 6, and time series diagnostics, discussed in chapter 9, provide tests for the predictability of individual cases based on the event sequence data. Other evidence for predictability beyond what is available in the process data may also be employed.

(f) *Do conflict or contradictions influence the development or change process?* The dialectical and evolutionary models give conflict an important role. The teleological model takes the opposite tack, assuming that the consensus which underpins concerted action can be achieved; conflict is either nonexistent or short-lived in a process governed by the teleological model. Life cycle models may allow for conflict in one or more stages. Evidence for the presence or absence of conflicts can be obtained from event sequence data utilizing coding procedures described in chapter 5. Stochastic modeling, phase analysis, and event time series methods can all be used to explore the role of conflict in a process. Evidence external to the event sequence may also be utilized to establish the degree to which conflict is important in the process.

SUMMARY

Table 4.1 summarizes the tests that can be used to establish the plausibility of the four models. Notice that each row has a different pattern of answers to the questions, thus ensuring that if all questions are validly addressed a unique model can be established. A development or change process shaped by one model is relatively simple. As we noted in chapter 3, development and change theories often combine more than one model in their explanations. In such cases, it is important for researchers to "localize" tests and to

Table 4.1   Tests for the Four Basic Change Models

TEST	LIFE CYCLE	TELEOLOGICAL	EVOLUTIONARY	DIALECTICAL
Is there a unitary sequence?	Yes	No	Possible	Possible
Program, code, sequencing device?	Yes	No	Yes	No
Is there a goal-setting process?	Possible as one stage	Yes	Possible in units	Possible in units
Is the central subject an individual or set of interacting entities?	Individual	Individual	Set	Set
Are individual cases unpredictable?	No	No	Yes	Possible
Is conflict or contradiction important to the change process?	Possible as one stage	No	Yes	Yes

eliminate as much interference as possible in the evaluation of each individual model.

For each specific version of the four models, there will be additional assumptions that must be tested, such as the particular number and types of stages in a life cycle model, how consensus is reached in teleological motor, how entities clash in a dialectical motor and how resolution occurs, and how retention occurs in an evolutionary model. In some instances, these tests can be conducted from the event sequence data, while in other instances special supplementary data will be required.

POSTSCRIPT

Table 4.2 indicates which process research tasks are addressed by the methods discussed in subsequent chapters. As the table suggests, process research may require a combination of several methods.

We will use a common dataset to illustrate how the various methods enable researchers to tackle different process research problems. This should

Table 4.2   Methods and the Tasks They Address

TASK	EVENT CODING	STOCHASTIC MODELING	PHASIC ANALYSIS	TIME SERIES ANALYSIS	NONLINEAR MODELING
Event identification	✔		✔		
Characterize event sequences			✔	✔	
Identify temporal dependencies		✔		✔	✔
Evaluate formal/final causal hypotheses		✔	✔	✔	✔
Recognize overall narrative patterns		✔	✔	✔	✔
Is there a unitary sequence		✔	✔	✔	
Program, code, sequencing device?					
Goal-setting?	✔		✔		
Single or set of central subjects?	✔				
Are individual cases unpredictable?		✔		✔	
Is conflict/contradiction important?	✔	✔	✔	✔	

facilitate comparison of the methods and help researchers make judicious choices that match their own preferences and presumptions about the process. The next section describes this dataset in more detail.

A PROCESS DATASET

The data used in most of the examples in this book come from the Minnesota Innovation Research Program (MIRP). As described by Van de Ven, Angle, and Poole (1989), this program consisted of longitudinal field studies undertaken during the 1980s by 14 different research teams (involving over 30 faculty and doctoral students). These studies tracked the development of a wide variety of product, process, and administrative innovations from concept to implementation or termination.

Although the research teams adopted different methods and time frames, depending on their unique circumstances, they adopted a common conceptual framework. This framework focused on tracking changes in five concepts that were used to define innovation development. The process of innovation was defined as the development of new *ideas* by *people* who engage in *transactions* (or relationships) with others within a changing environmental *context* and who change their behaviors based on the *outcomes* of their actions. Comparisons of innovations in terms of these five concepts permitted the researchers to identify and generalize overall process patterns across the innovations studied. Many of these patterns are discussed in Van de Ven, Angle, and Poole (1989).

More specific evidence for some of these developmental patterns was gained from a few innovations that were studied using detailed real-time observations of the innovation process. In this book we will take as our example a fine-grained study of the development of cochlear implants by the 3M Corporation that was conducted by Garud and Van de Ven (1989). This example will be carried through the rest of the book to provide a common frame for exemplifying process research methods. We will describe this study and its data in some detail here in order to set the stage for subsequent chapters. Specifically, we will introduce the nature of the data gathered, the basic event constructs, and how they were operationalized. We will also discuss the theory that Van de Ven, Garud, and Polley developed to explain new product development processes. Definitions of constructs in the dataset and coding categories are detailed in the appendix to this chapter.

The cochlear implant program (CIP) ran from 1977 to 1989 as an internal corporate venture to create an implanted device allowing profoundly deaf people to hear. Following the event sequence methods discussed in this book, this longitudinal field study focused on the events that occurred throughout the development of the cochlear implant program until the termination of the project.

This study, and a related study of therapeutic apherisis technology (TAP) in 3M by Van de Ven and Polley (1992), examined a model of trial-and-error learning for explaining the process of innovation development. The core of this model focuses on the relationships between the actions taken and outcomes experienced by an entrepreneurial unit as it develops an innovation from concept to reality, and the influences of environmental context events on these action-outcome relationships. Following March (1991), the model assumes that people are purposeful and adaptively rational. To develop an innovation, entrepreneurs initially take a course of action, for example, A, with the intention of achieving a positive outcome. If they experience a positive outcome from this initial action, they exploit it by continuing to pursue action course A; if a negative outcome is experienced, they will engage in exploratory behavior by changing to a new course of action, B, for example. Subsequently, if positive outcomes are experienced with action course B, they exploit B by continuing with it, but if negative outcomes are experienced, they continue exploration activities by changing again to another course of action, C, for example, which may appear as the next best alternative course at that time. This anchoring-and-adjustment process of negative outcomes leading to changes in the prior course of action continues until positive outcomes are experienced, which, in turn, serve as the retention mechanism for continuing with the prior course of action.

MIRP researchers (Garud & Van de Ven, 1992; see also Van de Ven & Polley, 1992) tracked events in the development of the CIP as they occurred from the time funding and efforts began to initially develop the innovation ideas until the innovations were implemented and introduced into the market. The researchers collected their data by attending and recording the proceedings of monthly or bimonthly meetings of the CIP team and periodic administrative reviews by top managers, by conducting semiannual interviews with all innovation managers and questionnaire surveys of all innovation personnel, and by obtaining documents from company records and industry trade publications throughout the developmental periods of the CIP innovation. Each raw observation was termed an *incident*. Observations were defined as incidents when changes were observed to occur in the innovation idea, innovation team personnel and roles, the activities and relationships they engaged in with others, the external context beyond the control of the innovation team, and judgments of positive or negative outcomes associated with these events.

These incidents were entered into a qualitative computer database which recorded its date, the action that occurred, the actors involved, the outcomes of the action (if available), and the data source. Chronological event listings were shared with innovation managers in order to verify their completeness and accuracy. The CIP database contained 1,007 event records.

Events were then coded according to a number of conceptual categories in the learning model. These included:

- *Course of action:* The direction of actions that occurred in each event were coded according to whether they represented (a) a continuation or expansion (addition, elaboration, or reinforcement) of the course of action underway on the topic, versus (b) a change in the action course through a contraction (subtraction, reduction, or deemphasis) or modification (revision, shift, or correction) from the prior event.
- *Outcomes:* When events provided evidence of results, they were coded as either (a) positive (good news or successful accomplishment), (b) negative (bad news or instances of mistakes or failures), (c) mixed (neutral, ambivalent, or ambiguous news of results), or (d) null (events provided no information about outcomes).
- *Context events:* This category includes external environmental incidents that occurred beyond the control of the innovation participants but were reported by participants as relevant to the innovation.

These and a number of other event constructs utilized in the CIP and TAP studies are outlined in the appendix.

Two researchers independently coded the events into the relevant categories of each event construct. Garud and Van de Ven (1992) agreed on 93% of all codings of CIP events (Van de Ven and Polley [1992] agreed on 91% of all event codes for the therapeutic apheresis project). The researchers resolved all differences through mutual consent.

In chapter 5 we will present more detailed examples of procedures for creating event sequence files, including coding categories and procedures and various transformations of the data that can be undertaken to convert it into forms appropriate for different types of analysis.

To put the data into perspective it is useful to know something about how the investigators interpreted their results. Two temporal periods reflecting very different patterns of relationships between actions and outcomes were found in the development of CIP: (a) an initial premarket development period of mostly expanding activities undertaken once decisions were made to launch the innovation efforts with corporate venture capital support, followed by (b) an ending market-entry development period of mostly contracting activities that concluded with decisions to terminate CIP. This delineation of the event sequence into two stages was based on qualitative interpretation of the time series, supplemented by quantitative analyses discussed shortly. Chapter 7 illustrates the application of more systematic, formal phase mapping procedures to the attempts that the CIP team made to form alliances and joint ventures with researchers and other businesses.

Event time series analysis (chapter 8) supplemented qualitative interpretation to suggest the following narrative for the CIP innovation process: The initial development period began when the innovation team was formed and funded to explore an innovative idea. This was an ambiguous period where it was not clear which of several possible technical designs should be developed. During this initial ambiguous period, external environmental events (not the actions of entrepreneurs) had a significant negative effect on outcomes. When negative outcomes occurred, they subsequently led the entrepreneurs to continue with, and not change, their prior course of action. These actions, in turn, had no effect on subsequent outcomes in either positive or negative directions. These findings suggest a faulty learning process of action persistence, despite the occurrence of negative outcomes during the beginning development period.

Major problems of market entry punctuated the beginning and ending development periods; in particular, product failures necessitated a product recall for CIP. The ending period largely dealt with uncertain but less ambiguous problems of scale-up manufacturing and market entry of the technical designs that were chosen in the earlier period. During this period, strong evidence for the learning model was found for CIP, as well as for the therapeutic apheresis effort. Adaptive learning was evident in the positive reciprocal relationships between actions and outcomes.

In explaining these results, Van de Ven and Polley (1992) concluded that the process of learning seems random and unpredictable during the initial period of development, but not during the concluding period of development. Garud and Van de Ven (1992) speculated that trial-and-error learning seems to guide innovation development under conditions of uncertainty (i.e., when it is not clear what means to pursue to achieve known ends), but action persistence appears to occur when the developmental process is ambiguous (i.e., when it is not clear what specific ends are worth pursuing). Finally, Cheng and Van de Ven (1996) applied some of the methods described in chapter 9 to reexamine the event sequence time series for nonlinear patterns. Their findings suggested a chaotic process during the initial period of development and more orderly periodic patterns in the ending developmental periods of the two innovations. One set of methods that were not used to study the CIP process are the stochastic modeling approaches described in chapter 6. We will rectify this oversight by presenting a detailed example of how CIP can be illuminated through stochastic modeling.

With these preliminaries behind us, we are ready to continue our journey. Our road will take some unusual twists and turns, and it may be a bit bumpy at times. At some points we will have to slow down, as we pass through a zone of "methods under construction." We hope that readers will find this an interesting and rewarding journey. And we fully expect that when this road is traveled twenty or so years from now it will be an interstate highway, rather than the treacherous two-lane country road we now embark.

APPENDIX: DEFINITIONS AND CODING RULES FOR CIP EVENTS

This appendix is adapted from the codebook for the CIP event data file. It specifies rules for defining events and definitions and coding rules for event constructs, the variables that capture various characteristics and properties of events. These events and event constructs will be used in the illustrations of each type of analysis in subsequent chapters. The original codebook has been changed as little as possible; most changes were intended to maintain subject confidentiality.

CRITICAL INCIDENTS

An event sequence file contains records of the critical incidents in the development of the innovation. *Incidents* can be divided into *events* and *observations on events* that occur on specific dates over the course of an innovation's development.

- *Events* are major cyclical activities and changes in the core MIRP concepts of innovation ideas, people, transactions, context, and outcomes.
- *Observations* are judgements or interpretive statements about events made on specific dates by key stakeholders (innovation participants, resource controllers, and researchers).

Some subjective judgment is involved in determining whether an incident is critical. Incidents will be judged as critical (and therefore recorded in the event sequence file) (a) when the events or observations are important (i.e, are stated by a stakeholder to have a noticeable impact) and (b) when they approximate the level of specificity (from fine to coarse grain) called for in the conceptual categories or coding rules for key concepts in the research framework (defined below).

Discrete Time

We take a discrete view of time when incidents occur. This means that events and observations are actions that take place at a particular time; incidents are a function of the unit of time measurement. For example, if an action takes less time than the smallest unit available to measure it, then the action may be attached to the closest measurement unit. In our case, the day of an incident is our temporal unit of measurement.

Thus, the occurrence of each critical incident in the event sequence file is coded by *day/month/year*, with two columns for each variable.

- Where the specific day, month, or year of an incident is not known, this will be stated in the incident description.
- Where events take longer than one unit of measurement, they may be said to have duration. This problem is handled by specifying the dates and incidents that started and concluded the event.
- When exact dates of changes cannot be ascertained, they are estimated based on the information obtained and are entered in the incident date field. Only as a last resort is the date when the information is received used to indicate the date of an incident.

We reserve the terms "patterns," "trends, "paths," and "trajectories" for processes that represent aggregations across several related events or observations. An example would be when several related observations of competitive action are given the label of "competitive awareness."

CODING OF CRITICAL INCIDENTS

A coding scheme refers to the set of labels that are used to identify critical incidents into either event or observation types or to identify characteristics or types of events. The data may be coded multiple times into whatever constructs are useful for further research and theory construction and evaluation. To permit comparisons of incidents across MIRP studies, the following major types of classifications will be made. Additional codings may be added as necessary.

Events versus Observations

Incidents are coded as *events* when the actions are either major cyclical "milepost" activities or when changes are observed in the core MIRP concepts of innovation ideas, people, transactions, context, and outcomes.

Incidents are coded as *observations* when judgments or interpretive statements are made by key stakeholders (innovation participants, resource controllers, and researchers) about events. Coding incidents as observations requires a referencing of the event (by number) on which interpretive statements are made, the stakeholders making the observation, and what the statement is about (i.e., the innovation idea, people, transaction, context, and outcomes).

The reason for distinguishing events from observations is to capture both objective—or factual—descriptions of events and the more subjective, cognitive, and partisan perspectives of various stakeholders about events. Both factual events and interpretive observations are needed to have a complete story or narrative of the development of an innovation.

Activity Events

Throughout the MIRP project, we have conceptualized events as incidents when changes occur in the core MIRP concepts of ideas, people, transactions, context, and outcomes. In addition, it is useful to consider a classification of events that includes *activities* that represent major cyclical "mileposts" in the innovation's development, even though they may not represent changes in the other constructs.

- Examples of activities include administrative reviews, resource procurement and budgeting cycles, strategy meetings, major trade or professional conferences, and other recurrent "mileposts" that are structured to direct or evaluate the innovation's development.
- A less obvious example of an activity is when a previously determined goal (outcome) is publicly communicated to upper management via a management review. This might be subsumed as a change in context, but it assumes effects not necessarily in evidence and is different from resource allocations or organizational changes that would otherwise constitute contextual events.

Idea Events

An incident is coded as an idea event when there is a change in the ideas that are deemed to be significant to the overall development of the innovation by the innovators. Changes in innovation ideas are classified into those that pertain to core or related ideas.

- *Core* ideas are those that pertain to the central technology, product, program, or service that makes up the essence of the innovation.
- *Related* ideas are those that support the development of the innovation, but do not constitute a change in the core embodiment of the innovation.

In general, changes in core innovation ideas often represent new pathways or trajectories of the innovation (as drawn in our charts), whereas related ideas often pertain to organizing, coordinating, or funding a given pathway or trajectory.

- For example, a change in the core idea for CIP was the shift from claiming to develop an implant device to that of forming a Hearing Health Program that included the CIP device. A related idea to this core idea change was a reallocation of resources in the program.
- Evidence of idea changes is most often marked by debate at management meetings or general announcement by management responsible for the overall innovation. This may also suggest that when a potential change is considered and not implemented it should be coded as an idea event.

People Events

An incident is coded as a people event when there is a change in the staffing (turnover) or assignments (roles) of people holding key positions in the innovation (as suggested by the innovators). In addition, key individuals responsible for the management of the innovation environment would also be included. (This relates to the definition of context given below.)

Transaction Events

An incident is coded as a transaction event when there is a change in the legal or social contracts associated with the innovation. This may relate to key transactions between the innovation and other organizations in the environment and also to transactions between people within the innovation unit. Efforts to change or modify existing transactions may also receive this code. For example, when the company initiates efforts to create a new contract or relationship involving the innovation, it is coded as a transaction event.

- *Resource controller interventions* is one form of transaction we want to track over time. Resource controllers may be venture capitalists, top managers, or board members who have invested capital in the innovation being studied. When a resource controller is behaviorally involved in activities or administrative reviews of the innovation unit, it is defined as a transaction event and coded as a resource controller intervention.

Context Events

A context event is an external incident that is related to the innovation but occurred beyond the control of the innovation team. It may involve an environmental change in technology, structure, or market that is related to the innovation's development. Context events are subdivided into *organizational* and *external context*. The line of demarcation between these falls at the boundary of the working organization that houses the innovation. For CIP, the internal context includes the strategic business unit and all organizational elements under their control. Other environmental changes (such as changes at 3M or changes in resource availability) are allocated to the external context.

Outcome Events

An incident is coded as an outcome event when a change occurs in the criteria or values of criteria used to judge the progress or outcomes of the innovation. Outcomes include both tangible results of innovators' courses of action and completions of innovation components or products, as well as less tangible value judgments about the success or failure of an innovation's development by key resource controllers and innovation managers.

Outcomes are further coded as representing either:

- *positive* (good news or successful accomplishments),
- *negative* (bad news or instances of failures or mistakes), or
- *mixed* (neutral or ambiguous news or results indicating elements of both success and failure).

These categories for coding outcomes are useful for empirically examining the success-failure action loops model of innovation development.

- Another outcome event category is *dates,* which refers to changes in schedules, milestones, or anticipated dates for meeting objectives. This category is added to the coding of outcomes in order to measure the progress of an innovation in meeting its timetable. Thus, changes in dates that merely extend proposed timetables for courses of action are to be coded as changes in outcomes-dates.
- Outcome events are also recorded when there is a *shift in outcome criteria*. When an innovation team leader or resource controller states a goal or an outcome criterion for judging the innovation's success that is different from the past, it is recorded as an outcome criterion shift event.

Course of Action

The directions of the actions that occur in each event will be coded according to whether they represent a continuation or change in the course of action from the previous event related to the topic. Specifically, the course of action involved in each event will be coded according to whether it represents an

- *expansion*—an addition, elaboration, reinforcement,
- *contraction*—subtraction, reduction, deemphasis,
- *modification*—revision, shift, correction, or
- *continuation*—repetition or ongoing progression

in the current direction of the course of action underway on the topic.

This coding of event action course requires identifying the prior event pertaining to the topic, and then judging if and how the action course in the present event differs from the prior event.

Summary List of Core MIRP Codes

In summary, the event sequence files for all MIRP innovation studies consist of the following core Fields (columns) and Labels (or categories):

- Incident Number
  A sequential numbering of incidents in chronological order
- Incident Date
  Month/Day/Year
- Record Entry Date in File
  Month/Day/Year
- Data Source
  Sources of data on incident
- Incident Type
  Event or observation
- Core MIRP Index
  Activity (major recurrent events; e.g., reviews, funding)
  Idea-Core (the central product, program, or business idea)
  Idea-Related (to the development of the core innovation idea)
  People (turnover and role changes)
  Transaction (relationships with other units and organizations)
  Resource Controller Intervention
  Context-Internal (in the organization housing the innovation)
  Context-External (to the organization housing the innovation)
  Outcome
  Action Course (change in direction from prior event on topic)

Unique Innovation Codes

Each innovation contains numerous incidents about substantively different topics, products, programs, pathways, or trajectories. In order to examine developments in each of these substantively different areas, more specific content codes are needed for each incident in the event sequence file. These content codes are unique to each innovation study and represent another layer of classifications under some of the major classification categories listed in the previous section. The codes in this section are unique for the CIP case.

- Activity (major recurrent events; e.g., reviews, funding)
  Actions: Types of behaviors that occurred in an incident (each of these has a more specific definition in terms of the parenthetical terms, which are in turn defined in a coding manual):
    Introduce (search, study)
    Propose (report, claim)
    Evaluate (judge, review)
    Negotiate (offer/discuss/modify terms of relationship)
    Commit (agree, appoint, grant, confirm, acquire)
    Execute (perform, carry out, administer)
    Correct (adapt, revise, problem solve)
    Conflict (disagree, fight)
    Withhold (forebear, table, defer, reject)
  Functions: Topics of action, that is, the innovation function it serves:
    Overall development of organization/program
    Links between organizations
    Financing
    Competence development/training
    Technological R&D and design
    Testing/comparing technologies
    Clinical trials/Regulatory approval
    Manufacturing and quality control
    Marketing/Endorsement/Distribution
- Idea-Core (the central product, program, or business idea)
  Device: A number of particular devices were listed. [These are not given here to protect subject confidentiality.]
- People
  Actors: A list of specific actors involved in the case; they are listed by name and also classified into general types (e.g., Associations, Regulators, Firms, Funders, etc.). [This list is not included to protect subject confidentiality.]
- Context-External (to the organization housing the innovation):
  Industry/Technology Development Patterns: Incident types pertaining to the following patterns of technology and industry development:
    Uncertainty: Evidence of uncertainties perceived by innovation participants about action outcomes and technologies.
    Market: Estimates of market size and potential by industry participants.
    Anticipatory retardation (or postponement): Incidents where actors declined or deferred innovation adoption in anticipation of a future improved version.

Upgradability/design continuity: Efforts or incidents to make generations of products, services, or structures compatible with each other.

Creative destruction: Efforts or incidents that made existing products, services, or structures obsolete.

Barriers: Blockage, patent protection, or preemptive tactics used by actors to secure protection or private gains from their developmental or commercial efforts.

Substitutes: Any product or service that acted as a substitute for cochlear implants.

Transfer: Exchange or sharing of information or competence between firms.

- Outcome:

  Outcome-Positive (good news)

  Outcome-Negative (bad news)

  Outcome-Mixed (neutral or mixed good and bad news)

  Outcome-Date (shfiting schedules)

  Outcome Criteria shift (change in goals or evaluation benchmarks)

- Action Course (change in direction from prior event on topic):

  Expand path (add, elaborate, reinforce)

  Contract path (subtract, reduce, deemphasize)

  Modify path (revise, shift, correct)

  Continue path (in current direction)

The categories and subcategories listed here will be used in the example analyses in later chapters.

5 Issues in the Design of Process Research

PROCESS RESEARCH DESIGNS are premised on systematic analysis of event series. They presume that understanding change and development depends on understanding dynamics. As Miller and Freisen note:

> It is very hard to draw inferences about the operations of machines by looking at snapshots of a diverse array of them. It is much more instructive to watch a few machines in motion, seeing how their parts interact while examining their inputs and outputs. We can then distinguish between moving and static parts; active and passive ones. Such knowledge is essential to any designer. Theorists do seem to realize this, at least at one level. They are constantly couching their theories in dynamic terms. Unfortunately they tend to examine only cross-sectional data to generate and to test theories. (1982, pp. 1014–1015)

Methods that rise to the challenge of process research make special demands on the researcher. To identify patterns, uncover narratives, and discriminate among developmental models requires detailed longitudinal data on a number of comparable cases, as well as systematic methods for analyzing these observations and the context in which they are embedded. As a result, process research designs require revisions and extensions of traditional research methods.

In particular, we noted in chapter 1 that longitudinal case studies can provide useful data for studying change processes because they are often based on event chronologies that can be interpreted to isolate unique or important event sequences. However, most case studies do not take advantage of the power afforded by more formalized analytical methods. Case study reports are often subject to nagging questions about the validity and generality of conclusions. It is difficult for interpretive researchers to enunciate the process by which they draw their conclusions. Hence, it is difficult to assess the validity of interpretive claims or to engage them in critical discussion. At the end of the day, the interpreter can always take refuge in the claim, "I saw it and you did not," which effectively stops all discussion.

Such arguments can be avoided if researchers present their data as distinct from their data analysis, so that different perspectives can be publicly assessed and tested. Data on a series of events in the development of organizational units can be interpreted and analyzed from a variety of perspectives. A properly designed and documented process study offers researchers the opportunity to analyze the data from a wide spectrum of interests—to discover new patterns, to test hypotheses about developmental models, to understand the rich, historical context of change, and to specify the form of developmental functions.

The foundation for this approach is the construction of a data file that systematically presents the events that were observed to occur in the organizational entities being investigated. The construction of this data file should achieve two objectives. First, it should meet the same standards of reliable and valid measurement and documentation as found in good quantitative survey studies. Second, the data file should also reflect the careful attention to qualitative nuances and detail that are often found in well-conducted case studies. In other words, process research methods should harness the sensitivity of case analyses to the power and generalizability of quantitative methods. Achieving these dual goals often requires considerable ingenuity on the part of the researcher. One way to serve both ends is to utilize a mix of methods and to bolster interpretation of quantitative results with qualitative data (Miller & Freisen, 1982).

The purpose of this chapter is to introduce a set of concepts and methods for designing process research studies that can achieve these dual objectives of qualitative richness and quantitative generality. As used here, *research design* refers not just to procedures for gathering data, but to the entire enterprise of conceiving and conducting a longitudinal study. Design decisions must be informed both by the theory and questions that direct the study and by the methods of analysis that will be employed. Design cannot be understood independently of theory or analysis. In the case of longitudinal process research, theory and analysis are important determinants of the observational schemes employed, the frequency and types of data sampled, and how observational data are interpreted and transformed for purposes of pattern discovery or theory testing.

This chapter is divided into three parts, corresponding to three important concerns in process research design: formulating the research plan, establishing and validating the observational systems, and transforming

Table 5.1   Overview of Process Research Design Topics

Formulating the Research Plan

1. Tailoring the Study to the Research Question
   Deductive and retroductive approaches
   Developmental motors
   Examine a single model vs. compare alternative models
   Direct real-time observation vs. archival studies
   Component sources of change
2. Sampling
   Sample size
   Sample diversity
3. Fitting the Design to Methods of Data Analysis

Gathering Longitudinal Process Data

1. Defining Incidents and Events
   Parsing incidents from "raw data"
   Duration and granularity of incidents and events
2. Observational and Archival Sources of Data
3. Identifying Events from Incidents
4. Reliability and Validity of Incident Construction
5. Coding
   Design of coding systems
   Layered coding
   Reliability and validity of coding systems
6. Chronicles: Event Sequence Data Files

Transforming Coded Data Into Forms Suitable for Analysis

1. Types of transformations
   Summary data
   Bitmaps
   Phase maps
   Continuous variables

observational data into useful forms for analysis. Table 5.1 provides an overview of the topics in each part. While these topics are discussed in sequential order, we emphasize that they are interdependent. Designing a particular research project requires making numerous interdependent decisions and trade-offs on these topics listed in Table 5.1.

FORMULATING THE RESEARCH PLAN

The design of any research should depend on the nature of the research questions or hypotheses to be investigated. Tailoring a study to its research questions and hypotheses entails several choices, including whether the researcher emphasizes a deductive or retroductive approach, whether to observe processes directly or rely primarily on retrospective accounts, whether the research will test a single theory or compare alternative models, and how to sort out different sources of change. Another set of issues revolves around the research sample. These include sample selection, sample size, and breadth of sampling. Finally, an adequate design must satisfy the requirements of analytical methods. These three sets of issues overlap, so the following sections will build on each other.

TAILORING THE STUDY

Deduction, Induction, and Retroduction

Deductive and retroductive approaches define a continuum of strategies researchers may employ. While *deduction* is familiar to most readers, retroduction, and its relationship to the more popular term, induction, may not be. *Induction* refers to the inference we draw from direct observation of a phenomenon which results in assigning a probability of the likelihood of an occurrence in the future. Induction leads only to probabilistic statements. *Retroduction*, defined by Peirce (1955), refers to the inference in which we posit a theory or substantive hypothesis to explain previously observed patterns. Such theory or hypothesis is supposed to go beyond the specific case. We believe this pattern of inference more accurately describes what occurs in social scientific research than does the pattern corresponding to induction, and so we use the term retroduction as the opposite of deduction.

If a deductive approach is taken, the basic steps in designing research might consist of adopting one or more of the basic process theories described in chapter 3, operationalizing the theory(ies) into a template, and then using this (these) template(s) to determine how closely an observed process matches the theory. One could also proceed by retroduction: observe processes of stability and change over time in a few organizational entities, sort the data into meaningful categories, and then develop a theory or hypothesis to explain the observations. This theory or hypothesis would need to be verified with a different sample or on the same sample at a different time. One could also start somewhere in between, with a partial theory and flesh it out through retroduction and induction.

In the course of a research program, most researchers will move back and forth between deduction and retroduction. Deductive studies will raise questions or adventitious observations that lead to retroductive theory building. Retroduction will generate theories that stimulate deductive research.

Identification and Testing of Developmental Motors

We noted in chapter 3 that deriving or verifying a theory of development and change is ultimately dependent on assessment of whether the conditions for one or more of the four motors is met. For example, distinguishing between a life cycle or teleological motor depends in part on whether development follows a unitary, set sequence of stages (indicating a life cycle motor) or may follow multiple sequences (suggesting, but not sufficient, for a teleological motor). Deductive research would assess the fit of the two models to the data directly, while retroductive research might examine a number of cases and note the uniformity of sequence, suggesting a life cycle. The conditions listed in Table 3.3 set up an ensemble of tests that can be employed to determine which models hold for a given process. Testing becomes more complicated when multiple, layered models hold, but it follows a similar logic.

The specific context of an organizational change process is also important to examine. For example, if initial tests indicate that a teleological model offers a plausible account for startup of international organizations (as Etzioni, 1963, posited), we might also need to conduct additional tests to ensure that it holds in the format to be expected for this context. We might test whether the particular sort of goal-setting processes to be expected in international organizations holds for this case. Only if there were support for both the general and specific conditions for a motor (or motors) to hold could we conclude with some certainty that the motor was a plausible explanation. Therefore, a critical issue in the formulation of any research plan is how to garner the proper data in a form that permits identifying the context-specific conditions when each of the four motors might be operating.

Examining Single Models versus Model Comparison

Is it better to study a single model or to compare the fit of two or more models? Working with a single model of development or change has the advantage of forcing the researcher to make definite "bets" and clear hypotheses. A study focused on a single model makes it easy to test for specification errors and to improve a model that is close to fitting.

Although most research is conducted with only a single model or theory in mind, we believe a stronger case can be made for designs that compare alternative models or theories of change. First, as Stinchcombe (1972) argued, having two or more models enables the researcher to make stronger inferences by conducting critical tests of assumptions that differentiate among the models. For example, as we noted above, one test to differentiate a life cycle from a teleological model is to determine whether events follow a single general sequence or multiple sequences. Finding a general sequence supports the assumptions of the life cycle model, whereas multiple sequences would support the teleological alternative. The advantage of comparative testing is that null results for one model do not leave the researcher in a cul-de-sac where he or she knows only what is *not* likely. Studies that compare plausible alternative models have a high probability of making a positive contribution to knowledge.

Second, most "real-world" processes are exceedingly complex to a point in which they are beyond the explanatory capabilities of any simple theory found in the literature. Hence, we suggest exploring several alternative theories that capture different aspects of the same process. This not only gives a fuller picture, but also encourages rigorous and critical appraisals of theories. As Mitroff and Emshoff (1979) observed, when scholars and practitioners work from a single perspective or theory, they are subject to the temptation to unintentionally twist and rationalize facts to fit their preconceptions. One way to counteract this temptation is to develop and juxtapose alternative theories that throw one another's assumptions and weak points into clear relief. Although results are seldom clear-cut, comparative analysis will generally enable researchers to determine which theory better explains the data or how they can be combined.

The comparative approach is particularly advantageous when a retroductive research strategy is employed. Trying out several different models facilitates exploratory investigations by giving conceptual guidance to the analysis of large bodies of field data. Consideration of several models or theories enables researchers to tack back and forth between different assumptions and premises, gauging which seem to fit the data best. Each perspective serves as a comparison point for the others. It is always difficult to rule out the possibility that the data are being selectively assimilated toward a promising model. Judicious contrast of two or more promising and workable, but distinctive theories offers perhaps the best way of keeping our minds "alive" and critical of emerging accounts. It is also consistent with the principle that knowledge advances by successive approximations and comparisons of competing, alternative theories (Diesing, 1991).

Observation of Processes in Real Time versus Reliance on Retrospective Accounts

Studying organizational change processes necessarily entails collecting longitudinal data. These data can be obtained either by observing the sequence of change events as they occur in real time or by relying on historical archival data to obtain a retrospective account of the change process. Most studies of organizational change to date have been retrospective case histories, conducted after outcomes were known. Retrospective studies provide the advantage of knowing the "big picture," how things developed, and the outcomes that ensued. This post hoc knowledge is helpful for interpreting events and for constructing a narrative of the developmental process. When researchers conduct real-time observations of a change process as it unfolds, they do not have this advantage of afterthought and may miss occurrences or events that later may be viewed as critical. Until we have the compass of the entire process, we have no way of knowing what will be important and what will not.

However, there is another side to this: prior knowledge of the outcome of an organizational change process invariably biases a study's findings. This is especially true if the final assessment valorizes the outcome as a success or failure, effective or ineffective. There is a tendency to filter out events that do not fit or that render the story less coherent. This tendency to reduce the "difficult" nature of the data may result in censorship of interesting dynamics and minority views. However, historical analysis is necessary for examining many questions and concerted efforts can be undertaken to minimize bias.

A promising approach is to initiate historical study before the outcomes of an organizational change effort become known. It is even better to observe the change process throughout its unfolding. This approach maximizes the probability of discovering short-lived factors and changes that exert important influence. As Pettigrew notes, "the more we look at present-day events, the easier it is to identify change; the longer we stay with an emergent process and the further back we go to disentangle its origins, the more likely we are to identify continuities" (1985, p. 1).

For example, if the purpose of a study is to understand how to manage the formulation or implementation of an organizational strategy, it will be necessary for researchers to place themselves into the manager's temporal and contextual frames of reference. Presumably, this would initially involve conducting a retrospective case history to understand the context and events leading up to the present strategy being investigated. However, the major focus of the study would entail conducting real-time observations of the events and activities in strategy development while they occur in time, and without knowing a priori the outcomes of these events and activities.

Regularly scheduled and intermittent real-time observations are necessary to observe if and how changes occur over time. Repetitive surveys and interviews provide comparative-static observations of the organizational unit or strategy being tracked over time. Difference scores between time periods on these dimensions would determine if and what changes occurred in the organizational unit or strategy. But to understand how these changes came about, there is a need to supplement regularly scheduled data collection with intermittent real-time data. For example, this would involve observing key committee meetings, decision or crisis events, and conducting informal discussions with key organizational participants. Thus, while difference scores on dimensions measured through regularly scheduled surveys and interviews identify *if* and *what* changes occurred, real-time observations are needed to understand *how* these changes occurred. Over the years, Chris Argyris (1968, 1985) has forcefully argued that significant new methods and skills of action science are called for to conduct this kind of longitudinal real-time research. It requires researchers to identify the principal users of their research project and to negotiate the research plan with these principal users. Typically, this entails designing the research observations from the frame of reference of these users. It further implies significant researcher commitment and organizational access, which few researchers have achieved to date. As a consequence, few developmental studies of organizational change efforts have been conducted with real-time observations.

Organizational scholars often state that the purpose of their research is to develop new scientific knowledge that will improve management practice (Van de Ven, Angle, & Poole, 1989). In other words, these researchers view managers as the principal users of their research. Obviously, researchers must obtain informed voluntary consent of participants to study any organizational change process in which they might be engaged. One reason why gaining such consent and organizational access has been problematic is because researchers seldom place themselves into the manager's frame of reference to conduct their studies. Without observing a change process from a manager's perspective, it becomes difficult (if not impossible) for an investigator to understand the dynamics confronting managers who are directing the change effort, and thereby generate new knowledge that advances the theory and practice of managing change.

Furthermore, if organizational participants do not understand the relevance of a study, there is little to motivate their providing access and information to an investigator. At issue here is *not* that researchers become consultants. The issue is one of negotiating and addressing important research questions that capture the attention and motivation of scholars and practitioners alike. Clearly, the outcomes of research on an important question may not provide immediate pay-off to practitioners or academics. Many important research questions do not have clear solutions until after the research has been conducted. If solutions are well known in advance of the research, the question may be appropriate for a consulting practice or an internal management study, but clearly not for basic scientific research. Thus, at the time of designing research and negotiating access to organizations, prospective solutions to applied problems are secondary in comparison with the importance of the research question. A good indicator of such a research question is its self-evident capability (when properly articulated) to motivate the attention and enthusiasm of scholars and practitioners alike.

For example, in launching the Minnesota Innovation Research Program (see Van de Ven et al., 1989), we found that a useful way to begin longitudinal research is to conduct meetings with small groups (eight to twelve) of managers or representatives from various organizations that were about to initiate comparable organizational change efforts or ventures in their natural organizational settings. In these hour-and-a-half meetings we introduced our research question (e.g., "How and why do innovations develop over time?"), discussed why it is important to advancing theory and practice, and outlined a longitudinal real-time research strategy for studying the research question in comparable field settings over time. Participants then shared their opinions of the research question, why it was important or useful to study the question, and how the research design might be modified to make it workable in their organizational settings. The meetings concluded by thanking participants for their useful ideas and indicating that we would contact them individually to negotiate access to study the question in their organizations. Following these meetings, the research design was modified as deemed necessary, and negotiations began with individual organizations. A substantial subset of those represented at the meetings agreed to provide access to conduct the research.

Component Sources of Change

In the study of human development, Schaie (1965, 1973; Wohlwill, 1973) discussed three common sources of temporal change:

1. *Age:* The age or temporal duration of the individual at the time of measurement. This variable represents that part of development and change that is produced by unfolding biological or institutional processes.
2. *Cohort:* The set of characteristics of all individuals who are born at the

same time and go through similar developmental processes, such as classes in school. This variable represents the common historical conditions that shape the development of a given cohort.

3. *Transient:* All the temporary or immediate and noncumulative factors that influence outcomes or the dependent variables at the time of measurement.

Schaie argued that developmental research should be designed to distinguish these three effects—those that are due to age, to external factors in the history of the developing organism (cohort), or to immediate external factors (time of measurement).

It is important to design organizational change studies so they can disentangle these three sources of change. What appears to be a developmental change due to some immanent mechanism could well be due to a cohort effect or to a unique effect at the time of measurement. For example, a sudden shift in morale compared to previous levels may result from a general improvement in social mood at the time of measurement. Interpreting this as a function of solidification of a developing culture would be incorrect, though it would be easy to see why a researcher whose attention was focused only on the organization under study might draw this conclusion. In the same vein, what appears to be a general developmental pattern might be due to cohort effects, unique events occurring only to the group of organizations which were founded in a given time and place. By this reasoning, for example, it would be risky to try to generalize principles of effective development of organizational startups in the relatively benign 1950s to organizations in the "lean and mean" 1980s, because they belong to different cohorts. They started under different resource constraints, had employees with different attitudes, and a different external environment.

This is not to imply that it is impossible to develop generalizable findings concerning development and change. Rather, it is important to consider from what source observed changes originate and to rule out alternative explanations for the ones we advance. It is also important to consider the limits of our conclusions. Taking into account age, cohort, and time of measurement, as well as organization type and context, will result in more effective research designs.

SAMPLING ISSUES

Sample Selection

There is no one best sampling scheme for process research. In determining the nature of the sample to be drawn, researchers must consider the balance among four factors: sample size, sample diversity, intensity of data gathering, and cost. In general, the cost of a study in terms of time and effort increases as sample size, sample diversity, and intensity increase. To keep costs in check, compromises must be made on one or two of the three factors.

Consider sample size. The larger the sample the more valid the study and the more generalizable the results (provided cases are drawn in a representative fashion). However, large samples create problems of analysis and interpretation (Miller & Freisen, 1982). These problems stem from the time required to gather data from a large sample and from the volume of data researchers must handle. When the data are event descriptions, as process research requires, rather than quantitative responses, the cost of data gathering increases still further. If costs are held constant, there is an inherent trade-off between the intensity of data gathering—the richness and amount of data that can be acquired for each case—and sample size. A smaller sample enables more intense data collection, but also may result in nongenerality of results.

Next consider sample diversity. Should the researcher attempt to obtain a homogeneous uniform sample or a broad, heterogeneous sample? For example, if a researcher sets out to study the process of innovation development from concept to implementation, should s/he sample units that are all pursuing the same type of innovation, such as a biomedical device, or sample a wide variety of units that are pursuing different kinds of technical and administrative innovations in different industries and sectors? A case can be made for both strategies.

A homogeneous sample has the advantage of keeping to a minimum the multitude of alternative explanations for developmental processes. This is especially advantageous in the case of lengthy sequences of events, because they are particularly vulnerable to accidental or adventitious occurrences that shift the course of development. Comparing cases that are similar in as many respects as possible facilitates identifying whether change processes are due to such transient events or to more basic developmental models, but does not control for cohort effects. A homogeneous sample also facilitates the development and investigation of very precise, focused questions or hypotheses. Hence, homogeneous sampling is useful when a well-specified theory of change or development is available.

On the other hand, a case can also be made for a broad, heterogeneous sample, because it provides a better opportunity to detect whether sources of change are due to temporal development, cohort, or transient factors. Critics have questioned the wisdom of this heterogeneous sampling of innovations, since it may result in "trying to compare apples with oranges." Our position is that researchers will never know the limits where valid comparisons end and where invalid comparisons begin unless they empirically examine the broadest possible range of cases to which our definition of innovation applies.

The comparative method is perhaps the most general and basic strategy for generating and evaluating valid scientific knowledge. This strategy involves the selection of comparison groups that differ in the scope of the population and conceptual categories of central interest to the research. As Kaplan pointed out, scientific knowledge is greatly enhanced when we divide the subject matter into concepts and cases that "carve at the joints" over the widest possible ranges, types, conditions, and consequences (1964, p. 52). In this way researchers can develop and evaluate the limits of many important propositions about the subject matter.

A broad sampling scheme also permits a researcher to make empirical links between different specialties or schools of thought that have emerged for different organizational settings in which the change process occurs. For example, because organizational structures for business creation are different in small company startups, internal corporate innovation projects, and interorganizational joint ventures, it is widely believed that the process of entrepreneurship in these organizational settings must also be different. Van de Ven et al. (1989) questioned this conventional belief and proposed the plausible alternative that creating a new business entails fundamentally the same process regardless of organizational setting. If empirical evidence is obtained to support this proposition, then significant benefits and efficiencies can be gained by applying principles for business creation from new company startups to internal corporate venturing and interorganizational joint ventures, and vice versa.

In view of the trade-offs between homogeneous and heterogeneous samples, Pettigew suggests four useful guidelines for selecting cases to study:

1. "Go for extreme situations, critical incidents and social dramas." By choosing cases that are unusual, critically important, or highly visible, researchers select cases in which the process is "transparently observable." One thing researchers should be cognizant of is that such cases may have nongeneralizable features precisely because they are uncommon. It is important to assess how typical are the conclusions derived from such cases.
2. "Go for polar types." Choose cases that seem very different in terms

of the processes under study. For example, researchers might compare successful and unsuccessful program startups. Alternatively, they might choose cases that differ from patterns in earlier cases. By successive sampling of polar types, it will eventually be possible to cover the field of possible cases.

3. "Go for high experience levels of the phenomena under study." Choose cases that have a long track record of experience with a process. For example, in the studies of innovation, choose companies with reputations as highly successful innovators. This strategy may not be possible for some cases: new program startups, for example, may best be illuminated by inexperienced agencies, since they will make the mistakes and experience the learning that highlights key requirements for successful startups.

4. "Go for more informed choice of sites and increase the probabilities of negotiating access." Selecting a case for one's sample is fruitless if one cannot obtain cooperation. Often, cases must be selected on the basis of who will cooperate, rather than on grounds of optimal sampling. As Campbell and Stanley (1963) noted long ago, this introduces a bias in sampling that should be considered in drawing conclusions from the study. (1990, pp. 275–277)

While process studies, with their rich data requirements, are costly, Paul Nutt's (1984a, 1984b, 1993) strategy of gradual expansion seems to be one way of handling resource requirements. Nutt has developed a standard data collection format that he has employed over a period of 10 years to gather narratives of strategic decisions. By dint of patient and persistent pursuit of accounts, Nutt has developed a large database of decisions. While resource limitations may reduce the number of cases we can acquire at first, if we continue our pursuit, our confidence in our results can increase over the years.

THE RELATIONSHIP OF DATA AND ANALYTICAL METHODS

The research plan sets the parameters for the type of analytical methods that can be employed. However, some analytical methods are likely to be better than others for exploring certain research questions or testing certain models; hence, the proposed analysis should also be a constraint on the research plan.

Two important dimensions of research design which influence the choice of analytical methods are (1) the number of cases collected and (2) the number of events that are observed in the temporal development of the average case.

Most treatments of sample size in research methodology texts focus on the number of cases (not the number of temporal units) that are selected for data collection. The larger the number of cases that are sampled from a population of interest, the more generalizable are the results (provided that the cases are drawn in a representative fashion). Furthermore, in experimental designs researchers are advised to select the number of cases needed to obtain enough power from statistical tests to equate statistical significance with practical significance in hypotheses testing (Walster & Cleary, 1970). In addition to these statistical considerations, in practice, the number of cases selected also depends on the availability of sites and the costs involved in collecting data on each case.

In longitudinal research, an equally important consideration of sample size is the number of temporal intervals or events on which data are obtained from beginning to end on each case. The number of temporal intervals or events observed depends on what constitutes the "natural" flow of experience in the organizational change cases being studied. Organizational change processes vary in temporal duration and granularity. In terms of temporal duration, some organizational change processes, such as group decision making, may occur in committee meetings lasting no more than a few hours. Other change processes, such as the development of technological and administrative innovations, may span several years. Granularity refers to the preciseness or discreteness of events that are recorded throughout the temporal duration of a case being studied.

The granularity of events may vary greatly, ranging from events of such large scope that only 5 to 20 might be observed to exhaust the period of study to events of such small scope that several thousand occur during the period under study. Event granularity typically increases with the microanalytic detail of the change process being investigated. Psychological studies of change in individuals tend to sample fine-grained events, such as speech acts, time allocation, or role behavior, whereas sociological or economic studies of organization change tend to sample more coarse-grained events, such as structural reorganizations, mergers, or stages of organizational growth.

Another consideration is the cost of coding events. Events that require a great amount of time and effort to observe and code are likely to be observed in shorter sequences than less costly ones. For example, it might require a great deal of time and effort to compile the complete record of all the transactions between researchers in the field of gallium arsenide semiconductor research; however, to get a shorter (and probably just as representative) record of some transactions by coding which researchers attended the same meetings and which labs entered into joint projects would

Table 5.2 Analytical Options for Different Types of Process Datasets

	FEW EVENTS	MANY EVENTS
Few Cases	Summary Case Studies	Summary Case Studies Phasic Case Studies Time Series Analysis Markov Analysis
Many Cases	Multivariate Analysis	Multivariate Analysis of Summary Data
	Phasic Analysis with Optimal Matching	Phasic Analysis with Optimal Matching
	Event History Analysis	Markov Analysis Time Series Analysis

be much less costly. Due to the inherent trade-offs between the temporal duration and granularity of events that can be sampled, studies of relatively brief change processes can afford to utilize categories that code fine-grained events, while studies of lengthy change processes tend to adopt categories that tap coarse-grained events.

Crossing these two dimensions of number of cases and number of events yields a 2×2 table, each of whose cells corresponds to a different set of appropriate data analysis methods, as shown in Table 5.2. Each method will be mentioned only briefly here, to give an overview of the relationships between sampling schemes and methods of data analysis. Data-method relations will be discussed in more depth in subsequent chapters.

Studies consisting of *few cases, few events* are not suited for most of the methods discussed in this book. However, there are many important phenomena in which the focal events occur only a few times. For example, consider a comparative study of strategic decision making where the sequence of search, screen, and choice activities is the object of investigation. As Nutt's (1984a & b) studies show, there may be relatively few instances of these activities for each decision, resulting in short event series. Other studies may focus on critical incidents, unusual or uncommon events such as conflict or key turning points in development of industries. Provided there are enough cases for systematic comparison and induction across the instances, Yin's (1984) comparative case study designs are useful in this situation.

Studies with *many cases, few events* enjoy more options. *Summary measures* for each case can be derived by collapsing the data along the time dimension (e.g., counting the number of conflicts that occur during innovation regardless of when they occurred), or through use of surrogate measures of temporal order (e.g., did the conflict occur during the first or second halves of the innovation process?). Such measures can then be treated as variables in traditional statistical methods. One method to preserve information about temporal order which clusters cases with similar sequences is *phasic analysis*. As discussed in chapter 7, once clusters of phasic sequences have been derived they can serve as the basis for variables that can be entered into traditional statistical analyses. Alternatively, Tuma and Hannan (1984) discuss how *event history analysis* can be used to determine when critical events occur, provided the length of time until they occur is recorded. Supplementary analysis can in some cases divulge causal factors underlying event occurrences (Willett & Singer, 1991).

Several additional avenues are open for studies with *few cases, many events*. Comparative analysis of *qualitative case studies* using Yin's designs are one option. Chapter 7 discusses how events can be parsed into phases that represent coherent periods of activities subsuming two or more events in sequence. These phases can then be used as bounded units to provide temporal divisions in case studies, as Holmes (1992, 1997a, 1997b) did in his studies of hostage-taking situations, and Polley and Van de Ven (1989) did in the study of a biomedical innovation. Various types of *time series* analyses can also be used when many events are available for each case. As discussed in chapter 8, these generally involve transforming the event series into some continuous form. Chapter 6 discusses the application of *stochastic modeling*, which preserves the categorical qualities of the event series and enables us to track temporal dependencies among events.

For studies with *many cases, many events* a number of powerful statistical techniques are available. As with the many cases, few events situation, simple *descriptive summaries* of the frequency with which coded events occur provide useful displays for examining stages or phases in the developmental progression. However, with such pooling of the data one can lose the temporal order of events that figure prominently in most process research studies. As discussed in chapter 7, the technique of *optimal matching* can be used to derive measures of similarity among large samples of phase sequences derived through phasic analysis for the cases. These measures can then be analyzed in at least two ways. First, they can be used as input to cluster analysis and multidimensional scaling (MDS) techniques that can identify clusters of similar sequences; the resulting clusters can then be used to define variables for causal or correlational analysis, as in Poole and Holmes

(1995). Second, these distances can be used to test for causal factors that create the differences between pairs of sequences.

Chapter 8 discusses how *trend analysis or multiple time series methods* can be used to identify patterns of change across many cases, provided the events can be used to define continuous variables. Chapter 6 also shows how *stochastic modeling* of multiple cases can provide maps of temporal dependencies among events. Causal factors leading to such dependencies can then be identified.

As noted previously, the relation between the two dimensions and analysis is a two-way street. A researcher who chooses a certain method of analysis will want to design her/his research so that the proper number of cases and events are sampled. However, in some cases the researcher is limited by what is feasible. Then it is important to select an appropriate method and find some way of creating the type of data it requires from what is there.

Concluding Comments on Formulating the Research Plan

The issues discussed here do not exhaust those that confront the researcher, but they represent several critical choices. Other good sources for the design of longitudinal organizational studies include Galtung (1967), Kimberly (1980), Miller and Freisen (1982), and the *Organization Science* special issues on longitudinal field research (1990, Volume 1, Numbers 3 and 4). Though it poses thorny design problems, longitudinal process research is a worthwhile challenge. It offers the best chance we have of evaluating the stories that hold our theories together.

At the heart of any design is data gathering. This section has considered general choices we must confront in planning how to get our data. The next section discusses in much greater detail techniques for gathering and validating data.

DATA GATHERING IN PROCESS RESEARCH

Consider the challenge confronting researchers who attempt to implement a typical process research design. Over one to three years of real-time field study, they use a survey to collect quantitative and qualitative data every six months, conduct interviews with key managers and technicians, attend and make direct observations of regularly scheduled (monthly or bimonthly) organizational meetings, and maintain a study diary to record and file frequent informal discussions with participants, organizational memos and reports, and stories in trade journals or newspapers about the innovation.

As studies such as these proceed, the volume of data mounts astronomically and quickly overloads the information-processing capacity of even the most insightful mind. Rigorously drawing inferential links between the data and theory require methods which go beyond subjective "eyeballing" of raw qualitative data to identify patterns. Unfortunately, data analysis methods are rarely reported in detail in published case studies or ethnographic reports. One cannot ordinarily follow how a researcher got from hundreds of pages of field observations to the final conclusions, even though the research may be sprinkled with vivid—yet idiosyncratic—quotations from organizational participants. The sheer mass of data overload our information-processing capacities and threaten us with what Pettigrew calls "data asphyxiation." Confronted with such a mass of raw data, how should the researcher convert it into a form useful for developing and testing process theories of organizational change or innovation?

Data gathering in process research can be divided into several distinct operations. First, researchers must get the *raw data*. Then they must identify *events* in this raw data that capture key aspects of the process. These events are then arrayed in a *chronicle* of the process. In moving from raw data to events to chronicle, *coding* is often employed. This part of the chapter will offer guidelines for each of these operations. This will be followed by a section discussing the final operation in the preparation of data for process analysis, its transformation into a *final form* suitable for various process analysis methods. The appendix to this chapter describes step-by-step the process of building an event sequence file in the CIP project. It covers the technical aspects of the research process that will be the focus of the remainder of this chapter.

Longitudinal observation depends on a set of categories or variables to describe the developmental process. Whether they are implicit or explicit, these concepts help to focus observation of the change process; one cannot study everything. Category systems provide the "measurement" necessary to connect theoretical models of development with empirical events. When the model(s) is known beforehand, category development proceeds as a form of operationalization of theoretical constructs. In the process of developing a category system, the constructs themselves are respecified and fine-tuned, but generally category development is a top-down process in this case. On the other hand, when study of organizational development processes is at an embryonic stage, these initial categories emerge as "sensitizing constructs" for conducting exploratory research. The categories become clearer as they are put to use, and eventually they can be codified into a formal scheme.

For example, the MIRP studies began with five "sensitizing categories"

Table 5.3 Evolution of Innovation Concepts During the Minnesota Innovation Research Project

CONCEPT	INITIAL DEFINITIONS BASED ON THE LITERATURE	WHAT THE PROJECT FOUND
Ideas	One invention to be realized	Reinvention, proliferation, reimplementation, discarding, and termination of many ideas
People	An entrepreneur with a fixed set of full-time people	Many entrepreneurs, distracted fluidly engaging and disengaging in a variety of roles over time
Transactions	Fixed network of people/firms working out the details of an innovation idea	Expanding and contracting network of partisan stakeholders converging and diverging on innovation ideas
Context	Environment provides opportunities and constraints on the innovation process	Innovation process constrained and created by multiple enacted environments
Outcomes	Final result orientation: A stable order	Final results may be indeterminate; multiple in-process assessments and spinoffs; integration of new order with old

that seemed important to innovation development: ideas, people, transactions, context, and outcomes (Van de Ven et al., 1989). As the study progressed, these assumptions and concept definitions changed substantially and became successively clearer over time. Table 5.3 compares the starting assumptions related to these concepts, as reflected in the literature at the time (summarized in the left column), with how the MIRP researchers came to view them as a result of two years of field studies (in the right column). The latter disclosed a different reality from the rather orderly and simple concepts of the former. As this example illustrates, the development of research constructs involves an iterative process of developing initial conceptual categories, observations, and progressive redefinition and refinement of categories. This iterative process underlies many of the data collection and coding steps discussed in this section.

INCIDENTS AND EVENTS

As stated before, a theory of development consists of statements about the temporal sequence of events that explain an observed stream of incidents or occurrences. To make such a theory operational, and hence testable, Abbott (1984) emphasizes that it is important to distinguish between an *incident* (a raw datum) and an *event* (a theoretical construct). Whereas an incident is an empirical observation, an event is not directly observed; it is a construct in a model that explains the pattern of incidents. For each event one can choose any number of incidents as indicators that that event has occurred.

This definition implies a particular kind of relationship between incidents and events. Incidents are descriptions of happenings, documentary records of occurrences. Events are meaningful parsings of the stream of incidents. They are constructions based on a more-or-less systematic interpretation by the researcher of what is relevant to the process. The stream of incidents, a first-order construction, is translated into a sequence of events, a second-order construction. This implies that some incidents may be emplotted in different ways, utilized as constituents of different events. And this is not just a matter of different interpretations, that is, that incident k indicates event A versus event B, as a brief consideration of the nature of events will show.

Events may vary in several respects. First, they may differ in temporal duration. For example in the CIP case, a meeting with a potential partner is a bounded event of three to four hours duration, but the clinical trial of a design to meet FDA approval was an event that stretched over a much longer period. Events may also overlap or nest. For example, the meeting in question might occur during the period covered by the clinical trial. Or a relatively long event such as the clinical trial may be decomposed into shorter constituent events, such as a meeting to plan the trial, several different tests conducted as part of the trial, and an evaluation session, all of which are nested within the trial. Events may also differ in spatial extension. The meeting with the partner occurred in one room and stretched to a meal at a restaurant, whereas the clinical trial involved implantation in the hospital and monitoring the effectiveness of the device in the day-to-day life of the subjects. The clinical trial stretched over a much wider space and involved more people than did the meeting.

That events may differ in temporal and spatial scope suggests that incidents may well indicate more than one overlapping event. For example, the meeting with the potential partner can indicate the event "meeting with a partner," but it may also indicate a longer event, "negotiation with firm Q regarding partnership." Events may be embedded within other, different types of events of larger scope. Both levels may be important for understanding the change process, because interleaving narratives clarify it better than either narrative could on its own. Abbott gives an example from his studies of the rise of professions in society:

I once set out to explain why there are no psychiatrists in American mental hospitals. The exodus, which dates from 1900–1930, reflects not only the rational individual mobility decisions that are specifiable annually, but also outpatient community developments that are specifiable only decadally, and changes in knowledge and social control taking place over even longer periods (1992, p. 439).

Another complication is the possibility that the incident-event relationship may change over time (Abbott, 1984). As we noted in chapter 2, the significance of events may change as the process unfolds. The same change is possible in incident-event relations. For example, the first time a potential partner is encountered may signal the expansion of a program such as CIP, whereas the sixth encounter with a potential partner may signal desperation for ideas or resources.

To sum up, events are constructs indicated by incidents. However, the indication relationship is more complicated for qualitative data than it is for quantitative scores. Psychometrics and scaling theory presume a uniformity across respondents and responses that may not be the case for the data used to define events. What quantitative analysis would relegate to the domain of "error variance" may be quite an important nuance for qualitative analysis.

A final consideration in defining events is identification of the central subject(s) that the events refer to. Narrative analysis depends on defining a central subject for the narrative. This subject may be many things—a person, group, organization, idea, product, innovation, interorganizational field, almost any social unit that develops or changes over time may serve as a central subject. As we noted in chapter 2, the nature of the central subject may change over the course of the narrative, so it is imperative to have a clear sense of who or what the central subject is. This involves defining its essential characteristics and cues that will enable the research team to track it over time.

For example, in the CIP study, the central subject was the business startup within 3M, which revolved around a technology-based product, the cochlear implant. The development of the central subject and technology were intertwined, so anything that was relevant to either was included in the incident record. Data was also considered relevant if it concerned any of the principals in the innovation unit and any competing technology with the 3M technology. The resulting categories of events and interpretations of events are detailed in the appendix to chapter 4. Decisions that data was relevant hinged on its connection to any group of people or technologies; these served as the cues for preliminary inclusion of the incident in the data file.

There is, of course, another way to interpret this example. Instead of one central subject, the CIP case had two—the startup and the technology—or even more than two—the startup, the technology, and the three or four principal movers of the innovation. Narratives with multiple central subjects are possible. However, they may become quite tangled and complicated as the multiple strands of narrative are tracked.

DEFINING AN INCIDENT: A QUALITATIVE DATUM

In quantitative survey research, the datum is typically assumed to be sufficiently clear to require no explicit treatment. However, this is not the case with qualitative data, where it is important to define a *datum,* which is the basic element of information that is entered into a data file for analyzing temporal event sequences in the development of organizational entities.

In survey research, a *quantitative datum* is commonly regarded to be (1) a numerical response to a question scaled along a distribution (2) about an object (the unit of analysis) (3) at the time of measurement, which is (4) entered as a variable (along with other variables on the object) into a record (or case) of a quantitative data file, and (5) is subsequently recoded and classified as an indicator of a theoretical construct. In comparison, we can define a *qualitative datum* as (1) a bracketed string of words capturing the basic elements of information (2) about a discrete incident or occurrence (the unit of analysis) (3) that happened on a specific date, which is (4) entered as a unique record (or case) in a qualitative data file, and (5) is subsequently coded and classified as an indicator of a theoretical event.

Parsing Incidents from "Raw Data"

As the definitions just stipulated indicate, the basic element of information in a qualitative datum is a bracketed string of words about a discrete incident, while in a quantitative datum the element of information is a number scaled along a predetermined distribution of a variable. Raw words, sentences, or stories collected from the field or from archives cannot be entered into a series until they are bracketed into a datum (data). Obviously, explicit decision rules are needed to bracket raw words. Many diverse types of rules are possible and their common denominator is that they should reflect the substantive purposes of the research.

In the case of CIP, the decision rule used to bracket words into a qualitative datum was the definition of an incident that occurred in the development of the innovation. An *incident* was defined as a major recurrent activity or whenever changes were observed to occur in any one of the five core

Table 5.4 Examples of Incidents and Event Codes from CIP Database

	INCIDENT NUMBER: 312 INCIDENT DATE: 06/01/87	INCIDENT NUMBER: 313 INCIDENT DATE: 06/01/87	INCIDENT NUMBER: 314 INCIDENT DATE: 06/18/87	INCIDENT NUMBER: 315 INCIDENT DATE: 06/25/87
INCIDENT DATE:				
Incident	MN firm executive states he will not support TAP beyond 1988. The MN firm has been investing about $4M per year in TAP, and the MA firm is only spending between $1 and $1.5M. The MN executive thinks the MA firm should contribute more. SK met with JB and offered several options such as donating modules, writing a check for $1M, or taking less royalties. JB will see iff the MA firm is still interested.	June SBU meeting canceled.	Emergency meeting conducted of MN firm's core TAP team to discuss restructuring finances as a result of recent internal management review. Items for discussion included 10–15% across the board reductions, omission of diagnostics, assumption of improved electronics by 1/1/88, 70% of sales by 1995 will come from tubesets manufactured outside of the MI firm, and no significant research beyond LDL and immune complex.	Joint administrative review of TAP by MN and MA firm executives. MN executive suggests bringing in a third partner to reduce financial burden. He suggests that TAP be spun off into a joint venture with a third partner. No conclusion reached. The MA firm executive asks "Why has my partner blinked?" He questions if the MN firm is really committed to TAP. The MN firm executive suggests that it is just an issue of financing and additional opportunities for investment.
Data Source	Phone calls with SK and JB, 6/1/87.	Phone call with SK 6/1/87.	Internal memo of 6/10/87 and 6/18/87 meeting notes.	AHV notes of 6/25/87 administrative review meeting
Core MIRP CODES	Outcome-negative Context-internal Context-external Transaction, Contraction	Context-internal Contraction	Transaction Idea-core Context-internal	Transaction Context-internal Context-external Outcome-negative

concepts in the MIRP framework: innovation ideas, people, transactions, context, and outcomes. Examples of incidents from a business startup case are shown in Table 5.4. The definitions for incidents can be found in the appendix to chapter 4, and some of the guidelines for defining these incidents can be found in the appendix of this chapter.

When each incident was identified by MIRP researchers, the bracketed string of words required to describe it included: date of occurrence, the actor(s) or object(s) involved, the action or behavior that occurred, the consequence (if any) of the action, and the source of the information. As with any set of decision rules, some further subjective judgments were involved in defining innovation incidents in an operationally consistent manner. These were resolved in discussions among the researchers that took additional information and special circumstances into account.

Duration and Granularity of Incidents

Decision rules may vary in the level of specificity and the temporal duration of incidents they construct. Some rules specify fine-grained definitions of incidents that interpret each action as a separate incident; others adopt coarse-grained definitions that require longer episodes for incidents.

The proper granularity of incidents should depend on the rates of development of various kinds of innovations, and the differing research questions associated with these rates. For example, two MIRP researchers working on a different innovation (Knudson & Ruttan, 1989) found that the rate of hybrid wheat development is governed by biological laws that require several decades in order to move from basic research through technology development to market introduction. They observed that hybrid wheat's innovation process has been following this "biological time clock" since the late 1950s. In studies of biomedical innovations such as CIP (see also Garud & Van de Ven, 1989), the rate of development appears to be governed by an "institutional regulation time clock," in which the design, testing, and commercial release of devices entailed extensive review and approval steps by the U.S. Food and Drug Administration, sometimes lasting five years. Finally, rates of development of other processes, such as group decision making (Poole & Roth, 1989) or the development of novel administrative programs (Bryson & Roering, 1989; Roberts & King, 1989) are more rapid and appear to be limited only by entrepreneurial time and attention. As these variations suggest, researchers need to develop operational procedures for tracking developmental processes that are congruent with the temporal scope of development and the corresponding granularity of incident detail appropriate to the organizational entities being examined.

OBSERVATIONAL AND ARCHIVAL SOURCES OF DATA

In an earlier section we discussed planning research to study change processes in real time or in retrospect. Here we expand on this by addressing the advantages and disadvantages of gathering data from direct observation and from secondary archival sources.

Incidents can be identified either through direct observation or through archival research. By direct observation we mean study of the process *as it unfolds,* through participant observation, interviews with key principals and informants, and study of emerging records and documents. The hallmark of direct observation is that the research is carried out contemporaneously with the unfolding process. By archival research we mean study of the process *after it has occurred,* through analysis of documents and records, retrospective interviews, bibliometric analysis, and other historical-reconstructive methods. The two data-gathering methods are often used together, as when researchers conduct a historical case study prior to a direct observational study in order to better understand the context and meaning of current incidents.

With direct observation, researchers have the opportunity to judge immediately how adequate their data is and to follow up on questions or uncertain areas. Direct observation also grants flexibility to the research team. If necessary, researchers can expand or contract data collection activities. They can alter procedures to solve emerging problems and respond to unique opportunities. Being close to the process is also likely to give researchers a special feel for what is immediately significant at any given moment. By experiencing the process with key actors, researchers have a chance to gauge its emotional tenor and impact on participants far better than researchers removed in time and space.

There are also disadvantages to direct observation. Adjusting data collection procedures later in the game means that earlier data are incomplete. Researchers are then faced with the task of reconstructing earlier observations. The very immediacy of the process in direct observation may also blind researchers to significant patterns because they cannot see the forest for the trees. Often it is only after the fact, when the process can be understood as a whole, that key drivers and turning points can be discerned. Finally, studying a whole process may be very time-consuming. Direct observation can in some cases require a commitment of several years, with no date certain for an end to the process.

The quality of data from direct observation depends on several factors:

1. *Access* to important sources, activities, and documents is critical. Being available to study a process in real time means little if researchers are not able to observe critical events. Private discussions, secret actions, and classified documents may contain the key to understanding the process. To the extent that researchers miss or are not aware of these, their conclusions are limited. Of course, the catch-22 in this admonition is that in many cases researchers are not aware of what they are denied access to.

2. *Distortions and biases* may be introduced by those with a vested interest in the process. In some cases they are intentional, designed to make the informant look good or to protect him or her. In more cases, biases and distortions are simply the product of cognitive and social processes that simplify, consolidate, and assimilate to the expectations of subjects' recall and reportage.

3. *Data may be so bountiful* that researchers cannot capture it properly. For example, a sleepy meeting may suddenly turn into a major decision-making session, and a single researcher lulled into complacency may be unprepared to record key arguments or conclusions. Information overload may cause loss of data or inaccurate recording into conceptual categories. Investigators can take these factors into account when designing observational research. If these problems cannot be counteracted, they can at least be factored into the conclusions.

Archival research, the other data-gathering strategy, also has several advantages. Researchers have the benefit of hindsight, which lends valuable perspective to their efforts. Others' judgments of the process and its outcomes can inform the researchers' analyses. Provided adequate records are available, the data can be combed and recombed, coded in multiple layers, and otherwise interrogated until the full story emerges. A second advantage of archival research is that it takes much less of the researchers' time: very lengthy processes can be investigated in comparatively brief periods. Researchers with access to a good record may be able to explore a process lasting decades in a year's research, as Knudson and Ruttan (1989) did in their study of the emergence of hybrid wheat strains.

A major disadvantage of archival research is its limited flexibility. Researchers must make do with what has been preserved, either materially or in informants' memories. There is no possibility of adding measures or observations; data that is lost is gone forever. Then too, knowing how things turn out can bias one's perceptions and interpretations. A researcher studying a failed startup may well have a tendency to find events that seem to lead "downhill" more salient than those which are commonly thought to lead to success. The former may find a prominent place in the chronology, while the latter are passed over or explained away. Distance in time and space also decreases the researchers' ability to identify with and to empathize with participants. While much has been written about procedures for hermeneutic reconstruction of activities and events, this is a poor substitute for experiencing or witnessing them first hand (or even second hand, if contemporaneously).

The quality of data used in archival studies depends on several factors:

1. *The extent to which relevant records are kept* varies greatly. Some organizations and people are fastidious about keeping records, whereas others are not. Some activities lend themselves to recording better than others. For example, there are often legal requirements that minutes of board meetings be kept, but there are no such requirements for dyadic conversations among key actors.

2. Even if relevant records are kept, there may be *loss of data due to archival practices*. Confronted with a mass of historical data, archivists must appraise what is worth keeping and what is not. They may either discard (the worst case) or not catalog or organize data (a bad case, but sometimes recoverable), depending on whether they judge the information and its creator to be significant and worth study (see Baer, 1997, for some of the theories that might guide archivists confronted with organizational records).

3. *Contradictions among records* also must be reconciled. Different observers may have different perceptions of the same event, and one set of records may yield a different set of incidents than another. Researchers differ in their attitudes toward contradictions. Historians have long worked to refine methods for adjudicating and resolving inconsistencies in the historical record (Walsh, 1967). Pettigrew (1990) exemplifies a different tack: Acknowledge the validity of different perspectives and accept the fact that there are multiple layers of socially constructed reality. He argues that our understanding will be enriched by taking into account the alternative views that invariably develop, because they indicate the differential views that shape the development of multiply determined processes.

4. *Biases and self-serving distortions* occur in records just as they do in direct observation. Records may be intentionally destroyed or falsified, and they may be unintentionally neglected. Key events may not be recorded at

all. There is the same catch-22 for archival data as well. Researchers dealing with incomplete data may never get a clue that it is incomplete.

5. *Inconsistent quality of records* is a common problem in archival research. For some events excellent, clear, detailed records survive, while for others the records are spotty and confusing. As a result, there is variation in the degree of confidence that can be placed in the accounts of different incidents or events in a historical record.

Archival research can plan to minimize these problems, or at least, to acknowledge and allow for them. Some good sources of advice on archival research strategies are Baer (1997), Hill (1993), Elder, Pavalko, and Clipp (1993), and especially O'Toole (1997).

RELIABILITY AND VALIDITY OF INCIDENT CONSTRUCTION

It is important to establish the reliability of classifying raw data into incidents. An equally important, though often neglected issue, is the validity of this bracketing procedure (Folger, Hewes & Poole, 1984; Poole, Folger, & Hewes, 1987). Researchers often assume that the meaning of incidents is clear and that establishing reliability is equivalent to showing clear meaning of codings. However, attaining reliability among coders simply indicates that the meaning of incidents is clear to the particular group of researchers who designed the coding system. Of course, this does not mean the classifications correspond to the way participants see them. Thus, it is important to distinguish between classifications meaningful to researchers and those meaningful to organizational participants. These two types of classifications may not overlap, and researchers must be clear about what sorts of claims they make about the meaning of the incidents they record. It is necessary to test empirically whether researchers' classifications are consistent with practitioners' common perceptions of events. If the evidence indicates inconsistency, then no claims about the meaning of events to the participants are valid. Researchers can still sustain claims about the meaning of the incident from their theoretical position, but no claims about the "social reality" of the event are appropriate.

Two basic procedures are useful to enhance the reliability and validity of the incidents entered into the qualitative data file. First, the entry of incidents from raw data sources into a data file can be performed by at least two researchers. Consensus among these researchers increases the consistency of interpretations of the decision rules used to identify incidents. Second, the resulting list of incidents can be reviewed by key informants. It is useful to ask these informants if any incidents that occurred in the development of the organizational change process are missing or incorrectly described. Based on this feedback, revisions in the incident listings can be made if they conform to the decision rules for defining each incident. Typically, these two steps result in a more complete listing of incidents about an organizational change process.

In getting this information from subjects it is important to be sensitive to where the brackets are being put, that is, whether the incidents divide up the flow of "raw data" into units which are sensible and natural to participants. Studies of the parsing of social behavior into units indicate that people are capable of attaining high agreement on their unitizing of interaction (Planalp & Tracy, 1980). However, these studies also show that unitizing depends on the goals of the actor, so it is probably a good idea to check, with several informants if possible, whether incidents represent "wholes" or should be subdivided or combined. Unitizing is likely to be more difficult in cases when the investigator has to identify incidents directly from ongoing interaction or occurrences than in the case of incidents defined through interviews, which are likely to already come in "predigested" bits.

Finally, it is important to recognize that the resulting list of incidents, no matter how painstakingly wrought, is only a sample of occurrences in the development of an organizational entity. In the case of studies based on records and interviews, the sample is limited to what informants know and can recall and what the records contain. Even with real-time field observations, it is not humanly possible to observe and record all possible incidents. Researchers are limited to what they can observe and the particular layers of meaning they can pick up. Thus, as in classical test theory of item sampling (Lord & Novick, 1968), the incidents represent a *sample* of indicators of what happened over time in an organizational change process. This has important implications for event identification.

IDENTIFYING EVENTS FROM INCIDENTS

As they stand, the incident listings are only one step above the raw material for analysis, because each incident is just a qualitative summary or indicator of what happened. The next step is to identify theoretically meaningful events from the incident data. We will discuss the coding procedures that can be used to translate incidents into event indicators in some detail in the next section. Before describing these procedures, we will discuss a prerequisite issue of moving across levels of abstraction between indicators and theoretical constructs.

Indicators can correspond to a theoretical construct in several different ways. As is the case in psychometrics, some indicators are usually better representatives of the construct than others. Some indicators are also easier to measure or detect than others, resulting in differential reliability across indicators. Sampling error also presents a problem, with the result that some indicators will not be included in a given sample, while others will be oversampled. In the study of ongoing processes, there is the troubling possibility of "right censorship," that is, that relevant incidents are not being sampled because they have not yet occurred. So we have better knowledge of the beginning of an event than of its end in many cases. Such problems suggest a need to think through the indicator-construct relationship carefully.

Several options exist to map indicators to constructs (Abbott, 1984). The first and most straightforward strategy is to give all indicators of an event equal weight. For temporally extended events, this means that the event commences when the first indicator is observed and continues until the last occurs. For example, a "resource controller intervention" into a new business startup might begin when the resource controller first contacts the unit and continue through all contacts until the outcome of the intervention for the business is noted. This event would then stretch across a number of incidents. For short-term events, this means that they occur as many times as indicators are observed. For example, idea development might be defined as occurring each time a change in an idea occurs; there would be as many events as there were incidents in which a previously held idea was changed or a new idea was advanced. One weakness of this strategy is that it does not allow for error; it assumes every incident is observed reliably and validly. Another weakness is that the strategy assumes each indicator is equally critical to the event, which is at odds with the narrative approach. The advantage of this strategy is that it takes the data at face value and does not attach any particular assumptions to incidents. It also avoids the uncertainties and possible biases involved in trying to weight incidents in terms of their importance to the event.

A second strategy is to make judgments concerning whether indicators signal an event on a case-by-case basis. This is the common approach in historical studies, where the researcher establishes whether an event occurred by considering the indicators in context. The researcher uses her or his judgment and contextual knowledge to determine the occurrence and duration of events, as well as other characteristics, such as intensity and impact. For example, resource controller interventions could be defined by having one or more researchers read a string of incidents connected with the resource controller and, based on their knowledge of the case and its context, make a judgment of when the event began and ended. This judgment may not include some of the incidents that seem to relate to the resource controller in the definition of the event. One advantage of this strategy is that it gives a much more nuanced reading of the process. A large number of attributes of an event can be discerned, including narrative properties such as how much impact it had on subsequent events. This approach assumes the researcher is able to make holistic judgments based on context much more adroitly than could any algorithm. One possible problem stems from the biases introduced by this holistic knowledge and the value judgments that may come with it. A second problem is the difficulty of making such interpretations consistently across a large sample of processes. Carried to an extreme, this approach could reduce an event sequence to the researcher's preferred story or byline.

A third strategy is to use indicators as some measure of central tendency, such as the median occurrence of an incident, the mean time when incidents occurred on the timeline, or the mean number of times an incident occurred within a given time segment. For example, resource controller intervention might be defined as an event at the midpoint (median) of contact between the business startup and the resource controller on a given topic. This enables a "single resource controller intervention" event to be pinpointed in the sequence. Even more subtle rules are possible, such as "the first time two medical schools are founded within ten years of each other will indicate that medical education is institutionalized" (Abbott, 1984). The advantage of these indicators is that they allow for error in the data. Except for the degenerate case when only one or two indicators are observed, they correct for unreliability and sampling error by relying on composite indicators. Just as multiple items make a scale more reliable, so multiple indicators correct for error. This strategy is only workable, however, when multiple indicators are available.

One workable option is to employ strategies 1 or 3 for initial classifications and then use strategy 2, interpretive judgment, to adjust the event sequence. Using conceptual and practical reasoning to correct for the bluntness of classifications that employ objective rules can greatly improve the accuracy of process analyses. Insofar as possible, this should be done at the "local" level, avoiding the use of knowledge about the overall sequence or outcomes to guide reclassifications. This will minimize the intrusion of biases and value judgments into the event classifications.

The process of classifying incidents into events is also likely to spark a return to the "raw data" by raising questions about the incident list. This may stimulate the collection of more data to fill in gaps in the account or to answer troubling queries. It may also lead to a revision of the incident list itself, as problems with event identification lead researchers to rethink their incident descriptions. Handled carefully, this circling from data to incidents to events and back again can greatly enhance the fidelity of the data in process analysis.

The appendix to chapter 4 provides examples of event categories developed by MIRP researchers. These were defined after repeated discussions over a period of about a year among MIRP researchers. A preliminary set of categories was identified, then tried out, then refined, and tried again, in five cycles of this process until the final set of categories emerged.

CODING: A KEY METHOD IN PROCESS RESEARCH
Design of Coding Systems

There are several approaches for tacking back and forth among theory, category, and data to develop coding schemes such as the one presented in the appendix to chapter 4. *Inductive* approaches go first to the data—the incidents—and sift through the various instances, deriving categories from the ground up, using the constant comparative method. This is quite time-consuming and may make it difficult to link observation with current theory. However, it is likely to lead to interesting innovations. *Deductive* approaches use theory to specify expected categories, which are then written into rules.

In practice, the two approaches are often combined using a *retroductive* approach that often includes a literature search to derive a synthetic category scheme that seems to fit what the researcher sees in the data, then adjustment of categories in view of what is workable and informative after trying them out on the data. Poole used this approach to derive his decision functions coding system (Poole & Roth, 1989a & b). Another retroductive approach is to generate a set of categories based on theory and then refine and adjust them as they are applied to data. This permits the theoretically driven scheme to grow and to adapt in response to the exigencies of the data. Bales (1950) used this approach in developing Interaction Process Analysis.

Key choices in generating coding systems for longitudinal process research include (1) the type of unit to be used; (2) the type of coding to be made; (3) the latitude of judgment accorded to the coders; (4) univocal versus multifunctional coding; and (5) the domain of meaning the classifications are meant to tap.

1. *Type of unit.* This involves two issues, selection of a "natural" unit versus an "artificial" unit, and the granularity of the unit. Natural units are those whose bounds are set in the phenomenon itself, such as a speaker's turn, or a quarter's performance in a firm, or a meeting. Artificial units are those specified by the researcher, such as a 30-second period of discussion or a summary of climate concerns for one-month periods. Artificial units are easier to delimit and are useful if real time is the central metric of the analysis, but they may require subjects to distort the meaning of events to them. As stated previously, the granularity of the unit may vary greatly as well, since events differ in duration and scale. Granularity probably needs to be established independently for each phenomenon studied.

2. *Type of coding.* Several different types of codings are possible. The most common, of course, is to code events into the qualitative categories typical of most classification systems. However, it is also possible to have coders assign a numerical rating to an incident, for example, coding it on a 5-point scale, reflecting intensity of conflict exhibited in the event. Such global judgments can be just as reliable and valid as classifications, though they tend to gloss details and lead to distortions if the unit to be coded is a large or lengthy one (Poole et al., 1987).

3. *Latitude of judgment accorded to coders.* Coding systems incorporate the coder's knowledge of language and social context into the measurement process. Though the researcher would probably not want to eliminate use of this background knowledge, there are variations in the degree to which the coder is allowed to exercise this knowledge in making judgments. At one end of the scale are mechanical devices and computer software that greatly constrain human judgment. For example, content analysis programs based on dictionaries automatically classify sentences. A less-stringent alternative specifies a choice tree that presents a complete set of classifications and a series of simple binary questions that "lead" the coder to the proper classification (e.g., Anderson, 1983). The most common method emphasizes utility and pragmatic impact rather than logical completeness. Researchers compile as complete a list of categories as possible (or necessary), write enough rules to enable coders to recognize and distinguish the categories, and rely on coders' native knowledge and skills for the rest. This strategy is advantageous for complex meanings for which it is difficult, if not impossible, to develop complete classification rules. However, reliance on coder judgment makes the procedure harder to control and may result in inconsistent classifications if categories are not sufficiently defined.

4. *Univocal versus multifunctional coding*. Many traditional sources recommend that coding categories be mutually exclusive and exhaustive. But assigning a single code to each incident (mutual exclusivity) may be problematic if more than one social function is served by an act or if more than one meaningful thing happens in the same incident. In view of the fact that social life has multiple layers of meaning and that more than one consequence can be taken from any incident, multifunctional coding may be preferred for many applications. For example, the CIP study utilized multifunctional coding. As the appendix to chapter 4 indicates, incidents could be assigned a number of different codes and the same incident could receive more than one code from a given category.

The notion of multifunctional coding fits well with Abbott's concept of processes as multiple, intertwining narratives (chapter 2). To track the participation of incidents or events in more than one narrative simultaneously requires multiple codings.

5. *Domain of meaning to be coded*. The last issue involves determining what sort of meaning the classification scheme is intended to capture. Though finer distinctions are possible, Poole et al. (1987) distinguished observer-privileged meanings from subject-privileged meanings. Observer-privileged meanings are those accessible to outside observers, whereas subject-privileged meanings are those understandings that insiders and participants would have of the same incidents. Clearly a coding scheme designed to pick up subject-privileged meaning is harder to design than an observer-privileged system. In the section on validation below, we briefly discuss how to test whether a system can get at subject-privileged meanings.

Layered Coding

The five issues just discussed cover many important issues that researchers confront in designing category systems. It is also the case that often codings are recoded into higher-order categories. The simplest examples of this has been described already: the translation (read coding) of raw data into incidents is then recoded into theoretically meaningful events. These events can then, in turn, be recoded into higher-order variables.

A limitation of many coding systems is that they reduce rich qualitative data to a single dimension of meaning. For example, a failure to get renewed funding for an innovation may influence the development of the idea behind the project; it may also result in layoffs of innovation personnel; and it may signal a change in the relationship of the innovation to external resource controllers. If we code this incident simply as the termination of an idea, we omit other dimensions of meaning of the event. To avoid this problem, incidents may be coded on several dimensions. For example, we might code the incident on four event dimensions: a negative outcome (resource cut), a change in the core innovation idea, people leaving, and a change in transactions (relations with resource controllers).

One way to organize these multidimensional data into a format to analyze change processes is to array them on multiple tracks that correspond to conceptually meaningful categories. The procedure of coding incidents along several event tracks evolved in Poole's (1983a & b) studies of decision development in small groups. Poole argued that previous models of group decision development—which commonly posited a rational decision process of three to five stages—were too simple. He was interested in testing the hypothesis that decisions did not follow a fixed sequence of phases, but instead could follow several different paths. He also believed that the previous practice of coding only one dimension of group behavior, such as task process, was responsible for previous findings supporting the single sequence models. To examine a richer model of group development, he developed a three-track coding system: one track coded the impact an incident had on the process by which the group does its work (in this case, an incident was a member's statement), a second coded the same incident in terms of its effect on group relationships, and a third track indexed which of several topics the incident referred to. By coding an incident on several conceptually relevant dimensions simultaneously, Poole was able to derive a richer description of group processes than had previous studies.

The CIP researchers, along with other MIRP investigators, also coded each innovation incident according to multiple dimensions or constructs of events. Their coding scheme captured key dimensions of changes in innovation ideas, people, transactions, context, and outcomes in an observed incident. Figure 5.1 summarizes the general MIRP categories and displays them as a set of layered tracks. Within each conceptual track a number of more specific codings are possible, depending on the particular questions being addressed by the researchers. For example, in their MIRP study Ring and Rands (1989) coded incidents in terms of more refined dimensions of transactions in order to examine their model of formal and informal transaction processes, while Garud and Van de Ven (1989) expanded the context track into a number of dimensions to examine their model of industry emergence. Thus, the coding scheme can be tailored to meet the needs and interests of individual MIRP study teams.

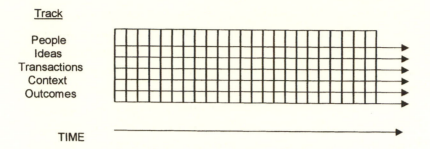

People Track: a coding of the people/groups involved in an incident, the roles and
activities they perform at a given point in time.

Ideas Track: a coding of the substantive ideas or strategies that innovation group
members use to describe the content of their innovation at a given
point in time.

Transactions Track: a coding of the formal and informal relationships among
innovation group members, other firms, and groups involved in the
incident.

Context/Environmental Track: a coding of the exogenous events outside of the
innovation unit in the larger organization and industry/community
which are perceived by innovation group members to affect the
innovation.

Outcomes Track: when incidents provide evidence of results, they are coded as
representing either positive (good news or successful accomplishment),
negative (bad news or instances of failure or mistakes), and mixed
(neutral or ambiguous news, indicating elements of both success
and failure).

Figure 5.1 Coding tracks on core MIRP dimensions

Assessing the Reliability and Validity of Coding Systems

A number of steps can be taken to enhance the reliability and validity of coding incidents into indicators of event constructs or events into higher-order
constructs. First, operational definitions and coding conventions can be
drafted for the coded constructs. Periodic meetings can be conducted with
researchers and other colleagues to evaluate the construct validity of these definitions; that is, the extent to which operational definitions appeared to be
logical and understandable indicators of the constructs under consideration.

Van de Ven and Ferry (1980) found that a useful way to conduct these
meetings is to begin with an overall presentation of the conceptual model
being studied. Then participants are handed a paper that defines each con-

struct in the model and the sugggested indicators to be used to measure each construct. Participants can then be asked to "suggest better indicators for measuring this construct as defined previously." Often using a Nominal Group Technique format (see Delbecq, Gustafson, & Van de Ven, 1975), reviewers are provided a brief period to think and respond to the questions in writing. Then a general discussion ensues to obtain group opinions. The qualitative written comments from these review sessions are especially helpful to sharpen the norms of correspondence (Kaplan, 1964) between definitions of constructs and event indicators, and to clarify ambiguities in decision rules for coding event indicators.

In addition to incorporating these protections into the construction of categories, it is also important to assess reliability and validity of coding systems based on empirical performance. Reliability refers to the consistency of coding classifications across raters. Two types of reliability can be distinguished (Folger, Hewes, & Poole, 1984): Unitizing reliability refers to consistency in dividing the stream of activity into units. Classificatory reliability refers to consistency in assigning units to categories. The two sorts of reliability must be assessed separately. One widely used index of unitizing reliability is Guetzkow's U (Folger et al., 1984, pp. 119–120). Folger et al. describe a more sensitive method of assessing unitizing reliability based on comparison of lengths of units, which Guetzkow's U takes into account only indirectly. The best measure of classification reliability is Cohen's kappa, available in most nonparametric statistics programs (Popping, 1988). In addition to reliability across the entire category system, it is also important to compute reliability for each individual category. This helps identify problem categories.

While consistency of classification (reliability) is an important criterion, equally important is accuracy of interpretation (validity). It is not common to assess the validity of coding systems, but it is just as important to do so as it would be to assess the validity of a scale. What evidence is necessary to establish the validity of a coding system depends on the type of meaning it is designed to capture. If the system is designed to capture only observer-privileged meanings then the same types of evidence used to assess face and construct validity for quantitative measures can be obtained to evaluate the validity of the category system. To the extent that the constructs in the coding system relate to other constructs in ways that would be expected based on the theory of the construct, then the coding system has a measure of validity (see Folger et al., 1984).

Things are more complicated when the researcher aspires to capture subject-privileged meanings with a classification system. In such cases, face and construct validity must be established, but they are not sufficient to ensure validity of the system as a whole. In addition, the researcher must show that the interpretations yielded by the coding system correspond somehow to those of the participants or insiders. This involves mapping participant or insider intepretations and comparing them to the interpretations of the system. Folger et al. (1984) discuss several ways of doing this.

CHRONICLES: EVENT SEQUENCE DATA FILES

Moving from raw data to incidents results in a stream of data consisting of a chronological listing of all incidents observed in the development of an organizational change process. Each incident represents a datum that is entered as a unique record into a qualitative data file for each innovation. Table 5.5 shows an example of a few incidents in such a data file. A variety of database software programs can be used to organize and manage the qualitative data files. MIRP researchers used R:Base©, but Access™ or any other relational database program can be used equally well. Weitzman and Miles (1995) provide a compilation of qualitative data analysis programs that could also be used for recording such data.

When events and higher-order constructs representing types of events are identified from the sequence of incidents, they can be recorded in the database in several ways. The appendix to this chapter describes the steps involved in creating a qualitative chronicle similar to that used in the MIRP research. This example utilizes the MIRP categories discussed above and presented in detail in the appendix to chapter 4.

While these examples from MIRP are useful for illustrative purposes, it should be noted that many other types of developmental processes can be represented, such as decision-making discussions and other deliberations (in this case the actual verbiage and the data are almost identical, save what is left out by transcription rules), critical events in organizational careers, occurrences during the implementation of information technologies, and the history of the addition and adaptation of features of a organizational structure in a firm.

The chronicle, or event sequence, presents the basic data to be analyzed with the methods outlined in the rest of this book. To render the data suitable for analysis, some transformations are required.

Table 5.5 Partial Bitmap of Incidents in CIP Study

INCIDENT NUM	DATE	DAYS	IC	IR	PE	TR	CI	CE	OP	ON	OM
1	01/01/68	1	1	0	0	0	1	0	0	0	0
2	01/01/68	1	0	0	0	1	0	0	0	0	0
3	01/01/68	1	0	0	0	0	0	1	0	0	0
4	01/01/68	1	0	0	0	0	0	1	0	0	0
5	01/01/68	1	1	0	0	1	0	0	0	0	0
6	01/01/68	1	1	0	0	1	0	0	0	1	0
7	01/01/74	2193	1	0	1	0	0	0	0	0	0
8	01/01/74	2193	0	0	1	0	0	0	0	0	0
9	12/01/78	3988	0	0	1	0	0	0	0	0	0
10	10/01/79	4292	1	0	1	1	0	0	0	0	0
11	10/07/79	4298	1	0	0	1	0	0	0	0	0
12	01/01/80	4384	0	0	0	0	0	1	0	0	0
13	01/04/80	4387	1	0	0	0	0	0	0	0	0
14	01/08/80	4391	0	0	0	1	0	0	0	1	0
15	01/12/80	4395	1	0	0	0	0	0	1	0	0
16	04/01/80	4475	1	0	0	0	0	0	0	0	0
17	04/07/80	4481	0	0	0	1	0	0	1	0	0
18	05/01/80	4505	0	0	0	1	0	0	1	0	0
19	10/01/80	4658	1	0	0	0	0	0	0	1	0
20	10/07/90	4664	0	0	0	1	0	0	1	0	0
21	11/01/80	4689	0	0	1	1	0	0	0	1	0
22	11/07/80	4695	1	0	0	0	0	0	0	0	0
23	11/15/80	4703	0	0	0	1	1	0	0	1	0
24	11/21/80	4709	0	0	0	1	0	0	0	1	0
25	12/01/80	4719	1	0	1	1	0	0	0	0	0
26	12/11/80	4729	0	0	0	1	0	0	0	1	0

Variables (number in [] represents the frequency of 1s):

num: Incident Number

date: Incident Date

days: Number of Days from 01/01/68

  (thr first incident)

ic: Idea-core [68]

ir: Idea-related [4]

pe: People [49]

tr: Transaction [165]

ci: Context-internal [8]

ce: Context-external [22]

op: Outcome positive [58]

on: Outcome-negative [59]

om: Outcome-mixed [7]

TRANSFORMING CODED DATA INTO FORMS SUITABLE FOR ANALYSIS

We will go into greater detail on transformations appropriate for each of the data analysis methods in subsequent chapters. At this point, we will discuss in general terms several transformations of the qualitative data that have proven useful.

SUMMARY DATA

One transformation involves converting the sequence data into summary statistics, such as the total number of events in various categories in the entire sequence or in segments of it; or the total number of phases in the process (see below for definition of phase). This data can then be used to test developmental models with variance analysis. For example, if a three-phase life cycle model holds, then the monthly count of events characteristic of phase 1 should be highest early in the process and decline, the monthly count of events characteristic of phase 2 should peak after phase 1 events start to decline and then decline thereafter, and the count of events characteristic of phase 3 should peak near the end of the process, as shown in Figure 5.2. This transformation, one of the most common in developmental research, essentially collapses the data over time, removing any temporal information. The remaining three transformations preserve temporal information.

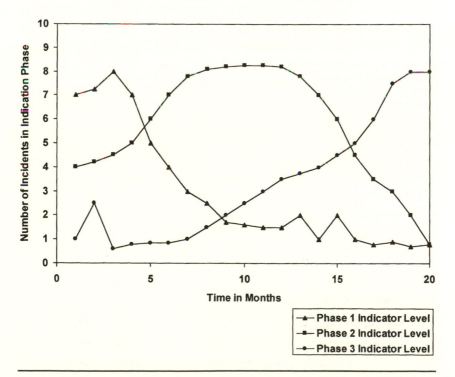

Figure 5.2 Patterns of indicators expected if a three-phase life cycle holds for a process

Bitmaps

Bitmaps (Frey, 1986) can be used to represent nominal level constructs, such as the occurrence or nonoccurrence of a certain type of event. One such bitmap is shown in Table 5.5. In a bitmap a column in the database is created for each event category. If a given type of event, such as an idea event, can be classified into events affecting the core idea or events affecting related ideas, two different columns are created (columns ic and ir in Table 5.5). When an event occurs that affects the core idea, a "1" is entered into column ic; otherwise, the value for a given incident is coded as "0." Any data which can be exhaustively described by a set of nominal categories can be represented as a bitmap. This bitmap can then be subjected to analysis with various statistical methods to examine time-dependent patterns of relations among the event constructs. In a bitmap such as the one shown in Table 5.5, the chronological listing of qualitative events is time-dependent, meaning that the sequential order of the rows is crucial and should be taken into account when information is to be extracted, although the columns are interchangeable. A method that returns the same results when the rows of an event sequence bitmap are interchanged is not appropriate for identifying dynamic patterns because the information contained in the temporal order of the incidents is not used.

Phase Maps

Phasic analysis presumes that individual events are indicators of underlying phases. It transforms the sequential event stream into a series of phases of various lengths, using procedures to be described in more detail in chapter 7. Phase mapping adopts the third strategy for event identification from indicators: it uses a summary measure to define events or higher-order constructs. For example, one algorithm defines a phase based on three consecutive occurrences of an indicator. Fewer than three is considered an error and does not define a phase. Phase maps assume and try to correct for some unreliability in the indicators of events or higher-order constructs.

Continuous Variables

Some methods require continuous data. In these cases the sequence data, bitmaps, or phase maps may be transformed into continuous data by (a) dividing the sequence into segments of uniform length containing more than one event and (b) calculating the number of events of various types in the segments; the number of events represents a continuous measure. For example, Van de Ven and Polley (1992) coded whether innovation units persisted in their current actions or changed. They subdivided their event sequence into one-month intervals and counted how many of each category of behavior (persist or change) occurred in each month. This served as continuous data for a time series analysis of action persistence.

COMMENTS

These transformations generate data that can be used in a wide variety of analyses, ranging from qualitative interpretation of the data stream to multivariate statistical analysis. Specific applications require quite a bit of tailoring of the original event data, as subsequent chapters illustrate. The important thing is to be ever cognizant of the possibilities for testing models and hypotheses and flexible with respect to methods of analysis.

CONCLUSION

This chapter introduced methods for designing longitudinal research for studying how and why change unfolds in organizational entities. The chapter outlined a host of choices available to researchers, all of which entail difficult decisions and trade-offs. As always, research design requires the exercise of what Aristotle called "practical wisdom." There is no definitive best design for a given project, and any design requires giving up some data in order to get others.

One objection that might be registered is that the methods proposed here may "overquantify" analysis. This conclusion may be the inadvertent result of our objective in this chapter, which was to introduce some systematic methods to overcome the tendency in much research of relying exclusively on subjective "eyeballing" and anecdotal information in qualitative data. However, in practice, our objective is to combine the special information that quantitative and qualitative approaches provide to understand organizational change processes. After all, by themselves quantitative data provide only a skeletal configuration of structural regularities, often devoid of life, flesh, and soul. Qualitative data, by themselves, are like an amoeba, rich with life but squishy, soft, and absent of apparent structure. Only by combining quantitative and qualitative data in a balanced way do we come to understand the richness of life in its varied regularities.

APPENDIX: BUILDING AN EVENT SEQUENCE FILE
David N. Grazman and Andrew H. Van de Ven

INTRODUCTION

This appendix takes the researcher, step-by-step, through the mechanics involved in building an event sequence file, from defining a qualitative datum to analyzing the temporal relationships in event sequence data. While each longitudinal study of organizational change processes is characterized by its own specific requirements, this discussion will utilize the CIP data to illustrate the steps. By design, this appendix leaves substantial room for interpretation and application. We do not intend for it to serve as a manual for any particular software program, but as a general guide to the steps involved in collecting, managing, and analyzing large sets of event data.

The methods described here relate to recording and analyzing event data (consisting of descriptions of actors, actions, outcomes, dates and sources) from real-time or archival longitudinal, qualitative research. We refer to the "researcher" as the person who participates in all steps of the research, including collecting data, designing the database, managing the data, and analysis. Although field studies may require the involvement of many data collectors, we find that the fewer the number of individuals involved in managing or changing the actual event database, the less likely major inconsistencies or errors arise in constructing the dataset. Keeping responsibility for entering and working with raw event data with as few individuals as possible is one way to ensure higher levels of data consistency.

HARDWARE AND SOFTWARE REQUIREMENTS

Computers are a crucial factor in determining how easy or difficult data entry and manipulation tasks become. Most longitudinal field studies entail collecting enormous amounts of data often obtained over lengthy time periods. Therefore, it is important to use computers with sufficient RAM and hard drive storage space. Most software programs basic for this research require large amounts of RAM and are significantly slowed (or do not run at all) when adequate memory is not available.

To minimize data management errors, we suggest that data files be stored on a single computer and that one version of the file serve as a master. If more than one researcher is involved in entering or managing data, it becomes crucial to have a single data storage site so that the most up-to-date and complete data file will always be used. Research files grow quickly and data file backups are best made often and kept by one researcher separately from the working master copy. Without these precautions, it is inevitable that changes made in one copy of the file often do not find their way to other copies and people begin to work with slightly different versions of the database, creating a problem that is difficult to pinpoint and even harder to correct.

We are using two commercially available software packages, R:Base© and RATS©, though these are by no means the only programs on the market that have the necessary capabilities for longitudinal research. We are currently evaluating newer, more powerful software packages. Whatever programs you choose to use, all must be able to store and read data files in unformated ASCII code in order to facilitate transfer of data from program to program. Fortunately, it is increasingly common for software packages to import and export data formated by other packages, and at some point this requirement may no longer be necessary.

R:Base© (Microrim, Inc.) is a Windows-compatible, relational database program that allows information to be entered via predesigned forms into data tables that can be sorted, indexed, reorganized, and accessed quickly and easily, with minimal training. Many of the procedures we cover are tailored toward R:Base but can be easily adapted to other database programs. At the time of our review of database software, we found that R:Base had a unique advantage of allowing unlimited length "note" fields. For qualitative event data, it is useful to have the freedom to enter as much information as necessary without worrying about hitting the end of the data field.

Regression Analysis of Time Series© (RATS, VAR Econometrics) is a statistical analysis program focused on time series analysis and the graphing of results. RATS is a relatively straightforward program to use, however, it takes familiarity with its syntax before one feels comfortable using the program and knowing its capabilities. We are currently examining other software programs that may be more well suited and powerful than RATS, as well as more user-friendly. We do not anticipate, however, that the fundamental issues involved in event data analysis would change if we were to use another package. As with R:Base, our example uses RATS because that is what we currently use. However, the principles relate to most time series analysis packages available.

PLANNING, PLANNING, PLANNING

Even with appropriate hardware and software, we are still *not* ready to begin entering data. The data management process described here is fairly complex and may involve many data files, many variables, and literally thousands of observations. Careful planning at the outset helps ensure (though it does not guarantee) that problems down the road are few and that when they do arise, they can be corrected. Planning ahead also helps to maximize the effectiveness of data analysis; indeed, analyses that could have resulted in valuable findings may be impossible to carry out if data is coded or stored sloppily. The value of this appendix comes not only from the detailed instructions it provides, but also from pointing out the lessons we have learned over time from our own mistakes, many of which were completely preventable.

The process of building an event sequence data file is pictured in Figure 5.3. The following sections describe how to complete the research tasks outlined in Chapter 5 that relate to data collection, management, and analysis. The steps covered in this appendix do not necessarily correspond one-to-one with the sections in the discussion in chapter 5, but are presented in sequential order and are logically integrated with and connected to the contents of chapter 5. We will assume that the researcher has decided on a design, chosen an appropriate sample, and has obtained data. At this point, the researcher must prepare that data for further analysis. This process can be broken into five steps, which will be discussed in turn. Following this, we will describe a sixth step, conducting a time series analysis; theory and methods for this type of analysis will be outlined in chapter 8.

STEP 1. DESIGNING A DATABASE FILE TO RECORD AND MANAGE EVENT DATA

First, the research team must define a qualitative datum, enter raw data into incidents, and assess the reliability and validity of the incidents. Chapter 5 provides a conceptual overview of incidents and discusses the processes involved in validating meaningful incident records. However, before incidents can be recorded, a database file must be built to handle the raw event data. The design of the database file is the heart of the first step outlined in Figure 5.3.

Setting the Incident Format

As we observed in chapter 5, before data collection or file creation takes place, researchers must agree upon the components of an event for theoretical reasons. There is also a mechanical reason: Researchers involved in collecting the information that will be used to specify incidents must have in mind clear definitions of the minimum bits of information necessary to document events in a standard manner. This is true whether the informa-

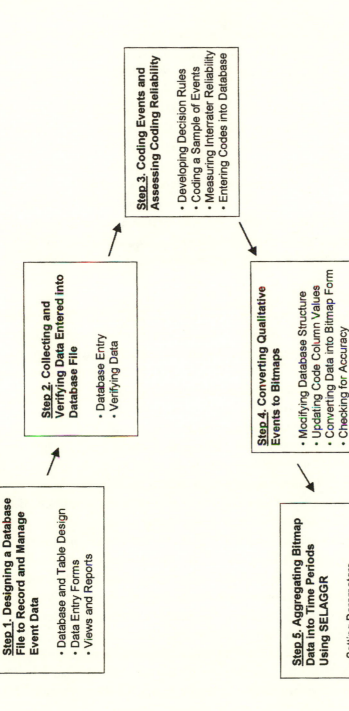

Step 1. Designing a Database File to Record and Manage Event Data

· Database and Table Design
· Data Entry Forms
· Views and Reports

Step 2. Collecting and Verifying Data Entered into Database File

· Database Entry
· Verifying Data

Step 3. Coding Events and Assessing Coding Reliability

· Developing Decision Rules
· Coding a Sample of Events
· Measuring Interrater Reliability
· Entering Codes into Database

Step 4. Converting Qualitative Events to Bitmaps

· Modifying Database Structure
· Updating Code Column Values
· Converting Data into Bitmap Form
· Checking for Accuracy

Step 5. Aggregating Bitmap Data into Time Periods Using SELAGGR

· Setting Parameters
· Running SELAGGR
· Checking for Accuracy

Figure 5.3 The process of building an event sequence data file

tion is gathered from archives or in the field. If the needs of the project are unclear, there is a danger that data will be incomplete. And without standardization it is hard to compare events or to understand how one event leads to another.

For example, for the CIP study, the decision rule used to specify an incident in the CIP study was that each incident should contain, at a minimum, the name of a primary actor (and secondary actor, if appropriate), a description of the action taken or change made, the date the action took place, and if known or discernible, the outcome of the action, why the action took place, and the source of the information. Agreement about these components prior to the initial database design saved time and effort and prevented having to go back to the raw events to change them later. Though it is possible to change data after it has been entered, it is a tedious task.

Database and Table Construction

Once a standard event format has been set, a researcher must design the database file where the data will be stored. This is a crucial step in the data management process because the design of the database determines how data are accessed for editing, analysis, and reporting. Various database programs have different structural capabilities. Our example uses R:Base©, though the principles covered relate to most current database programs.

A database file can consist of a number of tables with relational connections, meaning one data field can link together related entries in different tables. We have found that one table is adequate for many longitudinal cases, as long as the data coding scheme allows for sufficient complexity. Therefore, we do not go into detail here about the use of multiple data tables.

The researcher needs to create and define the table into which collected data will be entered. A table gives the data an organized structure and allows for access, viewing, and editing. Each row represents a single event and each column or "field" contains information relating to that event. Each column should represent the event components agreed upon earlier and be placed into the table in a logical order for manipulation. For example, if an event is composed of a date, an actor, and an action, it is easiest to place the date column to the left of the others, so that it is easy to see the date for each event when rows are chronologically sorted. Figure 5.4 shows a sample data table.

When defining columns (fields) in a table, each column's format must match the information that will be entered into it. Fields need to be defined

Days	Event	Observation	Source	Keywords	
01/01/77	Researchers in Los Angeles conduct the 1st cochlear implant in the US by implanting a limited number of patients using a single electrode device.	The event was published in W. F. House and K.. Berliner's "Cochlear Implants: Progress and Perspectives," Annals of Otiology & Rhinology, 1982, pp. 1-124.	ASHA, May, 1985	House, Academics	More Data Fields →
	↓ More Events				

Figure 5.4 Sample event data table from R:Base

as date fields, text fields, note fields, or integer fields. Field definition sets the format for the data and determines how that data can be used. Formats include the length of the data in the field. However, the length of note fields in R:Base© does not need to be specified and can be approximately 4,000 words. Unlike text fields, the content of note fields cannot be searched for key words or phrases. Allow for sufficient length in each text field because it is difficult to expand the size once data are entered. Events, or rows in the table, can be alphanumerically sorted using any field as a key. Once columns are defined, the table is saved as the central component of the database file.

Along with columns for incident components, we also suggest including a separate column to be used for code words (keywords) to allow for sorting and grouping of events on their coded dimensions. We discuss coding and keywords later in this appendix, but this section warrants their mention. With a simple coding scheme, a single keyword field (usually, a text field), is sufficient. Make it long enough to contain multiple codings. More complex coding schemes can often be simplified by adding more than one keyword field. For example, if three general categories of codes are used (for changes in transactions, people, or ideas), with subcodes for each category, adding three uniquely named keyword fields may be the most useful way to handle coding and grouping. Different coding schemes are addressed in more detail below.

Data Entry Forms

Although data can be entered directly into the table, we suggest using customized data entry forms for quicker and more accurate data entry. Directly linked with the data table, data entry forms are designed to match column names and data types. Data entry forms give researchers an easier way to input data because all fields related to a unique incident are visible at one time. Figure 5.5 shows an example of a data entry form. The field order in which data are entered can be programmed in the data entry forms and can be designated with efficient entry in mind. Data entry forms serve as templates for incoming event data, and while they can be adjusted to reflect new linkages with a table, we suggest limiting modifications in order to keep entries as consistent as possible.

Data entry forms are also useful as printed copies that can be distributed to data collectors to fill in all fields on the sheet before submitting it for entry. By doing this, not only is the researcher more likely to get complete events, but also event information will be compatible with the entry form for the file itself, greatly speeding up and ensuring the integrity of the data entry process.

Date:__________ Event #: ______

Event:____

____

____

Observation: ________________________________

____

Source: ____________________________________

Keywords: __________________________________

Figure 5.5 Sample data entry form

Views and Reports

Views and Reports offer tools with which researchers can systematically view, manage, or print incidents in a data file. Though these steps of database construction may be better discussed or understood following an introduction to coding, it is an important element of the file's infrastructure and should, at least, be considered throughout the planning process.

Because we advocate using one data table, all incidents are entered into a data file for each individual case. Although one table makes data management easier, it makes it more difficult to look directly for certain classes of events separately. R:Base offers a filterlike option called a "View" that allows a predetermined subset of events, based upon codes, dates, or other criteria, to be viewed independently from the entire set of events. To construct a view, the researcher must gain access to the data table itself, then follow the same procedures as called for by a database query. R:Base's on-line help command walks an operator through these steps. Views can be continually and easily updated and changed.

Predesigned reports allow the researcher to create text or screen output of the entire set or any particular subset of events sorted by date or other criteria. Reports can be formated to include any and all columns in the data table. In R:Base, the "Reports" menu contains an option to "Create/Modify," from which a report can be built and stored for future use. At the very least, we recommend setting up an initial report that prints all fields basic to each event. This report is crucial because it will be used in the iterative process of verifying data, coding events, and determining the reliability of the coding scheme. Table 5.4 from chapter 5 shows an example of a printed summary report of events.

STEP 2. COLLECTING AND VERIFYING DATA ENTERED INTO A DATABASE FILE

Once the structure of a data file has been constructed and stored, researchers can begin entering real-time and archival data. The data collection process can be tedious as well as exciting; most longitudinal projects will consist of periods of both. As always, planning and organization are key to managing the data collection process from beginning to end. Researchers should strive to enter complete event information; however, if only partial information is available for an event, it is best to enter partial data and return to update or correct it at a later time.

Data Entry

Once a database structure is defined, researchers can begin entering the event data that will serve as the raw materials upon which keyword coding and time series analysis are based. A general rule for data entry in the case of longitudinal, real-time studies is to enter the information as soon as possible after it is collected. Event data piles up very quickly and the researcher who waits to enter data after too much has been collected can become overwhelmed. Moreover, the sooner information is entered into a database, the more likely it is to be accurate. If it is inaccurate, the sooner it is noticed, the more likely the researcher will be able to track down the original source of the information and correct the incident record.

In the case of archival studies, systematic searches of databases, company documents, library records, newspapers and magazines, academic journals, and other sources should be conducted at regular intervals over the time span covered by the research so that as much relevant event information as possible can be gathered and entered into the database. Interviews, conversations, and correspondence should be recorded, transcribed, and entered into the database as soon as possible after they occur to minimize the risk of forgetting nuances of the interview or other important issues relating to the conveyed information. Expediency in entering data is important to prevent misstatements or errors from becoming part of the permanent data file.

Original source documents should be recorded and stored in an orderly way to ensure that if discrepancies in the data exist, researchers can reexamine the original documentation to verify or correct event information. Files should be kept by the researcher in a safe and organized way and should be easily accessible. One useful strategy for keeping data sources organized is to use uniform classifications in the source field in the event table. This way, events can be quickly and easily linked back to their original source.

Verifying Data

Data entered into the database must be repeatedly checked for completeness and accuracy. As was the case for data entry, verifying data is an easier task if it is done while it is being entered or shortly thereafter, instead of waiting until the entire data file is complete and then returning to check for accuracy. In general, there are two types of verification that can be done in order to minimize the possibility of errors in the events that are included as part of the database. One involves checking original documentation, and the other involves printing events in a report and sharing it with informants who can verify its accuracy.

First, all of the categories that are chosen to make up the event construct—dates, actors, outcomes, etc.—should be verified. If researchers uncover references to the same event from two or more different sources, each account should be entered so that any biases due to a data collector or source are minimized. Later, researchers can decide which account is more accurate or if multiple accounts of a single event need to be included.

Second, data accuracy can also be judged by organizational informants, participants, or others familiar with the events being observed. Input from these informed sources is particularly useful in detecting perceptions and unrecorded events and can, itself, serve as an important source of additional information. In conducting this type of study we have found that organizational informants are very effective in pinpointing errors in the data, elaborating on the data already collected, and leading us to new sources of information that we did not previously know existed.

STEP 3. CODING EVENTS AND DETERMINING CODE RELIABILITY

Once event data have been entered and verified, we can move to tasks three and four described in chapter 2: coding incidents into event constructs and assessing the reliability and validity of our coding scheme. These tasks comprise the first steps in the analysis of the accumulated data. Figure 5.6 summarizes the tasks involved in translating a database of incident listings into a reliable set of coded, theoretically meaningful events.

Developing and Refining Decision Rules

An effective coding scheme accomplishes two objectives. First, it captures the theoretically important dimensions of the phenomena that the researcher is interested in tracking. Second, it provides a guide to the classification and categorization of incidents in the database.

To accomplish the first objective, the researcher should be clear about the theoretical grounding for his or her concepts. This requires clear definitions of event concepts, constructs and indicators, and decision rules for achieving high construct validity as concepts move up and down the ladder of abstraction. The development of decision rules should specify operational steps for classifying incidents into event constructs the researcher has chosen to address a particular research question.

For the second objective, the evolving decision rules should be frequently checked against the data to ensure they are meaningful and complete guides for classification. Decision rules should initially be developed independently of the data and based upon the theoretical perspective of the

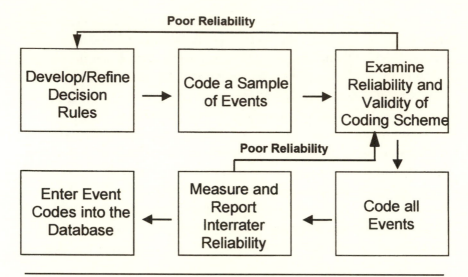

Figure 5.6 Steps for coding events and determining reliability

study. As events are coded, some events may not fit into any decision rule, while others may indicate the need to expand the decision rules to include a new event coding. In the CIP case, we made the development of decision rules an iterative process where we used the rules, read through the set of events, and then discussed whether the coding scheme was adequate and sufficient. If it was not, we added a code or new decision rule and reviewed all events again using the new codes. These discussions about the coding scheme invariably resulted in clearer, more complete, and more valid decision rules.

A few other practical guidelines are useful to make decision rules easy to use. First, be very clear about the boundaries of a decision rule, that is, the incidents that a particular decision rule does *not* include, as well as what it does include. Second, provide examples of incidents that would fall within a particular decision rule along with the rule. Third, keep decision rules short and concise.

Coding a Sample of Events to Measure the Reliability of the Coding Scheme

Once the researcher feels that the decision rules are both theoretically valid and clearly written, the rules should be tested with a sample of events to examine the extent to which they provide a reliable coding guide. One important measure of the reliability of a coding scheme is the extent to which two (or more) individuals agree on the appropriate codes for a sample of events when applying the decision rules independently. We examine one method for calculating interrater reliability here.

We suggest using a sample of events (at least 25) taken from different chronological points in the database. For example, one might code every nth event or select events at random from different points in the dataset. At least two coders, working independently, should assign codes to each event in the sample using the same set of decision rules. At earlier stages in the development of the decision rules, the researcher can act as one of the coders. At some point, however, an individual who has not been involved in the development of the coding scheme should be asked to code the events. This fresh perspective helps to ensure that interrater agreement is due to the clarity of the decision rules and not just to converging interpretations among the researchers involved in writing the decision rules.

The agreement between the two coders can be measured using a matrix similar to the spreadsheet printout in Figure 5.7. The vector of possible codes should be placed along the top and down the side of the matrix. The codes assigned by Coder A will be placed along the rows and the codes assigned by Coder B will be placed down the columns. Often, an additional category will need to be added to the vector to account for those cases

Coder B

	NEG	CMT	EXEC	CXT	NULL	
NEG	5		1			6
CMT		5				5
EXEC			7			7
CXT				6		6
NULL				1		1
	5	5	8	7	0	25

(Coder A labels the rows)

Overall Agreement: .92
Chance Agreement: .24
Cohen's Kappa: .89

Figure 5.7 Coding reliability matrix (using EXCEL)

where no code is assigned. For each event in the sample, the coders compare their codes and add a 1 to the appropriate cell in the matrix.

For example, assume that Coder A in Figure 5.6 assigned an "NEG" code to a particular event and Coder B also assigned an "NEG" code to that event. This implies that a value of 1 should be added to the (NEG, NEG) cell of the matrix which lies on the diagonal. On the next event, Coder A assigned an "NEG" code, but Coder B assigned a "EXEC" code. We would then add a 1 to the (CMT, EXEC) cell of the matrix which lies off the diagonal.

Once the codes assigned to all of the events have been entered, the overall agreement between the coders can be calculated as follows:

overall agreement $= \Sigma(r_i, c_i)/N$,

where (r_i, c_i) represents the value of the cell designated by row i, column i, and N is the total number of codes assigned. In some cases N may be greater than the total number of events, because single events are assigned multiple codes.

While overall agreement provides one measure of reliability, it is also important to employ a statistic such as Cohen's kappa (Cohen, 1960) that corrects for chance agreement. Cohen's kappa is calculated as follows:

$$\kappa = \frac{(\text{overall agreement} - \text{chance agreement})}{(1 - \text{chance agreement})}$$

where,

chance agreement $= \Sigma(R_i C_i/N)/N$
R_i = sum of all codes in row i
C_i = sum of all codes in column i

Values for κ can range from -1 to 1. If $\kappa = 0$, agreement is equal to chance. If $\kappa < 0$, agreement is less than chance and if $\kappa > 0$, agreement is better than chance. Values of $\kappa > .80$ signify reasonable interrater agreement. In some cases, the researcher may decide that certain misclassifications are more serious than others. In such cases, each cell of the agreement matrix may be assigned a weight and the kappa can be calculated to include these weights (see Cohen, 1968 for a description).

We have found that interrater reliability can be low for two typical reasons. First, individual coders may have different understandings of the meanings and applications of the decision rules. If this is the reason for the disagreement, the decision rules should be revised to improve clarity and comprehensiveness and the above process should be repeated. We should not be surprised if the first few cuts at a coding scheme yield low reliability scores. In our experience, it takes several iterations before clear and unambiguous decision rules that are appropriate for the dataset are developed.

A second typical reason for disagreement is that coders disagree on how a particular event in the database should be interpreted. Since disagreement based on event interpretation does not reflect on the reliability of the decision rules, this source of disagreement should be eliminated whenever possible. One approach to eliminating this source of error is to allow coders to discuss the interpretation of an *event* (not a decision rule) either with one another or with a third person who is familiar with the case while coding. This process can also help the researcher to clarify the wording of events in the database.

Coding All Events and Measuring Interrater Reliabilities

Once the interrater reliabilities calculated for samples of events have attained an acceptable level, the decision rules are ready to be applied to the entire sample of events. This process should involve two or more coders who have a basic understanding of the case and who work independently. The actual coding can be done in at least two different ways. First, both coders can code the entire sample of events and interrater reliabilities can be calculated on the entire sample. Second, one coder can code the entire sample and a second coder can code a *random* sample of events (at least 25) taken from the larger dataset. Interrater agreement can then be calculated on this random sample. Since the second approach does not compromise reliability, it may be a preferable approach for most purposes.

In cases of disagreement at this stage of the research, coders can engage in discussions to see whether or not consensus can be reached on specific events. As was mentioned above, these discussions will often reveal two sources of disagreement: (1) the event was interpreted differently by the two coders or (2) the coders interpreted the decision rules differently. In the former case, the event can be clarified and consensus can usually be reached. In the latter case, the decision rules may need to be revised, in which case the researcher will need to work on obtaining basic reliability with samples of data before coding the entire sample.

Entering Event Codes into the Database

When coding is complete, the event codes should be entered into the keyword column in the database. Event codes should be no more than two or three letters long and codes should be separated by a space or comma.

STEP 4. CONVERTING QUALITATIVE EVENTS TO QUANTITATIVE BITMAPS

Because R:Base© is a database program, its statistical capabilities beyond event counts and frequencies are limited. One important transformation mentioned in chapter 5 was that qualitative codes must be translated into quantitative indicators for statistical analyses. Once events have been coded, the translation from qualitative events to quantitative bitmaps requires only a few mechanical steps to modify the database and convert the data. Note that there are many opportunities throughout this process for small errors. Do not become discouraged by having to repeat certain steps; we have yet to complete this process in its entirety without having to go back to correct some sort of error.

Modifying the Database Structure

After all events have been coded, the database structure must expand to include a unique new column for every code that is selected to classify or represent an event construct (or variable). For example, if 36 total possible codes are applied to events, the table must be expanded by 36 unique columns, each corresponding to one and only one new variable. Because each column is independent of the others, multiple codings for a single event are easily accommodated by this procedure. We suggest that column names be as short and informative as possible regarding their content to eliminate unnecessary confusion. Neither code nor column names can be repeated, nor can they consist of any reserved words (reserved words are protected words that the database program will not allow a user to use).

Updating Code Column Values

New code columns should be defined as integer fields which do not require that any length be specified. The new columns represent the binary indicators of the presence or absence of a particular event construct (e.g., code). Initially, the value of each column for all events should be set to 0 and then updated to reflect the occurrence of a change in a construct for a particular event.[1] Column values are dichotomous and can only be 0s or 1s, representing either the presence or absence of a particular event dimension according to the set of decision rules. As described in chapter 2, multiple

---

1. Note, however, that although the default value in R:Base looks like a zero (-0-), it is actually a text string variable rather than an integer, and cannot be downloaded into a bitmap. While each program differs, other databases are likely to follow the same default convention.

codes on a single event are created by updating more than one column in an event record with a 1. An example of the syntax entered at the R> prompt needed to execute this step is given below.[2] For this example, the code/column name is *OP*(outcome-positive), the table is named *CIPT* and all events took place after 01/01/76.

> Update set OP =0 in CIPT where DATE Gt 01/01/76
> Update set OP =1 in CIPT where DATE Gt 01/01/76

Downloading Column Data into Bitmap Form

Once values are updated to reflect changes in key constructs, the columns of 0s and 1s combine to form the matrix downloaded into a bitmap used by RATS and other data analysis programs. The downloaded data from these procedures should contain each unique event number, the event date, the number of days elapsed since the first event occurred, followed by single columns for each possible codes. The syntax for downloading can be written outside of R:Base in ASCII format and used as a command file. The file should be written in this format:

> Set Variable start to 01/01/76
> Output CIPEXA.DAT
> Select number=4 date (date-.start)=4 +
> ac=1 ic=1 ir=1 pe=1 tr=1 ci=1 ce=1 op=1 on=1 om=1 on=1 +
> a01=1 a02=1 +
> From CIPT Sorted By date

In this example, actual command syntax is in bold and database variables are in italics. The Set Variable command allows R:Base to calculate the number of days elapsed from the initial event to the current event. This calculated variable is necessary for time series analyses as it establishes both a temporal ordering and scaling of events. The date inserted at the end of the first line (01/01/76) should be the occurrence date of the first event.

The Output command names the output file to be created. Unless a path is explicitly given, R:Base will write the file to its current directory. Using a .DAT extension for the file will help keep different types of files easy to distinguish.

The Select command tells R:Base which columns you want downloaded

---

2. As with any command in R:Base, the syntax file can be written in ASCII outside of R:Base and submitted to run at the R> screen. To execute a syntax program, type "run [filename]", making sure that the file is either in the current directory or the path is specified.

into the output file, the number of characters allocated to each field, and the order in which they appear. For this example, each event has an ID number, followed by the DATE, the calculated day count, then each of the coded variables. At the end of each line, a "+" indicates that commands continue on the next line.

The From command identifies which table (or file) the data are coming from and the Sorted By command indicates the order of the events in the output file. Sorted By is usually either the event number or another unique field for each event.

Once data are transferred, they must be formated before any analysis can be performed. Because R:Base prints column headings every 20 lines, these headings must be removed throughout the entire file before it can be read into another program for analysis. To do this, either work in a text editor or word processing package to delete the lines, and then resave the file (keeping it in ASCII format). Once the editing has been completed, the bitmap should resemble the sample bitmap shown in Table 5.5 in chapter 5.

Checking the Downloaded Bitmap File for Accuracy

Despite every attempt to prevent errors, it is almost inevitable that errors will appear somewhere in the bitmap. Before any further analysis begins, we suggest that a small sample of events be tested in order to be sure that the column codes (downloaded 0s and 1s) accurately reflect the coding found in a particular incident record. For example, choose 10 or 20 rows from the bitmap. After identifying the unique event represented, examine the codes used to describe its content. Then, check the columns of 0s and 1s following the event number and date in the bitmap. Column values should correspond precisely to coding in the event. So, if an event had three codes assigned, those three code columns should each show 1s rather than 0s. Choosing a small number of events distributed throughout the bitmap and finding them to be correct is a good assurance that the bitmapping process was successful.

STEP 5. AGGREGATING BITMAP DATA INTO TIME PERIODS USING SELAGGR

The bitmap described above contains unique rows for each individual event included in the entire time series. For some types of time series analyses, such as log-linear and logit analysis, a bitmap of unique events is appropriate. If continuous data is required, however, it is necessary to aggregate event counts into temporal intervals as described in chapter 5. This involves another step of transforming an event bitmap to an aggregated bitmap, reflecting a count of event types occurring during defined time periods (e.g., week, month, year). The format of an aggregated bitmap is similar to an event bitmap but consists of a fixed temporal period (e.g., Year 1, Year 2) rather than an event date or observation number, and columns which represent aggregated variable counts rather than individual observations. The Day Count column in the event bitmap is excluded in an aggregated bitmap. SELAGGR[3] converts event bitmaps into aggregated event bitmaps.

The SELAGGR program is an ASCII text file which contains RATS-compatible commands and requires RATS to operate. However, before an event bitmap can be aggregated, SELAGGR's parameters must be adjusted to fit the event bitmap's content and structure.

Modifying SELAGGR Parameters

The SELAGGR program file must be in the same directory as the event bitmap. RATS© must also be installed on the computer, though it can be located in any directory as long as it is part of the general path. SELAGGR requires parameter changes based on dimensions of the bitmap, so it is necessary to know the exact number of events (rows) in the bitmap and the number and order of columns. These format items are required by SELAGGR and RATS©. Also, columns representing event numbers, dates, and codes must be identified to make sure that event numbers and dates are not aggregated.

Using any text editor, bring up the SELAGGR program copy. Only two sections of the program need to be changed: the beginning "input format" section and the ending "output format" section. No other section needs adjustment. The "input format" and "output format" sections are shown in Figure 5.8.

The file itself is self-explanatory. The OPEN DATA command should be followed by the full name of the event data file bitmap (including its extension and path if not in the current directory). The NOFS variable should be the total number of columns. Our convention for dates has been to count them as three separate columns (MM/DD/YY) and to adjust the format line accordingly (see below). The FIRSTBS variable is the column number of the first variable to be aggregated. Obviously, not every bitmap column

---

3. SELAGGR was written by Tse-min Lin for aggregating events for the Minnesota Innovation Research Program. Contact the authors for a copy of this program.

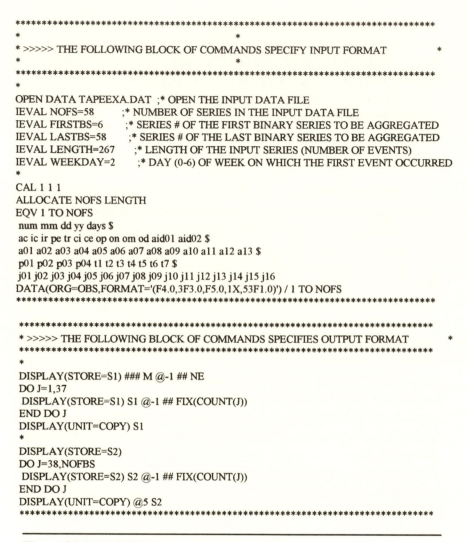

```
**************************************************************************
*                              *                                         *
* >>>>> THE FOLLOWING BLOCK OF COMMANDS SPECIFY INPUT FORMAT              *
*                              *                                         *
**************************************************************************
*
OPEN DATA TAPEEXA.DAT  ;* OPEN THE INPUT DATA FILE
IEVAL NOFS=58        ;* NUMBER OF SERIES IN THE INPUT DATA FILE
IEVAL FIRSTBS=6      ;* SERIES # OF THE FIRST BINARY SERIES TO BE AGGREGATED
IEVAL LASTBS=58      ;* SERIES # OF THE LAST BINARY SERIES TO BE AGGREGATED
IEVAL LENGTH=267     ;* LENGTH OF THE INPUT SERIES (NUMBER OF EVENTS)
IEVAL WEEKDAY=2      ;* DAY (0-6) OF WEEK ON WHICH THE FIRST EVENT OCCURRED
*
CAL 1 1 1
ALLOCATE NOFS LENGTH
EQV 1 TO NOFS
 num mm dd yy days $
 ac ic ir pe tr ci ce op on om od aid01 aid02 $
 a01 a02 a03 a04 a05 a06 a07 a08 a09 a10 a11 a12 a13 $
 p01 p02 p03 p04 t1 t2 t3 t4 t5 t6 t7 $
 j01 j02 j03 j04 j05 j06 j07 j08 j09 j10 j11 j12 j13 j14 j15 j16
DATA(ORG=OBS,FORMAT='(F4.0,3F3.0,F5.0,1X,53F1.0)') / 1 TO NOFS
**************************************************************************

**************************************************************************
* >>>>> THE FOLLOWING BLOCK OF COMMANDS SPECIFIES OUTPUT FORMAT           *
**************************************************************************
*
DISPLAY(STORE=S1) ### M @-1 ## NE
DO J=1,37
 DISPLAY(STORE=S1) S1 @-1 ## FIX(COUNT(J))
END DO J
DISPLAY(UNIT=COPY) S1
*
DISPLAY(STORE=S2)
DO J=38,NOFBS
 DISPLAY(STORE=S2) S2 @-1 ## FIX(COUNT(J))
END DO J
DISPLAY(UNIT=COPY) @5 S2
**************************************************************************
```

Figure 5.8 SELAGGR's input and output sections

should be aggregated. For example, if the event file includes an event number, three columns for the date, and the number of days since the first event, the first variable or series to be aggregated would be the sixth, so "6" would be entered. The LASTBS variable should indicate the last column number to be aggregated. The LENGTH variable should be changed to reflect the number of rows in the bitmap. The WEEKDAY variable can remain 2, unless it is important to the aggregation that day of the week be specified.

Following the input format variables to be changed is a section which reads the data from the bitmap into the SELAGGR program. The format convention used here is taken from RATS and will be duplicated when creating source code files for RATS. The first three lines of the program (CAL, ALLOCATE, EQV) should not change.

The remainder of this section looks for variable columns to be read. Each variable is reflected with a simple name and must be ordered as it was downloaded from R:Base. A "$" follows each line until all variables have been listed.

The DATA line contains the FORMAT code vital for reading data. The FORMAT section of the DATA line must be only on one line.[4] This string indicates each series' location and its character width. All series must be accounted for in the string. In the example below, F4.0 represents the first series (num) as a 4-digit series with no decimal point. The 3F3.0 represents the entire date field, but is separated into 3 3-digit, no decimal point series (mm,dd,yy). An integer preceding an F code tells SELAGGR to repeat the F coded value. Xs are used to represent empty columns in the file (e.g, 1X represents one blank column). The combination of codes must capture the *exact* layout of the file. Unless this FORMAT code is completely accurate, the program will not aggregate data correctly. In our experience, aggregating errors are frequently eliminated by readjusting the FORMAT string. Be patient, however; detecting errors here can sometimes be frustrating.

At the end of the program, the "output format" section needs to be changed before running SELAGGR. A maximum of 36 series can be aggregated and printed to an output file during any single pass through the program. The number following the "J=1," needs to be equal to (LASTBS - FIRSTBS + 1) in order to be sure that all aggregated data series are included in SELAGGR's output. If more than 36 series need aggregation, the second DISPLAY block must be included (as in the example). However, if less than 36 series are aggregated the "37" should be replaced by the correct number and the second DISPLAY section should be erased from the program. Like the FORMAT line, it is important that this section be completely accurate or data will be printed incorrectly.

Running SELAGGR

Once all parameters fit the event bitmap, SELAGGR can be run using RATS. The current directory must contain the edited SELAGGR copy and

---

4. The DATA line, however, can be separated by placing a "$" after ORG=OBS, and putting the FORMAT string onto the next line.

the event bitmap. At the DOS prompt, type "RATS SELAGGR.xxx," depending on the exact name under which you saved SELAGGR. Any name can be used for the file. Once executed, SELAGGR prompts the researcher for two items of information needed to complete the aggregation procedure. First, the length of the temporal interval must be specified. The choice of time period depends on the total time span of events, theoretical requirements, and meaningfulness of statistical interpretation. Second, SELAGGR asks for an output file name to be used for the aggregated bitmap. Make sure that the name you choose is different from the event bitmap or the original data will be erased inadvertently.

When SELAGGR writes an outfile with the new bitmap, the first column indicates the period number, the second column indicates the number of aggregated events in that time period, and aggregated variables begin in the third column. This has been a problem for us more than once and is essential for checking data accuracy.

Checking Data for Accuracy

As in all previous steps, it is important to check the aggregated bitmap data to be certain that columns total to the correct sum and are in the correct order. To do this, we recommend choosing a few codes, summing up the total figure in the columns, and checking it against the sum of event types in the R:Base file. If columns do not add up correctly, it is likely that the problem lies in how the data was read into the SELAGGR program or printed to the output file. Check the input and output sections for errors in the FORMAT line, errors in the listed variables and their order, and the number of iterations (in the output section after the J) for printing.

CONCLUSION

It is our hope that this appendix will make the procedures for coding and data entry more concrete and "doable" for the reader. While the packages mentioned in this chapter have been useful for us, many other similar ones are now available. It should be possible to translate the steps outlined here without too much difficulty.

6 Stochastic Modeling

W E NOTED IN CHAPTER 2 that among the basic requirements of process research are the ability to identify and characterize event sequences and the capacity to identify temporal dependencies in event sequences. Stochastic modeling of event sequences is directly applicable to both tasks, because it captures dependencies among sequential observations. Stochastic modeling can also contribute to the evaluation of developmental models based on formal and final causality and to the identification of macrolevel narrative structures.

Anderson defines stochastic models as "time series [models] in which the characteristic and useful properties appropriate to the time series are not the deterministic mean value functions, but the probability structure itself" (1971, p. 164). In other words, stochastic models are oriented toward predicting changes in probability distributions of events as a function of time. To illustrate what this entails, let's return to the case of social service agency startups discussed in chapter 1. In an event sequence describing the actions taken in a startup, the following event types might be distinguished: (a) *definition events* (those which help define the nature of the program, its organization, and the services it offers); (b) *boundary spanning events* (those in which members of the program development team interact with people or organizations outside the program itself, for example, resource controllers or potential constituents); and (c) *management events* (those involved in actually managing the day-to-day operation of the unit). To study how the process unfolds, it is useful to determine whether there are patterns in sequencing of these three types of events.

Consider two hypotheses about the nature of the process. Hypothesis 1 posits that effective startups will continuously engage in all three types of actions, because they represent key functions that reinforce each other. This implies that the observed event sequence should be constituted of a mixture of the three types of events, with no single type dominating. Hypothesis 2 proposes that effective startups first focus primarily on defining themselves and then shift their focus to linking with resource controllers and constituents, while management should be emphasized only in the final stage of the process. This implies that the event sequence has three distinct segments: the first is comprised primarily of definition events, the second primarily of boundary spanning events, and the third of management events. Moreover, the first two phases should be longer than the third phase.

These two hypotheses can be distinguished in terms of the distribution of activities that should be observed during startups. Hypothesis 1 implies that activities should be equally distributed across all three categories in effective startups and that unequal distributions will be found in ineffective startups. The three events should be observed in proportions of the overall distribution of acts approximately as follows: defining = .33, boundary spanning = .33, and management = .33. Hypothesis 2 suggests that effective startups will focus mostly on definition and boundary spanning and to a lesser extent on management. Moreover, definition events should occur early in the sequence; management events, on the other hand, should be concentrated primarily at the end of the event sequence, after the general form of the startup has been negotiated. This might yield the following summary distribution for effective startups: defining = .40, boundary spanning = .40, and management = .20. One way to test these hypotheses is to compare the distributions of events in observed startups to these two hypothesized patterns, allowing for level of effectiveness. If either hypothesis were correct, then the event sequence from the effective startups should conform to the pattern, while the event sequence from the ineffective startups would not.

While comparing overall distributions is useful, it portrays only part of the whole picture. It tells us about the nature of the overall pattern of events across the entire startup, but not about the dependencies among events in the startup. To explore the generative process, it is necessary to identify the model that gives rise to these summary event distributions via temporal linkages and dependencies among events. Such a model not only shows the final distribution of event types, but also shows how the process "got there" by depicting the dependencies among events that generated the summary pattern.

For example, assume that the observed summary data distribution was similar to what would be expected if hypothesis 1 were true, that is, that .33 of all events were in each of the three categories. This equal distribution of events across all three categories could be generated by a number of processes. For instance, there might be "true mixing," in which the definition (D), boundary spanning (B), and management (M) events occurred as follows: D-B-M-D-B-M-D-M-D-B-B-M-D-M-D- etc. This would yield a summary distribution of events such that (D, B, M) = (.33, .33, 33). However, a very different process could also produce the same summary distribution. For example, it might be the case that the startup activities are divided into three phases, as specified in hypothesis 2, but researchers misestimated the length of the phases. If each phase was approximately the same length, then the following event sequence would be observed: D-D-D-D-D-D- . . . -D-B-B-B-B-B-B- . . . -B-M-M-M-M-M-M . . . -M. This, too, would yield the summary distribution of events (D, B, M) = (.33, .33, .33). The only way to distinguish the two cases would be to determine the event-to-event dependencies in the event sequence. In the first case, these dependencies would be such that each event type was about equally likely to follow each other event; in the second case, when there are three phases, events of the same type are much more likely to follow each other than to follow an event of a different type. Hence, we would find different patterns of event-to-event dependencies in the two cases.

Such dependencies could be detected by developing models that depict the probabilities of events following one another in sequence. For example, if hypothesis 1 were correct, the probability of a definition event occurring after another definition event would be .333, the probability of a definition event occurring after a boundary spanning event would be .333, and the probability of a definition event occurring after a management event would be .333. Because the sequence in hypothesis 1 is mixed so that all three events occur together, the probability of any event following any other is equal. If hypothesis 2 were true, the probabilities of definition following definition, boundary spanning, and management respectively are 1.00, .00, and .00 (as the sequence shows, definition events always follow definition events and none follows any other type of event). The forms of stochastic modeling discussed in this chapter are designed to describe event dependencies in these terms, and they go beyond description to specification of a relatively simple model that generates the sequence.

Stochastic modeling is also useful to evaluate hypotheses concerning developmental motors. When a developmental model suggests that the event sequence should exhibit particular properties, stochastic modeling can be employed to determine whether this is the case. For example, a life cycle model implies a sequence like the one connected with hypothesis 2. This entails a definite structure for event-to-event linkages, and the tenability of this probability structure can be evaluated by fitting the appropriate stochastic model to the data. Its ability to test for patterns in events makes stochastic modeling useful to test hypotheses of formal and final causality. This can also be extended to illuminate entire narratives, provided researchers can work out the pattern of event dependencies implied by the narrative.

This chapter will focus primarily on discrete time stochastic modeling, rather than continuous time processes, because it best fits the discrete nature of events. The following section begins with a discussion of the basic assumptions underlying stochastic modeling and defines discrete-time, discrete-state stochastic models. We then describe the fitting of homogeneous Markov models to event sequence data, which involves testing assumptions of order, stationarity, and homogeneity. We then turn to analysis of the fitted models, techniques for describing event interdependencies and for testing hypotheses about event sequences. The next sections briefly discuss other approaches for modeling stochastic processes, lag sequential analysis, event history analysis, and semi-Markov modeling, and their application in process research. Following this, we present an extended example of stochastic modeling of the CIP data described in chapter 4. The chapter concludes with a general consideration of the strengths and limitations of stochastic modeling as a process research methodology.

DISCRETE-STATE, DISCRETE-TIME STOCHASTIC MODELS

Our discussion will focus on a particularly useful class of stochastic models for process analysis: discrete-state, discrete-time models. These models are tailored to identify dependencies among nominal level variables such as event types and will enable us to conduct the analyses outlined in the previous section. They presume that time is best considered as broken into discrete intervals, usually of the same length. As we will see later on, this assumption can also be relaxed to allow for different event durations.

First, we will discuss some basic assumptions of discrete-time, discrete-state stochastic models and position them in relation to other types of stochastic models. Then we will explain how to fit these models and test whether a given case meets their basic assumptions. Following this, we will explore various methods for extracting information about development and change processes from these models.

SOME BASIC ASSUMPTIONS AND DEFINITIONS

As we have noted, stochastic models are designed to enable the prediction of future events based on prior events. Rather than predicting specific occurrences, stochastic models predict the *probability distribution* of a set of possible events at a given point in time. For example, rather than predicting that a definition event will occur at time t, a stochastic model attempts to specify the probability that each of the three events in the set (definition, boundary spanning, management) will occur at time t.

Prediction to a probability distribution may not seem as neat as a deterministic prediction of a particular event, but there are reasons to believe that it is useful and may even be preferable to deterministic modeling, at least in terms of modeling microlevel event dependencies. To make a deterministic prediction of a singular event, it would be necessary to assume that all conditions other than those in the deterministic model are constant, an unrealistic assumption in most organizational contexts. Indeed, there is so much interference in most cases that a deterministic prediction is unlikely to fit, even if the theory behind it is correct. As we noted in chapter 2, (a) a multitude of local forces that differ across cases influence a developing entity; (b) how they influence the unfolding event sequence is path dependent, contingent on the events that have previously occurred to the entity; and (c) these events are themselves influenced in idiosyncratic ways by the particular constellation of local forces that hold at a given point in time, and so the causal forces imparted by these events may be somewhat different in each instance. In view of the amount of noise in a development or change process, prediction to a probability distribution is the pragmatic choice over attempts to specify a deterministic model at the event level.

Stochastic models of event-to-event connections may also be more consistent with the basic assumptions of many theories of organizational change and development. In theories that focus on the role of active agents and strategic choice in change and development, probabilistic prediction is expected and assumed. The actions of agents are assumed to be affected by other actors and environmental forces which are not well understood and which are, in any case, too numerous to be explicitly incorporated into the theory. Under such circumstances, a stochastic model is consistent with theory, because there is the assumption that the world has an important component of nonpredictability due to other agents and the complexity of the action system. In such cases theory indicates that the best that can be done is to predict to probabilities of occurrence of a set of possible events.

A wide variety of stochastic models have been considered by social scientists (Coleman, 1964; Howard, 1971; Suppes & Atkinson, 1960). This chapter will focus on a class of models termed *homogeneous Markov processes*, which are models that predict the probability distribution of a set of events X_{t+k} at time t + k based on the probability distribution of the same set of events X_t at time t (our notation in this chapter will use the boldface capital letter to refer to the entire set of events and the small case to refer to a particular category or variable in the set). So, for example, a homogeneous

Markov process would use the probability distribution of the three events, definition, boundary spanning, and management, at one time to predict the distribution of the three events at a later point. The structure of this model would depict the temporal dependencies among events. For example, if definition events tended to be followed by boundary spanning events (perhaps because the innovation team is eager to assess the political acceptability of its attempts to define the program with outside stakeholders), then a high probability of definition events at time 1 would imply that at time 2 there would be a high probability of boundary spanning events.

The number of time periods k that the model projects into the future is termed the *order* of the process. If the current time period t is used to predict t+1, the Markov process is first-order; if we use two time periods, t and t−1 to predict t+1, the process is second-order; if we use three, t, t−1, and t−2 to predict t+1, it is third-order, and so on.

Homogeneous Markov processes should be distinguished from *nonhomogeneous Markov processes,* which add other variables than the events themselves to the predictive model. For instance, in addition to predicting the probability distribution of the three events in our example—definition, boundary spanning, and management—based on their own prior occurrence, they could also be predicted based on other events not in the set, such as environmental shocks, and variables, such as level of resources available at a point in time. These models are more difficult to work with than homogeneous Markov processes, and considering them in depth would move this chapter well beyond its intended scope. However, they are a viable option and we hope they will be explored in the future. The ability to explain event dependencies with exogenous variables is one of the attractions of nonhomogeneous models, and we will detail how this can be accomplished with homogeneous process models later in this chapter.

Homogeneous Markov process models assume discrete-time intervals, and therefore must be distinguished from *continuous stochastic models.* The structure of event sequences suggests that discrete-time stochastic models are most useful for analysis of typical process data, because each event can be viewed as corresponding to a discrete time point in the process. However, it is also desirable to incorporate some continuous aspects of event sequences into the model to represent events with different durations. Incorporating duration into Markov processes creates what has been termed the *discrete time semi-Markov process* model (Howard, 1971).

True continuous stochastic models will not be considered in this chapter. They do not offer a natural match to nominal event data. However, continuous stochastic models may well have useful application when event data can be translated into continuous variables, as it is for event time series. Continuous stochastic models are quite complex mathematically, but Coleman (1964) and Leik and Meeker (1975) have provided generalized solutions for many of the equations necessary for applying continuous time processes.

FITTING HOMOGENEOUS MARKOV MODELS

Several assumptions must be met for a homogeneous Markov process model to give a satisfactory representation of event sequence data. The model we will focus on is the Markov chain, which predicts the probability of occurrence of an event at time t+k as a function of the events occurring at immediately earlier time periods. This model is to be preferred for the analysis of event sequences because it provides a powerful and useful summary of the nature of event dependencies. It also can be used with a single event sequence; it does not require a large sample of cases, so long as the cases under analysis are sufficiently long.

The Basic Markov Chain

Our analysis starts with a set of mutually exclusive and exhaustive events, X. To introduce the model we will consider a set of two events; the generalization of the model to more than two event types is straightforward. We will use the example of events which can be coded to indicate the *adoption* of an innovation and its opposite, *no adoption* of the innovation (Rogers, 1995), for illustrative purposes. The probability of the occurrence of the two events at time t+k is represented as a vector V_{t+k}. If the two events are labeled i and j,

$$V_{t+k} = [p_i(t+k), p_j(t+k)]$$

For instance, if the probability of adoption of an innovation (i) at t+k is .35 and the probability of no adoption of an innovation (j) at t+k is .65, then $V_{t+k} = [.35, .65]$.

The *transition matrix* **T** models probabilities of transition from one event to another over time. **T** contains the elements, q_{ii}, q_{ij}, and so on, in the following manner:

$$\mathbf{T} = \begin{bmatrix} q_{ii} & q_{ij} \\ q_{ji} & q_{jj} \end{bmatrix}$$

where q_{ii} in a discrete time system is the probability that event i will be followed immediately by another event i in the next time interval, q_{ij} is the probability that an event i will be followed immediately by an event j during the next time interval, and so on. The first row of the transition matrix shows the probabilities that an event i will be followed either by itself (q_{ii}) or by the other event (q_{ij}); the second row shows the probability that event j will be followed either by event i (q_{ji}) or by itself (q_{jj}). In cases when there are more than two events, the form of the matrix is the same: the rows contain probabilities of the transitions from one event to either itself or to the other events. In this transition matrix $q_{ii} + q_{ij} = 1.0$. All entries in a row of a transition matrix sum to 1.0 because in a set of mutually exclusive and exhaustive categories each event can only be followed by itself or by each of the other possible events; if we sum the probabilities of all possible transitions we obtain 1.0.

For example, the transition matrix for the innovation adoption case might be:

$$
\mathbf{T} = \begin{bmatrix} .80 & .20 \\ .50 & .50 \end{bmatrix}
$$

The first row of this transition matrix indicates that if a person has adopted the innovation at $t+k$, then by $t+k+1$ their probability of still using it is .80 and their probability of having moved into a state of no adoption, that is, of rejecting the innovation is .20. The second row pertains to the behavior of persons who have not adopted the innovation at $t+k$; by $t+k+1$ they have a 50% chance of having adopted the innovation and a 50% change of remaining in the "no adoption" state. Note that the rows of this matrix sum to 1.0, because, whatever their state during the event that happened at $t+k$, people can only be adopters or nonadopters at $t+k+1$.

This transition matrix represents a first-order Markov process, in which each event is dependent only on the event immediately preceding it. A second-order Markov process represents the probability of an event's occurrence based on the preceding two events. Using our two-category example, the transition matrix for a second-order Markov process would be:

$$
\mathbf{T} = \begin{bmatrix} q_{iii} & q_{iij} \\ q_{iji} & q_{ijj} \\ q_{jii} & q_{jij} \\ q_{jji} & q_{jjj} \end{bmatrix}
$$

The first entry in the matrix, q_{iii}, represents the probability that a person who had been in state i at time $t+k$ and remained in state i at time $t+k+1$ would remain in state i at time $t+k+2$. This entry corresponds to the case in which a person who had adopted at time $t+k$ continued to adopt during a second event at $t+k+1$ and then continued to adopt during a third event at $t+k+2$. This model predicts probabilities at a given point in time $t+k+2$ based on the preceding *two* events. Note that there are four rows in this transition matrix because it has to include all possible combinations of two sequential events as the predictors of the events in the time period $t+k+2$; so the first row represents the probabilities of events i and j, respectively, following the pair of events i and i, the second row represents the probabilities of i and j following the pair of events i and j, and so on. There are only two columns in this transition matrix because only two events are possible at any point in time in this example, i and j.

Following our example, a hypothetical second-order transition matrix might be:

	adopt	no adopt
adopt-adopt	.80	.20
adopt-no adopt	.40	.60
no adopt-adopt	.70	.30
no adopt-no adopt	.40	.60

In this transition matrix, we have labeled each row with the corresponding sequence of prior events and the columns with the predicted event. The top left entry in this matrix corresponds to the probability that the person will adopt during an event when they have adopted in the preceding two events; the top right entry represents the probability that the person will not adopt during an event when they have adopted in the preceding two events (that is, the probability of rejecting a previously adopted innovation), and so on.

Now that we have introduced transition matrices, we can state the basic form of a Markov chain. This model postulates that the probability vector V_{t+k+1} can be calculated by multiplying the probability vector V_{t+k} from time $t+k$ by the transition matrix T.

$$V_{t+k+1} = V_{t+k}T \qquad [6.1]$$

If we can assume that T is constant over time—that is, if we can assume that the values of the qs do not change with time—then the value of V for any time interval can be predicted using equation [6.1], as follows:

$$V_{t+1} = V_{t+0}T$$
$$V_{t+2} = V_{t+1}T$$
$$V_{t+3} = V_{t+2}T$$

and so on, for any time interval.

In general, we can predict from time $t+0$ to time $t+k$ by simply multiplying V_{t+0} by T k times, which is equivalent to multiplying V_{t+0} by T raised to the kth power.

$$V_{t+k} = V_{t+0}T^k \qquad [6.2]$$

Equation [6.2] is a powerful generalization. Starting with any known vector of event probabilities and a transition matrix, we can predict the probability vector for any time interval $t+k$ so long as T remains constant and some other assumptions are met. We will discuss these assumptions shortly.

To illustrate, let us return to our example with the first-order transition matrix. If $V_{t+0} = [.35 \ .65]$ and

$$T = \begin{bmatrix} .80 & .20 \\ .50 & .50 \end{bmatrix}$$

then, we can calculate V_{t+1} by multiplying V_{t+0} by T, as follows:

$$V_{t+1} = V_{t+0}T = [.35 \ \ .65]\begin{bmatrix} .80 & .20 \\ .50 & .50 \end{bmatrix} = [.605 \ \ .395]$$

$$V_{t+2} = V_{t+1}T = [.605 \ \ .395]\begin{bmatrix} .80 & .20 \\ .50 & .50 \end{bmatrix} = [.6815 \ \ .3185]$$

From this it is can be seen that $V_{t+2} = V_{t+0}T^2$. We could go on to project as many time periods into the future as we wished. To project the probability structure for events 50 periods into the future, we would have to take $V_{t+0}T^{50}$ (hopefully with the aid of a computer!).

From the example calculation we can see that the probability of adoption gradually increases as we move from time 0 to time 2, since the probability of adoption, the first entry in the vector V, increases from .65 to .6815, while the probability of no adoption, the second entry in the vector, decreases from .35 to .3185. In view of the structure of this transition matrix, we can expect probability of adoption to increase as time passes. Looking back at T for the first-order process, we can see from row 2 that while there is a 50–50 chance that someone who has not adopted will adopt during the next event, but there is an 80% chance that, once a person has adopted, they will continue to adopt. There is thus a "try it, you'll like it" tendency built into the probability structure for this event sequence.

Study of the trajectory of probabilities of event transitions over time and the structure of the transition matrix can yield useful insights into the nature of the change and development process. The relative sizes of different transition probabilities can suggest the preferred paths for microlevel changes. The second- and higher-order transition matrices are particularly interesting, because they shed light on longer sequences of activities. The second-order transition matrices show the probability of occurrence of double interacts, which Weick (1979) and others have argued are the basic building blocks of organizational processes.

To determine whether a Markov chain fits a given event sequence requires testing three interdependent assumptions: the assumptions of stationarity, order, and homogeneity. For the model to fit, all three assumptions must be supported, and if any one is not met, the model must be respecified until they are satisfied. We will consider these three tests in turn. However, before we do this, it is necessary to discuss how event data must be set up for these tests.

Data Transformation

Once the event data has been coded into the categories that are of interest for the analysis, no further data transformation is required. Discrete-state stochastic modeling can be applied directly to categorical data with no need to alter it from its original form. However, in order to prepare the data for the analyses discussed in the remainder of this section, it is necessary to create supplementary lagged variables. Table 6.1 illustrates this.

Most statistical analysis programs take as their basic unit the case, which is represented by data in a single "line" of the database. To fit models of different orders it is necessary to be able to model dependencies between time t and $t-1$, $t-2$, $t-3$, and so on. As we noted previously, if state at time t is dependent only on the state at time $t-1$, then the data fits a first-order process; if state at time t is dependent on states at time $t-1$ and $t-2$, then it is a second-order process; if state at time t depends on states at time $t-1$, $t-2$, and $t-3$, then it is a third-order process, and so on. In order to create a dataset that enables such dependencies to be investigated, data must be lagged as shown in Table 6.1. In order to compute a first-order transition matrix, columns one (lag 0) and two (lag 1) can be cross-tabulated. To compute the second-order matrix, columns one (lag 0), two (lag 1), and

Table 6.1 Data for Stochastic Modeling

ORIGINAL DATA (LAG 0)	LAG 1 DATA	LAG 2 DATA	LAG 3 DATA	LAG 4 DATA
A				
B	A			
C	B	A		
D	C	B	A	
E	D	C	B	A
F	E	D	C	B
G	F	E	D	C
H	G	F	E	D
I	H	G	F	E
J	I	H	G	F
K	J	I	H	G
L	K	J	I	H
M	L	K	J	I
	M	L	K	J
		M	L	K
			M	L
				M

three (lag 2) can be cross-tabulated. This process can continue for as many orders as desired.

Stationarity

Stationarity refers to the assumption that the same transition matrix T operates through the entire series. From the preceding examples, it is evident that we can only use **T** to model the event series if it does not change during the course of the series. More generally, the assumption of stationarity is crucial to the predictive power of the whole class of stochastic models that includes Markov chains and various continuous state models and autoregressive models (see chapter 8 on event time series). This assumption must be empirically validated before other aspects of a Markov chain model are examined.

The logic of the test for stationarity is as follows: First, the event sequence is divided into shorter segments and transition matrices are computed for each segment. Second, these transition matrices are compared to each other. The null hypothesis for this test is that any differences between matrices are due to chance alone. If the null cannot be rejected, then the assumption of stationarity is supported.

A number of specific tests for stationarity have been developed

(Anderson & Goodman, 1957; Kullback, Kupperman, & Ku, 1962). Some involve comparing pairs or sets of transition matrices for segments, and others compare each transition matrix to the pooled transition matrix that represents the entire event sequence. Bishop, Fienberg, and Holland (1975) describe a procedure for testing the stationarity assumption with loglinear models. In view of the widespread availability of software for loglinear analysis, we will center our discussion on this approach.

The first step is to segment an event sequence into several pieces and compute a transition matrix for each sequence. Here we will expand our example somewhat, adding a third category to the adopt-no adopt pair, *experiment*, which refers to trying the innovation out on an experimental basis. This gives us a triple of possible states an event might be in: no adopt, experiment, and adopt. We will take a series of 300 events which have been coded into one of the three states and segment it into three 100-event sequences. The 3 × 3 contingency matrices that indicate the first-order sequential structure for each of these segments and the entire segment are shown in Table 6.2. These are I × I square matrices, where I is the number of events in set **X**; the rows represent the first event in each pair (lag 1), and the columns represent the second (lag 0), as illustrated in Table 6.1. Of course, these matrices represent a first-order process. They would be larger and more complex for a second-order process or higher.

These contingency matrices can be converted into transition matrices by dividing each entry in a row by the row total. This yields the transition matrices shown in Table 6.3. Inspection of these matrices suggests that the first-order contingencies and transition matrices for each of the three segments differ at least to some extent and that these are also not particularly similar to the matrices for the entire segment. Hence, an "eyeball" assessment would conclude that the assumption of stationarity is not met.

A statistical test for the assumption of stationarity can be conducted by fitting a loglinear model for the I × I × T contingency table formed by stacking the contingency matrices for the three segments according to temporal order. In this table I represents the number of rows (prior events, lag 1), the second I the number of columns (second events, lag 0), and T the number of segments (where segments are arrayed in the order of temporal occurrence). The model to be fit is

$$L=[12][13] \tag{6.3}$$

In this model 1 corresponds to the row factor, 2 to the column factor, and 3 to the temporal ordering. Notice that the model is missing the term

Table 6.2   Transition Matrices for the Entire Sequence and the Three Segments

Entire Sequence

	No Adopt	Experiment	Adopt
No Adopt	21	33	2
Experiment	30	84	50
Adopt	4	48	27

Segment 1

	No Adopt	Experiment	Adopt
No Adopt	2	9	2
Experiment	9	23	24
Adopt	1	25	3

Segment 2

	No Adopt	Experiment	Adopt
No Adopt	7	13	0
Experiment	11	27	16
Adopt	2	14	10

Segment 3

	No Adopt	Experiment	Adopt
No Adopt	12	11	0
Experiment	10	34	10
Adopt	1	9	14

[123], which would indicate dependency between time and the structure of the contingency matrices, that is, nonstationarity. The term [13] is included in the model because the row probabilities must sum to 1 for each time period; this creates an artifactual association between time and row values that this term models (Bishop, Fienberg, and Holland, 1975).

Testing the goodness of fit of this model, we get $G^2 = 35.11$ and $\chi^2 = 33.07$ with 12 degrees of freedom. The probability of this test is less than .005, so it is reasonable to conclude that this model does not fit (recall that for a loglinear model test, a model that fits will have a nonsignificant test value).

Tests of partial associations for the significance of individual effects are displayed in Table 6.4. In these tests, a significant value indicates that removing the effect from a model containing all possible effects results in

Table 6.3 Transition Probabilities for the Entire Sequence and the Three Segments

Entire Sequence

	No Adopt	Experiment	Adopt
No Adopt	.375	.589	.036
Experiment	.183	.512	.305
Adopt	.051	.608	.342

Segment 1

	No Adopt	Experiment	Adopt
No Adopt	.154	.692	.154
Experiment	.161	.411	.429
Adopt	.034	.862	.103

Segment 2

	No Adopt	Experiment	Adopt
No Adopt	.350	.650	.000
Experiment	.204	.500	.296
Adopt	.077	.538	.385

Segment 3

	No Adopt	Experiment	Adopt
No Adopt	.522	.478	.000
Experiment	.185	.630	.185
Adopt	.042	.375	.583

worse fit; terms with significant tests should be included in the final model. A third event type (event 3, which corresponds to lag 2 in Table 6.1) has been inserted in this analysis because a test for partial association cannot be generated for the model that incorporates dependencies among event 1, event 2, and time unless the fourth term is included. In Table 6.4, event 3 is indicated by factor 3 and the time effect is now indicated by factor 4. The results in Table 6.4 suggest that the terms [124] and [12] should be included in any final model, but not [14]. The significance of the term [124] suggests that the structure of event-to-event relationships for the first order model does change over time. This indicates that the model in equation [6.3] does not fit and that the first-order process is not stationary.

What is the next step if the assumption of stationarity is not supported? One option is to attempt to model the nonstationarity using other variables.

Table 6.4 Tests of Partial Association for Stationarity

MODEL: EVENT 1 × EVENT 2 × EVENT 3 × TIME

EFFECT	df	PARTIAL χ^2	PROBABILITY
[123]: Event1*Event2*Event3	8	20.04	.010*
[124]: Event1*Event2*Time	8	25.03	.002*
[134]: Event*Event3*Time	8	21.27	.007*
[234]: Event2*Event3*Time	8	14.19	.077
[12]: Event1*Event2	4	22.68	.000*
[13]: Event1*Event3	4	53.18	.000*
[23]: Event2*Event3	4	22.91	.000*
[14]: Event1*Time	4	2.06	.724
[24]: Event2*Time	4	1.78	.775
[34]: Event3*Time	4	1.34	.855
[1]: Event1	2	63.24	.000*
[2]: Event2	2	63.24	.000*
[3]: Event3	2	62.55	.000*
[4]: Time	2	.03	.987

This would involve moving to a nonhomogeneous Markov model, in which a state is predicted based on its previous value and some other independent variable. For example, transitions between various states related to adoption might be explainable as a function of influence from opinion leaders, as well as prior state. Another possibility is that a Markov chain model of higher order fits and will yield stationarity. We will explore this option in the next section. Finally, it is possible that a Markov chain does not fit the event sequence, that it is essentially unpredictable based on prior states.

In general, the more segments that are included in the test, the more sensitive the test for stationarity, and the more likely investigators are to discover uneven parts of the process. However, the segments must be sufficiently long to produce contingency matrices whose expected values meet the assumptions of loglinear statistics. A very conservative expected value is 5 per cell (Fienberg, 1980). With fairly uniform marginal distributions of the contingency matrix, this would require a minimum of 45 acts per matrix; but as marginal distributions become more uneven, more acts are needed, perhaps as many as 100 per matrix. However, Monte Carlo studies have suggested that both χ^2 and G^2 perform adequately under most conditions with expected values as low as 1 per cell (Fienberg, 1980). These studies suggest that the chi-square (χ^2) statistic is more stable and reliable than the log-likelihood (G^2) statistic, which yields too many false negative conclusions. Even with an average expected value of 1.0, there may still be many zero cells in a transition matrix, that is cells with 0 expected or observed values. One way to deal with this situation is to define certain cells as structural zeros, if one knows a priori that no cases will fall into them. Most loglinear programs have the capacity to do this. The major problem with this corrective is that theory often gives little guidance as to which cells should be zero. Another measure, adjusting the degrees of freedom downward to allow for zero cells (Bishop et al., 1975), often yields too conservative a test. The unadjusted test statistics should be regarded as upper bounds of the true values of the statistic in this case.

A different situation arises when researchers have a very large sample of events and cells have very high expected values. For example, when a researcher has an event series with 1,200 units and three categories, the resulting 3×3 first-order transition matrix would have expected values in excess of 100 per cell. In such cases, the tests have such great statistical power that it is difficult to discriminate between models with good and bad fit; using the standard alpha level of .05, almost all models would fail to fit due to high statistical power. One solution is to tighten the alpha level, thus lowering the statistical power of the χ^2 and G^2 tests. For instance, employing alphas of .001 or even .0001 to lower power to .80 or so would enable judicious assessment of model fit.

Order

A second assumption that must be tested to fit a Markov chain is that the process has a definite order. If the stationarity test for the first-order chain had supported the stationarity assumption, we would then be looking for a first-order process to fit. However, in view of the fact that it did not, we can look to a second- or higher-order process. In any case, we cannot presume to know the order of a Markov process; we must conduct tests to establish what order structure exists in the data.

The logic of the test for order is to compare the fit of models of successive order. The fit of the first-order model is compared to that of the zeroth-order model (a model that assumes no sequential structure in the event sequence). Then the fit of the second-order model is compared to that of the first-order model, the third-order model to the second-order model, and so on. Generally, testing goes only as high as the fourth- or fifth-order models for two reasons. First, it is difficult to understand what longer sequences of microlevel events mean; though researchers may be able to make sense out of some possible 5–6 unit event sequences, many are not meaningful; a model of this order does not increase our understanding of the event sequence. Second, moving to longer and longer sequences increases the size of the transition matrix considerably; for example, for the two-category scheme used as our first example, a second-order matrix has 8 cells, a third-order matrix 16, a fourth-order matrix 32, and a fifth-order matrix 64. Unless researchers have a very large sample of events, the expected values of the cells reach levels that do not support statistical inference.

Tests specific to Markov process for order are reported in Kullback et al. (1962). Bishop, Fienberg, and Holland (1975) describe how to test for order assumptions using loglinear analysis. Again, we will employ the latter approach because it can be conducted using generally available loglinear programs.

The tests for order use a number of lagged event variables equal to the maximum order of Markov chain to be considered. The lagged variables indicate earlier events whose interdependence to the event at lag 0 are being tested. So, for example, if we were interested in evaluating Markov chains for the adoption data up to fourth order, we would need to create lagged variables back four periods. In the second step we would use this data to test for order using a sequence of tests. Initially, we would determine the fit of a model for no temporal dependencies, which corresponds to a zeroth-order process. If this model is true, then none of the lagged events should be related to the lag 0 event. Then we test for a first-order model using lag 0 and lag 1 variables, for a second-order model using lag 0, lag 1, and lag 2 variables, for a third-order model using lag 0, lag 1, lag 2 and lag 3 variables, and so on. In judging between models, we take the highest-order model that fits.

Log linear analysis can be used to test for order. The model for a zeroth order process is [1][2][3][4][5] in cases where a fourth-order model is the highest model of interest (in this case the number of the effect corresponds to the lag plus 1; so lag 0 is effect 1, lag 1 effect 2, and so on); the notation indicates that events at all lags are independent of each other. For the first-order process the hypothesized model is [12][3][4][5], indicating that each event is interdependent with the immediately preceding event; for the second-order process it is [123][4][5]; for the third-order process is it [1234][5]; for the fourth-order process it is [12345], the saturated model.

Table 6.5 displays the tests for partial association for the five-effect model. A conservative significance level of .01 was set. As these tests indicate, the second-order model fits the data best. The tests for partial association indicate that the terms [123], [234], and [345] should all be included in a five-way model. This is consistent with the assumption of a second-

Table 6.5   Tests of Partial Association for Order

MODEL: EVENT 1 × EVENT 2 × EVENT 3 × EVENT 4 × EVENT 5

EFFECT	df	PARTIAL χ^2	PROBABILITY
[1234]: Event1*Event2*Event3*Event4	16	19.10	.264
[1235]: Event1*Event2*Event3*Event5	16	.80	.999
[1245]: Event1*Event2*Event4*Event5	16	6.78	.977
[1345]: Event1*Event3*Event4*Event5	16	.28	.999
[2345]: Event2*Event3*Event4*Event5	16	14.43	.567
[123]: Event1*Event2*Event3	8	22.08	.005*
[124]: Event1*Event2*Event4	8	7.93	.441
[134]: Event1*Event3*Event4	8	7.63	.471
[234]: Event2*Event3*Event4	8	29.47	.001*
[125]: Event1*Event2*Event5	8	13.50	.010*
[135]: Event1*Event3*Event5	8	25.52	.001*
[145]: Event1*Event4*Event5	8	18.89	.016*
[245]: Event2*Event4*Event5	8	16.73	.033*
[345]: Event3*Event4*Event5	8	22.85	.004*
[12]: Event1*Event2	4	24.62	.001*
[13]: Event1*Event3	4	20.33	.001*
[23]: Event2*Event3	4	12.15	.016*
[14]: Event1*Event4	4	14.81	.005*
[24]: Event2*Event4	4	50.28	.000*
[34]: Event3*Event4	4	9.48	.050*
[15]: Event1*Event5	4	23.52	.000*
[25]: Event2*Event5	4	15.13	.004*
[35]: Event3*Event5	4	27.63	.000*
[45]: Event4*Event5	4	18.61	.001*
[1]: Event1	2	63.43	.000*
[2]: Event2	2	61.25	.000*
[3]: Event3	2	62.70	.000*
[4]: Event4	2	64.20	.000*
[5]: Event5	2	62.03	.000*

order process, because it indicates that there are interdependencies in sequences of three consecutive events. In this data the best-fitting model is [123][234][345][135] (χ^2 = 192.15, df= 176, p=.198; there were a number of zero expected values, so we did not use G^2 for this test).

In view of this, it is worthwhile doubling back to consider whether a second-order Markov chain is stationary for this data. Table 6.6 contains the second-order transition matrix for this data. To test for stationarity we calculate the second-order transition matrices for the three time segments and compare them with loglinear analysis. The appropriate model to fit in this case is [123][124], where 1 refers to event 1, 2 to event 2, 3 to event 3, and

Table 6.6   Second-Order Transition Matrix

	No Adopt	Experiment	Adopt
No Adopt-No Adopt	.476	.524	.000
No Adopt-Experiment	.300	.633	.067
No Adopt-Adopt	.500	.500	.000
Experiment-No Adopt	.273	.697	.030
Experiment-Experiment	.238	.583	.179
Experiment-Adopt	.021	.255	.723
Adopt-No Adopt	.000	.500	.500
Adopt-Experiment	.080	.640	.280
Adopt-Adopt	.000	.556	.444

4 to time segment. If this model fits, then the process is stationary, because there is no interdependency with the time variable. The [124] term is included to allow for the constraint introduced by the fact that the rows of the second-order transition matrix sum to 1.0. Table 6.7 shows the tests for partial association.

The test indicated that the model had good fit to the data ($\chi^2 = 19.30$, df = 24 p=.736; $G^2 = 19.87$, df = 24, p=.704), which suggests that the assumption of stationarity is tenable.

Homogeneity

The final assumption of a Markov chain is that the same model holds for all subgroups of the sample; this is termed the assumption of homogeneity. Generally, homogeneity is evaluated by comparing the transition matrices of subgroups that might differ, with the null hypothesis that there is no difference between subgroups. Following our example, we might compare the transition matrices for male and female innovators to determine whether they differ. The test for homogeneity depends on the researcher's knowledge of subgroups in the sample that might have different interdependency structures.

Procedurally, the test for homogeneity would first partition the sample into meaningful subgroups. Then contingency and transition matrices would be computed for each subgroup and compared across subgroups. Again, loglinear analysis could be used to conduct these comparisons. The null hypothesis in this test is that there is no difference across subgroups, that is, that the Markov process is homogeneous. In form, these tests are

Table 6.7   Tests of Partial Association for Stationarity of the Second-Order Process

EFFECT	df	PARTIAL χ^2	PROBABILITY
[1234]: Event1*Event2*Event3*Time	16	2.78	.999
[1235]: Event1*Event2*Event3*Event4	16	11.74	.762
[1245]: Event1*Event2*Time*Event4	16	3.72	.999
[1345]: Event1*Event3*Time*Event4	16	1.82	.999
[2345]: Event2*Event3*Time*Event4	16	2.21	.999
[123]: Event1*Event2*Event3	8	22.45	.004*
[124]: Event1*Event2*Time	8	26.53	.001*
[134]: Event1*Event3*Time	8	24.19	.002*
[234]: Event2*Event3*Time	8	10.58	.227*
[125]: Event1*Event2*Event4	8	23.73	.003*
[135]: Event1*Event3*Event4	8	14.71	.065
[235]: Event2*Event3*Event4	8	15.94	.043*
[145]: Event1*Time*Event4	8	23.97	.002*
[245]: Event2*Time*Event4	8	25.29	.001*
[345]: Event3*Time*Event4	8	10.76	.215
[12]: Event1*Event2	4	21.85	.000*
[13]: Event1*Event3	4	46.60	.000*
[23]: Event2*Event3	4	11.10	.026*
[14]: Event1*Time	4	2.17	.704
[24]: Event2*Time	4	1.32	.857
[34]: Event3*Time	4	1.36	.851
[15]: Event1*Event4	4	12.90	.012*
[25]: Event2*Event4	4	53.44	.000*
[35]: Event3*Event4	4	16.39	.002*
[45]: Time*Event4	4	1.62	.805
[1]: Event1	2	62.24	.000*
[2]: Event2	2	62.24	.000*
[3]: Event3	2	63.71	.000*
[4]: Time	2	.06	.970
[5]: Event4	2	63.04	.000*

similar to those for stationarity and order, with subgroup forming a factor rather than time segment or order. For this reason, we will not describe them in detail.

Summary

To fit a Markov chain to the data requires satisfying some quite rigorous assumptions. If these assumptions can be met, the Markov chain provides a powerful model and useful summary of the interdependencies among events.

No method is without limitations. One assumption of the Markov process that may prove problematic for some researchers is that a single process of a definite order generates the entire sequence of events. This simplification enables a powerful model to be advanced, but it presumes that all temporal dependencies in an event sequence are of the same order. Some investigators may find this a difficult assumption to accept. Consider the following sequence of events:

a. John Jones reads a book about quality improvement.
b. John Jones is contacted by his supervisor and asked to join a quality improvement team.
c. John Jones joins the "Ratebusters" quality improvement team.
d. John Jones takes some ideas from the book he read in event (a) and in order to determine if they are worthwhile he applies them in the "Ratebusters" team.

These events would be coded as follows with the simple scheme we have employed in our example:

a. No adoption
b. No adoption
c. Adoption
d. Experimentation

It is entirely possible that a first-order Markov chain would fit an event sequence that contained this segment of John Jones's adoption behavior. If such a model fit and we were not familiar with the specific four-act sequence other than in terms of the first-order model, we would be likely to conclude that act (a) led to act (b) which led to act (c) and then to act (d). There is some justice to this conclusion, since all actions involve quality improvement, and since it is difficult to separate with certainty reading the book and joining the team. However, a close reading of the segment suggests that a case could be made that the most plausible dependencies are between events (a) and (d)—a lag three dependency—and events (b) and (c)—a first-order dependency. The tendency for dependencies of different orders and types to be embedded in the same sequence may lead some researchers to consider that no single stable order exists in a sequence, regardless of whether a Markov chain of definite order fits the data. In sum, while a Markov chain can be found to fit many event sequences, whether it provides a compelling representation is a matter of judgment.

A second limitation of Markov chain models—and of all stochastic models—is that a good amount of data is required to fit them. To comfortably fit a five-category, first-order Markov chain requires at least 150 data points. This is because the test of first- versus second-order processes necessitates calculating a transition matrix with 125 cells, and 150 data points in this instance will only guarantee an average expected value of 1.0 per cell if the acts are distributed fairly homogeneously. If they are not, then 300–500 data points may be required. This places heavy demands on the researcher and may preclude the use of Markov chains for relatively short event sequences.

Bearing these limitations in mind, we now turn to analysis of the structure of the Markov chain itself. We assume that a model can be fit for one or more event sequences and concentrate on characterizing the model and testing hypotheses about it.

FURTHER ANALYSIS OF HOMOGENEOUS MARKOV CHAINS

Once a Markov model has been fit to the event sequence, it can then be interrogated to discover characteristics of the process and to test developmental models. One way to do this is through descriptive analysis of the transition matrix. Another approach is to predict or explain transition values. This section will discuss characterizing Markov processes and exploratory identification of interdependent sequences through lag sequential analysis.

Exploring and Explaining the Structure of Markov Chains

PATTERNS IN THE TRANSITION MATRIX. Some useful information about the processes underlying an event sequence can be derived simply by inspecting the transition probabilities. We can inspect the patterns of the numbers themselves or their visual representation. A transition matrix reports the probabilities of moving between various states; therefore, it can be represented visually as a *state transition diagram* or *digraph* (directed graph). Bakeman and Gottman (1986) note: "Such diagrams have the merit of rendering quite visible just how events (or time intervals) were sequenced in time" (p. 127). In a digraph for a transition matrix, circles represent states (in our case, the state of a given innovation course of action having occurred), and labeled arrows connecting the circles represent the transitional probabilities among them. In complex diagrams, line weight may be used to indicate various levels of probability and lower-probability transitions may be omitted for clarity. Figure 6.1 displays digraphs for three example transition matrices.

One property that can be inferred from the structure of the transition matrix is the existence of *absorbing states,* states that have zero probability

A. Transition probability matrix with
   absorbing state

B. Reducible transition probability matrix

C. Hypothesized three-phase sequence

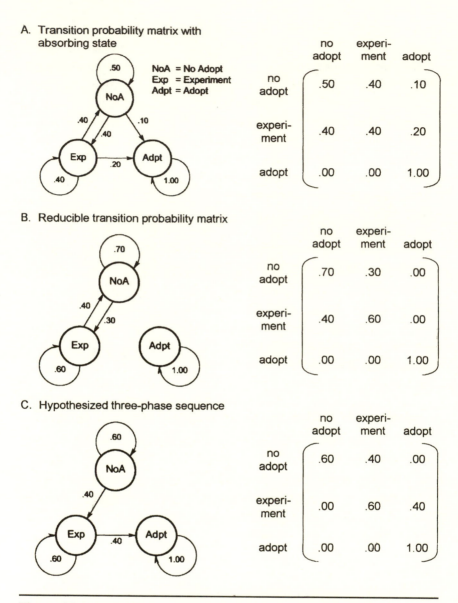

Figure 6.1 Digraphs for course of action transition probability matrices

of transition to any other state (Leik & Meeker, 1975). Once a process enters an absorbing state it never moves into a different state; it remains in the absorbing state permanently. Having one or more absorbing events means that, over time, all events in the system will end up in the absorbing states. They will move into it and never move out again. In our example of the three adoption events, a first-order Markov chain with an absorbing state is

	No Adopt	Experiment	Adopt
No Adopt	.50	.40	.10
Experiment	.40	.40	.20
Adopt	.00	.00	1.00

In this example, once someone has adopted the innovation they continue to use it. Those who have not adopted have a .40 probability of making the transition into experimentation, and a .10 chance of adopting. Once a person has experimented, they adopt with a 40% probability. As a result of this process, everyone in the population will move to adoption; at some time in the future, there will be no events in the experimentation and no adoption categories.

Absorbing states may signal the end points of development and change processes. For example, that adoption is an absorbing state indicates that it is the final phase of the innovation process and not just another state that people pass through in trying out an innovation. Working backward from adoption to earlier events—in this case to experimentation and then to no adoption—enables researchers to specify a typical sequence for the process. Identification of end points may also facilitate identification and testing of final and formal causal patterns.

Another piece of information that can be derived from the pattern of transition matrices is the existence of *noncommunicating states*. Noncommunicating states are defined as those that never make transitions with each other. In terms of our example, a transition matrix with noncommunicating states is

	No Adopt	Experiment	Adopt
No Adopt	.70	.30	.00
Experiment	.40	.60	.00
Adopt	.00	.00	1.00

This transition matrix is unlikely to exist, but is shown here for illustrative purposes. In this matrix the pairs adopt–no adopt and experiment–no adopt never make transitions into each other. There is no way for events to move from no adopt to either of the other two states. Moreover, if we take this transition matrix to higher powers, as we would for transitions in to time t+k, the no adopt event will never make any transitions into the other events. This suggests that the transition matrix can be split into two matrices, that is, that the transition matrix is *reducible*. A reducible transition matrix has the following properties (Greybill, 1983): (a) it must have at least n-1 elements equal to zero; and (b) by permuting the rows and columns it is possible to transform it into a matrix of the form:

$$\begin{bmatrix} \mathbf{A} & \mathbf{0} \\ \mathbf{0} & \mathbf{B} \end{bmatrix}$$

where the bold zeros indicate matrices composed of all zero transition probabilities and **A** and **B** are matrices of transition probabilities in which no column contains all zeros. This arrangement of values indicates that there are really two different processes operating among the events.

The existence of a reducible transition matrix suggests that at least two distinct subprocesses operate in the event sequence. One way to make sense of such a finding would be to return to the qualitative event data to determine what might account for interdependencies among the two subsets of events. In terms of the motors of change discussed in chapter 3, this may indicate a composite explanation that relies on two or more motors to account for development and change.

The formal definitions of absorbing state and reducible transition matrix specify perfect probabilities as their thresholds: absorbing states must have a probability of 1.0 for remaining in state and .00 for transitions into other states, while the submatrices of reducible matrices must have zero probabilities of transition into each other. However, for descriptive and interpretive purposes, it seems useful to relax these criteria somewhat. For example, a state with .95 probability of remaining in state and only .05 for transition into other states is, for all practical purposes, an absorbing state, and may indicate an end point in a process, as described above. In the same vein, nearly reducible matrices can also be considered to define distinct processes.

EQUILIBRIUM VALUES. Over time many Markov chains will eventually reach a state of equilibrium where the probability distribution of events no longer changes as the transition matrix is taken to successively higher powers. At equilibrium, although individual events may indicate a shift from one category to another as time passes, the probability distribution of events across categories does not change over time. The equilibrium distribution has the useful property of being independent of earlier states of the system; the probability of an event being in a given category remains constant over time once equilibrium has been reached. The equilibrium distribution represents the stable state toward which the system is tending; all rows of the transition matrix T^q, where q is the power needed to reach equilibrium, are equal. By the mathematical rules, q must go to infinity to reach equilibrium, but practically, we can find whether there is an equilibrium by raising the matrix to powers until its rows are equal within a certain tolerance. This stability over time suggests that the equilibrium distribution provides a glimpse into essential characteristics of the process.

The equilibrium distribution can be calculated by solving a system of simultaneous equations as indicated by Leik and Meeker (1975). However, this is difficult to do when a large number of categories are involved. For small transition matrices it is often possible to do the calculations by hand, though for larger ones it is necessary to use specialized programs. Moreover, there may not always be a solution for a given set of simultaneous equations, which indicates that there is no equilibrium. Another way to obtain an equilibrium matrix is by raising the transition matrix to higher and higher powers until its row values are equal within some tolerance level. Most statistical packages, such as SAS®, support calculation of powers of matrices. Though not elegant, this "brute force" method may be easier than programming solutions for a large matrix.

PERIODIC TRANSITION MATRICES. Periodic states can be discovered by raising the transition matrix to higher powers. A periodic state is defined as one in which the transition probability from state q to state q is zero for some powers and nonzero for others. Note that it is the probabilities along the diagonal of the transition matrix—the ones that show the probability of a state following itself—that define the periodicity. The powers at which the transition probabilities are zero are multiples of some integer, which accounts for the regular periodic nature of the zero values. For example, a transition probability in a periodic process might have a value of zero at T^2, T^4, T^6, T^8, and so on (i.e., for all powers that are multiples of 2). While it will be rare to find .00 transition probabilities in social processes, finding regularly recurring patterns that are near zero and then nonzero as the transition matrix is raised to higher powers signals a "dampening oscillation" toward an equilibrium point. To test for periodicity, simply raise the transition matrix to successively higher powers and look for recurrent near zero values along the diagonal for one or more states.

COMPARISON OF INDIVIDUAL VALUES IN THE TRANSITION MATRIX. Researchers may be interested in assessing differences, or the lack thereof, between individual transition probabilities. In our example, for instance, it would be useful to know if the transition probability for remaining an adopter once adoption has occurred for the first time, is greater than remaining a nonadopter. This could be assessed by comparing the transition probability t_{11} (no adopt-no adopt) to t_{33} (adopt-adopt) in the three-state transition matrix shown above. This comparison can be conducted using a simple test for equality of proportions, which is described in most introductory statistics texts (see, e.g., Blalock, 1960, and Ramsey & Schafer, 1997).

COMPARISON OF THE TRANSITION MATRIX TO A HYPOTHESIZED TRANSITION MATRIX. In some cases researchers will wish to compare the observed transition matrix to some hypothesized structure, or to compare two transition matrices to each other to assess similarity. Following our example, researchers may desire to determine if a transition matrix calculated from an event series is similar to the matrix used as an example of an absorbing state. Or researchers may have a hypothesized stage structure that they wish to compare to an observed transition matrix. For example, if the adoption process occurs in a three-phase sequence no adoption::experimentation:: adoption, then we might expect the transition matrix of an event sequence to resemble this pattern:

$$
\begin{array}{c c c c}
& \text{No Adopt} & \text{Experiment} & \text{Adopt} \\
\text{No Adopt} & \begin{bmatrix} .60 \\ .00 \\ .00 \end{bmatrix} & \begin{matrix} .40 \\ .60 \\ .00 \end{matrix} & \begin{matrix} .00 \\ .40 \\ 1.00 \end{matrix} \\
\text{Experiment} & & & \\
\text{Adopt} & & &
\end{array}
$$

This structure corresponds to the assumption in a set sequential model that there are only direct transitions from no adoption to experimentation and from experimentation to adoption, but no reverse transitions. This hypothesized pattern could then be compared to the observed matrix to test the hypothesis of a stage sequence. Singer and Spilerman (1979) describe how a number of different types of stage models could be evaluated with Markov and other stochastic models.

At least two ways of evaluating these sorts of hypotheses are available. Kullback et al. (1962) describe a direct statistical test to compare two contingency tables or transition matrices. A second approach is to employ the matrix correlation method developed by Hubert and his colleagues to determine the degree of similarity in the matrices (Hubert & Levin, 1976; Hubert & Schutte, 1976). Hubert's matrix correlation procedure provides a nonparametric statistical test for the null hypothesis of lack of correspondence between two matrices. This extremely flexible procedure is well suited for comparing two observed matrices, for comparing a hypothesized matrix to an observed one, or for predicting the values of one matrix from those of another. Matrix correlation and matrix regression procedures are available in the UCINET analysis package (Borgatti, Everett, & Freeman, 1992). This procedure is also used in phasic analysis, described in chapter 7.

EXPLAINING THE TRANSITION PROBABILITIES WITH EXOGENOUS VARI-ABLES. A final type of analysis considers the transition probabilities themselves as dependent variables and tests explanations for them. In order to use the transition probabilities as dependent variables there must be some variation in these probabilities across time or across cases. This implies that there must be a violation of the assumptions of stationarity or homogeneity in the data pooled across time or cases. Explaining the transition probabilities then involves partitioning the data so that Markov chains can be found that satisfy the assumptions of order, stationarity, and homogeneity. Factors that account for the differences between the transition matrices for the partitioned data can then be evaluated.

The explanation of transition probabilities can be best understood by considering some examples. Rogers' (1995) theory of innovation distinguishes early adopters from other individuals involved in the adoption process; early adopters are generally more open to innovation and change than are other types of individuals. This implies that any sample of innovation adoption processes is composed of two different Markov processes, those for early adopters and those for other individuals. The transition matrix for early adopters might resemble something like this:

	No Adopt	Experiment	Adopt
No Adopt	.20	.40	.40
Experiment	.60	.38	.02
Adopt	.00	.20	.80

The transition matrix for other individuals might resemble the following:

	No Adopt	Experiment	Adopt
No Adopt	.50	.30	.20
Experiment	.35	.40	.25
Adopt	.20	.30	.50

The transition matrix for early adopters reflects lower thresholds required to induce experimentation and adoption and a propensity to persist in adoption compared to other individuals. To test the hypothesis that early adopters and other individuals have different patterns of adoption, investigators would need a criterion or test to identify early adopters that is independent of the adoption process itself. They could then divide the sample into early adopters and others and test for homogeneity by determining if the individual characteristic resulted in two different transition matrices, as described in the previous section. If the hypothesis of no difference can be rejected, and if separate models that fit the assumptions of order, stationarity, and homogeneity could be fit to the two subsamples, then the theory of different processes for early adopters and others can be judged to be tenable.

Consider next a case in which transition probability structure for an event sequence changes over time. In our adoption example, this might occur as the innovation "matures." Early on, when most are unfamiliar with the innovation, there may be more difficulty in persuading people to try or to adopt it. Later on, when there is a large cadre of adopters, there may not be as much resistance to trying it out. The early period might be represented by a matrix such as

	No Adopt	Experiment	Adopt
No Adopt	.75	.20	.05
Experiment	.35	.45	.20
Adopt	.10	.35	.55

In the later stages of the innovation process, when the innovation is better known and has a track record, the transition matrix might be

	No Adopt	Experiment	Adopt
No Adopt	.45	.35	.20
Experiment	.15	.40	.45
Adopt	.10	.20	.70

The first matrix shows a situation in which there is relatively low likelihood that people will experiment or adopt, whereas the second illustrates a more benign situation for innovation, with greater likelihood of experimentation and adoption.

To test the hypothesis that there are temporal shifts in the transition matrices, researchers must identify a point at which such a shift is likely to occur. Subdividing the event sequence at this point, they would then fit two Markov chains. If the two models satisfied the assumptions of order, stationarity, and homogeneity, then they could be compared. Rejection of the hypothesis of no difference would lend support to the theory that a temporal shift had occurred.

It is worth noting that in both cases, key assumptions of Markov chains are violated—in the first case the assumption of homogeneity and in the second the assumption of stationarity. So the same tests that are used to fit Markov chains can be used to test hypotheses about differences over time or across subgroups. It also indicates that violations of Markovian assumptions do not always just provide negative information: they may suggest insights into the factors that determine the stochastic structure.

Both examples thus far involve relatively simple comparisons based on nominal level factors. Spilerman (1972) describes a technique for exploring numerous factors at continuous as well as nominal levels. It requires a large sample of sequences and uses regression analysis to identify influential factors and weed out less important ones. The essence of Spilerman's approach is to use the factors as predictors for transition probabilities in the regression equation. To the extent that the factors can account for variance in the transition probabilities, they can be used to explain the stochastic process.

The explanation of transition probabilities moves Markov modeling to a new level. Markov models provide useful and suggestive descriptions of interdependencies in event sequences. Theories about development and change can be tested and refined with such descriptive data. The analyses described in this section move beyond description and actively incorporate explanatory factors into stochastic modeling.

Lag Sequential Analysis

Lag sequential analysis, a technique closely related to Markov analysis, focuses on the identification of certain meaningful sequences of activities in a series of data (Sackett, 1979, 1980). While most stochastic models identify the overall structure of dependencies among events, lag sequential analysis targets particular sequences of events. As originally proposed by Sackett (1979, 1980) lag sequential analysis involved identifying a criterion event—experimentation, for example—and then determining which events match each occurrence of the criterion as the very next event (lag 1), the second event after it (lag 2), the third (lag 3), the fourth (lag 4) and so on, up to the Maximum Lag event after the criterion. The Maximum Lag is defined as the largest sequential step of interest. Sackett and colleagues have developed software to conduct this analysis (Sackett, Holm, Crowley, & Henkins, 1979). Lag sequential analysis has been used to identify contingencies among pairs of acts and also to identify sequences of acts that commonly occur together.

A researcher might, for instance, be interested in studying experimentation with innovations as a part of the adoption process. Using our example, experimentation would be chosen as the criterion and the acts that follow it identified at lags 1 through 6. The Maximum Lag (in this case 6) would be chosen on the basis of theory or other information the researcher had (for instance, 6 events per month might occur on average in the sample, so choosing lag 6 allows the researcher to follow experimentation impacts for about a month). Suppose that one finding was that adoption occurred with very low probability until lag 4, at which point the probability of adoption was .70, and then it dropped off again. This finding suggests that there is a latent period after experimentation during which the innovation is reevaluated and considered. At the end of this period (corresponding to lag 4), adoption occurred.

Lag sequential analysis can also be utilized to test hypotheses about interdependencies. For instance, a researcher might be interested in testing the hypothesis that cases with "decisive" experimentation will be more effective in retaining adoption than will cases with "tentative" experimentation. Decisive experimentation could be defined as a sequence of events in which experimentation is pursued for three or more consecutive events (which suggests careful, extended experimentation) and then there is a transition to adoption, which is pursued for the remainder of the sequence. On the other hand, tentative experimentation could be defined as a sequence of events in which experimentation is tried for one or two events and then there is a reversion to a state of no adopt, followed by more experimentation. Decisive experimentation would imply that sequences, experiment-experiment-experiment-adopt-adopt-adopt and experiment-experiment-experiment-experiment-adopt-adopt-adopt-adopt, would be common. Other sequences with mixtures of experiment, no adopt, and adopt would suggest tentative adoption. To test the hypothesis, two subsamples of effective and ineffective adoptions could be selected. Lag sequential analysis could then be employed to determine whether the decisive sequences occurred to a greater extent in the effective than in the ineffective cases.

The appeal of lag sequential analysis lies in its ability to help researchers dredge through sequential data to identify key interdependencies. It is well suited for retroductive research. Lag sequential analysis also does not require as large a sample of events as fitting a Markov chain does, because it analyzes dependencies among pairs of events rather than an entire matrix of interdependencies.

Two qualifications must be registered, however. Allison and Liker (1982) noted that Sackett's original tests for the fit of various lags did not take into account temporal dependencies in the data. They suggested a modified test that should be employed when evaluating lag sequential models. More serious is Kellerman's (1988) demonstration that although lag sequential models may provide good *descriptions* of lagged dependencies, they do *not* provide accurate models of the order of the stochastic process that underlies sequences of dependencies. Kellerman's analysis indicates that lag sequential analysis is useful as an exploratory technique, but that it should be used in concert with Markov analysis rather than as an alternative.

SOME DISCRETE-STATE, CONTINUOUS TIME STOCHASTIC MODELS

Discrete-time stochastic models presume "event time"; they define time in terms of the occurrence of events, with each event corresponding to one time unit. This conception of time is useful, but in some cases it is also desirable to introduce continuous time into our models. We noted in chapter 2 that events may differ in duration and scope, but utilizing event time assumes that, in effect, all events have the same duration. The introduction of continuous time into the stochastic model enables us to take the length of events into account. A second, pragmatic reason to consider the use of continuous time models is that process data often come with "real time" indicators, such as dates and times at which events occurred. Continuous models enable us to take advantage of the full information in our data.

SEMI-MARKOV MODELS

A general model that incorporates continuous time into a homogeneous Markov model is the *semi-Markov process* (Howard, 1971, Ch. 10). Whereas Markov models in effect assume that a transition occurs at every point in time (transitions in a Markov chain occur at $t, t+1, t+2$, etc. by taking the transition matrix T to higher powers), semi-Markov models assume that transitions do not have to occur at each point in time, but that a process has a probability of "holding" in a given state for a specified number of time periods. Incorporation of *holding time* into the model enables semi-Markov models to capture events with different durations, as the durations in a given matrix are reflected in the holding time probabilities. So if an event such as experimentation lasts for three weeks (and the week is our basic time unit), it would have a holding time of "3" in the state experimentation, if an adoption event lasts six weeks, it would have a holding time of "6," and so on. Since holding times differ for the same state, they are expressed as a probability distribution of times for each state, yielding probabilities of a process being in state S for 1 time unit, 2 time units, etc. up to the maximum number of time units considered.

It is useful to introduce the equation for a semi-Markov model and to contrast it with that for the Markov chain. Recall that the Markov chain equation is $V_{t+k} = V_{t+0}T^k$, where T is the transition matrix. The corresponding equation for semi-Markov models is $V_{t+k} = V_{t+0}M^k$, where M is the *interval transition matrix*. Thus, the two models are similar in form. The interval transition matrix M is a composite matrix.

$$M(k) = W(k) + \sum_{n=0}^{k} [T \square D(n)] M(k - n) \qquad [6.4]$$

In equation [6.4] each element of the interval transition matrix $m_{ij}(k)$ is the probability that the system will be in state j at t+k if it was in state i at t+0. Note that "being in state j" means arriving in state j at any time during the time period beginning at t+0 and running up to and including t+k.

The matrix $W(k)$ is the "waiting-time probability matrix," a diagonal matrix with elements $w_{ii}(k)$ on the diagonals and zeroes elsewhere. The elements $w_{ii}(k)$ of this matrix are the probabilities that a transition from state i will take longer than t+k (that is, occur in any period starting at t+k+1 or higher).

The matrix T is the transition matrix we are already familiar with from the Markov chain, the "event time transition matrix." This matrix contains no information about durations or times; it takes into account only the ordering of transitions. The matrix $D(n)$ is the "holding-time transition matrix," whose elements $d_{ij}(n)$ indicate the likelihood that a transition from i to j will occur in exactly n units of time. The symbol $\square$ indicates element-by-element matrix multiplication as opposed to the traditional method of multiplying matrices.

Note that there are n holding time transition matrices; to calculate $M(k)$ it is necessary to multiply T by $M(1)$, $M(2)$, . . . $M(n)$ and sum the results. As this operation suggests, fitting a semi-Markov model requires a complicated and lengthy set of calculations. They are so complex that we will not undertake them in this chapter. For applications of semi-Markov models see Ginsberg (1971) and Hewes, Planalp, and Streibel (1980).

As equation (6.4) indicates, the semi-Markov model builds information about duration into the traditional Markov chain. Hence, it is still a discrete-time model, that is, it relies on the division of time into discrete units that are used to time durations rather than regarding time as truly continuous. However, it enables us to model processes as though they were operating in continuous time by setting the units of time at the smallest transition time for the process or less. Other types of models incorporate continuous time explicitly.

EVENT HISTORY ANALYSIS

Event history analysis has received much attention in organizational research (Allison, 1984; Kalbfleisch & Prentice, 1980; Mayer & Tuma, 1990; Tuma & Hannan, 1984; Willett & Singer, 1991). This method is concerned with the question of how much time must pass before a specific type of change or a specific event occurs. Questions that might be addressed using event history analysis include: How long is the experimentation phase of innovation adoption? When does experimentation begin? Are periods of experimentation longer for some types of people than for others? Event history or survival analysis is appropriate for a multitude of research topics, including career dynamics, turnover, idea generation, and organizational demise.

Event history analysis requires a large sample of cases. For each case it requires data on the times during a specified continuous interval when transitions from one state to another occurred and the sequence of these transitions. The data for one case would be of the form: $\{t_0, y_0; t_1, y_1; \ldots t_n, y_n\}$ where n is the number of changes in state and t_0 is the starting time and y_0 the starting state. Usually, the value of n varies across cases, and t_0 may vary as well. In most analyses a single type of transition is the focus, for example, the transition from being employed to being unemployed. However, it is possible to study several different types of transitions simultaneously. The various methods that have been employed in event history analysis study the durations between transitions, that is the length of time between t_0 and t_1, how long it takes for a change in state to occur.

The most common type of event history analysis, *survival analysis*, models the probability distribution of durations prior to the occurrence of a state transition (an event can be considered a state transition in which y_0 is nonoccurrence of the event and y_1 is the occurrence of the event). Our example can be used to illustrate such a probability distribution: Assume that we are interested in durations prior to adoption of an innovation in a one-year period, using the month as our sampling unit. Assume we drew a sample of 288 potential adopters and followed them for a year. The resulting

Table 6.8   Durations Until Adoption of Innovation: 288 Cases

MONTH	NUMBER OF ADOPTIONS IN MONTH
1	5
2	10
3	20
4	30
5	50
6	70
7	30
8	20
9	10
10	9
11	5
12	4

data on adoption is in Table 6.8. Note that 25 cases had not adopted by the 12th month.

In survival analysis, two types of functions are often used to characterize the probability of making transitions during specific time intervals. The *survivor function* captures the probability of remaining in ("surviving") the original state as a function of time. Figure 6.2 shows the survival function for this data. Note that it continuously declines, but never reaches 0.0 in this sample, because after 12 months, 25 cases still have not adopted the innovation. The survivor function drops sharply when a large number of events occur at the same point in time, so changes in the slope of the survivor function may indicate typical points at which transitions tend to occur. A different characterization of event occurrences is the *hazard function*, which captures the risk that the event will occur at a certain point in time given that it has not previously occurred.

Some methods of analyzing these two curves are primarily descriptive; they generate summary statistics that provide an overall picture of the change process. A second type of analysis focuses on precise specification of the nature of the change process through modeling the two functions in terms of the rate of change over time. A number of different models are available to portray the rate of change function, depending on the theory used in a given case (see, e.g., Gross & Clark, 1975; Tuma & Hannan, 1984). A third analysis uses summary statistics and fitted models to identify factors that explain variation in the function. This may involve testing

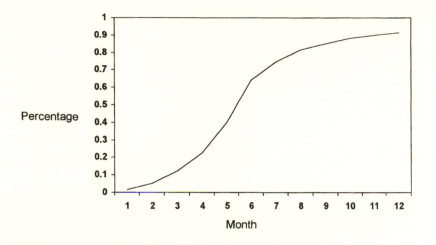

Figure 6.2 Survival function for the data in Table 6.8

whether two or more groups differ in their change processes, or it may involve identification of continuous variables that covary with the functions.

Most event history methods are designed for the study of nonrepeatable events that only happen once in each case. However, models are available to handle repeated events (see Mayer & Tuma, 1990). Amburgey (1986) describes the use of multivariate point process models to study repeated events.

We do not discuss event history analysis in depth because the requirement of a large sample makes it difficult to apply in typical, data intensive process research designs. However, event history analysis can prove a useful supplement for process research methods if a two-part procedure is employed, in which a large sample of cases are measured on a few event types and a smaller sample of cases is devoted to intensive process research.

CONCLUSION

Both semi-Markov modeling and event history methods place stringent requirements on the researcher. Semi-Markov models require complex computations and a large number of events to fit the model. Event history methods do not require large numbers of events, but they do require a large sample of cases. Both have great potential to contribute to process research under particular circumstances.

We will now turn to an example in which we use a homogeneous Markov chain to model the CIP data.

AN EXAMPLE: JOINT VENTURES AND ORGANIZATIONAL LEARNING

RESEARCH QUESTIONS AND DATA

Two of the characteristics captured in coding the CIP events were the *course of action* of the event and the *topic* the event pertained to. As the appendix in chapter 4 indicates, course of action referred to "the direction of the actions that occur in each event" coded "according to whether the event represents a continuation or change in the course of action from the previous event related to the topic." Four codes were possible for course of action:

a. *expansion* (P1), an addition, elaboration, or reinforcement of the course of action;
b. *contraction* (P2), a subtraction, reduction, or deemphasis of the course of action;
c. *modification* (P3), a revision, shift, or correction in the course of action;
d. *continuation* (P4), a repetition or ongoing continuance of the course of action.

Course of action, then, refers to what the event portended for the particular aspect of the innovation that it referred to. Courses of action were taken with respect to innovation topics. As the appendix to chapter 4 indicates, a topic could be coded into 19 categories. Of particular interest for this analysis were the last 9 topic categories, T10 through T19, which refer to the events in which the 3M innovation team discussed and negotiated joint or cooperative ventures with other organizations. These discussions are the focus of this example.

The research questions of interest pertain to patterns in the courses of action taken with respect to innovation topics. One interesting question is: Does momentum play a role in creation of joint ventures? Momentum can be defined as the tendency of a project to remain in its current course of action. So if a project is expanding, then there should be expansion and continuation actions, while once it begins to contract, then there should be a series of contractions. There might also be some correction actions at the transition points between expansions and contractions. If momentum is not important, then we would expect to see a good deal of movement among the four states, rather than a pattern that settles into one state and continues.

A second research question is: Can the negotiations among venture partners be explained in terms of a learning model? Van de Ven and Garud (1993) and Van de Ven and Polley (1992) reported evidence that innovation actions could be understood as a learning process, in which the innovation team responded to negative feedback by changing its course of action and to positive feedback by continuing and expanding the current course of action. The events in the CIP file were coded for valence of feedback they indicated, and the plausibility of a learning model can be evaluated by assessing the degree to which actions vary as a function of feedback.

FITTING A MARKOV MODEL TO THE CIP DATA

As we have noted, to fit a Markov model it is necessary to determine whether the assumptions of order, stationarity, and homogeneity are met. We will test each of these in turn for the basic course of action data—which will be referred to as "action" henceforth—in order to address the first research question. Then we will turn to the second research question.

Fitting the Model for Action

ORDER. First, we compute lagged variables as lags 1, 2, and 3 from the original action data. This will enable us to fit models that test the order assumption from zeroth to third orders. If the third-order process fits, we can then proceed to compare the fit of fourth- and higher-order models. As a quick screening device, we first conduct the tests of partial association for the model [12345], where 1 refers to action lag 0, 2 to action lag 1, 3 to action lag 2, 4 to action lag 3, and 5 to action lag 4. These tests are reported in Table 6.9. They indicate that a second-order Markov process is adequate to fit the data. A statistical test for the fit of second-order model [123] indicated good fit for this model ($G^2 = 149.01$, df=144, p = .370; $\chi^2 = 135.88$, df = 144, p = .673). In contrast, the third-order model [1234] did not fit.

STATIONARITY. The next step was to test for stationarity of the second-order process. The log linear model under analysis was [1234][124], in which 1 refers to action lag 0, 2 to action lag 1, 3 to action lag 2, and 4 to time segment. The tests for higher-order effects and partial associations are shown in Table 6.10. The tests for higher-order effects evaluate the hypothesis that three-way or four-way effects should be included in the model, and they indicate that these should not be included. The tests of partial associations suggest that no terms indicating dependence of time and any three-way factors should be included in the best-fitting model. The model for a stationary process fits [123][124] ($G^2 = 221.66$, df=216, p =.381; $\chi^2 = 208.54$, df = 216, p =. 630); recall that the term 124 is included because the row

Table 6.9 Tests of Partial Association for Order of the CIP Actions

EFFECT	df	PARTIAL χ^2	PROBABILITY
[1234]: Action0*Action1*Action2*Action3	81	57.57	.974
[1235]: Action0*Action1*Action2*Action4	81	63.90	.919
[1245]: Action0*Action1*Action3*Action4	81	68.04	.847
[1345]: Action0*Action2*Action3*Action4	81	67.42	.860
[2345]: Action1*Action2*Action3*Action4	81	76.76	.613
[123]: Action0*Action1*Action2	27	49.73	.005*
[124]: Action0*Action1*Action3	27	22.12	.731
[134]: Action0*Action2*Action3	27	33.22	.190
[234]: Action1*Action2*Action3	27	52.07	.003*
[125]: Action0*Action1*Action4	27	25.95	.521
[135]: Action0*Action2*Action4	27	23.62	.651
[235]: Action1*Action2*Action4	27	22.71	.700
[145]: Action0*Action3*Action4	27	22.84	.694
[245]: Action1*Action3*Action4	27	41.51	.037*
[345]: Action2*Action3*Action4	27	46.81	.010*
[12]: Action0*Action1	9	19.68	.020*
[13]: Action0*Action2	9	11.65	.234
[23]: Action1*Action2	9	18.20	.033*
[14]: Action0*Action3	9	15.18	.086
[24]: Action1*Action3	9	9.48	.394
[34]: Action2*Action3	9	18.56	.029*
[15]: Action0*Action4	9	12.16	.205
[25]: Action1*Action4	9	13.86	.128
[35]: Action2*Action4	9	11.39	.250
[45]: Action3*Action4	9	21.78	.001*
[1]: Action0	3	94.85	.000*
[2]: Action1	3	96.16	.000*
[3]: Action2	3	96.26	.000*
[4]: Action3	3	95.41	.000*
[5]: Action4	3	95.55	.000*

of probabilities of the second-order matrix sum to 1.0. Thus, the evidence suggests that the assumption of stationarity is tenable. The second-order transition matrix is illustrated in Table 6.11.

HOMOGENEITY. We assessed homogeneity with two different tests: (1) we compared a significant subgroup of events in CIP to the remainder of the sample; and (2) we divided the entire sample of events into two equal sub-samples through random assignment and compared the transition matrices for the two subsamples.

In the first test, we identified a potentially important source of

Table 6.10 Tests of Partial Association for Stationarity of the CIP Actions

EFFECT	df	PARTIAL χ^2	PROBABILITY
[234]: Action1*Action2*Time	36	38.63	.352
[134]: Action0*Action2*Time	36	36.12	.463
[124]: Action0*Action1*Time	36	34.44	.542
[123]: Action0*Action1*Action2	27	44.35	.019*
[34]: Action2*Time	12	94.94	.000*
[24]: Action1*Time	12	86.37	.000*
[23]: Action1*Action2	9	7.34	.601
[14]: Action0*Time	12	92.56	.000*
[13]: Action0*Action2	9	4.38	.885
[12]: Action0*Action1	9	6.89	.648
[1]: Action0	3	94.83	.000*
[2]: Action1	3	96.16	.000*
[3]: Action2	3	96.28	.000*
[4]: Time	3	2.40	.662

Table 6.11 Second-Order Transition Matrix for Course of Action

	Lag 0			
Lag 2–Lag 1	1: Expand	2: Contract	3: Modify	4: Continue
1–1: Expand–Expand	.31	.07	.20	.42
1–2: Expand–Contract	.06	.28	.44	.22
1–3: Expand–Modify	.17	.06	.31	.47
1–4: Expand–Continue	.36	.01	.17	.46
2–1: Contract–Expand	.40	.20	.13	.27
2–2: Contract–Contract	.04	.36	.24	.36
2–3: Contract–Modify	.13	.21	.29	.38
2–4: Contract–Continue	.21	.18	.36	.25
3–1: Modify–Expand	.10	.17	.35	.38
3–2: Modify–Contract	.41	.27	.23	.09
3–3: Modify–Modify	.15	.14	.35	.37
3–4: Modify–Continue	.21	.11	.21	.44
4–1: Continue–Expand	.35	.07	.16	.42
4–2: Continue–Contract	.15	.19	.19	.48
4–3: Continue–Modify	.21	.16	.28	.36
4–4: Continue–Continue	.30	.13	.20	.37

variation—negotiation partner—and tested the hypothesis that it resulted in violation of the homogeneity assumption. The model we have derived includes actions related to several different joint ventures. This is warranted because the CIP innovation team typically worked with several potential partners simultaneously, and actions in one negotiation were related to those others. The search for partners and viable technology during the CIP project comprised a unified effort to identify what was necessary to bring good products to market. It was neither a competitive bidding process, in which an advance in negotiations with one potential partner meant a loss for another partner, nor a series of independent discussions that could be clearly distinguished. Consideration of joint venturing as a whole provided the firmest foundation for initial model construction. It is, however, important to test this assumption.

Most of the negotiations with individual partners were too brief to allow modeling, but one—the negotiation for the House hearing device—had

Table 6.12 Second-Order Transition Matrix for Course of Action: House Subsample

	Lag 0			
Lag 2–Lag 1	1: Expand	2: Contract	3: Modify	4: Continue
1–1: Expand–Expand	.14	.07	.29	.50
1–2: Expand–Contract	.00	.25	.50	.25
1–3: Expand–Modify	.14	.00	.57	.29
1–4: Expand–Continue	.27	.00	.20	.53
2–1: Contract–Expand	.33	.00	.33	.34
2–2: Contract–Contract	.13	.38	.13	.38
2–3: Contract–Modify	.50	.50	.00	.00
2–4: Contract–Continue	.11	.44	.22	.22
3–1: Modify–Expand	.00	.00	.71	.29
3–2: Modify–Contract	.50	.00	.50	.00
3–3: Modify–Modify	.07	.20	.20	.53
3–4: Modify–Continue	.12	.00	.29	.59
4–1: Continue–Expand	.12	.12	.24	.53
4–2: Continue–Contract	.29	.14	.00	.57
4–3: Continue–Modify	.08	.33	.25	.33
4–4: Continue–Continue	.24	.14	.24	.38

Table 6.13   Second-Order Transition Matrix for Course of Action: Remaining Subsample

Lag 2–Lag 1	Lag 0			
	1: Expand	2: Contract	3: Modify	4: Continue
1–1: Expand–Expand	.34	.07	.17	.42
1–2: Expand–Contract	.08	.33	.33	.25
1–3: Expand–Modify	.17	.07	.24	.52
1–4: Expand–Continue	.40	.02	.16	.43
2–1: Contract–Expand	.46	.23	.08	.23
2–2: Contract–Contract	.05	.41	.23	.32
2–3: Contract–Modify	.09	.18	.32	.41
2–4: Contract–Continue	.22	.22	.35	.22
3–1: Modify–Expand	.13	.22	.26	.39
3–2: Modify–Contract	.43	.29	.19	.10
3–3: Modify–Modify	.21	.11	.40	.29
3–4: Modify–Continue	.26	.13	.21	.40
4–1: Continue–Expand	.40	.06	.15	.39
4–2: Continue–Contract	.09	.18	.23	.50
4–3: Continue–Modify	.23	.13	.28	.36
4–4: Continue–Continue	.31	.14	.19	.36

164 events, sufficient to allow fitting a Markov chain. The transition matrix based on the House negotiation was then compared to the transition matrix for the rest of the sample. If no differences were found due to subgroup, the results would suggest that the assumption of homogeneity was plausible.

The transition matrix for the House device is displayed in Table 6.12 and that of the remainder of the sample in Table 6.13. Tests indicated that both sets of data were best represented by a second-order process and that this process was stationary. The differences between the transition matrices are, for the most part, due to cells with low counts. The test for homogeneity fit the model [123][234], in which effect 1 refers to action lag 0, 2 to action lag 1, 3 to action lag 2, and 4 to the subgroup. The [234] term was included because the row probabilities sum to one in the second-order transition matrix (as recommended by Bishop et al., 1975); preliminary tests for partial association indicated that it should be included. The model had good fit ($G^2 = 60.34$, df = 48, p = .109; $\chi^2 = 52.15$ df = 60. p = .616). Moreover, the model [1234] did not fit. This indicated that there were no differences between the transition matrices for the two subgroups, consistent with the assumption of homogeneity.

The second test of homogeneity split the sample into two equal-sized random subsamples. The transition matrices for the two were then compared. Both subsamples were represented by stationary, second-order transition matrices, shown in Tables 6.14 and 6.15. Comparison of the two subsamples was conducted by fitting the model [123][234], where 1 refers to action lag 0, 2 to action lag 1, 3 to action lag 2, and 4 to subsamples. The model had good fit ($G^2 = 56.37$, df = 48, p = .190; $\chi^2 = 51.52$, df = 48, p = .334). Indeed, the best fitting model for this analysis was simply [123], which is preferred because it is the most parsimonious model that contains all terms. In addition, the model [1234] did not fit. That there were no associations due to subsample suggests that the assumption of homogeneity is tenable.

Table 6.14 Second-Order Transition Matrix for Course of Action: First Random Subsample

Lag 2–Lag 1	Lag 0			
	1: Expand	2: Contract	3: Modify	4: Continue
1–1: Expand–Expand	.29	.07	.16	.48
1–2: Expand–Contract	.10	.40	.50	.00
1–3: Expand–Modify	.27	.07	.20	.47
1–4: Expand–Continue	.47	.00	.14	.39
2–1: Contract–Expand	.33	.22	.11	.33
2–2: Contract–Contract	.07	.36	.36	.21
2–3: Contract–Modify	.22	.33	.22	.22
2–4: Contract–Continue	.22	.18	.39	.22
3–1: Modify–Expand	.00	.31	.39	.31
3–2: Modify–Contract	.31	.31	.31	.08
3–3: Modify–Modify	.07	.18	.32	.43
3–4: Modify–Continue	.20	.13	.30	.37
4–1: Continue–Expand	.39	.03	.15	.44
4–2: Continue–Contract	.08	.23	.23	.46
4–3: Continue–Modify	.19	.11	.37	.33
4–4: Continue–Continue	.35	.11	.26	.28

Table 6.15   Second-Order Transition Matrix for Course of Action: Second Random Subsample

Lag 2–Lag 1	Lag 0			
	1: Expand	2: Contract	3: Modify	4: Continue
1–1: Expand–Expand	.33	.08	.25	.33
1–2: Expand–Contract	.00	.12	.38	.50
1–3: Expand–Modify	.10	.05	.38	.48
1–4: Expand–Continue	.25	.03	.19	.53
2–1: Contract–Expand	.50	.17	.17	.17
2–2: Contract–Contract	.00	.36	.09	.55
2–3: Contract–Modify	.07	.13	.33	.47
2–4: Contract–Continue	.20	.20	.30	.30
3–1: Modify–Expand	.20	.06	.31	.44
3–2: Modify–Contract	.56	.22	.11	.11
3–3: Modify–Modify	.25	.08	.38	.29
3–4: Modify–Continue	.28	.08	.14	.50
4–1: Continue–Expand	.31	.12	.17	.41
4–2: Continue–Contract	.21	.14	.14	.50
4–3: Continue–Modify	.23	.19	.19	.39
4–4: Continue–Continue	.26	.14	.14	.46

Based on these two tests we conclude that the second-order Markov chain model met the assumption of homogeneity. However, we might well generate additional subsamples, using other variables or other splits, and continue testing for homogeneity until we are satisfied that the assumption is met. Because there are so many potential sources of nonhomogeneity, the decision to stop testing and "declare victory" is a judgment call.

CHARACTERISTICS OF THE MARKOV PROCESS FOR COURSE OF ACTION IN CIP

The second-order process suggests a large degree of interdependence among events in CIP. Inspection of the simple transition matrix (Table 6.11) does not reveal any absorbing or noncommunicating states. Event transitions are possible between every pair of categories with relative freedom, though there are some patterns of movement. The only very small transition probabilities are those for transitions between expansion and contraction events, specifically, t_{121}, t_{132}, t_{142}, t_{221}, and t_{412}. This is understandable, since such events should occur primarily at turning points in the event sequence and therefore should be relatively uncommon.

It is also useful to consider the characteristics of the transition matrix at equilibrium. In order to do this, we raised the matrix to successively higher powers. Once the values in the power matrix reach a point at which there is relatively little change as higher powers are taken, we have good estimates of the equilibrium transition probabilities. The matrix still had not converged after being raised to the 128th power, so we concluded that no meaningful equilibrium values existed for the matrix. There were also no patterns indicating periodicity in the data.

Other structural characteristics will be considered in the following sections, in which we explore the evidence related to the two research questions.

EVALUATING THE EVIDENCE ON RESEARCH QUESTION ONE

The first research question asked whether momentum could develop in innovation efforts. Recall that momentum was defined as the tendency of a project to remain in its current course of action. If a project were expanding, then there should be a series of similar types of actions. This implies that the transition probabilities that correspond to remaining in the current state—t_{111} (expand-expand-expand), t_{222} (contract-contract-contract), and t_{444} (continue-continue-continue)—should be large. It also implies large values for transition probabilities, in which expand and continue occur (t_{114}, t_{141}, t_{144}, t_{411}, t_{414}, and t_{441}), and transition probabilities in which contract and continue occur (t_{224}, t_{242}, t_{244}, t_{422}, t_{424}, and t_{442}). These 15 transition probabilities should be larger than the other transition probabilities if momentum applies in this case. To ascertain whether this is the case, we compared the sizes of transition probabilities in the rows containing each of the 13 target probabilities. In 10 of 13 cases, the probabilities were the largest ones in their rows of the transition matrix. The only exceptions were contract-continue-contract, contract-continue-continue, and continue-continue-contract.

It is useful to look at the interdependence structures in the contingency table as well. Since the values of the table are not converted into probabilities, we can compare the absolute magnitudes of the cells. The contingency table for the CIP data is shown in Table 6.16. Seven of the highest nine and eight of the highest fourteen values in the table are from the fifteen "target" transitions that indicate momentum. All seven of these relate to the expand-

Table 6.16 Second-Order Contingency Matrix for Course of Action

	Lag 0			
Lag 2–Lag 1	1: Expand	2: Contract	3: Modify	4: Continue
1–1: Expand–Expand	17	4	11	23
1–2: Expand–Contract	1	5	8	4
1–3: Expand–Modify	6	2	11	17
1–4: Expand–Continue	26	1	12	33
2–1: Contract–Expand	6	3	2	4
2–2: Contract–Contract	1	9	6	9
2–3: Contract–Modify	3	5	7	9
2–4: Contract–Continue	6	5	10	7
3–1: Modify–Expand	3	5	10	11
3–2: Modify–Contract	9	6	5	2
3–3: Modify–Modify	8	7	18	19
3–4: Modify–Continue	16	7	14	29
4–1: Continue–Expand	28	6	13	34
4–2: Continue–Contract	4	5	5	13
4–3: Continue–Modify	12	9	16	21
4–4: Continue–Continue	33	14	22	40

continue sequences. The contract-continue sequences are much less common. We conducted a formal comparison of the hypothesized and observed matrices with the matrix correlation procedure developed by Hubert and colleagues and included in the UCINET IV network analysis package. The matrix correlation between the hypothesized matrix, shown in Table 6.17, and the observed contingency matrix was .360, p=.168.

The remaining six of the highest fourteen values in the contingency table were for combinations of modify and continue events (t_{333}, t_{334}, t_{344}, t_{434} and t_{443}) and an expand- modify-continue sequence (t_{134}). This suggests that there may have been phases during which modification was the primary focus of activity. A modified hypothesis matrix, which posits that the large values will be the expand-continue and modify-continue sequences was generated, as shown in Table 6.18. Its correlation with the observed contingency matrix was significant (.482, p=.05).

Together, these results suggest that expansion and modification courses

Table 6.17   Hypothesized Pattern Matrix

	Lag 0			
Lag 2–Lag 1	1: Expand	2: Contract	3: Modify	4: Continue
1–1: Expand–Expand	1	0	0	1
1–2: Expand–Contract	0	0	0	0
1–3: Expand–Modify	0	0	0	0
1–4: Expand–Continue	1	0	0	1
2–1: Contract–Expand	0	0	0	0
2–2: Contract–Contract	0	1	0	1
2–3: Contract–Modify	0	0	0	0
2–4: Contract–Continue	0	1	0	1
3–1: Modify–Expand	0	0	0	0
3–2: Modify–Contract	0	0	0	0
3–3: Modify–Modify	0	0	0	0
3–4: Modify–Continue	0	0	0	0
4–1: Continue–Expand	1	0	0	1
4–2: Continue–Contract	0	1	0	1
4–3: Continue–Modify	0	0	0	0
4–4: Continue–Continue	1	1	0	1

of action both exhibited momentum such that once begun, they continued for some time. Contraction, however, did not exhibit momentum as defined here. Instead, contractions generally seemed to occur singly and mixed with other types of events. Even the pair contraction-contraction occurred infrequently. This is consistent with a view of contraction as a course of action that represents a decision to discontinue or table negotiations. Once a contraction starts it is over quickly, as the innovation team stops the negotiation and perhaps turns to other options.

The finding of momentum for expansion and modification events also suggests that there may be recognizable phases of expansion and modification, that is, periods during which there is coherent activity organized around definite functions. The next chapter, which is devoted to phasic analysis, will focus on this possibility.

EVALUATING THE EVIDENCE ON RESEARCH QUESTION TWO

One sign of learning is responsiveness to feedback. When things are going well, the organization should continue in its current course of action and

Table 6.18   Modified Hypothesized Pattern Matrix

| | Lag 0 | | | |
Lag 2–Lag 1	1: Expand	2: Contract	3: Modify	4: Continue
1–1: Expand–Expand	1	0	0	1
1–2: Expand–Contract	0	0	0	0
1–3: Expand–Modify	0	0	0	1
1–4: Expand–Continue	0	0	0	1
2–1: Contract–Expand	1	0	0	1
2–2: Contract–Contract	0	0	0	0
2–3: Contract–Modify	0	0	0	0
2–4: Contract–Continue	0	0	0	0
3–1: Modify–Expand	0	0	0	0
3–2: Modify–Contract	0	0	0	0
3–3: Modify–Modify	0	0	1	1
3–4: Modify–Continue	0	0	1	1
4–1: Continue–Expand	1	0	0	1
4–2: Continue–Contract	0	0	0	0
4–3: Continue–Modify	0	0	1	1
4–4: Continue–Continue	1	0	1	1

perhaps even expand its efforts. However, when the organization receives negative feedback, it should take corrective action, discontinuing the current course and searching for courses of action that can improve outcomes. The previous section suggested that there were some meaningful sequences of action related to expanding and modifying the course of action during innovation. If a learning model is consistent with innovation team behavior, we would expect that the sequences should be responsive to feedback, that is, there should be an interdependence between these sequences and feedback.

In order to test this hypothesis, we classified all possible three-event sequences into four categories that represented extended courses of action. These sequences are displayed in Table 16.19. *Cutback* occurs when the team is attempting to reduce its commitment to the current course of action. It is characterized by triples that include contract actions, usually at the end of the triple. A *correction* occurs when a contraction is followed by an expansion or modification; in corrections, some positive action is taken following a contract action, suggesting the team is changing course. A team

Table 6.19   Course of Action Sequence Types

1: CUTBACK	2: CORRECT	3: ADAPT	4: PERSIST
1-1-2	1-2-3	1-1-3	1-1-1
1-2-2	2-1-3	1-3-1	1-1-4
1-2-4	2-2-1	1-3-3	1-4-1
1-3-2	2-1-1	1-3-4	1-4-4
1-4-2	2-1-4	1-4-3	4-1-1
2-1-2	2-2-3	3-1-1	4-1-1
2-2-2	2-3-1	3-1-3	4-4-1
2-2-4	2-3-3	3-1-4	4-4-4
2-3-2	2-3-4	3-3-1	
2-4-2	1-2-1	3-3-3	
3-1-2	2-4-1	3-3-4	
3-2-2	2-4-3	3-4-1	
3-2-4	2-4-4	3-4-3	
3-3-2	3-2-1	3-4-4	
3-4-2	3-2-3	4-1-3	
4-1-2	4-2-1	4-3-1	
4-2-2	4-2-3	4-3-3	
4-2-4		4-3-4	
4-3-2		4-4-3	
4-4-2			

Key to Course of Action Types:
  1 = Expand
  2 = Contract
  3 = Modify
  4 = Continue

undertakes *adaptation* when it modifies its course of action as it expands or continues; adaptation involves adjustments that improve the current course of action. Finally, *persistence* involves expansion and continuation of the current course of action.

If learning is occurring, the action sequences should correlate with feedback. Specifically, we would expect that positive feedback would stimulate adaptation and persistence. Negative feedback should be followed by cutback and correction.

To evaluate these hypotheses, we created four variables to represent the action sequence types cutback, correction, adaptation, and persistence. At each point in time the lag 2, lag 1, and lag 0 actions for each point in time were used to code the action sequence type. For example, if at time 10, the lag 0 event was 1, the lag 1 event was 1, and the lag 2 event was 3, the action sequence type was coded as an adaptation. This is equivalent to transforming the data so that each point in the sequence represents three events:

the current event (lag 0) and the preceding two events (lags 1 and 2). In effect, we have moved a three-event "window" down the data and entered a code in the place of the last event that is based on that event and the previous two events. The result is a series of action sequences that can then be correlated with feedback.

Feedback was also coded for each event in the CIP dataset. Codes were assigned to each event, depending on whether the event represented positive or negative feedback. A number of events implied both positive and negative feedback, in which case the event was coded as mixed. Events in which no feedback could be discerned were not coded and are not included in this analysis.

One way to assess the degree of association between action sequences and feedback is to construct a contingency matrix similar to those we have dealt with throughout this chapter. The cross-classifications of action sequences with feedback for lag 0 and lag 1 feedback are shown in Table 6.20. Both cross-classifications were generated to allow for two different conceptions of the feedback-action relationship. On the one hand, we might assume that each three-act sequence is constructed in response to feedback received during the first action; the next two can then be seen as the responses to the feedback contingent on the action that was occurring when the feedback was received. This implies that teams interpret feedback in light of their current course of action and use current action as the standard for determining what to do next. Another interpretation views each triple as a reaction in itself. This implies that the lag 1 feedback should be utilized, because it is the stimulus to which the triple is the response.

The results for the lag 0 table suggest that learning is occurring. The predominant response to positive feedback is adaptation and persistence, as predicted. Responses to negative feedback involve cutbacks, as predicted,

Table 6.20 Contingency Table of Action Sequence by Feedback (lag 0 and lag 1)

ACTION SEQUENCE	FEEDBACK TYPE (LAG 0)			FEEDBACK TYPE (LAG 1)		
	POSITIVE	MIXED	NEGATIVE	POSITIVE	MIXED	NEGATIVE
Cutback	4	2	86	13	0	62
Correction	15	4	22	7	3	47
Adaptation	38	12	88	38	15	83
Persistence	50	9	32	49	9	35

but relatively few corrections. Instead, adaptation was a common response to negative feedback. This makes sense if we consider that teams that have already invested considerable time and energy in negotiating joint ventures may be somewhat reluctant to abandon one altogether. Instead, they may try to repair reported problems and redirect the project to respond to negative information. Also of interest is the fact that persistence occurred in response to negative feedback. The predominant responses to mixed feedback were adaptation and persistence, suggesting that the positive feedback was accentuated over the negative information. Adaptation probably involved taking the negative feedback into account, while persistence indicated ignoring it.

The results for the lag 1 table are similar to those for the lag 0 table in many respects. The reactions to positive feedback were almost identical. There were fewer cutbacks in response to negative information and more corrections. This implies that the preferred responses to negative information were attempts to change the joint venture rather than scaling it down. This interpretation is also suggested by the fact that adaptation was somewhat more prevalent in response to mixed feedback than it was for the lag 0 table.

The majority of the evidence garnered from this analysis supports the learning hypothesis. However, some findings are inconsistent with it. Certainly persistence in the face of negative feedback does not indicate learning but may indicate that there are two different mechanisms for dealing with positive and negative/mixed feedback. Positive feedback seems to be received with less vigilance than negative feedback. The most common response to positive feedback involved simply doing more of the same, and the second was to continue but modify the current course of action. Negative feedback, on the other hand, seemed to invoke adaptation and correction as much as a simple contraction of a project. This may be consistent with first trying to fix things and then scaling down when the repairs did not work. The response to mixed feedback seems to emphasize the positive aspects over the negative aspects of the feedback.

This pattern of results suggests that the innovation team was generally optimistic, that it attempted to redirect its actions rather than simply giving in to negative responses. The marginal totals indicate that there was much more negative than positive feedback during the CIP project. It may be the case that the team "kept going" in the face of this negative feedback by attempting to repair or salvage the negotiations rather than by cutting them back. Another possibility is that the team turned to joint ventures as a means of responding to negative feedback about the project in general. In order to assess whether either of these interpretations is plausible, we must go back to the original data and interrogate it through further analyses or through qualitative approaches.

CONCLUSION

Stochastic modeling is valuable because it enables researchers to discern connections among events and uncover localized patterns in event sequences. Such connections and local patterns are important building blocks of larger change and development patterns. Stochastic modeling supports both derivation of developmental models through retroduction and testing of hypothesized development and change models.

While many stochastic models are quite complex, we have chosen to advance the relatively simple Markov chain as the foundation for our analysis. It is advantageous because it posits clear, easily interpretable relationships among events, because it fits progressively longer and longer interdependencies while looking for the simplest possible model, and because it can be used for grounded theory development, as well as hypothesis testing. The mathematics and properties of Markov chains are well understood, and standard statistical packages can be used to fit Markov models. However, this is not meant to imply that other stochastic formulations should not be explored. Where large samples of cases are available, event history analysis and point process models are valuable. For smaller samples of cases that still are composed of many events, yet other models are available.

We should note some limitations of stochastic modeling. First, any model is only as good as the event types it incorporates. There is no guarantee that a Markov chain will fit a given set of data. The probability that it will fit depends in part on the researcher's insight in specifying a meaningful set of categories that can map existing dependencies. If there are meaningful patterns in the data, we are most likely to detect them if our categories are valid and strongly connected to the regularities in the case. An insightful set of categories depends more on choosing appropriate distinctions than on multiplying categories to capture all the nuances of a process. Fitting higher-order processes requires large amounts of data, and requirements increase as the number of categories multiplies. Even an extensive dataset will not yield stable estimates for classification schemes with many categories.

Second, as noted above, Markov chains can model only regular dependencies among events, that is, those of a constant order, either first, second, third, or higher. Markov chains are not designed to model cases of mixed order, in which some events have dependencies of order k, others of order k-n, others of order k+2, and so on. Since events are likely to be related in mixed orders in most processes, the insights a Markov chain can provide are inherently limited. A Markov model can capture repetitive regularities in a process, and hence provides a powerful means for identifying the primary dynamics that organize the entire process. However, it cannot characterize unique or occasional dependencies that may still be quite important to understanding particular cases. These must be handled with methods more suited to idiographic study.

A third limitation of Markov modeling stems from its focus on local patterns. The strength of Markov models lies in their ability to characterize recurrent localized sequences of events. However, too much emphasis on such patterns may lead to myopic concentration on the microlevel, with no sense of how local patterns form into or nest in broader developmental patterns. While much can be learned from studying connections among closely contiguous events, these are not sufficient to understand development and change. The meaning of local patterns is often enhanced by considering them in the context of the overall developmental pattern, just as the overall pattern is illuminated by knowledge of local interdependencies. It is important to keep in mind the need to characterize the entire narrative, as well as its subplots.

In view of the importance of immediate connections among events, stochastic models—particularly Markov chains—offer valuable tools for process research. They enable researchers to characterize and describe dependencies among events, they can shed light on larger phasic patterns in event sequences, and they contribute to the evaluation of models of development and change. And if their reach is confined to local patterns, the problems this entails can be remedied by combining stochastic models with other methods that are capable of capturing broader patterns. The next chapter turns to one such method, phasic analysis.

7 Phasic Analysis ≡

$\int$TOCHASTIC MODELING DERIVES STRUCTURE from event sequence data based on event-to-event linkages. This approach yields an account of development in which each event is treated as meaningful in its own right. But it is often the case that there are broader patterns of development, phases or stages comprised of individual events. In this case, the events are meaningful not only in their own right, but also as constituents of a broader developmental sweep represented by the phase or stage. As we noted in chapter 5, events may vary widely in their temporal extension, and more macrolevel events (phases) may be comprised of microlevel events (individual events just one order above the incidents in the data file).

It is also possible that patterns among events are not reflected in the immediate one-, two-, and three-step linkages that stochastic analysis hinges on. Consider, for example, a period of idea development in an innovation team which is comprised of the following activities:

1. generation of idea 1
2. critique of idea 2 spurred by idea 1
3. bolstering of idea 1
4. critique of idea 1 by proponents of idea 2
5. bolstering of idea 2
6. tangential joke and laughter
7. refinement of idea 1
8. tangential joke and laughter
9. generation of idea 3
10. refinement of idea 1
11. critique of idea 1
12. refinement of idea 2
    etc.

This chain of acts reflects the development and progressive refinement of ideas through what Scheidel and Crowell (1964) called "reach-testing." In this sequence there is clearly a strand of development for idea 1 in acts 1, 2,

3, 4, 7, 10, and 11. There is also a strand of development of idea 2 in acts 4, 5, and 12. Idea 3 is also advanced in act 9, but later events indicate that it died out at that point and was not developed further. It would be difficult for a stochastic analysis to pick up the strands of idea development, because the related acts occur at different, uneven lags. A first-order process would be detected if acts were recoded as "Idea Development," regardless of the specific ideas involved, but this would hide the specific strands of development. It is often the case that events indicating a phase may not be temporally linked in the relatively simple relations assumed by stochastic analysis. Moreover, some events represent other possible trajectories that could be followed, but never develop. Should such events carry equal weight to others, as assumed by stochastic analysis? Or should they be considered "interesting, but inconsequential events" and "smoothed" out of the bigger picture?

Phasic analysis attempts to capture the overall coherency of development and change at a higher level than fine-grained microlevel structure. It provides a second way of viewing development and change, one that focuses on more global, longer-term patterns. As this chapter will show, phasic analysis is quite useful for testing the developmental models laid out in chapter 3. It also enables the researcher to tackle four of the critical tasks set for process research methods in chapter 2, including identification of macrolevel events, characterization of event sequences and their properties, evaluation of formal and final causal hypotheses, and uncovering the overall pattern of narratives.

THEORETICAL BASIS OF PHASIC ANALYSIS

A fine-grained, atomistic recounting of a lengthy episode, such as an organizational innovation, would tax the cognitive capabilities of most humans, as well as prove too lengthy to be practical. Cognitive psychologist Donald Norman notes two features of memory and cognition that serve our ability to make manageable sense of complex processes: "Human memory is well tuned to remember the substance and meaning of events, not the details. . . . Humans are pattern recognition animals, matching things that appear to be similar to past events" (1993, p. 131). One means to capture the substance and pattern of complex events is to view an event stream as a series of phases: a sequence of periods of coherent, unified, or focused activity with recognizable boundaries (Poole, 1981; Holmes, 1992). Phasic analysis exploits and formalizes this natural tendency to explain human experience in stories constructed from a finite set of familiar events.

ASSUMPTIONS OF PHASE MODELS

The fundamental assumption of phase models is that the flow of human behavior and social interaction can be described in units larger than the atomistic events of which it is composed. Our ability to recognize coherent, bounded social episodes which unify individual events is evidence for this colligation of the flow of social processes into discrete units (e.g., Forgas, 1975). A second key assumption of phase models is that phases are temporally, developmentally, or functionally related to each other; that is, they cohere, *in meaningful order,* into larger social events. The larger events are defined by the kinds and sequences of the phases they contain. A third assumption is that the sequential structure of the social event is the result of (a) an underlying process motor that drives shifts in behavior over time and (b) the influence of external forces on that motor (Holmes & Poole, 1991; Holmes, 1997a).

Given these assumptions about the nature of phases, it follows that phases are too global and complex to be measured directly with any degree of reliability or validity. Instead, coded or labeled social events serve as *indicators* of phases, much as test items are indicators of an underlying trait. Constellations of coded events can be used to define particular phase types, and from these phases developmental sequences can be derived.

TYPES OF DEVELOPMENTAL SEQUENCES

Developmental psychologist Leland Van den Daele (1969, 1974) argues that observed developmental sequences can be distinguished in terms of two dimensions, whether a progression is *unitary* or *multiple* and whether a progression is *simple* or *cumulative*. This defines at a conceptual level four basic types of sequences which must be discerned at the empirical level: simple, unitary progressions; cumulative, unitary progressions; simple, multiple progressions; and cumulative, multiple progressions. Based on mathematical set theory, this classification scheme is useful for appreciating alternative forms phase sequences may take. The dimensions delimit the domain of possible observable phenomena in phase analysis, defining the requirements researchers must meet to characterize and differentiate developmental sequences in longitudinal data.

A *unitary sequence model* posits that a developmental process unfolds so that only one possible order of phases can occur, a sequence of the form U → V → W. Each of the phases U, V, and W may consist of any number of elements, but in a unitary sequence these subsets are arranged such that the resulting overall sequence is always the same. Greiner's (1972) model of organizational growth, for example, posits a unitary progression through five stages: growth through creativity; growth through direction; growth through delegation; growth through coordination; and growth through collaboration.

The phases in a unitary sequence model may overlap to some extent, as the succeeding phase may emerge while the current one is winding down. However, if a unitary sequence model holds, there will always be periods when one phase is dominant, as Figure 7.1 illustrates. A primary empirical criterion for a unitary progression is the absence of between-case differences; all cases should have the same basic ordering of phases, taking overlap into account. This also points to a key problem in testing for a unitary progression: distinguishing the "true" phase progression from the noise introduced by overlap and differences in pacing across cases.

By contrast, a *multiple sequence model* assumes that a developmental process may generate more than one possible progression. Three general forms of multiple progressions can be defined. As Figure 7.2 illustrates, a *divergent* progression starts with a single phase, which is common to all cases, and develops through a branching and differentiating process. A *convergent* progression may start in any of a number of phases, but it develops through an integrative process toward a common final phase. *Parallel* progressions exhibit different types and orderings of phases. The parallel progression is probably the most commonly observed progression in organizational research. Mintzberg, Raisinghani, and Theoret (1976), for example, identified parallel multiple progressions in strategic decision making which

Event Sequence

AAAAAAAAAABABABBBBBBBBCBCBCCCCCCCCDCDCDDDDDDDDDEDEDEEEEEEEEEE

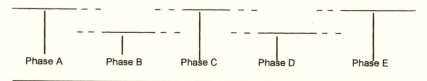

Phase A   Phase B   Phase C   Phase D   Phase E

Figure 7.1 Simple unitary phase sequence with phase overlap

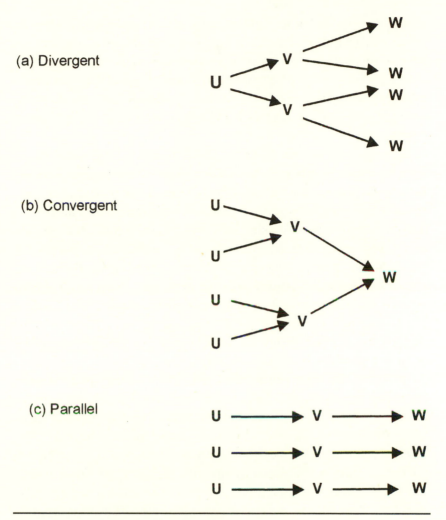

Figure 7.2 Types of multiple progressions

were composed of identification, development, and selection phases, each of which exhibited two or more "subroutines."

Empirical testing of multiple sequence models hinges on the ability to identify a basic set of progressions that articulate with the process theory (ideally the process theory would make prediction of progressions possible). Testing is complicated by the fact that there may be overlap among successive phases and differences in pacing between cases. Some studies have tested the multiple sequence assumption through comparative evaluation of the unitary and multiple sequence models. For example, Poole's (1981) study of small group decision development sought to establish the plausibility of a multiple sequence model through testing and rejecting the unitary sequence alternative. However useful this "negative" evidence is, it must be supplemented by "positive" demonstration that the range of observed progressions is consistent with a process theory which can explain their generation (Poole [Poole, 1983a & b; Poole & Roth, 1989a & b] later provided a theory that explained multiple sequences in group decision development).

Turning to the second dimension, a *simple model* assumes that the developing entity can only be in one phase at a given time, whereas a *cumulative model* assumes that the entity can be in more than one phase at once. In the simple case, development is assumed to progress from one phase to the next, with no carryover of properties of previous phases. Mintzberg et al.'s (1976) model of strategic decision making posits a simple progression. The decision unit moves from one phase of decision activity to the next, and activities from one phase do not carry over into successive stages. The three basic phases of identification, development, and selection are described as clearly separate activities, with unique subroutines; while the content of the decision clearly carries across the entire process, the activities themselves occur in unique, distinguishable "blocks" of time.

In contrast to simple models, cumulative models assume that properties of previous phases are carried into successive phases through accumulation of characteristics over time, much as a developing child adds to her or his intellectual capacities over time without losing many of them. Scott's (1971) stage model of corporate development posits a cumulative progression as the firm grows from (1) one with a single product and distribution channel and an entrepreneurial structure to (2) a larger firm with a single product and channel and a functional structure to (3) an even larger firm with multiple products and channels and a divisionalized structure. Earlier acquisitions are for the most part retained in this cumulative model. Cumulation can also be partial, with characteristics acquired in earlier stages persisting for a while and then dropping off. Partial cumulation is common in organizational contexts because losses of memory, mistakes, and terminated opportunities often occur in complex organizational environments. Quinn's (1980) "logical incrementalism" model of strategic decision making posits a long and complex sequence of 14 stages that partially cumulate decision elements, actors, and levels of awareness and resolve. These change as the process moves along, with gradual additions and deletions.

A cumulative progression may take the form of addition, substitution, or modification (Flavell, 1972). In *addition* a later-occurring characteristic supplements an earlier-occurring characteristic. The characteristics of two phases P_1 and P_2 are combined in the second phase, and both carry over into P_3, which enjoins additional characteristics. For example, in Scott's (1971) model of corporate development, the stage 3 multiple products divisionalized structure results from the addition (with slight modification) of more functional divisions to the stage 2 single product functional structure.

With *substitution* a later characteristic largely replaces an earlier one in a cumulative structure. As the process moves into P_2, some characteristics of P_1 carry over, but one or more are replaced by newer acquisitions. For example, in Greiner's (1972) model of organizational growth, crisis at the end of each stage leads the organization to shift (substitute) its focus as it moves into the next stage. Many of the remaining characteristics of the organization carry over from one stage to the next, and as the stage matures some of these are replaced by attributes acquired during the current period of growth. Thus, there is, so to speak, a "moving average" progression, with characteristics emerging, persisting for a few phases, and then dropping off.

In *modification,* a later event represents "a differentiation, generalization, or more stable version of the earlier one" (Flavell, 1972, p. 345). In this case, the characteristics of P_1 are revised or modified in P_2. For example, in the strategic planning model of Gluck, Kaufman, and Walleck (1980), the planning process and focus of each stage are modified and made more elaborate in the next stage. Modification cannot be reduced to addition; although characteristics persist from stage to stage, they are changed to a greater or lesser extent in the development process, rather than simply being added to.

Since simple and cumulative models represent mutually exclusive and exhaustive alternatives, empirical tests of these assumptions require comparative evaluation of the models. This hinges on establishing the extent to which successive phases share elements; if elements are replicated in more than one phase, there is evidence that the progression is cumulative, and the pattern of element occurrence and co-occurrence can be used to establish the form of the progression, that is, whether it depends on addition, substitution, or modification. Hence, the first step in testing the simple versus cumulative assumption is to define a distinctive set of empirically identifiable elements that compose the phases of the developmental model. A well-specified developmental theory, such as Greiner's (1972) or Gluck et al.'s (1980), would indicate whether the expected model was simple or cumulative, and the researcher could test for the expected pattern of elements. For example, the researcher might look for an accumulation of elements over time, if the theory predicted a cumulative, additive progression.

In cases where more than one developmental progression is consistent with the theory, the researcher is faced with the problem of distinguishing cumulation from overlap among phases. Even if the true model exhibited a simple progression, overlap among phases might make it appear that some elements were retained in succeeding periods. If the overlap is not severe, then the assumption of "cumulativeness" can be tested by determining whether elements are retained over more than one phase. Elements persisting due to overlap should fall off regularly and fairly soon after the central point of their phase has passed. In cases where overlap is severe, however, it may not be possible to distinguish equally plausible theories that posit simple, overlapping progressions and cumulative progressions.

Cumulative, modification progressions present a more difficult case. It is hard to distinguish empirically instances in which elements are being modified from simple progressions (in which old elements drop off and new ones are added) from cumulative progressions which exhibit both addition and substitution. The key to identifying a modification progression is to define the essential character of elements so that these can be tracked even as they change. Hence, a clear theory of the nature of modification is indispensable. For example, Gluck et al. (1980) describe how strategic planning structures are modified through elaboration as firms grow. Basic financial planning (Phase I) is succeeded by forecast-based planning (Phase II), which initially builds on financial tools but eventually integrates them with modeling methods, yielding a fundamentally different planning system. The tools can be identified, but they have a different character and function in the forecasting mode; for example, the Phase I budget is incorporated into forecasting models as a key variable. Externally oriented planning (Phase III) reorients features of the first two phases toward increasing response to markets and competition, eventually elaborating them with more advanced planning methods. These features can be picked out, but their character changes as they are incorporated into the Phase III system; for example, forecasting models are recast into dynamic terms and become part of a set of means of evaluating strategic opportunities. Definition of essential features facilitates separation of case, in which elements change from those where intact elements simply drop from or join a progression. And, as in the case of additive and substitutive progressions, analysis is further complicated by the need to distinguish persistence and modification from overlap among simple phases.

Taken together the two dichotomies and their variants define a wide array of possible developmental progressions and criteria for distinguishing them empirically. It is important to bear in mind that this typology describes *observed* progressions; it does not specify theories that explain the generation of the developmental path or account for multiple sequences, cumulation, modification, or the like. This highlights the importance of a well-specified theory. The process of developing a phase model involves the articulation of theoretical models with descriptions of phase progressions. Combined, theoretical and descriptive frameworks provide a powerful way to characterize change and development processes and to test for the plausibility of particular theories.

PROPERTIES OF DEVELOPMENTAL SEQUENCES

Once sequences have been characterized, it is also useful to identify their summary properties. These indices can be used to compare and classify sequences, and they reduce considerably the complex task of evaluating similarities and differences among sequences. They are also of interest in their own right. Structural properties of developmental sequences include phase cycles or repetitions, breakpoints between phases, and complexity (Poole & Doelger, 1986).

Repetitions of phase units and *cycling* are important indicators of regularities in developmental sequences. They may signal the operation of a rapidly repeating motor or of a persistent cause or problem which produces the cycling. For example, Poole and Roth (1989b) found that cycling through problem analysis and solution development phases characterized the decision paths of groups working on complex problems, suggesting that groups progressively tested and modified solutions.

Breakpoints are junctures where the nature of the developmental progression changes suddenly due to a critical event or external shock (Mintzberg et al., 1976; Poole, 1983a). Breakpoints may be precipitated by temporal breaks, such as annual reviews or the closing of the fiscal year, or by external shocks, such as economic disruptions or top management decisions, or by internal events, such as a conflict or transition to a different task step.

Complexity refers to the degree to which the developmental pattern departs from a simple unitary sequence. This indicator is useful because it enables researchers to separate progressions driven by relatively simple, static, or efficient motors from those that are more complex, unstable, and complicated by multiple factors. More complex progressions may also indicate the interplay of multiple motors in the developmental process.

These and other properties of sequences can enhance phasic descriptions considerably. We turn now to how the four developmental models outlined in chapter 1 can be explored using descriptions of developmental progressions.

DEVELOPMENTAL MODELS AND PHASIC SEQUENCES

Assumptions behind the *life cycle* model can be tested relatively easily with phasic analysis. If a life cycle motor holds, we would expect to find a unitary sequence of phases which is invariant across cases. The degree of overlap among phases varies and would be determined by the specific mechanism that governs phase transition. However, as noted above, there must always be some period when a phase is the dominant feature of the developmental progression, and hence, if the "pure" periods could be identified, their sequence would indicate the plausibility of the model. The degree to which a life cycle theory accurately predicts overlap provides a second way of evaluating its tenability.

Depending on the nature of the life cycle model, either simple or cumulative progressions may occur. Activity-oriented life cycle models, such as those concerned with group decision making or planning, will tend toward simple progressions, because succeeding activities tend to supplant previous ones more or less completely. Life cycle models that portray the development of an organization or its characteristics, such as organizational structure or form of governance, will tend toward cumulative progressions, because the organization generally carries its history along with it in its current configuration and its organizational memory. Again, the specific content of the theory should enable the researcher to project some expectations regarding the nature of the progression, whether it is cumulative, and (if so) the type of cumulation that occurs.

The *teleological* model implies two different levels of analysis. If we track the abstract activity mode the organization is in, as depicted in Figure 6.1, a unitary progression would be observed—dissatisfaction, search, envision goals, implement goals. For a given development or change process, we might observe several cycles of these steps with varying degrees of overlap (the details of the theory would specify the number of cycles and the degree and nature of overlap).

However, if we track instead the specific work that the organization is doing to realize its goals through the teleological motor—the functions it is fulfilling, the actions it undertakes, the components it is building or realizing—we should observe multiple sequences, since there is, for the most part, no preordained order in which these actions must be undertaken. For most teleological theories, it is likely that we will observe multiple sequences that first diverge from a common beginning point and then converge to a common ending point. For example, the beginning point for a product development effort might be common for all product teams: perception of the need or opportunity. Following this origin, other requirements, such as obtaining upper management sponsorship, customer requirements, adequate technology, building a project team, testing the product, etc., can be accomplished in many different orders (though some contexts may constrain the order more than others). The end point, product launch, is common to all teams, resulting in convergence at the conclusion.

As was the case for life cycle models, whether progressions are simple or cumulative in teleological models depends on the specifics of the theory. When cumulative progressions are predicted, they are more likely to be additive than substitutive or modifications. This is because teleological models are generally based on the accumulation of components or the cumulative accomplishment of goals that build on each other in a noncontingent fashion.

For the *dialectical* model, two levels of phasic analysis are possible. If we track the conflict and its resolution, we will find three overall stages—development of opposites, conflict, and synthesis—which hold if the process plays itself out fully. This yields a simple, unitary sequence with sharp dividing points between phases, because according to dialectical theory conflict emerges quickly and sharply and the synthesis occurs in a sudden moment. If the dialectic does not play out fully and either thesis or antithesis "wins," this sequence would be truncated.

Within the three stages of the dialectical model, particular subphases may unfold in multiple sequences that are either simple or cumulative, depending on the specifics of the theory. For example, the thesis and antithesis may develop simultaneously or in alternating sequences. Multiple sequences for conflict resolution have also been found, depending on whether the conflict is resolved by various types of confrontation or by lower key, more accommodative processes. Sambamurthy and Poole (1992), for example, found over 10 different conflict management sequences which fell into four major sequence categories.

For the *evolutionary* model, the three generic stages of variation, selection, and retention imply cycles of unitary sequences. Overlap depends on the specific theory. If change proceeds gradually and incrementally, the three phases should overlap; if change is radical, there should be less overlap.

Within these major phases, as with the dialectical model, there are likely to be multiple sequences of events that lead to variation and selection. Work by Mintzberg et al. (1976) and Nutt (1984a, 1984b) suggests that the creation of options and their winnowing may occur through more than one possible path. These are most likely divergent or parallel multiple sequences, because there is no common ending point. Cumulative progressions of all three types are likely in evolutionary models, since many incorporate ideas akin to inheritance in their developmental motors.

Another option for phase analysis is to decompose the population and map each unit's developmental path separately. The resulting sample of maps could be analyzed to define characteristics of processes within each phase. If the developmental theory provides the specifics of how the motor operates, phase analysis can help determine whether predictions based on the motor's operation are consistent with observed developmental progressions. With enough specifics, the fit of different theories can be compared with the same dataset, enabling identification of a best-fitting model.

When a theory incorporates more than one developmental motor, as many do, empirical analysis becomes more complicated. The researcher must sort out the various levels on which different motors operate and map the data on those levels. These data can then be treated as distinct progressions and analyzed on their own. This strategy will work well as long as the motors do not influence each other's operation. To the extent this occurs, some ingenuity may be required to tease out their effects.

DATA TRANSFORMATIONS FOR PHASIC ANALYSIS

The starting point for phasic analysis is a series of time-ordered, categorical event codes that serve as indicators of those aspects of organizational activity in which the researcher is interested. The coding unit may vary: particular actions, actions during timed intervals (e.g., one-day or one-week periods), or complete organizational episodes (e.g., a product life cycle). Bakeman and Gottman (1986) note three approaches to generating sequential event descriptions: retrospective reports (which they referred to as "narrative reports"), systematic observation (categorical coding), and rating scales. The former two can produce categorical data suitable for phasic analysis; the third approach produces data more suited to sequence methods for continuous data, such as time series analysis, which are covered in chapters 8 and 9.

The data to be analyzed must meet the requirements of consistency and accuracy; that is, it should be both reliable and valid. Bakeman and Gottman (1986) and Folger, Hewes, and Poole (1984) provide useful introductions to problems of reliability and validity in sequence descriptions, and some of these concerns, as well as methods for addressing them, were covered in chapter 4.

CODING EVENTS FROM RETROSPECTIVE REPORTS

Retrospective reports of event sequences typically operate at a fairly high level of analysis because they are narratives that describe complex events extended in time and/or space. Such descriptions rely upon the human tendency to organize events into stories consisting of a sequence of bounded episodes or events. For example, Nutt's (1984a, 1984b,1993) "process reconstruction" of organizational decision processes applies a vocabulary of decision process elements to translate multiple case studies of a given decision process into a process profile. In a similar fashion, the MIRP event process analysis reduced the content of each innovation event to one or two summary sentences.

Data reduction is the strength of the retrospective representation of a complex event stream. As Nutt notes, case studies provide a "mass of detail which makes it difficult to tease out patterns in the data" (1984a, p. 415). The short narrative descriptions characterististic of retrospective reports, especially if guided by a formal event typology and/or story grammar, reduce the bulk of the data while still preserving the core of the "story."

The key weakness of the retrospective approach is that there are few assurances that it systematically and thoroughly retrieves the "real" sequence of events. Smoothing of complex event sequences into larger events is accomplished in the storytelling and summarization and therefore may be influenced by a wide variety of factors. As Bakeman and Gottman warn, "narrative reports depend mightily on the individual human doing them, and judgments about the worth of the reports are inextricably bound up with judgments about the personal qualities of their author" (1986, p. 3). Retrospective case studies based on participant or observer recall are prey to all of the interpretation and reconfiguring inherent in post-hoc sense-making.

CATEGORICAL CODING

Categorical coding attempts to provide a systematic, valid, and reliable description of a process as a sequence of discrete events. The coding proceeds through (1) parsing the event stream into theoretically meaningful units and (2) reliably categorizing the content of the units according to a valid scheme consisting of a finite set of well-defined categories of events (unitizing and coding are sometimes performed concurrently in practice). For example, Saberwhal and Robey (1993) classified 1,088 events in 53 cases of information systems implementation according to an inductively derived 15-category coding scheme that included such categories as "assignment of personnel," "submission of proposal," and "approval or authorization."

If properly performed, categorical coding produces trustworthy sequence descriptions. It allows the researcher more hope that cases are consistently described, even if there is a large number of cases, than can be provided by narrative reconstruction. The systematic nature of the approach makes it reasonable to apply methods requiring consistency in process descriptions, whether nonsequential (such as summary measures to describe time budgets for different activities) or sequential (such as gamma analysis and optimal matching analysis, described below).

The weaknesses of categorical coding are (1) the sequence description is rigidly constrained by the coding system and the relatively small vocabulary of most coding systems does not provide great descriptive richness, and (2) the method is difficult and time consuming. Neither of these problems is insurmountable, and categorical coding remains a powerful tool for studying change processes.

PARSING EVENT SEQUENCES INTO PHASES

Complex episodes or phases are typically defined by constellations of acts: characteristic events, in combination, serve as indicators of the phase to which they belong. Narrative descriptions, such as Nutt's (1984a, 1984b) translation of case study stories into phases, are already compound representations of complex combinations of activities and typically require no further parsing. In the case of categorically coded data, the process of moving from coded events to a phasic description is a series of rule-driven, incremental data transformations. In those cases where there is direct correspondence between event codes and phase types (as in narrative reconstruction), the original codes are phase markers and no translation is needed prior to sequence mapping. In other cases, the event coding system may contain a number of codes that—alone or in combination—indicate a given

Event Sequence

AAAAAAAAAABABABBBBBBBBCBCBCCCCCCCCCDCDCDDDDDDDDDEDEDEEEEEEEEEE

Parsing Rules:

1. Phase start rule: A phase begins when three contiguous codes share the
   same phase marker value; i.e., they are identical or translate to the same
   phase marker value.

2. Phase end rule: A phase ends when three contiguous codes of different
   phase marker value(s) are encountered.

3. When a phase end rule is applied, and the next three elements match the
   phase start rule, search backwards in a sliding two-element window and
   include in that phase any elements which serve as markers for that phase
   until the two-element window shows no such elements.

Parsed and smoothed phase sequence

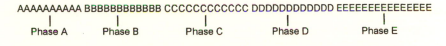

AAAAAAAAAA BBBBBBBBBBBB CCCCCCCCCCCC DDDDDDDDDDDD EEEEEEEEEEEEEE

Phase A   Phase B   Phase C   Phase D   Phase E

Figure 7.3 Example event sequence smoothed and parsed using phase mapping rules

phase. For example, "manufacturing" and "marketing" events may both serve as indicators of an "execution" phase of an organizational innovation.

To generate the sequence of phase markers from the original sequence, translation rules are applied which define the codes or combinations of codes that indicate various phases. The rules for sequence parsing define the minimum conditions indicating a phase and the various conditions identifying a boundary between phases. Parsing rules are used as a translation mechanism or as a sequential data-smoothing technique. An example of a parsing rule set is provided by Holmes and Poole (1991). Using that rule set, the event sequence displayed in Figure 7.1 would be mapped as shown in Figure 7.3.

Parsing rules should allow for the possibility of "null" or disorganized portions of event sequences. If a portion of a sequence fails to trigger a phase definition rule, then that portion may be considered disorganized or not constitutive of a phase.

Parsing becomes more complex if multiple event tracks are necessary to identify phases; for example, a researcher might apply multiple coding of an event stream to generate a track of functional event codes and a track of relationship event codes. In such cases, the process of unitizing, categorizing, and parsing remains the same, but a final step is added to translate ordered n-tuples of event and relationship markers into phase indicators.

ANALYSIS OF PHASIC DATA

There are a number of methods that can be used in phasic analysis. We will discuss them in order of increasing complexity of both the sequences analyzed and the analytical method.

QUALITATIVE ANALYSIS OF SEQUENCES

The simplest way to categorize and group phasic sequences is through direct inspection and sorting. Poole (1983a), for example, used this approach to sort ten group decisions into a basic set of developmental types. Direct inspection enabled him to smoothe the developmental sequence in a more discerning fashion than would have been possible with algorithmic or statistical procedures.

Nutt (1993; cf. 1984a & b) used a theoretically driven model as a basis for qualitative analysis of developmental sequences in strategic decision making. Nutt developed a transactional framework to understand the steps and stages involved in decision making. This framework, depicted in Figure 7.4, breaks the decision making process into three major blocks, intelligence, choice, and development, which are further decomposed into six stages (represented by the boxes) and choices (represented by the circles) that are linked by "decision-making steps which identify actions called for by the decision maker and others involved in the decision process" (1993, p. 229). This nuanced and flexible system forms the basis for graphical representation of the temporal flow of the steps in the strategic decision process that Nutt combed from his narratives. Figure 7.5 shows a graphical representation of one decision process.

Nutt (1993) then took the graphical representations of 163 cases and sorted them into categories. This qualitative sorting was facilitated by the representations, which are fairly easily grouped through "eyeballing" the pictures. The resulting types reflected different modes of problem formulation in strategic decision making.

Qualitative classification and analysis of phasic data capitalizes on the researcher's background knowledge. It is highly probable, for example, that Nutt's typology was informed by his extensive knowledge of and experience with strategic decision making. Classification biases can be minimized by conducting several independent classifications of the same phases. This en-

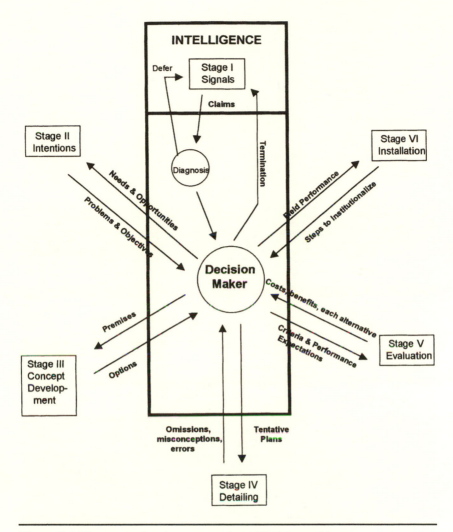

Figure 7.4 The transactional representation of decision making

ables the identification of biases and the reconciliation of inconsistent classifications.

Qualitative approaches run into difficulty when there are many phases in a developmental sequence or when there are many distinct types of phases. In both cases, the developmental sequences may be so complex that discerning patterns and grouping similar sequences is difficult.

A number of quantitative methods are available to help researchers tackle complex phasic datasets. Quantitative methods are also useful for researchers who desire checks on their classifications, or who wish to be

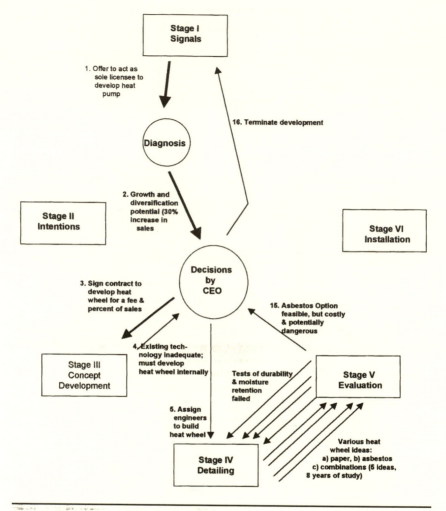

Figure 7.5 Profile of a failed innovation

guided by systematic and objective procedures through at least the initial stages of analysis. We now turn to a series of these methods that address various questions in phasic analysis.

TESTING THE NULL HYPOTHESIS

In phasic analysis, the null hypothesis is that there is no order in the event sequence, that is, that events occur randomly rather than in meaningful phasic patterns. One cause of such disorder might be a series of repetitive random shocks that drives the system and never allows it to settle into a self-organized state. In such a case, the events are best explained as a function of the external shocks and not in terms of a coherent narrative structure that might be reflected in the phase sequence.

The stochastic methods described in the previous chapter provide a straightforward test for the null hypothesis of no order. In fitting a Markov chain model, tests are conducted comparing zero-order, first-order, second-order and higher-order process models in terms of how well they account for patterns among events. If the zero-order model is shown to fit and higher-order models rejected, then the pattern is essentially random and a case can be made that there is insufficient order among events for phasic models to be workable. While phasic models capture more complex event relationships than stochastic models allow, if a phasic model is tenable, there will be many first-order event-event linkages that should yield good fit for a first-order Markov model. The inability to fit such a model suggests the sequence is random and that phasic models are inappropriate.

TESTING FOR UNITARY SEQUENCES

Over the past several decades psychologists, sociologists, and statisticians have worked out a number of procedures for testing hypotheses regarding developmental sequences. Because most of their theories posited unitary, set developmental sequences driven by life cycle models, these tests primarily evaluate the hypothesis that development follows a unitary sequence. Almost all of these methods require data to be displayed in a contiguity matrix as shown in Figure 7.6(b). The values in the matrix consist of codes for pairs of contiguous events, with the row values being defined by the first event and the columns by the second event in each pair. The code categories are arranged along the horizontal and vertical axes in the order they are expected to occur if the unitary sequence hypothesis holds. Assuming that we have multiple indicators for each phase, as shown in Figure 7.6(a), we would expect high contiguity values near the diagonal and decreasing values as we move away from the diagonal. The expected pattern is shown in Figure 7.7.

A number of tests have been developed to evaluate the fit of contiguity data to such a pattern. Several tests are based on the similarity of the pattern in Figure 7.7 to the pattern of interitem correlations that would be observed if the items formed a Guttman scale. Kugelmass and Breznitz (1967) and Leik and Matthews (1968) describe tests for unitary sequences based on the Guttman scalability assumption. Coombs and Smith (1973) describe a similar test based on a different approach to scaling. Davison and his col-

(a) Phases and Indicators

Stage	Indicator
A: Orientation	a_1: Ask for information a_2: Express ambiguity
B: Evaluation	b_1: Express opinion b_2: Criticize b_3: Defend
C: Control	c_1: Suggest plan of action c_2: Elaborate suggestion c_3: Suggest criteria for suggestion

(b) Contiguity Matrix

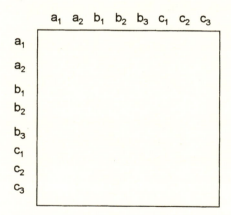

Figure 7.6 Unitary sequence data in a contiguity matrix

leagues (Davison, King, Kitchener, & Parker, 1980; Davison, Robbins, & Swanson, 1978) describe a different method of evaluating unitary sequence hypotheses based on factor analysis and multidimensional scaling.

A more general approach to evaluating sequence hypotheses that is quite well suited for testing the unitary sequence assumption is the matrix correlation procedure developed by Hubert and his colleagues (Hubert & Levin,

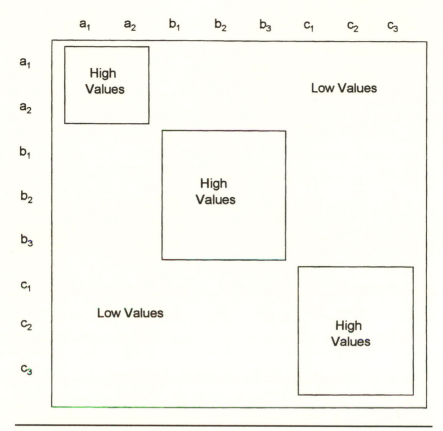

Figure 7.7 Hypothesized contiguity matrix for unitary sequence model

1976; Hubert & Schutte, 1976) and described in chapter 6. As indicated there, this method enables researchers to compare an observed matrix to a hypothesized ideal pattern. In the case of the unitary sequence hypothesized in Figure 7.7, the comparison matrix would be composed of values of 1, where high values were expected in the contiguity matrix and 0 elsewhere. Hubert's method provides a statistical test for the null hypothesis of lack of fit between the two matrices, as described in chapter 6. Because matrix correlation can be used to evaluate the fit of the contiguity matrix to any hypothesized pattern, it can also be used to evaluate more complex phasic hypotheses. Coombs and Smith (1973) also describe methods of evaluating more complex developmental hypotheses in their framework. Gamma analysis, discussed in the next section, is also a useful method for typing complex sequences.

Event Sequence

AAAAAAAAAABABABBBBBBBBBCBCBCCCCCCCCCDCDCDDDDDDDDDEDEDEEEEEEEEEEE

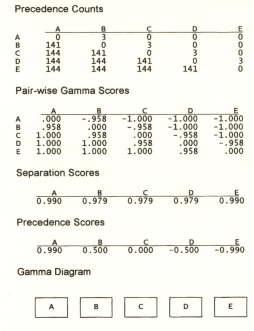

Precedence Counts

	A	B	C	D	E
A	0	3	0	0	0
B	141	0	3	0	0
C	144	141	0	3	0
D	144	144	141	0	3
E	144	144	144	141	0

Pair-wise Gamma Scores

	A	B	C	D	E
A	.000	-.958	-1.000	-1.000	-1.000
B	.958	.000	-.958	-1.000	-1.000
C	1.000	.958	.000	-.958	-1.000
D	1.000	1.000	.958	.000	-.958
E	1.000	1.000	1.000	.958	.000

Separation Scores

A	B	C	D	E
0.990	0.979	0.979	0.979	0.990

Precedence Scores

A	B	C	D	E
0.990	0.500	0.000	-0.500	-0.990

Gamma Diagram

A	B	C	D	E

Figure 7.8 Gamma analysis tables and diagram for a simple unitary sequence

IDENTIFICATION OF DEVELOPMENTAL TYPES WITH GAMMA ANALYSIS

Gamma analysis, based on the Goodman-Kruskal gamma (Pelz, 1985), describes the general order of phases in a sequence and provides a measure of the distinctness or overlap of phase types. It is especially appropriate for use with simple unitary developmental models. Sequence length information is ultimately discarded in gamma analysis, so the method is also appropriate when comparing sequences of different length if the length differences themselves are unimportant to the research question. A gamma score is a measure of the proportion of A events that precede or follow B events in a sequence. A pairwise gamma is given by P-Q/P+Q, where P is the number of A events preceding B events and Q is the number of B events preceding A events. Gamma analysis of a sequence yields a table consisting of gamma scores for each possible pair of phase types (Figure 7.8).

The mean of pairwise gamma scores for a given phase type constitutes its precedence score; this score indicates the location of the element in the overall ordering of element types and can range from -1 to 1. The separation score for a phase type is given by the mean of the absolute value of its pairwise gamma scores. It provides a measure of the relative distinctness of the phase type and can range from 0 to 1. Separation approaches 1 as more of the units of a given phase type occur contiguously.

Precedence and separation scores are used to construct gamma diagrams. Phase types are ordered sequentially from smallest to largest precedence scores. Phase separation can also be indicated on the diagram by "boxing" phases to show degree of separation (i.e., whether the phases tightly cohere as discrete periods or if their indicators are mixed together). For example, phases with a separation score greater than .50 might be boxed. Those with separation scores between .50 and .25 could then be indicated with an incomplete box. Those with separation below .25 would not be boxed at all, as phases with separation scores below .25 are not clearly separated from other phases (Poole & Roth, 1989a). If the separation score for two phases is less than .25, those phases could be boxed together to indicate their substantial overlap or intermixing.

Gamma diagrams provide a simple phasic description that allows for visual examination and comparison of sequences. From the gamma analysis tables and diagrams, sequences can be examined and characterized according to phase order, the degree of phase separation, and which phase types overlap or fail to cohere. These summary properties can serve as guidelines for qualitative grouping of a set of diagrammed sequences.

SEQUENCE COMPARISON WITH OPTIMAL MATCHING

In their study of implementation sequences in information system development, Sabherwal and Robey(1993) note that it is common to develop taxonomies of event sequences by visually sorting charts of the sequences into sets. This method is adequate for a small collection of sequences (and, as noted above, it is one way to use gamma diagrams), but such qualitative sorting is likely to miss important distinctions within larger collections of complex sequences. Large data sets of long sequences would be better compared if the similarity or dissimilarity of any two sequences could be quantified in a numerical distance index. However, in cases where elements in a sequence may repeat, the familiar methods of enumeration, permutation statistics, or scaling are not appropriate (Abbott & Hrycak, 1990). Optimal matching analysis provides a generic tool for sequence comparison for those situations in which each sequence is represented by well-defined elements drawn from an alphabet of a relatively small set of (repeating) event types. It is especially appropriate for exploring and testing multiple sequence models, as such models can generate diverse progressions through phases. The diversity of paths can be described by their intersequence distances, and possible path typologies can be generated.

A Sequence Distance Index

Optimal matching produces an index of the relative "distance" between any two sequences. This index, the Levenshtein distance, is the smallest possible cost of operations of insertion, substitution, and deletion of sequence units required to align two sequences, that is, to transform one sequence into the other. The more similar the sequences being compared, the fewer operations required to align them and the smaller the index of distance or dissimilarity. Before considering how such an index is calculated, this definition will be demonstrated in a more intuitive fashion. For the purposes of this discussion, we'll use a simple alphabet of three possible sequence elements: A, B, and C, and three short sequences composed of these elements:

> Sequence 1: A B A A A A A B A A
> Sequence 2: A B C A B C A B C A
> Sequence 3: C B C C C C C B C C

An informal comparison of these three sequences based on the positions of shared elements would conclude that sequence 1 and sequence 3 are most dissimilar, with sequence 2 resembling both 1 and 3 more than they resemble each other. The basis for this informal judgment—the "lining up" of shared elements and intuitive evaluation of how difficult it would be to align all elements of each sequence pair—is formalized in optimal matching analysis. Figure 7.9 displays the optimal matching alignment of the three sequences.

SEQUENCES ONE AND TWO. Figure 7.9 shows that there are six elements already aligned in this comparison. Four substitutions will align the two sequences completely. The cost of the alignment of the ten elements is four operations; the "distance" between the sequences is .40 (the number of alignment operations divided by the sequence length).

SEQUENCES TWO AND THREE. In this case there are five aligned elements. Five substitutions are required to complete the alignment, producing a distance index of .50.

Event Sequences

Sequence 1: A B A A A A A B A A
Sequence 2: A B C A B C A B C A
Sequence 3: C B C C C C C B C C

Alignment of Sequence 1 and Sequence 2

A B A A A A A B A A
| | | |
A B C A B C A B C A

Four substitutions are required to
align the two sequences

Distance: .4

Alignment of Sequence 2 and Sequence 3

A B C A B C A B C A
| | | | |
C B C C C C C B C C

Five substitutions are required to
align the two sequences.

Distance: .5

Alignment of Sequence 1 and Sequence 3

A B A A A A A B A A
| | | | | | | |
C B C C C C C B C C

Eight substitutions are required
to align the two sequences.

Distance: .8

Diagram of the relative distances between the three sequences

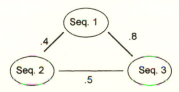

Figure 7.9 Optimal matching analysis of three short sequences

SEQUENCES ONE AND THREE. The final sequence pair displays only two aligned elements. Eight substitutions are required to complete the alignment, so the distance index is .80.

The final diagram in Figure 7.9 arranges the three sequences in space on the basis of their distances: the configuration echoes our earlier judgment of the relative similarity of the three sequences. Of course, sequence alignment is seldom as simple as these examples. Consider this pair of sequences:

Sequence 1: A B A B A B A B A B
Sequence 2: B A B A B A B A B A

There are no aligned elements in this pair. Ten substitutions are required to align the two sequences, at a total adjusted cost of 1.0; however, visual inspection of the sequences suggests they aren't that different. It takes only two operations to align them if we delete the initial element from, and add a terminal element to, either sequence.

These examples show how sequences can be aligned by operations of substitution, insertion, and deletion of units. There are many possible sets of operations to align any two sequences. In the last example, substitutions could have been used to align the first five elements and then an element inserted to align the rest. However, at six operations, rather than two operations, this is a less efficient alignment. Optimal matching analysis applies a dynamic programming algorithm to reveal the least possible cost for the alignment. An introduction to the algorithm and its variations can be found in Sankoff and Kruskal (1983).

Using the Distance Index

A single distance index provides a numerical value of the dissimilarity between two sequences. In itself, this index may not be especially interesting. Typically, more sequences are compared and the results are used in one of two ways. First, if there is a model or ideal sequence, perhaps from prior research or theory, a set of empirical event sequences can be compared to the expected sequence in order to gauge their relative fit to the model. Second, given enough event sequences, we can compare all the sequences in a dataset to each other. The resulting distance matrix can then be used in cluster analysis and/or multidimensional scaling to generate a sequence typology (cf. Holmes, 1997b; Poole & Holmes, 1995; Saberwhal & Robey, 1993). We will illustrate this in the following example.

AN EXAMPLE OF PHASIC ANALYSIS

This example will focus on the complex web of interorganizational cooperation between the CIP program and several governmental or private partners. It will utilize the coded event data that tracked the changing status of the innovation relationship through its negotiation, commitment, and execution by the parties. The small number of cases available (4) precludes full-blown theory development and testing, but suffices for a simple demonstration of phasic analysis. In part of this analysis we will evaluate the fit of the four cases to two hypothesized sequences that represent different developmental models.

The sequence descriptions of the cases are based on the stage model of interorganizational transactions described by Ring and Van de Ven (1994). They postulate a cyclical sequence of negotiations, commitments, and executions. The negotiation stage is marked by a focus on "formal bargaining processes and choice behavior" (p. 97). In the commitment stage, the parties "reach an agreement on the obligations and rules for future action in the relationship" (p. 98). The commitments and rules of action are then carried out in the execution stage. Sensemaking and assessment occur throughout the stages. Bargaining and sensemaking constitute the formal and informal dimensions of negotiation; as sensemaking can occur in other contexts, our model separates the two. Formal negotiations are labeled Bargaining in this analysis, and Sensemaking is treated as a discrete activity that may occur in any phase.

The data are the event sequence data described in chapter 4. Bunderson, Dirks, Garud, and Van de Ven (1995) coded the CIP data with a category system developed from the Ring and Van de Ven (1994) model of interorganizational relationships. This system coded those events that pertained to interorganizational relationships into one of four categories: Bargaining, Commitment, Execution, and Sensemaking. The Bunderson et al. analysis was based on a qualitative, multiple-sequence "event process mapping" of the cases (a formalized narrative analysis). We reanalyzed their data using the more systematic gamma diagramming and optimal matching techniques to explore the fit of the sequences to a unitary phase model. In view of the fact that the Ring and Van de Ven model posits that interorganizational innovation project relationships are negotiated, confirmed, and executed, we might expect an "ideal" unitary sequence to follow a progression of Bargaining, Commitment, and Execution events. In the case of complex projects, we might expect several cycles of the three phases. Sensemaking activities can happen at any point in the process; they represent generic, multipurpose occasions for actors to work out the implications of previous moves and future actions.

We chose to work with smoothed sequences. The four-code category system did not require further translation of event codes into phase markers. However, based on a preliminary scan of the data, we defined two additional composite phases, conceptually compatible with the Ring and Van de Ven (1994) framework. The composite phases are comprised of repetitive patterns of the four basic codes. "Commitment Bargaining" is marked by cycles of these commitment and bargaining phase markers. From a theoretical point of view, this phase represents a form of incremental bargaining in which parties make commitments and then progress to other areas or issues, building on previous commitments. "Experimentation" is marked by Execution and Bargaining cycles or by Execution and Sensemaking cy-

Table 7.1   Interorganizational Innovation Case Event Sequences in 3M's Cochlear Inplant Program

CASE	SMOOTHED SEQUENCE IN RUN-LENGTH ENCODED FORMAT	EVENT FREQUENCY	
FDA (61 events)	5Expr 2Comm 7Barg 2Exec 4Comm 2Expr	Expr	7
	2Comm 5Barg 5Cbar 4Exec 3Cbar 4Exec	Barg	12
Cochlear implant (CI)-	4Comm 6Cbar 6Exec	Cbar	14
based regulatory		Comm	12
relationship with		Exec	16
Food and Drug		Snsm	0
Administration			
HEI (82 events)	7Expr 5Cbar 5Barg 6Exec 3Barg 2Exec 4Comm	Expr	34
	7Expr 2Snsm 5Expr 2Comm 4Snsm 6Expr	Barg	10
House Ear Institute	3Comm 6Expr 5Comm 3Expr 3Comm 2Barg	Cbar	5
Single channel CI	1Comm 1Exec	Comm	18
		Exec	9
		Snsm	6
HOCH (51 events)	6Barg 4Comm 10Exec 18Snsm 4Exec 5Comm	Expr	0
	2Exec 2Comm	Barg	6
Hochmairs, University		Cbar	0
of Innsbruck		Comm	11
Second-generation CI		Exec	16
		Snsm	18
NUCL (67 events)	20Cbar 2Exec 2Comm 28Exec 3Snsm 5Exec	Expr	0
	2Snsm 5Cbar	Barg	0
Nucleus Corporation		Cbar	25
Multiple-channel CI		Comm	2
		Exec	35
		Snsm	5

cles. As its name indicates, it represents a form of learning through experimentation in which parties take actions, then try to make sense of the actions, and/or bargain with each other about what to do next.

In a first pass, we smoothed the data by identifying the composite phases and substituting them for the original phase markers. The smoothed sequences for the four cases are listed in Table 7.1. Each entry in the sequence represents the phase indicator of the event and the number of events in a row with the same phase indicator. The FDA-CIP negotiation is listed in the first row of Table 7.1. It is made up of 61 events, of which the first five are Experimentation, the next two Commitment, followed by seven Bargaining events, two Execution events, four Commitment events, and so on.

The far right column of the table lists the event frequencies for each of the cases.

Table 7.2 lists projected patterns of events for the two hypothesized models. Model 1 represents a unitary sequence innovation process model consistent with Ring and Van de Ven's theory. It is set to a typical length for the four cases, 65 events, and the events are evenly distributed among three consecutive phases of Bargaining, Commitment, and Execution. Model 1 assumes that interorganizational linkages form through a steady process that logically builds through the three phases with little or no backtracking. Model 2 also posits that the negotiations follow the three-phase sequence, but in this case it assumes that linkages form by cycling through these phases. For this analysis three cycles through the phases are assumed, and phase lengths are set constant. The assumption that there will be three cycles is arbitrary, but three is sufficient to enable us to detect cyclicity in an event sequence with between 40 and 80 datapoints, even if there are more cycles than three.

Gamma diagramming of the six sequences in Table 7.1 produced the maps displayed in Figure 7.10. Visual examination of the diagrams focuses on phase coherence and sequence. We used a conservative rule for appraising phase separation in the gamma diagrams in Figure 7.10 because data smoothing tends to enhance separation scores. Phases must exceed .50 separation to be boxed with a broken line and exceed .75 separation to be boxed with a solid line. The strongest and most consistent separation is

Table 7.2 Sequences Representing the Two Hypothesized Models

CASE	SMOOTH SEQUENCE IN RUN-LENGTH ENCODED FORMAT	EVENT FREQUENCY	
Model 1 (65 events)	22Barg 22Comm 21 Exec	Expr	0
		Barg	22
Unitary sequence		Cbar	0
innovation process		Comm	22
model		Exec	21
		Snsm	0
Model 2 (66 events)	8Barg 7Comm 7Exec 8Barg 7Comm 7Exec 8Barg 7Comm 7Exec	Expr	0
		Barg	24
Unitary sequence		Cbar	0
innovation		Comm	21
process model		Exec	21
with cycling		Snsm	0

| Case | Phase | Gamma Values | | Diagram |
		Separation	Precedence	
1. FDA	Expr	0.827	0.827	
	Barg	0.703	0.370	
	CBar	0.708	-0.601	
	Com	0.510	0.028	
	Exec	0.624	-0.624	
2. HEI	Expr	0.340	-0.168	
	Barg	0.547	0.147	
	CBar	0.918	0.918	
	Com	0.644	-0.644	
	Exec	0.642	0.145	
	Snsm	0.561	-0.398	
3. HOCH	Barg	1.000	1.000	
	Com	0.477	-0.477	
	Exec	0.470	-0.197	
	Snsm	0.508	-0.326	
4. NUCL	CBar	0.600	0.600	
	Com	0.829	0.429	
	Exec	0.771	-0.219	
	Snsm	0.810	-0.810	
5. Model 1	Barg	1.000	1.000	
	Com	1.000	0.000	
	Exec	1.000	-1.000	
6. Model 2	Barg	0.333	0.333	
	Com	0.333	0.000	
	Exec	0.333	-0.333	

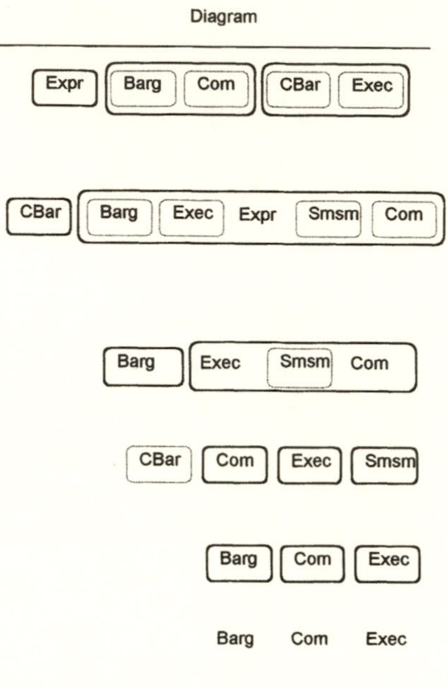

Figure 7.10 Gamma analysis summaries and diagrams for the four CIP innovation cases and two innovation process models

found in the Model 1 sequence because its pure progression of Bargaining, Commitment, and Execution markers does not intermingle events; in contrast, the phase cycling of Model 2 produces low separation scores. Note, however, that the general order of Bargaining, Commitment, Execution in Model 2 is revealed by the gamma analysis despite the cycling.

The phase sequences in Figure 7.10 suggest some patterns despite the small number of cases. Three cases reveal a Bargaining-Commitment-Execution progression, though that sequence should be seen as a tendency embedded in a more complex progression of events. All four cases tend to front-load bargaining activity. Sensemaking appears in three of the four cases; interestingly, it appears mid-to-late sequence in the diagrams.

The same sequences were compared with each other through optimal matching analysis. The alignment parameters are provided in Table 7.3. The substitution cost matrix was based on conceptual distinctions between the phases. Execution was given the greatest substitution cost because it constitutes a performance stage rather than a preparation stage, while

Table 7.3 Optimal Matching Analysis Parameters

Event vocabulary

BARG	Bargaining
COMM	Commitment
EXEC	Execution
CBAR	Commitment Bargaining
EXPR	Experimentation
SNSM	Sensemaking

Sequence element substitution cost matrix

	BARG	COMM	EXEC	CBAR	EXPR	SNSM
BARG						
COMM	0.3					
EXEC	0.5	0.5				
CBAR	0.2	0.2	0.5			
EXPR	0.2	0.4	0.2	0.3		
SNSM	0.1	0.1	0.1	0.1	0.1	

Insertion/Deletion cost for any element: 1.00
Length adjustment: Alignment cost is divided by length of the longer sequence in each comparison pair.

Sensemaking was given the lowest substitution cost because of its "wild card" function in the process. Combination phases (Commitment Bargaining and Experimentation) were given lower substitution costs for phase types that shared one of their elements.

The results of the optimal matching sequence comparison are summarized in Figure 7.11. To adjust for length differences (the sequences ranged from 51 to 82 events), the calculated alignment cost for each comparison pair was divided by the length of the pair's longer sequence. The resulting distance matrix displays sequence distance indexes ranging from a low of 0.257 (FDA to Model 2) to a high of 0.432 (HEI and HOCH). The distance matrix was subjected to Johnson's hierarchical cluster analysis; as shown in the icicle plot, this yielded two clusters (Model 1 and NUCL; Model 2, FDA, and HOCH) and one isolate (HEI). Nonmetric multidimensional scaling based on the MINISSA MDS(X) algorithm produced a two-dimensional solution with 0 stress after 24 iterations. The MDS results suggest two neighborhoods of cases: (1) Model 1 and NUCL and (2) Model 2, FDA, and HOCH. The HEI case is not adjacent to these neighborhoods. Figure 7.11 includes the plot of this two-dimensional MDS solution with the cluster analysis results superimposed.

Sequence alignment distances, adjusted by length of longer sequence in each pair.

	FDA	HEI	HOCH	NUCL	MOD. 1	MOD. 2
FDA						
HEI	0.363					
HOCH	0.302	0.432				
NUCL	0.327	0.330	0.330			
MODEL 1	0.282	0.370	0.383	0.284		
MODEL 2	0.257	0.344	0.282	0.330	0.285	

Hierarchical cluster analysis icicle plot.

```
            N M H   M
            H U O O F O
            E C D C D D
Level       I L 1 H A 2
0.2570      . . . . XXX
0.2840      . XXX . XXX
0.2887      . XXX XXXXX
0.3156      . XXXXXXXXX
0.3667      XXXXXXXXXXX
```

Multidimensional scaling solution in two dimensions.

	Dim 1	Dim 2
FDA	-0.57	-0.07
HEI	1.47	0.17
HOCH	-0.57	1.13
NUCL	0.52	-0.57
MODEL 1	-0.29	-0.91
MODEL 2	-0.55	0.24

Plot of multidimensional scaling solution in two dimensions with cluster analysis results superimposed.

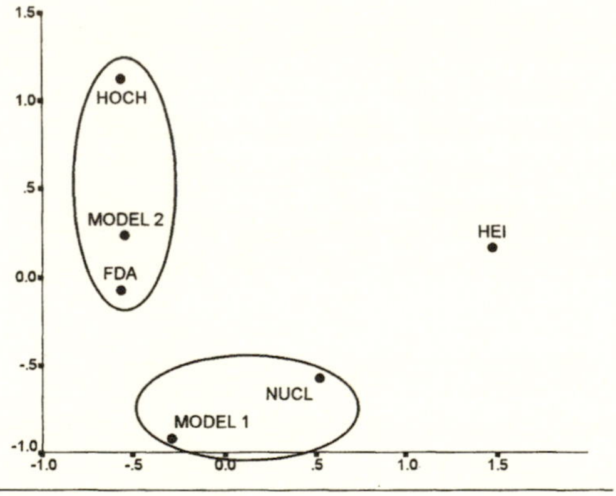

Figure 7.11 Summary of optimal matching analysis comparison of innovation case sequences and two model sequences

Review of the original sequences (see Table 7.1) suggests that the resemblance of Model 1 and NUCL is likely the result of the extended (20 unit) Commitment Bargaining phase early in the NUCL sequence and the even longer (28 unit) Execution phase late in the sequence; these provide opportunities for relatively low-cost alignment with the initial Bargaining and terminal Execution phases of Model 1. The close resemblance of the FDA and Model 2 sequence likely emerges from cycles of shorter (3 to 7 unit) phases of Commitment Bargaining and Execution in FDA that can align, with relatively low cost, to the repeated cycles of 7 and 8 unit phases of Bargaining, Commitment, and Execution that make up Model 2. The HOCH case also shows repeated short phases, but cycles of Commitment and Execution dominate the middle and later sequence; the only coherent Bargaining phase appears at the beginning of the sequence.

These results suggest that the cases unfold either as somewhat "noisy" instances of the simple unitary sequence of Bargaining-Commitment-Execution or as instances of repeated cycles of the three activities. There may be a sequence length artifact in the results, as the sequence pair with the greatest distance index (HEI and HOCH) consists of the longest and shortest sequences. The longest sequence, HEI, is the only sequence not to join with other sequences in the cluster analysis and to emerge in a different neighborhood in the multidimensional scaling. However, it is also the most complex sequence and its dissimilarity from the other sequences may arise in part from that complexity.

The analysis thus provides some support for the Ring and Van de Ven model of interorganizational relationship formation. However, it also yields evidence for at least two versions of the model, simple and cyclical sequences. Moreover, complex cases such as HEI may require a different or more complex developmental model.

This example is constrained by the small number of cases, but it shows that gamma analysis and optimal matching analysis provide powerful means of describing and comparing sequences for the purpose of developing and testing sequence models.

CONCLUSION

Phasic analysis enables researchers not only to capture global patterns, but also to make sensitive qualitative discriminations among types of events and activities. The flexible phase analysis procedures described in this chapter enable researchers to identify unitary, set sequences of events, but they do not force such models onto phenomena. These procedures can also detect complicated sequences of events, such as cyclical patterns or multiple sequences. They do not require all phases to be the same length, but are capable of mapping phase events of different lengths. The mapping procedures can also be adapted to detect "layers" of phases, as more microlevel phases are recoded and smoothed to yield macrolevel phases. Phasic procedures can contribute to testing the fit of all four basic developmental models. They can also support most of the key tasks of process research methods.

Used together, stochastic modeling and phasic analysis are a potent combination. Stochastic modeling can detect regularities in event sequence data that operate at the event-to-event level. Phasic analysis moves up a level to detect regular and irregular patterns that operate across multiple events and also enables identification of composite events with longer time horizons. A particularly promising combination is the use of interacts—pairs of contiguous events—as indicators of phases (see Poole, 1981 & 1983b). Stochastic modeling and phasic analysis can also be used to validate each other's assumptions. For example, a phase shift may be signaled by nonstationarity in a stochastic process. And a phase structure can be used to inform stochastic model building.

Stochastic modeling and phasic analysis procedures work with categorical event data, preserving a good deal of continuity with the initial qualitative data. Another class of methods, discussed in the next two chapters, transforms event data into continuous variables that can be analyzed using adaptations of multivariate statistical methods.

8 Event Time Series Regression Analysis ≡

CHAPTERS 6 AND 7 INTRODUCED MARKOV and phasic analysis, which help us understand the probabilistic and temporal relationships among individual events. As we have noted, these techniques preserve the nominal character of events. Stochastic modeling uses event types directly, while phasic analysis explores structures of phases that reflect the event types which constitute them. A different and quite useful approach considers the intensity or level of one or more characteristics over the course of the event sequence. For example, it would be useful to consider the degree to which actors external to an innovation were active in its development at various points in time. One way of measuring this would be to assess the number of interactions between the innovation team and external actors each month. This gives a measure of the intensity of external actor involvement, and the shape of this intensity curve over a period of three years would indicate when and how much external influence was occurring. A steady rise in this curve would indicate that external actors are more and more involved as time passes. On the other hand, cyclic patterns might suggest that external actors are involved only at certain key junctures. We might also gain some insights into the dynamics of external actor involvement by correlating the intensity curve with the curve of amount of positive and negative feedback each month. If increases in external involvement closely follow increases in negative feedback, then the nature of the key junctures would be clarified.

In such cases the nature of the process and the causal system that drives it can be inferred by examining collections of events, aggregated together across some time horizon into a count. We call these count data *time series*. By examining the patterns that emerge in time series, one can develop an understanding of temporal and probabilistic and perhaps causal precedence.

While event time series analysis is always a useful complement or alternative to stochastic and phasic analyses, there are certain cases in which aggregate analysis is called for because the events in a given sequence are not likely to be related to each other on a local basis. It is clear that events are interdependent when we are dealing with a small, well-defined system of actors, for example, the discussions in a small decision-making group. Because the group is acting as a closed system (at least during the span of the meeting), all actors will tend to be cognizant of all the activity within the group in an instantaneous fashion. Therefore, one might expect that explicit actions by such actors would tend to follow one another in a sequential cause-and-effect fashion, leading to explicit relationships between individual (discrete) actions or events. At the macrolevel, the same strategy could be applied; by limiting event observations to a single, or few, organizations or to well-defined activities, the researcher may find direct correspondence between events occurring sequentially with one another.

However, there may not be a direct correspondence between individual events when there is a multitude of actors in the observed system and when they do not know each other's actions immediately or cannot keep track of one another. In such cases there will be various time lags between cause-and-effect events and/or parallel cause-and-effect sequences intermingling together in a complex web of sequentiality. Lack of correspondence at the level of the individual event may also arise because events are observed at a level that is not easily distinguishable from "noise." For example, if events were collected at a sampling rate of one per day, one would not expect that there would be correspondence at the level of an individual event when examining a change process that occurred over a period of several years.

In phasic analysis, this issue is dealt with by transforming individual events into phase markers, via coding conventions and/or parsing rules. These phase markers stand as discrete, categorical data that is subsequently analyzed. One method that was described in chapter 7 smoothed the events by aggregating them into larger categories; for example, a time period dominated by events corresponding to "engineering design" and "market testing" might be labeled "detailed design" in an organizational innovation. Another common method is to label the phase marker according to the dominant event type; for example, in Figure 7.3, Phase "C" is denoted by a preponderance of event type C, with the single observation of event type "B" cancelled out (assumed as noise).

Let us consider an example where it might be advantageous for us to retain a measure of the *frequency* or time series of event counts. Suppose that in observing an organizational innovation, we identified numerous events over a period of a year. Consider that over a period of six months, from June

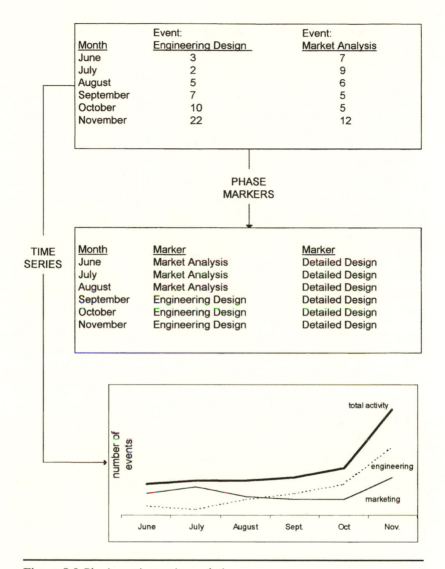

Figure 8.1 Phasic vs. time series analysis

to November, we found that there was a preponderance of event types "engineering design" and "market testing" (see Figure 8.1). In phasic analysis, we might code the entire period from June to November as "detailed design." Or we might filter the events into monthly phases via a majority count. Doing this, June to November would be labeled "Market Testing" (since during these three months "Market Testing" events predominated), and September to November, "Engineering Design."

Closer examination however shows some interesting detail that would have been left out. By examining the time series data for the two event types, we can see that while "engineering design" and "market testing" were both present during each of these six months, their relative frequency changed over the period. If one were to smooth the events of November into a phase marker, "engineering design," we would lose the important fact that market testing was still quite prevalent in that month. Additionally, the time series analysis indicates to us that the overall level of activity appears to be increasing steadily over the six months, culminating in a flurry of activity in November (right before the first prototype was made). Thus, time series analysis enables us to examine deeper patterns embedded within the temporal sequence of events.

So far, we have dealt with the more complex case where our longitudinal study produces qualitative events that we must make sense of. Of course, we also may collect substantive data that is already quantitative in form. For example, in examining an organizational restructuring, we may collect weekly or monthly data pertaining to such things as the number of employees, sales volume, public stock value, or even more process-related data, such as the number of e-mail communications between actors in the system. In such cases, these data form time series that can then be analyzed for patterns that might allow us to determine the causal influences in the system.

Time series analysis is useful for several of the key research tasks in process research. It enables researchers to identify long-term patterns in event sequences, and as such takes a broader view than phasic or stochastic analysis. A number of different types of patterns, including trends and cycles, can be identified with time series techniques. Time series methods also allow researchers to characterize the degree of order in an event series. Stochastic modeling, which tests whether there is order on an event-to-event basis, and time series analysis, which tests for longer-term predictability of the series, thus provide complementary tests of the assumption that an event sequence has regular processes, an assumption that is too often taken for granted.

Time series analysis can also detect critical points in long-term patterns. This opens the possibility of statistical identification of the unique events that shape development and change. In addition, many models of development posit transitions between different phases of a change process, and these too can be regarded as critical events. Insofar as a narrative explanation posits a turn of events that suggests a trend or some regular temporal pattern, time series analysis will find uses in testing formal and final causality. And, as we will see below, time series analysis can be used to evaluate whether specific developmental models hold, in particular, the four basic models outlined in chapter 3.

When time series data is the result of an event history research design, the subsequent data is called an *event time series*. The focus of this chapter and the next concern methods to analyze such event time series. In this chapter specifically, we cover the methods of *event time series regression analysis* or ETSRA for short. ETSRA involves the use of visual and computational methods to determine if simple, linear patterns exist in time series data. Different tools help us examine singular (univariate) time series and multiple time series. We shall discuss the theoretical basis for time series analysis, issues involved in transforming event data into event time series, and different methods for performing ETSRA. We will conclude with several examples using data from the CIP innovation study.

THEORETICAL BASIS

ASSUMPTIONS

Methods used for ETSRA share three common assumptions.

1. The time series is of sufficient length to determine appropriate model parameters with some degree of accuracy.

ETSRA typically involves fitting a parametric model to the time series. Model parameter estimates can be determined by ordinary or generalized least squares, or by other maximum likelihood methods. Parameter estimation algorithms require sufficient sample size to ensure asymptotic behavior in the statistical estimators. An estimator is considered valid if its statistical expected value approaches the true (but unknown) parameter being estimated in an asymptotic fashion as sample size is increased. A standard suggestion in time series analysis is to seek a minimum of 25–50 samples (Pandit and Wu, 1983).

2. The time series data follow a Gaussian (normal) distribution.

For event history data that is already quantitative in nature, this assumption may or may not be true. If it is not true, various statistical methods can be used to determine how the data can be transformed to make it more approximately normal (Box & Jenkins, 1976). For example, data pertaining to cost or time will often be right-skewed; it has a long tail on the right side of its frequency distribution (histogram). Taking the logarithm of data that is positively skewed will tend to shrink its tail and make its shape more approximately normal.

If however the time series data consists of event counts, these data are discrete and by definition not normally distributed. Event counts will tend to be distributed as a (discrete) Poisson random variable. Fortunately, many ETSRA methods are fairly robust to issues of nonnormality. Data transformations can help normalize discrete data. Data that is Poisson-distributed may well approximate normality if the mean number of periods until occurrence of an event is relatively large, above 10 or 15 (Montgomery, 1996). If results are ambiguous or diagnostic checks indicate the need for a transformation, it is possible to make Poisson variables more normal-like by using a square-root transformation. If counts are extremely low, then it may be more advantageous to treat the count as a discrete state (e.g., 2 = "two") and perform Markov chain analysis as discussed in chapter 6.

3. Data are subject to exogenous influences, including measurement error.

ETSRA assumes that time series are not completely deterministic. Data are subject to exogenous influences outside and beyond the context of the specified model, and such influences will tend to manifest themselves as "errors," normally and independently distributed with constant mean and variance. Errors include such phenomena as variations in the environment; small, random variations in model parameters; and measurement error. Various diagnostic tests can be performed to test the assumption of independent errors. In fact, detecting the presence of independent errors is an indicator that the modeling task is complete. We shall discuss this in more detail in a subsequent section.

TYPES OF TIME SERIES

A univariate time series y_t is a collection of quantitative observations arranged in time-sequential order, $\{y_1, y_2, \ldots y_N\}$. A multivariate time series is a collection of two or more univariate time series synchronized sample-by-sample. There are numerous ways in which time series can be analyzed and modeled. We shall cover four of the most common methods. The different models can be characterized by denoting the type of parameters associated with each model type:

- *Curve fitting:* "time" (t) is treated as an independent variable.
- *ARMA models:* independent variables capture path dependency (feedback) and exogenous influences.
- *Multivariate time series models:* Same as above. Additional parameters capture the simultaneous and lagged effects between different time series.
- *Change point time series models:* Can be used with any of the other three

model types. Additional parameters capture "change points" in the time series, where model parameters shift from one specific value to another.

In general, curve fitting is perhaps the most common statistical analysis performed on time series. Curve fitting is simple, and (depending on the complexity of the model) can be performed with ease in popular spreadsheet and data graphing computer programs. It tends to be somewhat atheoretical, however. Conversely, ARMA and multivariate time series models hypothesize specific generative mechanisms responsible for observed data. Such generative mechanisms may be useful in proposing specific, qualitative process theories. Change point time series models are appropriate when we either hypothesize a priori, or detect after the fact, a significant change that has occurred at some specific time. For example, a change point time series model would be appropriate for testing whether two qualitatively different "phases" were present within the observed event history. We shall explore each of these model types in more depth.

Curve Fitting

Curve fitting involves fitting a statistical model that mimics the shape of the observed time series, as temporally plotted. Curve-fitting models treat time (t) as an independent variable. The variable *time* cannot be a primary causal factor; however, it can serve as a surrogate factor for other, unidentified causal factor(s). For this reason a curve-fitting model can be helpful in determining what type of process theory should be entertained. If a linear trend or periodic cycle is present in the time series data, any process theory put forth should explain why such a trend is present.

Parameters can be estimated for many curve-fitting models via standard spreadsheet or data graphing computer programs. In some cases, the models are nonlinear, and a more powerful statistical modeling computer program must be used.

The simplest curve-fitting model is a linear trend (see Figure 8.2):

$$y_t = b_0 + b_1 \cdot t \qquad\qquad [8.1]$$

where $b_0 + b_1$ are parameters of the model and are empirically estimated. The null hypothesis involves testing whether the estimated parameter b_1 is statistically different from zero.

Another common curve-fitting model is a sine wave (see Figure 8.3):

$$y_t = b_0 + b_1 \cdot \sin \{\omega_1 \cdot t + \phi_1\} \qquad\qquad [8.2]$$

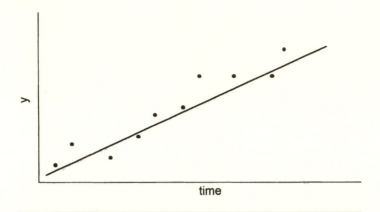

Figure 8.2 Straight line curve fit

where b_0, b_1, ω_1, and ϕ_1 are parameters of the model and are empirically estimated. The parameters ω_1 and ϕ_1 are referred to as the frequency and phase lag of the model. A sine wave captures periodic behavior in the time series. The frequency (ω_1 (in units of cycles per time unit) is related to the period of the sine wave, T_1 (in units of time). The period refers to how much time elapses between two "peaks" in the wave. The two are related by[1]

$$\omega_1 = 1 / T_1 \qquad [8.3]$$

For example, suppose data demonstrated an annual period—it "peaked" every 12 months. Equation [8.2] could be used to capture this behavior; in this case, the value of ω_1 would be (1 cycle/12 months), or 0.0833 cycles per month. In order to test whether or not a periodic trend is present, the null hypothesis consists of testing whether the estimated scaling parameter b_1 in equation [8.2] is statistically different from zero.

A time series may be composed of more than one frequency or periodic cycle. In this case, equation [8.2] can be generalized to:

$$Y_t = b_1 + b_1 \cdot \sin \{\omega_1 \cdot t + \phi_1\} + b_2 \cdot \sin \{\omega_2 \cdot t + \phi_2\} + \ldots \qquad [8.4]$$

In this case ω_i refers to the frequency of the i-th cycle. For example, event data may be subject to both seasonal (3-month), as well as annual (12-month) variation. Figure 8.4 depicts such a curve. Other common models that might be relevant to event time series include

---

1. More accurately, $\omega_1 = 2 * \pi / T_1$. The 2 * π term is necessary in order to complete the calculation correctly, as the sine function works in units of radians.

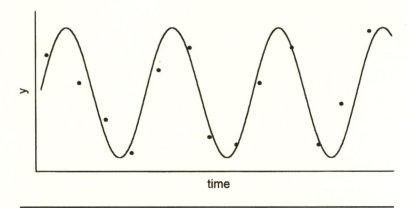

Figure 8.3 Sine wave curve fit

- *Exponential growth curve*—used to model a system's growth pattern that is rapid at first, and then decelerates as it reaches some upper bound (e.g., the cumulative money spent on a project).
- *Exponential decay curve*—used to model a system's natural reaction to some significantly sized, singular event (e.g., the number of e-mail communications per day as a response to a corporate message).
- *Logistic curve*—used to model event occurrence in a system, in which events occur slowly at first, then increase to a critical point, at which time event occurrence rapidly accelerates (e.g., innovation diffusion phenomena; Valente, 1995).

It is generally recommended that one examine the time series for the presence of these trends *prior* to application of other time series modeling. This is often referred to as *detrending* the time series.

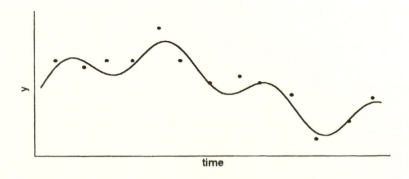

Figure 8.4 Sine wave with two periodicities

ARMA Models

The acronym ARMA is shorthand for "autoregressive, moving average." The parameters in an ARMA model capture two types of causal influence. Autoregressive parameters denote the existence of path dependency in the system. An autoregressive parameter links the current state of the system y_1 to some previous state y_{t-k}. Moving average parameters denote the dependence between the current state of the system y_t and some previous exogenous input a_{t-k}. These two causal components can stand alone or exist together. This leads to three different, standard types of time series models:

- autoregressive model of order p, AR(p)
- moving average model of order q, MA(q)
- autoregressive, moving average model of order (p,q), ARMA(p,q)

AR(P). The AR(p) model states that the system has memory of its previous behavior and that such memories influence future behavior. A random error-term a_t represents an exogenous input (disturbance, shock) to the system. Thus, at time t, the event count y_t is generated via an exogenous random input a_t (normally distributed with zero mean and constant variance) and some linear function of previous event counts, $(y_{t-1}, y_{t-2}, \cdots y_{t-k})$. The AR(p) system is defined by:

$$y_t = \sum_{k=1}^{p} \phi_k y_{t-k} + a_t \qquad [8.5]$$

where ϕ_k is the autoregressive parameter at lag k, and a_t is normally and independently distributed with mean zero and variance σ_a^2. The ϕ_k parameters can be estimated by ordinary least squares. Figure 8.5 shows the behavior of different time series following an AR(1) model, for different values of ϕ_1; 100 points are shown. Figure 8.5a shows a series with $\phi_1 = 0$, that is, a white noise or random series. Figures 8.5c and 8.5d show the oscillations that are inherent in AR(1) systems with negative ϕ_1 values. Figure 8.5b shows the special case when ϕ_1 is 1, or the random walk ($y_t = y_{t-k} + a_t$). The random walk series is sometimes called Brownian motion, and it represents an accumulation of random events. Many econometric time series can only be modeled as random walks, that is, the best prediction for tomorrow is what the data value is today. Figures 8.5e and 8.5f show the drifting tendencies of systems with positive ϕ_1 values.

In many cases organizational data can be adequately modeled by the simple AR(1) model. For example, suppose one is observing communication events between two parties engaging in a cooperative effort (see Figure 8.6). The number of messages sent between the two parties will tend to depend on the level of interaction required by the task at that moment in time. Assume that the level of required interaction remains relatively constant over several sampling periods; thus, the level of required interaction at time t will be roughly equivalent to that required at time t−1 and t+1. Subsequently, the number of message events at time t will be roughly equivalent to the number of message events at time t−1; likewise, the count at time t+1 will be similar to the count at time t. With the addition of a random error, this scenario yields an AR(1) model. In the extreme case, a random walk may be generated. For example, in an inventory process, the amount of product inventory on hand at a given time is equal to the amount on hand in the previous time unit, plus a random error (how much was replenished minus how much was used).

MA(Q). In contrast to the autoregressive process which states the system has memory of its past behavior but no memory of its random inputs, a moving average process has no memory of its past behavior but does have memory of its previous inputs. Alternatively, in a MA(q) system the influence of the random input lingers beyond the immediate time period. Thus, at time t, the event count y_t is generated via an exogenous random input a_t (normally distributed with zero mean and constant variance) and a linear function of previous exogenous random inputs, $(a_{t-1}, a_{t-2}, \ldots a_{t-q})$. An MA(q) model is denoted by:

$$y_t = \sum_{l=1}^{q} \theta_l a_{t-l} + a_t \qquad [8.6]$$

where θ_l is the moving average parameter at lag l. Figure 8.7 shows the time behavior of two different MA systems. Notice the series with the negative θ_1 value is considerably more variable.

The simple MA(1) model is often found to be adequate. For example, suppose one is monitoring the number of action events that occur in a system where actions are tightly coupled to resource allocations (see Figure 8.8). Further assume that resource allocations fluctuate randomly over time, due to random fluctuations in disposable income. At any given time t, the number of action events observed would depend directly on the amount of resources allocated (the exogenous input) at time t; but the

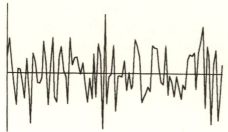

a. Random (White Noise)

b. $\phi_1 = 1.00$

c. $\phi_1 = -0.90$

d. $\phi_1 = -0.50$

Figure 8.5 Various AR models

e. $\phi_1 = 0.90$

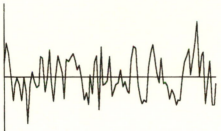

f. $\phi_1 = 0.50$

Figure 8.5 continued

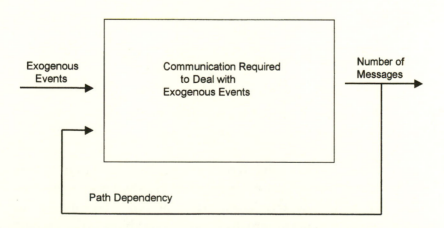

Figure 8.6 The AR(1) model

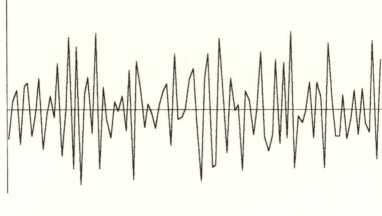

$\phi_1 = 0.60$

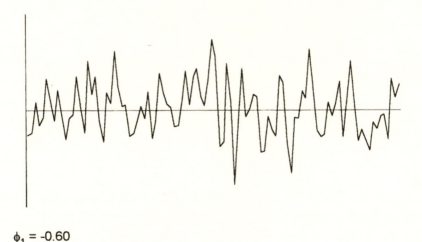

$\phi_1 = -0.60$

Figure 8.7 Various MA(1) models

count may also depend, somewhat less directly, on the resources allocated at time $t-1$. This scenario yields an MA(1) model.

ARMA(P,Q). Finally, it is possible to combine the AR(p) and MA(q) models into the autoregressive-moving average or ARMA(p,q) model. The ARMA(p,q) model states that the system is influenced by both its previous behavior, as well as a random error term and its recent history. Thus, at time t, the event count y_t is generated via an exogenous random input a_t (nor-

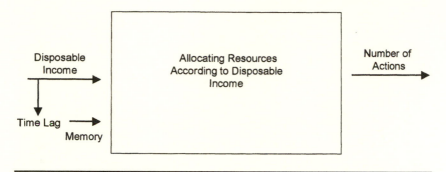

Figure 8.8 The MA(1) model

mally distributed with zero mean and constant variance), a linear function of previous event counts, $(y_{t-1}, y_{t-2}, \ldots y_{t-k})$, and a linear function of previous exogenous random inputs, $(a_{t-1}, a_{t-2}, \ldots a_{t-q})$. The ARMA(p,q) model is defined by:

$$y_t = \sum_{k=1}^{p} \phi_k y_{t-k} + \sum_{l=1}^{q} \theta_l a_{t-l} + a_t \qquad [8.7]$$

A particularly important form of the ARMA(p,q) model is the ARMA(2,1) model:

$$y_t = \phi_1 y_{t-1} + \phi_2 y_{t-2} + a_t - \theta_1 a_{t-1} \qquad [8.8]$$

This is the lowest order model that can capture periodic, oscillating dynamics. These dynamics are parameterized as the "natural frequency" and "damping ratio" of the system. The natural frequency implies the rate at which the system is oscillating, and the damping ratio indicates how quickly disturbances will die down in the system. A system with a damping ratio of greater than 1.0 is considered *overdamped,* and it behaves like an exponential decay system; a damping ratio of less than 1.0 is considered *underdamped* and will lead to oscillations. See Pandit and Wu (1983) for more discussion.

The ARMA(2,1) model is often adequate in describing a system with oscillatory dynamics. Figure 8.9 shows an underdamped ARMA(2,1) system; the oscillatory motion is obvious in the time plot. In this case the frequency is about 0.10 cycle per sample, and the damping ratio is relatively low (0.05), meaning that oscillations are not dampened much.

For example, suppose one is observing a system where staff hours can

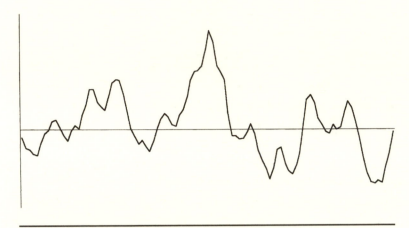

Figure 8.9 ARMA(2,1) model

fluctuate according to workload (see Figure 8.10). At a given instance in time, the random exogenous input may be the arrival of a service request, requiring a random amount of effort to fulfill. The decision maker (manager) may tend to overestimate or underestimate the amount of staff hours required for the task, and as a result, overshoot or undershoot the "optimal" staffing level; recognizing this error, the manager may then counter her original reaction, reversing the trend. Eventually, these oscillations will stop because the task has been completed. As these responses are aggregated over time (each new time interval brings a new service request and a new

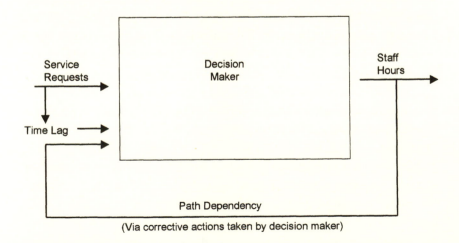

Figure 8.10 The ARMA(2,1) example

series of actions), the total staffed hours in a fixed interval of time may tend to follow an ARMA(2,1) model.

EQUIVALENCY OF MODEL TYPES. There is structural equivalency between AR, MA, and ARMA model forms, that is, one can transform a model from one structure to another without loss of information. For example, the AR(1) model transforms to an infinite order MA model, where $\theta_k = \phi_1^k$. Similarly, an MA(1) model can be transformed into an infinite order AR model. Any MA or AR model can also be transformed into an ARMA model and visa versa. If model forms are equivalent, how does one know which form to use? The following points can be considered:

- AR Models are the easiest to use in terms of parameter estimation, because ordinary least squares regression (which is commonly available) or Yule-Walker equations (which are computationally simple) can be used (see Pandit & Wu, 1983, for more discussion).
- MA models have equivalency to exponential smoothing techniques (Pandit & Wu, 1983); this may be advantageous since many social scientists have previous exposure to exponential smoothing via forecasting and econometrics. MA models must be estimated using nonlinear least squares.
- ARMA models will tend to yield the most parsimonious representation of the system, given that the system cannot be well represented by a simple MA or AR model. One may need an MA(q) or AR(p), where q and/or p is quite large, in order to represent a set of data which is easily modeled as an ARMA(2,1). ARMA models must also be estimated using nonlinear least squares.

Multivariate Time Series Models

Often it will be desirable to code events in several different ways. If these different codes are then aggregated into event counts, multiple event counts will exist—thus, multiple event time series will exist. Each of these event time series can be modeled independently, using curve-fitting or ARMA models. However, there may well be cause-and-effect relationships between the different time series. For example, in the CIP innovation study, it might be reasonable to hypothesize that the monthly event count for *actions* is positively related to the monthly event count for *outcomes*. More specifically, we might propose the following:

- When the monthly event count for actions is positive, the monthly event count for outcomes will tend to be positive.
- When the monthly event count for actions is negative, the monthly event count for outcomes will tend to be negative.

- When the monthly event count for actions is large, the monthly event count for outcomes will tend to be large.
- When the monthly event count for actions is small, the monthly event count for outcomes will tend to be small.

All of these relationships could be captured by a multivariate ARMA model. Let the monthly event count for actions in month t be denoted by x_t, and let the monthly event count for outcomes in month t be denoted by y_t. The four propositions above can be captured by the formulation:

$$Y_t = \phi_{1,2}^{(0)} * x_t + a_t \qquad [8.9]$$

where a_t is a normally, independently distributed error term and $\phi_{1,2}^{(0)}$ represents the parameter of the model to be determined empirically. It might also be reasonable to hypothesize that there is a lagged cause-and-effect relationship between actions and outcomes; namely, that the monthly event count for actions in month $t-1$, x_{t-1} is related to the monthly event count of outcomes in month t, y_t. This makes the reasonable assumption that actions have an impact on the system over a window of time longer than one month. Enhancing equation [8.9] leads us to:

$$y_t = \phi_{1,2}^{(0)} \cdot x_t + \phi_{1,2}^{(1)} \cdot x_{t-1} + a_t \qquad [8.10]$$

Generalizing this further, we could hypothesize that outcomes are affected over some longer period of time, thus resulting in the more general model:

$$y_t = \Sigma \, \phi_{1,2}^{(i)} \cdot x_{t-i} + a_t \qquad [8.11]$$

The monthly event count for outcomes in month t, y_t, may also have some path dependency; namely, the monthly event count in month t, y_t may be related to the monthly event count in months $t-1$, $t-2$, etc. (y_{t-1}, y_{t-2}, etc.). This leads us to the most general multivariate time series model:

$$y_t = \Sigma \, \phi_{1,2}^{(i)} \cdot x_{t-i} + \Sigma \, \phi_{1,1}^{(j)} \cdot y_{t-j} + a_t \qquad [8.12]$$

The relationship between the two time series may be bidirectional. For example, we might hypothesize that

- when the monthly event count for outcomes is positive, the monthly event count for actions will tend to be positive.
- when the monthly event count for outcomes is negative, the monthly event count for actions will tend to be negative.
- when the monthly event count for outcomes is large, the monthly event count for actions will tend to be large.
- when the monthly event count for outcomes is small, the monthly event count for actions will tend to be small.

This would enable us to propose the following companion model to equation [8.12]:

$$x_t = \Sigma\, \phi_{2,1}^{(i)} \cdot y_{t-i} + \Sigma\, \phi_{2,2}^{(j)} \cdot x_{t-j} + a_t \qquad [8.13]$$

By fitting equations [8.12] and [8.13] simultaneously, we are actually able to test for causality between the factors denoted by x and y. This form of causality is called Granger causality and shall be discussed in a later section of the chapter.

Change Point Time Series Models

The models discussed so far make a common assumption of weak stationarity—the mean and covariance structure of the data remains constant over time. It is possible, however, for the mean, variance, or dynamical (parametric) structure of the event time series to change over time. When this happens, we say that there is a *change point* present. The change point denotes the instance in time when a time series shifts from one model to another.

The simplest change point is represented by a change in the mean of the system (see Figure 8.11):

$$y_t = b_0 + a_t \qquad t < t'$$
$$y_t = b'_0 + a_t \qquad t \geq t' \qquad [8.14]$$

where b_0 and b'_0 are two different means, t' is the change point, and a_t is a random error series with constant variance and a mean of zero. In the CIP innovation study, for example, changes in the mean level of the monthly

Figure 8.11 Random system with a shift in mean

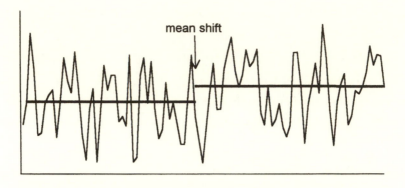

Figure 8.12 AR(1) system with a shift in mean

event count of actions may indicate a definitive transition from one phase of the innovation project to another (e.g., from research activities to premarket launch activities). Such a change in the mean is called a step-shift, denoting that the mean "steps" from one value (b_0) to another (b'_0). The step-shift structure is not limited to a random time series; for example, it could occur within an ARMA model:

$$Y_t = b_0 + \phi_1 \cdot y_{t-1} + a_t \quad t<t'$$
$$Y_t = b'_0 + \phi_1 \cdot y_{t-1} + a_t \quad t\geq t' \qquad [8.15]$$

An AR(1) model that has a step-shift in the mean is shown in Figure 8.12.

Another common way in which a time series may change is in its variance. For example, in the CIP innovation study, changes in the monthly event count of (external) context events may indicate a significant change in the environment, such as the presence of new competitors (which should also affect the mean level of context event counts). Within the model, this is depicted by a change in the variance of the exogenous (error) term a_t:

$$y_t = f() + a_t \quad t<t'$$
$$y_t = f() + a'_t \quad t\geq t' \qquad [8.16]$$

where $f()$ represents some time series model, a_t is normally and independently distributed with standard deviation σ, and a'_t is normally and independently distributed with standard deviation σ'. Figure 8.13 shows an AR(1) model where the standard deviation after the change point is twice that of before the change point. Finally, the parameters describing the dynamics of time series itself might change. For example, consider the AR(1) model that has its autoregressive parameter shift from one value (ϕ_1) to another (ϕ_1') after the change point:

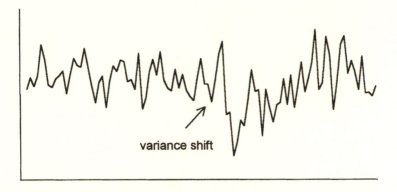

Figure 8.13 AR(1) system with a shift in variance

$$y_t = b_0 + \phi_1{}^* y_{(t-1)} + a_t \quad t<t'$$
$$y_t = b_0 + \phi'_1{}^* y_{t-1} + a_t \quad t\geq t' \qquad\qquad [8.17]$$

An example of such a time series is shown in Figure 8.14. For example, in the CIP innovation study, changes in the dynamical structure of the monthly event count of *actions* may indicate a change in the decision-making process (e.g., actions become more tightly tied to previous actions).

There are two ways in which the change point problem can manifest itself (see Figure 8.15). First, a change point may be present but unknown to the researcher. A multitude of methods exist for detecting (Box and Tiao, 1975; Dooley & Kapoor, 1990; James, James, & Siegmund, 1987) and diagnosing (Guo & Dooley, 1995) such changes. Unfortunately, the temporal stability of model parameters, especially those relating to the dynamical

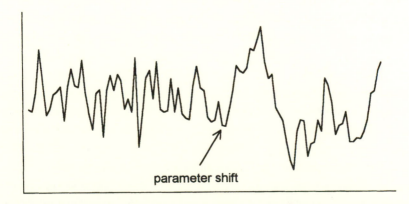

Figure 8.14 AR(1) system with a shift in dynamical parameters

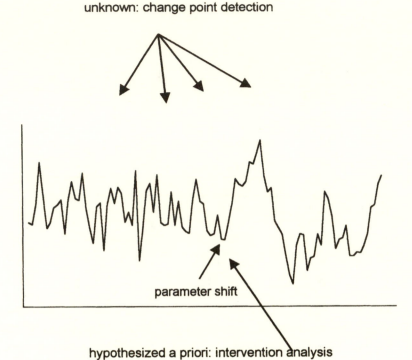

Figure 8.15 The nature of the change point

structure of the time series, is often left as an untested assumption (Isaac & Griffin, 1989).

Second, the researcher may hypothesize a change point of a specific nature a priori. This is the focus of "interrupted time series analysis," or "intervention analysis," in the social sciences (Cook & Campbell, 1979; McDowall, McCleary, Meidinger, & Hay, 1980). The purpose of intervention analysis is to determine whether a specific event has modified the structure of a time series; this is done by comparing the parameters of the time series models before and after the event. A key problem with intervention analysis as it is performed typically is that it is assumed that only the mean has been altered (as opposed to the variance or the time series model parameters). There is no need to make such a restrictive assumption. One can separate the time series into different periods (as we do later with the CIP data), and then estimate a ETSRA model for each of the periods. Because standard errors will be associated with all the estimated parameters, and parameter estimates will tend to be normally distributed, simple t-tests can be used to determine if any of the parameters differ significantly from one pe-riod to another.

PROPERTIES OF TIME SERIES

All time series possess two properties, autocorrelation and a spectral repre-sentation.[2] These two, in turn, are closely related to one another. Ad-ditionally, a multivariate time series possesses cross-correlation. These prop-erties can be thought of as different representations of the data; while there is not a unique correspondence between the raw data and these properties, there is a unique correspondence between a time series model and these properties. For example, an AR(2) model with specific values for its two pa-rameters has a unique correlation pattern and spectral representation. These properties turn out to be quite useful in helping determine what type of ETSRA model should be fit to the data. One can calculate these proper-ties empirically, and then examine the patterns (or lack thereof) embedded in these representations to postulate what type of model might best fit the data. The specific steps involved in such model fitting will be discussed in a subsequent section.

Autocorrelation

The time-dependent structure of the time series can be quantified using the autocorrelation function. Given a time series $(y_1, y_2, \ldots y_N)$, the sample autocorrelation $(r_1, r_2, \ldots r_{N-k})$, is given by:

$$r_k = \frac{\displaystyle\sum_{t=k+1}^{N} y_t y_{t-k}}{\displaystyle\sum_{t=k+1}^{N} y_{t-k}^2} \qquad [8.18]$$

The subscript "k" denotes the lag at which autocorrelation is estimated. The sample autocorrelations r_k lie between -1 and $+1$, where negative val-ues indicate an opposing tendency, positive values indicate a supporting tendency, and values near zero indicate independence. For example, if r_3 was 0.25, this would indicate that y_t was weakly and positively dependent upon (or coupled with) y_{t-3}—as y_{t-3} was either below/above the average, y_t would tend to be below/above the average. Conversely, if r_3 was -0.90,

---

2. Most statistical analysis software packages will have the capability to calculate and dis-play these properties.

this would indicate that y_t was strongly and negatively dependent upon (or coupled with) y_{t-3}—as y_{t-3} was either below/above the average, y_t would tend to be above/below the average.

Figure 8.16 shows the autocorrelation patterns for some different types of time series. The autocorrelation for a random (white noise) time series will simply be noise itself; small values centered on zero. The autocorrelation pattern for an AR time series model starts off somewhat large and positive at lag $k=1$, and then steadily decreases. This depicts the nature of path dependency in the AR system—process observations nearby in time are closely related, while those farther away in time are only weakly related. The autocorrelation pattern for an MA time series model will tend to be one of more positive autocorrelation at low lags, and then quickly decrease to zero. The autocorrelation pattern for an ARMA time series model, which captures periodicity in the time series, will tend to mimic the periodicity in the data. In reality, the sample autocorrelations are not as "smooth" as depicted in the figure. One typically evaluates r_k for lags between 1 and 20.

Closely related to the sample autocorrelation function is the sample partial autocorrelation function r^*_k (for more details on estimation, see Box & Jenkins, 1976). The partial autocorrelation function at lag k attempts to isolate autocorrelation at lag k by partialling out the contributions of autocorrelation at lags 1 through $k-1$. The pattern in partial autocorrelations is somewhat opposite that found in the regular autocorrelations. Namely, the partial autocorrelation pattern for an AR time series model will tend to have one of more positive partial autocorrelation at low lags, and then quickly decrease to zero. The partial autocorrelation pattern for an MA time series model starts off somewhat large and positive at lag $k=1$, and then steadily

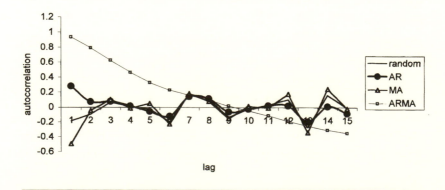

Figure 8.16 Autocorrelation patterns in various time series models

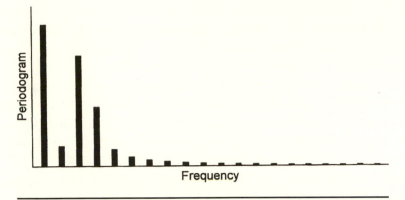

Figure 8.17 Periodogram for time series in Figure 8.4

decreases. Because of the "dual" nature of the regular and partial sample autocorrelations, and how they mirror-image their respective response to an AR versus MA model, the two can be examined simultaneously to see whether an AR or MA model is a more appropriate fit for the observed data.

Spectral Representation

A companion to the autocorrelation function is the sample spectrum or periodogram $f(\omega)$. Details on how to calculate the periodogram can be found in Pandit (1991). For an AR, MA, or ARMA model, there is a unique one-one correspondence between the periodogram and the autocorrelation values. The sample spectrum indicates whether periodic behavior is present in the data, and if so, what the period length is. For example, Figure 8.17 shows the periodogram for the time series data depicted in Figure 8.4. One can clearly see the "peaks" in the periodogram, corresponding to period lengths of 3 months and 12 months. The periodogram of an AR or MA process will tend to look linear, starting off large at small (slow) frequencies and decreasing rapidly for higher frequencies. The periodogram of of random (white noise) process will tend to be "flat" across all frequencies.

Cross-Correlation

The cross-correlation function $r_{xy}(k)$, where k can be either a positive or negative integer, defines the correlation between variables x_t and y_{t+k}. It has the same interpretation as the autocorrelation function, only it depicts relationships between two time series rather than within a single time series. Note that the index "k" can be positive *and* negative. For example, we could examine the correlation between x_t and y values into the future (k>0), which would imply x was a cause of y. Or conversely, we could examine the correlation between x_t and y values from the past (k>0), which would imply y was a cause of x. Also note that the value of "k" can be zero, denoting simultaneous correlation between the two time series.

For example, suppose that x_t was the amount of overtime used by a group at time t to complete a project, and y_t was a measure of group morale. If $r_{xy}(0)$ was negative, it would mean that overtime was instantaneously (within the timeframe of the sampling rate) observed with a loss of morale. If $r_{xy}(1)$ were negative also, it would mean overtime in one time period tended to be followed by morale decreases in the subsequent time period. If $r_{xy}(-1)$ were negative, it would mean overtime in one time period tended to be preceded by morale decreases in the previous time period. Finally, if $r_{xy}(k)$ is nonzero for both positive and negative values of k, it indicates overtime and morale tend to follow one another in a complex dance over time. The value of $r_{xy}(k)$ is defined by:

$$r_{x,y}(k) = \frac{\sum_{t=k+1}^{N} y_t x_{t-k}}{\sum_{t=k+1}^{N} y_{t-k}^2 \; \sum_{t=k+1}^{N} x_{t-k}^2} \qquad [8.19]$$

DEVELOPMENTAL MODELS AND EVENT TIME SERIES

Event sequence time series methods can be used to test the four motors of change presented in chapter 3. The life cycle motor is comprised of stages, each qualitatively different from one another. Within each stage of a life cycle, behavior may be quite simple. It would therefore be expected that an observed event time series on selected dimensions would show qualitatively different behavior in each of the stages. These differences would be observed as change points: within each stage of the life cycle, the time series data might be modeled by a simple AR, MA, or ARMA model; while between stages, the time series would undergo a change in mean, variance, and/or dynamical parameters.

Evidence of a dialectical process of change may even yield more dramatic and widespread changes. Each synthesis could potentially bring out qualitatively different behavior, leading to the same behavior described above. Additionally, the clash between thesis and antithesis is unlikely to unfold in the same manner each time, meaning that different behavior may exist even within a thesis-antithesis cycle. In particular, a dialectical process may demonstrate, within a cycle, increased variation (as the conflict escalates), followed by a sharp decrease in variance (as the conflict is resolved). One suggestion might be to aggregate the data in such a way that one could use the standard deviation of event counts, rather than the event counts themselves, as the time series. For example, if event counts were aggregated by the week, then one could find the standard deviation of event counts every four weeks and use that as a surrogate time series; such a time series would likely show linear trends up and down as cycles of dialectic change occurred.

A teleological process of change implies that once a goal is chosen, the system tends towards first-order change, where actions are taken to achieve a goal state. If the actions taken to achieve a goal were consistent over time, this would tend to yield a time series probably quite simple, such as a low-order AR, MA, or ARMA model.

Finally, an evolutionary model of change implies a certain relationship between variation, selection, and retention events of a particular form of organization. Multivariate time series could be used in this case to test for Granger causality between variation event counts, selection event counts, and retention event counts.

DATA TRANSFORMATION FOR ETSRA

Two basic steps are necessary to process and format event data before time series analysis can begin. First, event data, which are typically qualitative in nature, need to be transformed into a quantitative representation amenable to time series modeling. Some relevant data may already be in a quantitative form (e.g., chronological data on project monetary expenditures, the number of project personnel, or the number of project-related papers that were published over time). This topic has already been discussed in chapter 5, but some additional detail needs to be provided here. Second, these quantitative observations need to be aggregated into fixed temporal intervals. For example, should the event data for CIP be looked at in weekly, monthly, or yearly intervals?

Transforming Qualitative Events to Quantitative Data

Coded event data can be transformed into a quantitative representation for time series analysis in two ways: by event weights or counts. We will discuss considerations in using each method.

First, events can be weighted by their importance or intensity. This is especially relevant if the nature of events varies greatly, and intensity or importance can be quantitatively operationalized. For example, in their study of organizational change as punctuated equilibrium, Romanelli and Tushman (1994) code the event "power distribution changes" in three ways:

- the ratio between the number of new executive positions created and old positions eliminated, and the total number of executive positions,
- the percent change in the ratio between R&D spending and total spending for R&D, marketing, and sales, and
- the percent change in the ratio between R&D executive titles, and the total number of executive titles for R&D, marketing, and sales.

It may also be possible to obtain importance or intensity ratings via psychometric measurement of attitudes. As always, attention would need to be paid to scale reliability and validity. There is also the problem that in recalling and making sense of historical events, participants may not be able to accurately report their attitude toward or importance of an event at the time it occurred. It would probably be rare to find situations where participants maintained stable attitudes over time about selected events.

A second way of transforming raw event sequence data is by counting the number of times a particular type of event occurred in a fixed temporal interval (of a day, week, month, or year). Suppose events of type A, B, and C occur in the following sequence:

Date	Event	Date	Event
5/1	A	7/6	C
5/9	B	7/7	C
5/15	A	7/9	A
5/15	C	7/15	C
6/3	B	7/27	A
6/18	B	7/30	C

Monthly counts for A, B, and C would be {2, 0, 2}, {1, 2, 0}, and {1, 0, 4}, respectively. These monthly counts reflect the activity level of a certain variable. For example, if variable C denotes contextual events, then the time series would indicate that the change process was more greatly influenced by exogenous, contextual events during July than it was during May and June.[3]

---

3. Notice that we do not necessarily normalize the data with respect to the number of events. If one wanted to uncouple event type from the overall "activity level" of the system, then one could track activity level (the total number of events, e.g. {4, 2, 6}), and event proportions (the proportion of events that were of a particular type, e.g., A would be {.5, 0, .33}) separately.

CHOOSING A FIXED TEMPORAL INTERVAL

There are a number of considerations in selecting the fixed temporal interval for aggregating event count data. As discussed in chapter 5, the substantive considerations deal with the nature of the change process being investigated and the interval frequency of activities being observed in the field research setting. For example, if the study focuses on the development of project teams that meet regularly to conduct their business, the interval of these meetings (daily, weekly, or monthly) would represent a naturally meaningful temporal interval for aggregating event count data.

There are also four important statistical considerations in selecting a fixed temporal interval:

1. The need for resolution and normality in the data versus the need for an adequate number of samples or data points.

As the temporal interval, Δt, is made longer, counts of the number of events within intervals will become larger and resolution in measurement will be enhanced; however, sample size, or the number of data points in a time series, will decrease. As Δt is made shorter, counts will become smaller and less resolved, while sample size will increase. Thus, resolution plays against sample size.

The need for resolution stems from the nature of assumptions one typically has to make in order to employ standard statistical modeling techniques, such as ordinary or generalized least squares—namely, that the dependent data is Gaussian, and thus by definition, continuous.

2. The need to observe the least frequent event of interest.

The measurement span criterion (Arundale, 1980) states that if the frequency of the least frequent event in an interval is f_0, then one must choose the temporal interval, (t, such that $\Delta t > 1/f_0$. For example, if the least frequent event occurs at a frequency of 0.33 events per month, then Δt must be at least 1/0.33/months, or 3 months. This criterion assures that, on average, event counts for any given time period are one or greater.

3. The need to observe a difference in the frequency of occurence between two event-types.

The measurement span criterion (Arundale, 1980) also posits that if the frequencies of two different events must be differentiated, and the two events occur with frequencies f_1 and f_2, then one must choose the temporal interval, Δt, such that $\Delta t > 1/(f_2 - f_1)$. For example, if event A occurs at a frequency of 0.33 events per month, and event B occurs at a frequency of 0.25 events per month, then Δt must be at least $1/(0.33 - 0.25)$/months, or 12 months.

4. The need to resolve the highest oscillation of interest.

The Nyquist criterion (Arundale, 1980) states that if one is interested in estimating a period of oscillation f_n, then one must choose the temporal interval, Δt such that $\Delta t < 1/2f_n$. For example, if event A fluctuates at a frequency of 4 oscillations per month, then (t must be less than 1/8 months, or 0.125 months. In essence, this criterion ensures that at least two samples are observed within each oscillation.

For CIP data, monthly intervals were chosen because

- a project team met monthly to review status of the project,
- monthly aggregation yielded counts, ranging from 0–20, with infrequent periods where strings of zeros occurred, and
- monthly counts yield a total of 106 data points, considered adequate for subsequent time series modeling.

The Nyquist criterion states that the highest frequency oscillation that can be resolved with a Δt of 1 month is 0.50 oscillations per month.

Censored Data

A final issue that one may face in data preparation is the issue of temporal truncation: either the beginning (left-censored) or end (right-censored) of the time series may be missing because of data collection problems. If one is trying to estimate the birth or death of a particular event, methods have been developed that enable such extrapolation (see Tuma & Hannan, 1984).

If, however, one is trying to add additional quantitative data to the time series record, it is possible that some "missing data" can be supplied through archival analysis. If this is not possible, then one may have to confine the scope of one's theories to only that portion of the change process that has been observed. Unlike the case in event history analysis, it is not appropriate to extrapolate backward or forward to add more data. The choice of both a beginning and ending time should depend on sound theoretical (contextual and historical) reasons, rather than convenient statistical reasons (Isaac & Griffin, 1989).

ANALYSIS OF TIME SERIES DATA

After an event sequence time series of fixed temporal intervals has been obtained, the structure of the time series can be identified. Any analysis should be able to answer the following basic questions:

1. Are there time-ordered (path) dependencies in the data? The sample autocorrelation and partial autocorrelation function, as well as visual inspection of the time series, will help answer this question. The null hypothesis consists of testing whether the sample autocorrelation values are statistically different from zero.
2. Are the time-ordered dependencies periodic in nature? Simply, path dependency will manifest itself as an AR model, whereas more complex, periodic patterns will require an ARMA model, or curve-fitting sine waves, to properly capture embedded dynamics. Periodicities can be determined by visual inspection of the sample autocorrelation function and the periodogram.
3. Are there change points in the time series? Often change points make themselves obvious through visual inspection of the time series plot; or, they may be hypothesized a priori, due to qualitative data associated with the case events. More subtle change points are difficult to detect unless one uses some rather sophisticated statistical techniques.
4. How predictable is the time series? The more structure there is observable in the time series, the more predictable the system in question is. Whatever variation cannot be accounted for by the identified statistical model is considered random noise. As with most other statistical models, an r^2 value can quantify the predictability of the time series, as it denotes the fraction of the data variation captured by the specified model.

MODEL FITTING

The task of fitting models to time series data can be quite involved. Like statistical regression modeling, it sometimes is as much an "art" as a "science." Any given time series may be able to be modeled in several different ways, each with approximately equal predictive capability. The researcher should consider the qualitative nature of the process theory that they may likely put forward. For example, AR and ARMA models imply path dependency, so any process theory put forth in support of these models should also imply path dependency.

The exact details of the modeling task are beyond the scope of this chapter; rather, we shall outline the modeling steps at a broad level of detail. For an appropriate level of discussion concerning how parameters are estimated, and how the researcher makes particular decisions at various stages of the modeling process, we refer the reader to Box and Jenkins (1976) and Pandit and Wu (1983). We should also note that the actual task of ETSRA parameter estimation and model fitting is *not* something typically found in a standard statistical software package; one should carefully examine the capabilities of software packages to ensure that they have the capacity to perform these analyses.

Preliminary Steps

The preliminary steps in data analysis and model fitting are:

1. Estimate the mean μ of the time series $y_t = \{y_1, y_2, \ldots y_t, y_{t+1}, \ldots y_N\}$ and normalize the series by subtracting the mean, i.e., $y_t = y_t - \mu$.
2. Plot a run chart of the data (a plot that simply shows the data in a temporal fashion).
3. Generate the sample autocorrelation plot, sample partial autocorrelation plot, and the periodogram.
4. Analyze these to determine the order of the appropriate model.

Model Selection

The run chart should be examined first for obvious trends or cycles. A definitive peak in the periodogram is also indicative of a cycle. The sample autocorrelation and partial autocorrelation plots give the most useful evidence in determining model structure. Table 8.1 summarizes the behavior of the sample autocorrelation and partial autocorrelations for AR, MA, and ARMA models. Preliminary models should be hypothesized and model parameters estimated. The MA and ARMA are fit using generalized least squares (GLS) as opposed to ordinary least squares (OLS) because the subsequent loss function is nonlinear. In general, one can use OLS when error terms can be assumed to be independent (as in the case of an AR model);

Table 8.1   Behavior of Sample Autocorrelations and Partial Autocorrelations

	AUTOCORRELATIONS	PARTIAL AUTOCORRELATIONS
white noise	all lags: zero	all lags: zero
AR	decay like a damped exponential or sine wave lag k, k>p: zero	lag 1 thru p: nonzero
MA	lag 1 thru q: nonzero lag k, k>q: zero	decay like a damped exponential or sine wave
ARMA	lag k, k>q−p: damped exponential or sine wave	lag k, k>p−q: damped exponential or sine wave

Adapted from Cook and Campbell, 1979, p. 249.

when error terms are not independent (as in the case with MA and ARMA models), one must use GLS.

After a model has been fit, one must first examine whether the estimated parameters have generated a model that is stationary and invertible. The model is stationary if predictions based on the autocorrelation function remain bounded; the model is invertible if recent events have more influence on a prediction than more distant events. Models not meeting these criteria should not be entertained; see Box and Jenkins (1976) for more details on how these properties are estimated.

Residual Diagnostics

If the model is stationary and invertible, then one should find the series' prediction residuals e_t:

$$e_t = y_t - \hat{y}_t \qquad [8.20]$$

where the predicted value $\hat{y}_t$ is obtained by conditional expectations (see Box & Jenkins, 1976, for details). For example, in the AR(1) model:

$$e_t = y_t - \phi_1 y_{t-1} \qquad [8.21]$$

The residuals should be normally and independently distributed with zero mean and constant variance σ_e^2 (estimated by sample residual variance s_e^2); Box and Jenkins (1976) discuss residual analysis. Normality can be checked via a normal probability plot; gross departures from normality can be somewhat compensated for by nonlinear (e.g., log) transformations of the raw data. Standardized residuals (e_t/s_e) should be between -3 and $+3$; values greater than that may be considered outliers and should be investigated. One can plot e_t versus $\hat{y}_t$ to determine if variance is constant or varies as a function of mean response (if so, then a log transformation would be in order).

Any statistical software package performing such estimation procedures will also generate confidence intervals for the estimated model parameters. If any of the confidence intervals include (overlap) zero, then that model parameter could be considered statistically insignificant and should be dropped from consideration.

Model Fit

Finally, if residual analysis indicates an adequate model, then model fit can be quantified. The standard r^2 value can be obtained by taking $1-(s_y^2/s_e^2)$. Another fitness statistic is Akaike's Information Criterion, or AIC:

$$AIC = \ln s_e^2 + 2(p + q)/n \qquad [8.22]$$

where p and q are the order of the ARMA (p,q) model, and n is the sample size. The lower the AIC value, the better the model fit. The Hannan-Rissanen procedure (Granger & Newbold, 1986) uses AIC values in an "automated" modeling method; the user inputs the maximum values of AR(p) and MA(q) and the procedure returns the best AR, MA, or ARMA model available.

EXAMPLE ANALYSIS

In order to demonstrate these procedures, we examine two event time series from CIP: the action events during the initial period of development (n=59 data points, or months) and the action events during the second, final period of development (n=47). The time series is derived by taking the total numbers of action events in each month of CIP as follows: Each action was coded as $+1$ if it represented continuation of the project (actions coded as expansion or persistence) and as -1 if it represented a change in the project (actions coded as modification or persistence). For each month the total number of actions (now coded $+1$ or -1) were summed to yield a continuation score. High positive values on this score represented a general course of continuation during the month, high negative values represented a general course of change during the month, and low values indicated a mixture of continuation and change.

The overall time series was broken into the two periods—beginning and ending—based on a priori knowledge that the initial period constituted "research" and the second period constituted "development," as observed in chapter 4. This implies that a change point existed at the 60th observation in the series.

PRELIMINARY ANALYSIS

The time series for action events in the beginning phase is shown in Figure 8.18. The sample autocorrelations (Figure 8.19) and partial autocorrelations (Figure 8.20) are all statistically insignificant, and the periodogram (Figure 8.21) is essentially flat—thus indicating a random system. Randomness corresponds to "high dimensionality," meaning that there are many different sources of variation contributing to the data. Thus, any adequate process theory would have to incorporate this high dimensionality. This means that the theory would have to posit numerous causal factors contributing to action events. That a complex set of causal factors is oper-

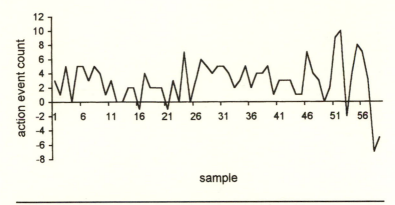

Figure 8.18 Beginning action time series—time plot

ating is consistent with an inability to predict a course of actions during this period.

The time series for action events during the ending phase is shown in Figure 8.22. The sample autocorrelations (Figure 8.23) indicate an MA(1) model, while the sample partial autocorrelations (Figure 8.24) indicate an AR(8) model. The periodogram (Figure 8.25) clearly has a single peak that is significantly higher than any of the other peaks; this indicates a periodic system, which minimally requires at least an AR(2) model. The length of the period found in the spectrum is 2.6 months.

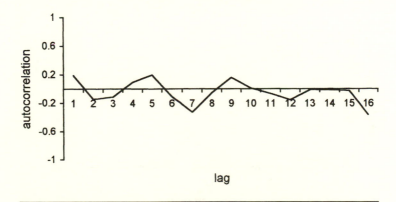

Figure 8.19 Beginning action time series—autocorrelation

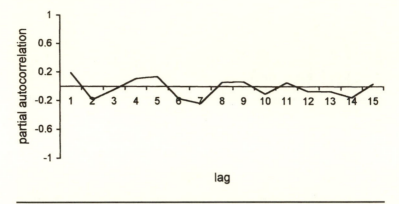

Figure 8.20 Beginning action time series—partial autocorrelation

Modeling Fitting and Comparisons

The next step is to run some different models and compare the quality of fit. The models here were fit using the "Time Series Module" (He, 1995) of *Mathematica* (Wolfram, 1988). Recall that in the preliminary statistics for CIP event sequence time series of beginning actions, a random series was indicated. For demonstrative purposes, a number of other models (AR(1), AR(2), MA(1), ARMA(2,1)) were run; results are compared in Table 8.2. While the other models had slightly better fit, their parameters were statistically insignificant (except for the MA(1) case), so the "random" model is preferable. In the case of the MA(1) model, a negative r^2 was generated, meaning that the variance of the residuals was actually larger than

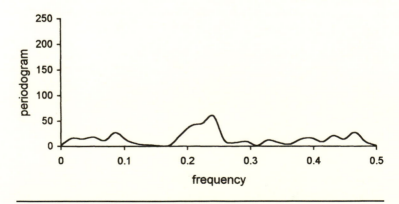

Figure 8.21 Beginning action time series—periodogram

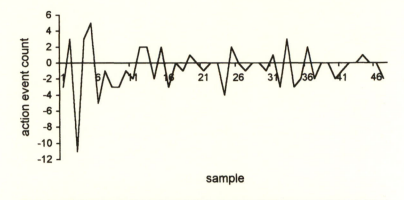

Figure 8.22 Ending action time series—time plot

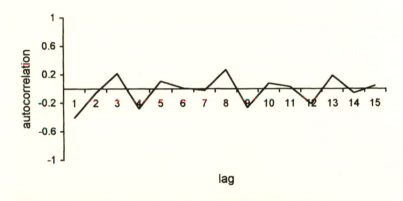

Figure 8.23 Ending action time series—autocorrelation

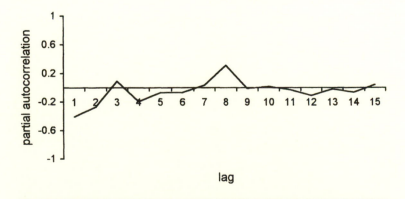

Figure 8.24 Ending action time series—partial autocorrelation

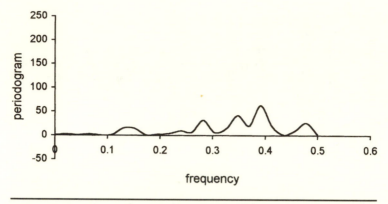

Figure 8.25 Ending action time series—periodogram

the variance of the original raw data. Thus, actions follow a random pattern in period one of the CIP innovation.

The preliminary statistics for the CIP event sequence time series of the second phase of ending actions indicated an MA(1) or AR(8) model, or something in between. A number of models were fit and results are shown in Table 8.3. The AR(8) model yields a low AIC, the best r^2 and Q values, and has significant parameters. Because all other AR parameter values from lag 2 through lag 7 are statistically insignificant, the model can be simplified to:

$$y_t = -.51y_{t-1} + .31y_{t-8} \qquad [8.23]$$

This implies that actions in the second period on CIP innovation are negatively correlated with the previous month's actions, and positively correlated with actions 8 months previous.

The overall pattern of results suggests that in the first phase, the CIP in-

Table 8.2   Model Estimates for Beginning Action Events

MODEL	STATIONARY	INVERTIBLE	AIC	s_e^2	r^2	Q	STATISTICALLY SIGNIFICANT
random	yes	yes	2.18	8.84	—	22.1	—
AR(1)	yes	yes	2.16	8.38	0.04	18.9	no
AR(2)	yes	yes	2.15	8.09	0.07	15.0	no
MA(1)	yes	yes	2.49	11.7	−0.20	28.99	yes
ARMA(2,1)	yes	yes	2.21	8.26	0.07	15.5	no

Table 8.3   Model Estimates for Ending Action Events

MODEL	STATIONARY	INVERTIBLE	AIC	s_e^2	r^2	Q	STATISTICALLY SIGNIFICANT
random	yes	yes	1.88	6.58	—	44.9	—
AR(1)	yes	yes	1.72	5.36	0.17	25.0	yes
AR(8)	yes	yes	1.78	4.23	0.35	4.66	yes
ARMA(2,1)	yes	yes	1.73	5.48	0.15	44.9	no
MA(1)	yes	yes	1.72	5.35	0.21	23.8	yes

novation team did not take actions systematically. They would build the project for a short time, then change it. While there may have been some logic or plan behind the CIP team's actions for short periods (as indicated in the Markov analysis in chapter 6), there is no longer-term pattern in the beginning phase. This may well have been because the fluid and complex situation in the beginning stages of CIP prevented any systematic development of lines of action.

In the second phase a pattern is evident, but it suggests that the CIP team was not sticking to a consistent course of action, but rather changing actions in a cyclical fashion. In particular, the negative relationship between actions at $t+1$ and actions at t suggests that the CIP team was rather reactive during this period, continuing to build the project one month and then changing course during the next month. The positive relationship with actions 8 months previous may be the result of the periodic swings between continuation and change in CIP activities. This pattern may be explainable in terms of a learning model if we also consider outcomes, because learning is defined as the systematic linkage of actions to feedback, either positive or negative.

The Multivariate Case

We now turn to a joint analysis of the actions and outcomes time series from the CIP study, to see whether:

- Actions tend to be tied to outcomes, indicating trial and error learning, and/or
- Outcomes tend to be tied to actions, indicating a relatively "closed" organizational system.

In order to test for causality, we can use *Granger causality,* which is an acceptable and common means by which correlation between two variables can be interpreted as causality (Granger, 1969). Given equations 8.12 and

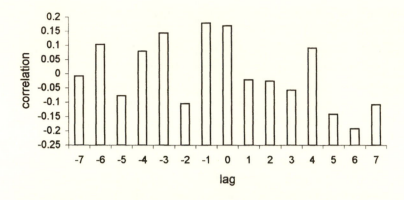

Figure 8.26 Beginning action time series—cross-correlation

8.13, Granger causality can be directly operationalized: if some ϕ^i_{12} is nonzero, then outcomes Granger-cause actions; conversely, if some ϕ^i_{21} is nonzero, then actions Granger-cause outcomes.

The specific nature of Granger causality can be described as follows. Let y^*_t be the predicted value of the dependent variable y_t. The value y_t can be predicted as some function of the previous values of y_t, for example, as a function of $(y_{t-1}, y_{t-2}, \cdots y_{t-k})$; let that prediction be $y^*_t{}^{(1)}$. The value y_t can also be predicted as some function of the previous values of both the dependent and the independent variable at time t, x_t, for example, as a function of $(x_{t-1}, x_{t-2}, \cdots x_{t-k}; y_{t-1}, y_{t-2}, \cdots y_{t-k})$; let that prediction be $y^*_t{}^{(2)}$. The independent variable x_t is said to "Granger-cause" the dependent variable y_t, if (on average) the predicted value $y^*_t{}^{(2)}$ is more accurate than the predicted value $y^*_t{}^{(1)}$. For example, in CIP, outcomes "Granger-

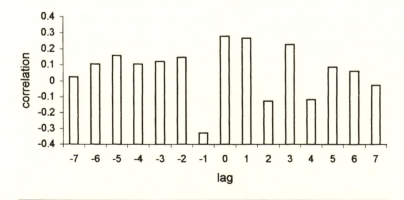

Figure 8.27 Ending action time series—cross-correlation

cause" actions if actions can be better predicted from the past actions and outcomes together than from past actions alone.

Figures 8.26 and 8.27 show the cross-correlation function between actions and outcomes for the two periods of innovation. In period one, actions and outcomes appear uncoupled. In period two, there is a statistically significant (negative) correlation between A_t (action at time t) and O_{t-1} (-0.327) (outcome at time $t-1$), and there are large correlations between (A_t, O_t), (A_t, O_{t+1}), and (A_t, O_{t+3}); in fact, it seems that A_t causes a second-order (oscillatory) response in subsequent outcomes. Note that these plots are based on the raw count data; Cook and Campbell (1979) also suggest that one may also examine the cross-correlations between the residuals yielded from the individual time series models.

In order to test this more rigorously, and based on the preceding results, the following models are fit:

$$A_t = \phi_{11}^{(1)} A_{t-1} + \phi_{11}^{(8)} A_{t-8} + \phi_{12}^{(0)} O_t + \phi_{12}^{(1)} O_{t-1} + e_t^{(1)} \quad [8.24]$$

$$O_t = \phi_{22}^{(1)} O_{t-1} + \phi_{21}^{(0)} A_{t-8} + \phi_{21}^{(1)} A_{t-1} + \phi_{21}^{(2)} A_{t-2} + \phi_{21}^{(3)} A_{t-3} \\ + e_t^{(2)} \quad [8.25]$$

Note that we have included certain terms in equations 8.24 (A_{t-1}, A_{t-8}) and 8.25 (O_{t-1}), based on the results of modeling the individual event time series.

Results show very strongly that there exists Granger causality in both directions. For actions, when $A_t = f(A_{t-8})$, an $r^2 = 0.159$ is obtained; when outcomes are included, the equation is $A_t = f(A_{t-8}, O_t)$ and $r^2 = 0.668$ is obtained. In this case, outcomes at one point in time cause actions at the same point in time. Now let us consider outcomes. When $O_t = f(O_{t-1})$, an $r^2 = 0.225$ is obtained; when actions are included in the equation and $O_t = f(O_{t-1}, A_t, A_{t-1})$, an $r^2 = 0.507$ is obtained. In this case, actions at one time cause outcomes at both the same time and actions at the prior time cause outcomes. This positive relationship is consistent with a learning model in which positive outcomes cause persistence, while negative outcomes cause change (indicated by negative action values). Moreover, these results suggest that there is mutual causation between the time series for actions and outcomes, with actions leading outcomes. This is consistent with the non-recursive (circular) causal model of learning advanced by Garud and Van de Ven (1992; see also Van de Ven & Polley, 1992), in which actions give rise to outcomes, which the team reacts to immediately with either persistence or change in course of action (depending on whether the outcome is positive or negative).

Tests indicated that errors in the two models were independent, as assumed. If error terms between the two models had been correlated, then GLS would have been used. Box and Jenkins (1976) explicitly model the covariance in the error structure by using vector-ARMA, or ARMAV models; while precision is gained in moving toward such a model, computational and interpretive complexity is also increased. Cook and Campbell (1979) discuss several other methods, using the cross-correlation function, which can be used as an alternative to parametric modeling.

CONCLUSION

The application of univariate and multivariate linear time series models allows one to understand the dynamics of event sequence data. This chapter presented the standard procedures for understanding the structure of event time series data. These procedures consist of the following steps:

1. Transform the event data into quantitative event sequence time series, either by weights or counts over fixed temporal intervals.
2. Examine the descriptive statistics of each individual time series and check for change points and linear or periodic in the time series; partition and/or detrend the data as necessary.
3. Using patterns observed in the descriptive statistics as indications of model form and order, fit various linear time series models to each data set; evaluate the quality of each model by its goodness of fit and validation of statistical assumptions; compare models and select the most appropriate.
4. Using the results from step 3, the sample cross-correlations between event types, and other relevant a priori knowledge, hypothesize multivariate model(s) and test for Granger causality.

STRENGTHS AND WEAKNESSES OF TIME SERIES MODELING

The strength of time series modeling lies in its ability to answer important questions concerning dynamic structure, stationarity, predictability, and causality in a system via the longitudinal observation of multiple variables. Because the model is parametric rather than probabilistic in nature, predictions of future behavior can be made.

One of the major weaknesses in time series modeling is its complexity. If a model chosen has dependent error terms (such as in the MA or ARMA models), then generalized (nonlinear) least squares must be used, which is computationally more complex than its companion, ordinary (linear) least squares. Additionally, the actual task of preliminary data analysis and model fitting is—despite how logically the sequence has been laid out here—somewhat of an "art." More experienced modelers will tend to develop better quality models than those with less experience.

One major assumption of the analysis in this chapter is that cause and effect can be modeled effectively using a linear approach. In complex systems this may not be the case. A variable may affect another in a positive way in part of the parameter space and in a negative way elsewhere. One also assumes that errors have little effect on the system; in a nonlinear system, errors may have very significant effects. A variety of nonlinear time series models exist (see Tong, 1990). The methodological route toward understanding such nonlinear systems entails event time series nonlinear dynamical analysis, the topic of the next chapter.

9 Event Time Series Nonlinear Dynamical Analysis

IN CHAPTER 8 EVENT TIME SERIES WERE SUBJECTED to event time series regression analysis (ETSRA) to determine what type of linear patterns existed in the temporal data. Recent advances in the theory and mathematics of *nonlinear dynamical systems* enable us to further distinguish between orderly, linear patterns of change and disorderly or random patterns of change. Specifically, we shall demonstrate that event time series that are classified as "random" according to the time series modeling techniques discussed in chapter 8 may in fact not be as random as we think. The methods of *event time series nonlinear dynamical analysis* (ETSNDA) will allow us to categorize time series data that would otherwise be classified as "random" into three different types of unpredictable behavior: chaos, colored noise, and white noise. Each of these patterns will be discussed in terms of their characteristics, how they manifest themselves in terms of statistical patterns, and what their implications are concerning social and organizational processes of change.

Traditionally, organizational researchers have taken two analytical approaches to model the process or sequence of events that unfold over time in the developmental sequence of an organizational entity. One approach assumes knowledge of the stages or phases of development (or the laws of motion) and the initial starting conditions. The states of events of a developing system can then be regarded as points whose future development occurs along a deterministic trajectory that settles down to an orderly stable or cyclical equilibrium. Life cycle models are of this nature. As Gordon and Greenspan note, most systems analysis "assumes that a system must be stable because only stable behavior persists; an unstable system exhibiting disequilibrium soon 'explodes' and therefore, is only of transient interest" (1988, p. 2).

However, as discussed in chapter 1, organizations are complex systems. Starting conditions for an organizational entity being studied may be uncertain, and observed events in the development of the entity may not settle down to a stable or quasiequilibrium. In fact, complex systems theory tells us that all "living systems," including social systems, exist at a far-from-equilibrium state; equilibrium in a living system is death (Dooley, 1997). As a result, attempts to examine and explain the development of the organization with a theory that is grounded in the assumption that organizations seek equilibrium may fail.

The indeterminate nature of many organizational change processes, such as innovation development, has lead some scholars to model change and development as a stochastic process of exogenous random events (Hannan & Freeman, 1989; Tuma & Hannan, 1984). To say that the process is random is to assume that either the source of a change is exogenous to the system being examined, and that events in the developmental sequence represent independent and equally likely draws from an underlying probability distribution of possible actions, or that there are so many unobservable and/or unidentifiable endogenous factors which affect change that we must rely on statistical description.

The basic problem with these assumptions are that they lead to an ad hoc explanation of organizational change processes that tends to mask important dynamics or assign unwarranted special significance to "key" exogenous events, particularly when this interpretation occurs ex post (Cottrell, 1993). As Koput (1992) argues, if one assumes that the process is random, then the only way to manage a change process is to either expose the organizational unit to a stream of external chance events and "blind" variations (Campbell, 1974) or give up any hope of managing change at all (Kiel, 1994). This amounts to admitting that the organizational process being studied is neither predictable nor manageable. "It just happens" (Aldrich, 1979).

However, a seemingly random process of organizational change may in fact not be; it may be the result of a nonlinear dynamical system. Advances in nonlinear dynamical systems theory provide mathematical tools for examining chaos and colored noise as an alternative explanation of an organizational change process. Dynamical systems theory is a branch of mathematics that can distinguish between five main types of temporal patterns that may exist in a time series of longitudinal data: fixed (static), periodic (cyclical), chaotic (strange), colored noise (pink, brown, or black), or random chance (white noise) (Morrison, 1991). Organizational researchers have tended to focus on static or cyclical models of behavior and to treat other seemingly random patterns as random Gaussian, Poisson, or other

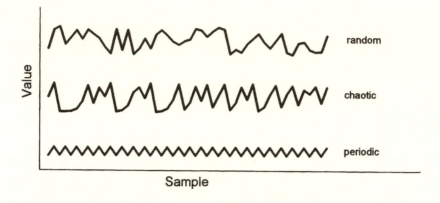

Figure 9.1 Periodic, chaotic, and random time series

forms of "error" distributions messing up their experiments (Abraham, Abraham, & Shaw, 1990; Tuma & Hannan, 1984).

The way in which nonlinear dynamics may manifest themselves has interesting theoretical implications for understanding processes of organizational change. The most commonly held model of nonlinear dynamics is that of chaotic dynamics arising from a stable and deterministic nonlinear system, possibly consisting of a small number of interacting variables, which produces behavior that appears irregular to the degree that it seems random moment-by-moment. Stepping back and viewing the system over a long period of time, however, yields distinctive patterns than clearly are not random. When this occurs, the resulting behavior has come to be called "chaos," to distinguish it from truly random behavior.

An illustration of the different types of dynamical behavior is shown in Figures 9.1 and 9.2. Figure 9.1 shows the time series data and Figure 9.2 the data return map.[1] The return map plots the point $(x(t), x(t+1))$ in order to see temporally related patterns in the data. Periodic, chaotic, and random systems distinguish themselves in terms of a prediction of path versus a prediction of pattern. Path is the specific temporal trajectory, or set of points, that a system follows moment-by-moment; pattern is the distinctive (often visual) temporal shape that emerges when one views the path over a long period of time, plotted in a particular manner. Periodic systems are predictable in both path and pattern. For example, both the time series plot and

---

1. The data correspond to the logistic equation $x(t+1)=k*x(t)*(1-x(t))$ with $k=3.2$ (periodic), $k=4$ (chaotic) (May, 1976), and a random number sequence.

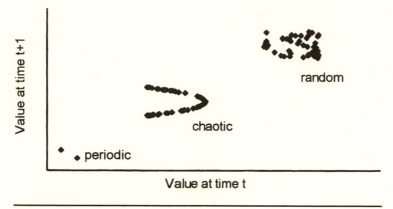

Figure 9.2 Return maps for periodic, chaotic, and random time series

the return map for the periodic data shown in Figures 8.1 and 8.2 demonstrate order and predictability. Random systems are predictable in neither path nor pattern. The corresponding plots for the random data demonstrate a complete lack of order and predictability. Chaotic systems are predictable in pattern but not path. The time plot of chaotic data in Figure 9.1 appears unpredictable, while the return map shown in Figure 9.2 demonstrates an obvious pattern.

Another discriminating characteristic of these different time series patterns is *dimensionality*. We know, for example, that a point has a dimension of zero, a line has a dimension of one, a plane has a dimension of two, and a cube has a dimension of three. Dimensionality refers to the number of dimensions of a geometric space that are required to plot all the points in a return map (or phase space) of a time series. When a time series is periodic, the alternating fixed points in a return map of a periodic pattern can be plotted on a line in one dimension (as illustrated in Figure 9.2). The return map of a chaotic time series is often known as a strange attractor, and plotting all its points may require anywhere from three- to six-dimensional space. Chaotic time series are low dimensional in comparison with the nearly infinite number of dimensions required to plot all points of a random time series.

Figure 9.2 illustrates that a phase plot of a random time series fills the two-dimensional space. If these random numbers are plotted against each other in three-dimensional space, $\{x(t), x(t+1), x(t+2)\}$, they will fill the cube. If we continue to plot the random time series in higher and higher dimensions, they will continue to fill the space into which they are embedded.

As Jayanthi and Sinha (1994) discuss, a major difference between a chaotic process and a truly random process is that while both appear random to the naked eye, a truly random process will have high to infinite dimension, whereas a chaotic process will have low dimension.

A good description of chaos and its origins is available in Gleick (1987). Complex dynamics in relatively simple nonlinear systems have been known since the late 1800s with the pioneering work of Poincaré. Only recently, with the advance of computers, have the implications of his work been explored. Examples of chaotic processes are being found in economics (Arthur, 1989; Brock, 1986), finance (Hsieh, 1991; Stutzer, 1980), psychology (Barton, 1994; Guastello, 1995), sociology (Dendrinos & Sonis, 1990), physiology (Freeman, 1991), and the physical sciences (Prigogine & Stengers, 1984). More recently, numerous applications in business, management, and organizational change are emerging (Cheng & Van de Ven, 1996; Dooley, 1997, Dooley, Johnson, Bush, 1995; Goldstein, 1994; Guastello, 1995; Jayanthi & Sinha, 1994; Kiel, 1994; Priesmeyer, 1992; Stacey, 1992; Thietart & Forgues, 1995).

The possibility of chaotic patterns in organizational behavior becomes apparent when we recognize the simple requirements for the presence of chaos. As Koput (1992) describes, chaos requires a dynamic nonlinear model that is sensitive to initial conditions. Dynamic means that the values a variable takes on at a given time are a function (at least in part) of the values of that same variable at an earlier time. Nonlinearity implies that the dynamic feedback loops vary in strength (loose or tight coupling) and direction (positive or negative) over time. Sensitivity to initial conditions means that small initial differences or fluctuations in variables may grow over time into large differences, and as they move further from equilibrium they bifurcate or branch out into numerous possible pathways resembling a complex decision tree. While we typically expect systems that start in very similar conditions to behave similarly over time, when a chaotic pattern exists, two initial starting conditions, no matter how close they are, diverge exponentially over time (Hibbert & Wilkinson, 1994). A consequence of this behavior is the impossibility of exactly predicting or forecasting an organizational change process in the long term. This irregular and unpredictable behavior arises endogenously—that is, without any exogenous, truly random inputs.

If a time series of organizational change events is found to be chaotic, this calls into question several of the most commonly held beliefs about organizational change and our ability to understand it:

- that change proceeds either in an orderly periodic progression of stages or phases, or that change proceeds in a random sequence of chance or "blind" events,
- that behavior which is unpredictable implies an underlying mechanism of either randomness or "many variables,"
- that organizational change processes converge to a common outcome somewhat irregardless of their initial condition (equifinality), and
- that organizational learning occurs in a predictable, cybernetic manner.

Chaos tells us that the organization can behave in such a manner that is neither stable and predictable nor stochastic and random; that unpredictability of behavior does not imply randomness; that organizations may be extremely sensitive to different initial conditions (path dependence); and that organizational learning processes may be much more complex than simple cybernetic mechanisms imply.

A further distinction can be made between different patterns of randomness. Recent discoveries show that not all randomness is the same; it comes in different colors. The most "basic" form of randomness is white noise. White noise is generated from a causal system where there is a multitude of causes acting in an independent fashion. When randomness is constrained—for example, by interdependencies between the causes—different types of noise patterns can arise. These patterns are still random, but they tend to exhibit a greater tendency to either trend in the same direction (brown and black noise) or reverse direction (pink noise) than white noise. These different noise patterns are collectively called colored noise. Pink noise has been found in a number of different organizational studies (Bak, 1996; Stanley et al., 1996), and so deserves special attention here. Figure 9.3 illustrates these three types of random behavior; one can see the tendency for brown noise to "follow itself" and pink noise to "reverse itself." Another distinguishing characteristic of pink noise is that unlike white noise, which shows no preference for certain frequencies of behaviors, pink noise tends to favor low-frequency over high-frequency behavior.

These findings sharpen the range of plausible explanations by identifying when and what dimensions of an organizational change process are orderly, random, and chaotic. Once we know this, then we have a better idea of what models to apply to understand the dynamics. As Morrison (1991) discusses, (1) use stochastic models and statistics (e.g., game theory) to explain random and colored noise processes; (2) use linear deterministic models (e.g., life cycle models) to explain periodic cycles or stable equilibria; and (3) use

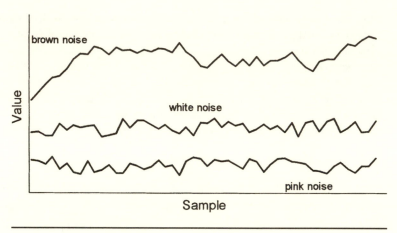

Figure 9.3 Colored noise

nonlinear dynamic modeling (e.g., the logistics equation) to explain chaotic processes.

THEORETICAL BASIS

TYPES OF NONLINEAR DYNAMICS

Chaos

To illustrate how a chaotic process might emerge in organization behavior, let us consider March's (1991) description of exploration and exploitation in organizational learning. Exploration includes behavior reflecting the search, discovery, experimentation, and play of new courses of action, while exploitation includes the choice, refinement, implementation, and execution of a particular course of action. March discusses a variety of trade-offs between exploration and exploitation; maintaining an appropriate balance is essential for organizational learning and survival. For example, in developing an innovation, entrepreneurs who allocate most of their limited time and resources to exploring new courses of action to the exclusion of exploitation are likely to find that they pursued too many undeveloped alternatives and developed too little distinctive competence in any one of them. Conversely, exploitation of a single course of action to the exclusion of exploring alternative pathways is likely to result in gaining competence in a suboptimal solution. March points out that finding the right balance between exploration and exploitation is complicated by the fact that outcomes from the two action options vary in terms of their expected value, timing, and distribution. He goes on to develop an argument that organizational processes which refine exploitation more rapidly than exploration tend to be effective in the short run but self-destructive in the long run.

For illustrative purposes, let us model this dynamic behavior with the following simple logistic difference equation[2]

$$X_t = kX_{t-1}(1-X_{t-1}) \qquad [9.1]$$

where X_t is the percentage of actions that entrepreneurs might devote to exploiting a course of action at time t (assumed to be 100% minus the percentage of actions devoted to exploration). This logistic equation states that the value of the variable X in a given time period is determined by its value in the previous time period and a constant, k. This parameter, k, which governs the degree of nonlinearity of the equation, might be substantively viewed as the relative demands placed on entrepreneurs to complete the innovation journey (e.g., in terms of targeted outcome criteria of quality, time, or costs). The logistic equation specifies a nonlinear inverse temporal relationship between the percentage of actions allocated to exploitation at time t with that at $t-1$. In other words, to maintain balance, entrepreneurs engaged in exploiting a given course of action at a particular time will experience pressure to allocate more time in the next period (perhaps in the next month) to exploring alternative courses of action, and vice versa.

This simple logistic map can produce fixed, periodic, or (seemingly random) chaotic behavior depending on the values of the parameter, k. Figures 9.4, 9.6, and 9.8 show the time series of the percentages of exploitation activities over 100 time periods when k = 2.0, 3.2, and 4.0, respectively. Figures 9.5, 9.7, and 9.9 show the corresponding phase plots (or return maps), in which the initial transitory points have been removed for the sake of clarity. In a phase plot, the values that a system takes on at any time, X_t, are plotted against the value in the previous time period, X_{t-1}, and connected in a time-phased order.

As Figures 9.4 and 9.5 show, when k = 2, the system exhibits a brief period of transitory behavior, but quickly levels off to its equilibrium value and

---

2. This example is motivated by and follows the quadratic formulation of a behavioral theory of chaos developed by Koput (1992). The logistic map is a simple equation often used to illustrate characteristics of chaos. These characteristics were initially developed by May (1976) and generalized by Feigenbaum (1979). We caution that the logistic map is presented for illustrative purposes only. The logistic equation may not be an adequate model of organizational innovation or learning processes.

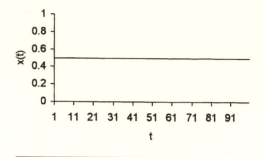

Figure 9.4 Logistic equation with k = 2.0

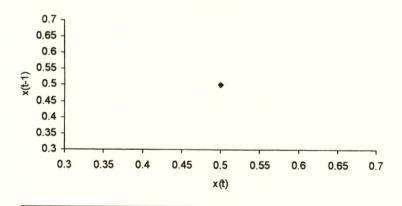

Figure 9.5 Logistic equation with k = 2.0, return map

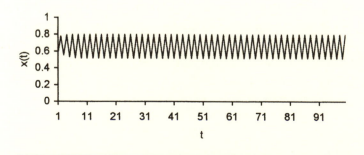

Figure 9.6 Logistic equation with k = 3.2

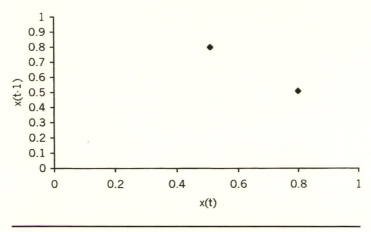

Figure 9.7 Logistic equation with k = 3.2, return map

remains constant at that fixed value for the remainder of the time series. When k = 3.2, after a brief transitory period, the system settles down to periodic or cyclical behavior of period two, alternating between low and high limits of exploitative actions (see Figures 9.6 & 9.7). Finally, Figures 9.8 and 9.9 show that when k = 4.0, the system never settles down to a repeating pattern, and the phase plot traces around a bounded outer edge, producing in this case a cup-shaped mesh.

A mathematical simulation of the logistic equation for different values of k produces the bifurcation structure shown in Figure 9.10, which shows the possible values the system may take at each value of k. This figure shows the attracting set in the logistic map as a function of k.[3] On the left of the map, k is set to 3.4 and has a cycle of period 2, indicated by the two points at approximately 5.6 and 8.2 at the y-axis of the graph where k = 3.4. This cycle of equilibrium values quickly bifurcates to periods 4, 8, and 16 as *k* increases, generating a period-doubling cascade; this is shown by the splitting of the line into 4, 8, and 16 branches as we move from k = 3.4 to k = 3.57 Above k = 3.57 the map exhibits deterministic chaos, indicated by the dark regions in the graph, interspersed with gaps where periodic motion has returned. For example, cycles of periods 6, 5, and 3 can be seen in the three larger gaps to the right.

---

3. The map is iterated until transients have died out, then the iterates are plotted on the y axis for each of 1150 values of k on the x axis.

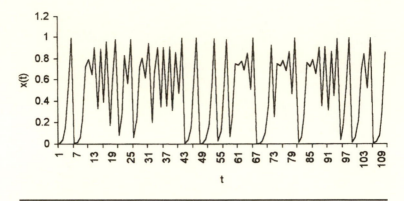

Figure 9.8 Logistic equation with k = 4

In the chaotic regions of the logistic map, the values of the variable X_t are sensitive to initial conditions. In order to determine this Campbell points out that one must observe how two initially nearby points in a time series separate as they are iterated by the map. Technically, this can be done by computing the first *Lyapunov exponent* λ. A value of greater than 0 indicates that the nearby initial points separate exponentially (at a rate determined by $\exp(\lambda)$). Figure 9.11 plots the Lyapunov exponent as a function of the values of the parameter k shown in Figure 9.10. It can be seen that in the chaotic regions $\lambda > 0$ and, moreover, the periodic windows in Figure 9.10 correspond to regions where $\lambda < 0$. "That such a filigree of interwoven regions of periodic and chaotic motion can be produced by a simple quadratic nonlinear map is indeed remarkable" (Campbell, 1989, p. 40).

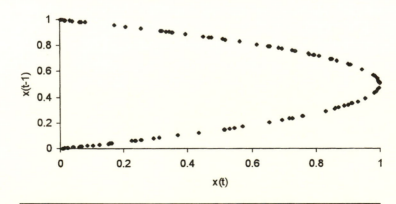

Figure 9.9 Logistic equation with k = 4, return map

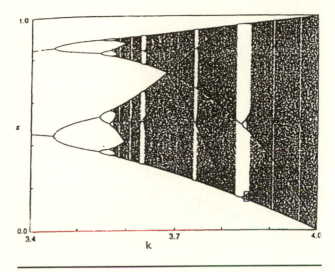

Figure 9.10 Logistic equation bifurcation map

Thus, for different values of k, the logistic map can produce fixed-point, periodic, or chaotic patterns of behavior. As Hibbert and Wilkinson (1994) point out, the parameters of the system set the pattern (i.e., fixed point, periodic, or chaotic), and the initial starting values determine the particular values in the time series. These alternative patterns are completely endoge-

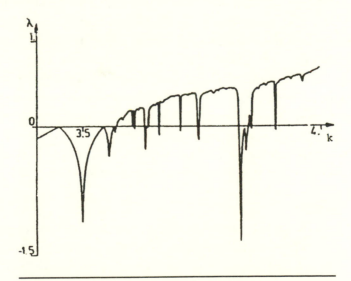

Figure 9.11 Lyapunov exponents of the limit set of the logistic map

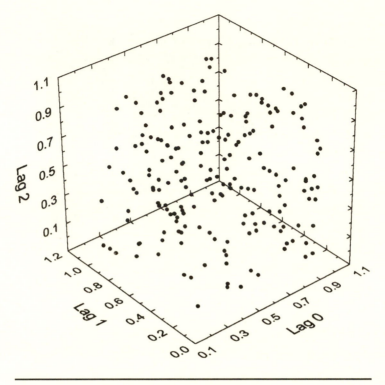

Figure 9.12 3-D return map of a random system

nous to the deterministic logistic system; no random exogenous influences are involved. If the system were produced by truly random, exogenous variations, the entire space of a phase plot of an infinite time series would be completely filled, as illustrated in Figure 9.12. Traditional linear statistical techniques, such as time series regression, assume that a system can produce irregular behavior only when subjected to random inputs. Researchers have treated the error term, reflecting the seemingly random component of the model, as meaningless noise when estimating patterns in event time series data. Nonlinear dynamical theory provides methods to determine whether the random component of behavior might arise endogenously.

Colored Noise

In the previous section, we described how seemingly random behavior can arise from nonlinear deterministic systems. The essence of chaos is that while path (the trajectory of the time series in a pointwise fashion) is not predictable, pattern (the attractor of the time series) is. One might conclude then that if both path and pattern are unpredictable, then the time series must be indicative of a system behaving randomly—and that is as far as explanation can go. Recent studies show, however, that even further distinctions can be made regarding phenomena classified as random (West & Deering, 1995). Conventional definitions of randomness describe *white noise;* this is not the only type of random noise that exists. Noise can also come in colors of pink, brown, and black (see Figure 9.3). Different colors of noise arise from different generative mechanisms. We shall examine the different types of colored noise and discuss the types of generative mechanisms that give rise to such behavior.

Assuming that the time series can been classified as "random" (according to ARIMA modeling and chaotic dynamics analysis), the color of the noise is determined by looking at the power law structure of the time series and at a statistic called the Hurst exponent. Before getting into the actual mechanics of such a diagnosis, let us first examine what power laws are and how they manifest themselves in the natural world.

A power law states that two variables x and y are related to one another via:

$$y = \beta * (x)^\alpha \qquad [9.2]$$

Systems following such power laws are said to be "fractal" because they show self-similarity across scale (scale invariance) and display complex behavior.

Numerous power law relationships have been found in nature and in social systems. Some examples include (Bak, 1996; Schroeder, 1991; Stanley et al., 1996; West & Deering, 1995):

- the body mass and metabolic rate of mammals
- the cumulative distribution of papers published by academic authors
- the spectral frequency of stock market changes
- the distribution of income (Pareto's law)
- the spectral frequencies of heartbeat rhythms
- the distribution of annual growth rates of organizations
- the distribution of city sizes

The diverse applications of power law relationships suggest that many behaviors in the social and physical world might be explained with a natural "scale-free" generating mechanism.

One can take the logarithm of equation [9.2] to obtain:

$$\log y = \log \beta + \alpha * \log x \qquad [9.3]$$

that is, if x and y are plotted on log scales, the power-law relationship will reveal itself as a straight line with slope α. If α is negative, the relationship is often referred to as an *inverse power law.* It is quite common to find that the

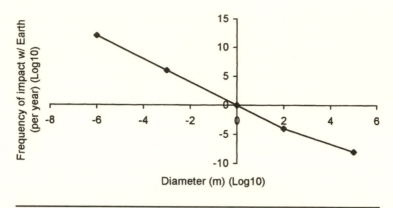

Figure 9.13 Power law (frequency vs. size of Earth-meteor collisions)

size of an event (x) and its frequency (y) follow an inverse power law. This type of power-law relationship is referred to as a *distributional fractal* (West & Deering, 1995), because the shape of the distribution of event sizes remains the same regardless of what scale is chosen (i.e., distribution is scale free). Thus, a histogram of the frequency of events between sizes A and B would look the same as a histogram of the frequency of events between sizes 2A and 2B.

If the size of an event and its frequency follow an inverse power law, then small events happen often, events of moderate size happen sometimes, and events of enormous size happen rarely. For example, Figure 9.13 (adapted from Schroeder, 1991) shows the diameter of meteoric sizes that collide with earth versus the frequency of impact. A few hits are huge; there are some of moderate sizes; and there are a large number of relatively small sizes.

The punctuated equilibrium theory of change reflects an inverse power function among organizational change events. As evidenced in Tushman and Anderson's (1986) studies of change in cement, minicomputer, and glass industries, radical transformation events seldom occur and punctuate long convergent periods of numerous incremental adaptation events.

Inverse power-law-based distributions occur in systems where a complex series of events must precede the onset of the actual event being measured or observed (West & Deering, 1995). For example, before the U.S. Food and Drug Administration approves any drug or biomedical device for market release, the developer must satisfy numerous requirements: (a) conduct clinical trials on animals in order to obtain permission to (b) conduct clinical trials on human beings, (c) which are needed to produce scientific evidence of the safety and efficacy of the drug or device, that (a) an FDA panel uses in its product market application decision. The likelihood of product market approval in such cases depends on the multiplicative likelihood that each of these necessary (but not sufficient) factors is satisfied.

When such systems of multiple causes exist and these causes are related to one another in a multiplicative (dependent) sense, a log-normal statistical distribution of events will arise. West and Deering (1995) show that as complexity in the system increases, the log-normal distribution will become wider and begin to approximate an inverse power law over a large portion of its values. This type of system can be contrasted to a system of multiple causes which are independent of one another, and thus aggregate additively, leading to a normal (as opposed to log-normal) distribution of events (West & Deering, 1995).

Colored noise not only shows the characteristics of a distributional fractal, but also demonstrates an inverse power-law behavior in its *periodogram* or spectrum (see chapter 8 for discussion of sample spectra). Thus, it is an example of a *dynamical fractal,* where x (in equation 9.2) is the time series' spectral frequency response and y is that frequency's corresponding magnitude in the periodogram. Dynamical fractals are often called $1/f$ systems, indicating that low frequencies dominate, moderate frequencies exist in a moderate amount, and high frequencies exist but are rare. Consider that the periodogram follows a $1/f^{-\alpha}$ relationship in log-log space; the value of α determines the type of colored noise:

$\alpha = 0$ implies *white noise,* which is commonly thought of as the "purest" form of randomness; white noise is *memoryless*

$0 < \alpha < 2$ implies *pink noise,* indicative of a system which is *antipersistent*

$\alpha = 2$ implies *brown noise,* or Brownian motion, which indicates that accumulation over time of white noise (brown noise which is differenced at lag one becomes white noise)

$\alpha > 2$ implies *black noise,* indicative of a system which is *persistent.*

Consider a time series made up of random, independent variates $\{x, x_2, \ldots, x_N\}$. Analysis of this time series' spectrum will indicate an α close to zero, indicating pure white noise. If a new series $\{y_1, y_2, \ldots, y_N\}$ is generated where y_i is the sum of x_1 through x_i, the series will now indicate an α close to 2, indicating brown noise.

Black noise demonstrates two behaviors: the "Joseph effect" and the

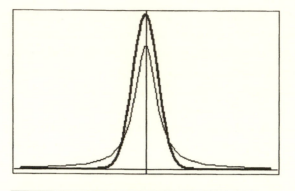

Figure 9.14 Levy-type distribution (Cauchy) vs. normal (thick-lined) distribution

"Noah effect." The long-term memory of black noise which causes aperiodic trends and cycles has been dubbed the Joseph effect (Peters, 1994), after the biblical story of seven fat years followed by seven lean years. Black noise is a more general form of Brownian motion; it can be generated by taking a weighted moving average of a finite range of random normal variates, where the weights are generated by a power law dependent upon α. The higher the value of (, the "smoother" the time series becomes, due to the averaging phenomena. Black noise also has catastrophes (dubbed the Noah effect), in that large, discontinuous changes can occur. Unlike the case of deterministic chaos, these catastrophes are rare, not common.

Statistically, a time series which is black noise will have a statistical distribution whose tails follow an inverse power law, for example, they are distributionally fractal. The overall statistical distribution will tend to be skinny and long-tailed, and follows a "Levy"-type distribution (Bak, 1996). Figure 9.14 shows a Levy distribution versus the standard normal distribution. Comparatively, a Levy distribution is more peaked, and has fat tails; in fact, one of the characteristics of these distributions is that they have no finite variance—hence, standard statistical characterization can be misleading. Mandelbrot first came upon the usefulness of Levy distributions in his analysis of stock market behavior (West & Deering, 1995). A Levy distribution is indicative of a time series which can be modeled as "fractal Brownian motion" (Falconer, 1990). Such a time series shows long-term *persistency* in apparent trends and cycles, and yet these patterns are nonlinear in nature.

The previous examples show how a distributional fractal can arise when a macrolevel event is generated by a single entity, due to a series of complex, interrelated microlevel events. Bak (1996) suggests that distributional fractals can also arise when a macrolevel event is generated by a single microlevel event that, because of coupling, cascades its effect across many interrelated entities. This phenomenon occurs when the system is in a state of *self-organized criticality* (SOC).

A metaphor and/or model often used to explain the behavior of a system at self-organized criticality is a *sandpile*. Imagine a box into which sand is to be poured one granule at a time. As the box is being filled, granules fall into the middle, and randomly push other granules aside until there is a somewhat uniform distribution of granules throughout the box. As additional granules are added, a sandpile begins to form, with a characteristic peak. Eventually that peak reaches a height that remains more or less stable. The sandpile is said to have reached a state of *criticality*.

As additional granules are added, the peak of the sandpile can no longer accommodate them, and "avalanches" occur. Most of these avalanches are small in size, for example, a single granule falls and causes no other movement, or perhaps only causes one or two other granules to move. Sometimes, however, a single granule causes many other granules to move, leading to a visible change in the structure of the sandpile. Even more rarely, a single granule will cause an avalanche of catastrophic proportion. If one plots the frequency of a particular sized avalanche versus the size, on double-logarithmic paper, it will show an inverse linear relationship (i.e., inverse power law).

When these types of "sandpile dynamics" occur, the subsequent time series is called pink noise. Pink noise tends to be *antipersistent* or mean reverting, that is, the time series tends to reverse its direction back toward the mean more often than a purely random system would. Intuitively, using the sandpile metaphor, moderately sized or catastrophic avalanches will tend to follow long periods of little movement, moderately sized or catastrophic avalanches tend not to occur back-to-back. Pink noise systems are so natural that it has been found that most popular music and visual arts display the spectral characteristics of pink noise (Schroeder, 1991; West & Deering, 1995).

Note that an avalanche in the sandpile is triggered when a particular site becomes too high or unstable. Thus, behavior is triggered by the attainment of a state representing a critical threshold; this critical threshold is key to pink noise systems, and the process of triggering is known as a "relaxation process." In general, a relaxation process is one where an agent moves from one discrete state to another (such as don't collapse, collapse; or take no action, take action) as a particular variable reaches a critical threshold value (Schroeder, 1991).

Suppose a two-dimensional grid represents spatial points where a grain of sand could be dropped. The rule modeling the relaxation process is that a particular site in the grid takes no action if it has less than four grains of sand; upon the fourth grain of sand being dropped, the pile at the site collapses and sends a single grain of sand to each of its spatial neighbors. Bak (1996) generalizes this to paperwork in an organization, where upon receiving a fourth "form," the bureaucrat releases a form to each of their neighbors. After a certain transient period, one will observe that for any single grain of sand dropped (this represents energy from the outside), avalanches of various sizes will occur: most small, some moderately sized, and a few of very large size, for example, the number of events triggered will be distributed according to an inverse power law (Bak, 1996).

In order to illustrate this, a one-dimensional example is used. Figure 9.15 shows the simulation of a one-dimensional sandpile grid. The threshold value is 2; when a particular site reaches a height of 2 or more, it sends a grain of sand to its neighbors to the left and right (sites at the end simply dump the extra grain out of the system). The system is started in a random, stable configuration. The first grain of sand falls in site 5, which changes it from a height of 0 to 1. The size of the avalanche is 0. The next grain of sand falls on site 5. This causes it to reach its threshold of 2, after which it sends a grain of sand to its right (and out of the system) and to the left to site 4, changing site 4's height from 0 to 1; the size of the avalanche was 1. Now, the next grain falls on site 4. We can follow the long chain of events that are triggered by the single grain; by the time everything has settled down, an avalanche of size 14 has occured. A further drop on site 4 causes an avalanche of size 4. If we were to look at the distribution of the size of avalanches over a long period of time, it would follow an inverse power law (approximately log-normal shape); if we were to calculate the spectrum of the time series resulting from this experiment, it would show an inverse power law with $0 < \alpha < 2$, implying pink noise.

Peters (1994) uses a different analogy to describe these pink noise systems, one that doesn't depend per se on self-organized criticality. Peters refers to these as "Hurst processes," because they have a significant Hurst exponent (to be discussed in the next section). A Hurst process arises from a system with a randomly time-varying mean: the random process proceeds with mean μ_i between times t_i and t_j, where μ_I, t_i and t_j are random variables. This model still depends on multiple relaxation processes; in essence,

drop site	grid					avalanche size
	0	1	1	0	0	
5	0	1	1	0	1	(0)
5	0	1	1	0	2	
	0	1	1	1	0	(1)
4	0	1	1	2	1	
	0	1	2	1	2	
	0	2	1	2	2	
	1	0	2	2	2	
	1	1	0	3	2	
	1	1	1	1	3	
	1	1	1	2	1	
	1	1	2	0	2	
	1	2	0	1	2	
	2	0	1	1	2	
	0	1	1	1	2	
	0	1	1	2	0	
	0	1	2	0	1	
	0	2	0	1	1	
	1	0	1	1	1	(14)
4	1	0	1	2	1	
	1	0	2	0	2	
	1	1	0	1	2	
	1	1	0	2	0	
	1	1	1	0	1	(4)

Figure 9.15 One-dimensional sandpile simulation

the mean changes whenever one of the parallel processes (or agents) reaches a critical level and changes from one state to another.

In summary, a complex system may demonstrate behavior whereby event sizes and/or magnitudes are distributionally and/or dynamically fractal, and follow an inverse power law. Such behavior emerges because the system's underlying causal mechanism consists of multiple, interdependent causes; and/or because the system has an aggregate behavior which depends on the simultaneous response of parallel relaxation processes. These systems, while random, will show specific patterns in either their distribution and/or power spectrum.

Thus, the first step in time series analysis is to determine if its pattern is behaving periodically, chaotically, or randomly. If the pattern is periodic, an explanation based on linear dynamics can be put forth; if chaotic, an explanation based on deterministic chaos can be put forth. If the system appears random, then further data analysis can show whether an inverse power law may be at work; if so, an explanation based on self-organized criticality can be put forth.

PROPERTIES OF NONLINEAR DYNAMICAL TIME SERIES
Attractors

All dynamical systems can be defined by the nature of their *attractor*. The attractor is defined as the set of states that a dynamical system passes through in its steady-state trajectory. It is called an "attractor" because while the system may start off (have initial conditions) in any number of different states, it is attracted over time to the set of states that is contained in the attractor. A vernacular definition of an attractor is a "recurrent pattern of behavior."

The state of a dynamical system is defined by n variables at time t, $X(t) = (x_1(t), \ldots, x_n(t))$. Geometrically, this is a point in an n-dimensional space called phase space. x_1 to x_n are called the state variables. Systems move in all sorts of directions, execute strange patterns, and sometimes stop. Consider a grandfather clock and its pendulum. The pendulum will come to rest at a stable vertical position when the clock mechanism stops. Such stable equilibrium points are called fixed-point attractors. An attractor is a set of points in phase space that represent the possible states that a system tends to take on over time. For the fixed-point system, the attractor is a single point. A periodic system's attractor consists of some finite number of points, connected in a close-loop. A periodic attractor and fixed-point attractor are much the same, in that both are generated from simple systems involving a few variables interacting in independent fashion.

Attractors play a very important role in dynamical systems. Their configuration can help us figure out whether or not the system is chaotic. The attractor known as a strange attractor is an important indicator of chaos. The term "strange attractor" is attributed to Ruelle and Takens (1971) to distinguish it from the simpler shapes of fixed-point or periodic attractors. Such attractors have complicated geometrical patterns. For example, they are nowhere differentiable and have noninteger or fractal dimensions. They are folded and stretched into all sorts of contortions. The trajectories of strange attractors diverge, and they are sensitive to initial conditions. This is characteristic of strange attractors and of chaos. Strange attractors are not necessarily chaotic. In proving this assertion, Grebogi, Ott, Pelikan, and Yorke (1984) explained that "strange" refers to the geometry of the attractor, while "chaotic" refers to the dynamics of the attractor. It is not unusual that chaotic attractors also happen to be strange.

Geometric evidence of the presence of chaos can be obtained by constructing a phase portrait, wherein one plots the values of several states through time (Schaffer & Kot, 1986). The method of time delay,[4] which is justified by embedding theorems (Takens, 1981; Whitney, 1936), is as follows: For almost every observable time series (say $x(t_i)$, $i = 1, 2, \ldots, N$), and embedding lag T, we can reconstruct the dynamics of the original system by a d-dimensional portrait constructed from the vectors $(x(t_i), x(t_{i-T}) \ldots, x(t_i - (d-1)T))$. Choice of T is critical: if it is too small, the reconstructed dynamics will be dominated by short-term, linear dependencies; if it is too large, all dynamics will be washed away. T is often chosen as the lag where the sample autocorrelation function diminishes to zero (Kaplan & Glass, 1995). Given an embedding lag T and embedding dimension d=3, we construct the following sequence of vectors

$$(x(t_1), x(t_{1-T}), x(t_{1-2T}))$$
$$(x(t_2), x(t_{2-T}), x(t_{2-2T}))$$
$$\vdots$$
$$(x(t_k), x(t_{k-T}), x(t_{k-2T})).$$

Plotting these points in three-dimensional space with connecting line segments, we obtain a phase portrait. Strange attractors theoretically can always be faithfully reconstructed using the above procedure, but the attractor will only appear to the eye if its dimensionality is relatively low. For example, the return map shown for the logistic equation (k=4) in Figure 9.4 depicts a dimension of about 1.60. A method about how to choose the time delay T and the embedding dimension d in order to obtain an optimal reconstruction of the strange attractor of a chaotic system from the time series of a single variable has been proposed (Schuster, 1989).

Lyapunov Exponent

A characteristic property of a chaotic system is that initial values of a time series that are close together separate exponentially. After N time periods, the

---

4. The idea of this method begins with Poincaré about the turn of the century. A much simpler alternative was suggested by Packard et al. (1980).

separation of two starting points that differ by Δ is $\exp(\Delta\lambda)$, where λ is known as the (first) *Lyapunov exponent* (Hibbert & Wilkinson, 1994, p. 227). As a comparison of Figures 9.10 and 9.11 illustrate, the Lyapunov exponent measures the rate of separation of trajectories with time in a phase portrait; that is, it is a measure of the degree of dependence upon initial conditions. If the system is chaotic, these trajectories are adjacent but have slightly different initial conditions, and over time they separate rapidly, which suggests instability.

A useful analogy for chaos is that of "kneading dough" (Peitgen, Jurgens, & Saupe, 1992). Take two points that are close together on the dough and observe the distance between them as the dough is repeatedly kneaded and folded. At first those two points will diverge exponentially from one another as the dough is stretched. Distant initial conditions may converge as the dough is folded back. The stretching action of a chaotic system represents sensitivity to initial conditions; the folding represents the presence of an attractor. Thus, chaotic systems contain both convergence and divergence. Without divergence, there is no chaos. Without convergence, there is no attractor. The repetitive occurrence of divergence and convergence can be considered a metamodel of chaos—indeed, the example used earlier regarding the logistics equation used constructs that implied divergence (exploration) and convergence (exploitation).

A positive Lyapunov exponent is a first indicator of chaos (Moon, 1987; Wolf, 1986; Wolf, Swift, Swinney, & Vastano, 1985). Wolf et al. (1985) present an algorithm that estimates the Lyapunov exponents from experimental data consisting of discrete measurements of a single time series (algorithms for small data sets have also been developed by Rosenstein, Collins, & DeLuca, 1993). The Lyapunov exponent is calculated as follows:

1. Generate the embedding vectors x_1, x_2, x_3, . . . , x_N where $x_k = (x(t_k), x(t_{k-T}), x(t_{k-2T}), . . . , x(t_{k-(d-1)T}))$, T is the embedding lag and m is the embedding dimension.
2. Locate the nearest neighbor point, y_1, using a Euclidean distance, to the point, x_1. Denote the distance between these two points L(1), $L(1) = |x_1 - y_1|$. Here, y_1 is one of the points of the embedded time series $\{x_k\}$, say $y_1 = x_j$, j not equal to 1.
3. At a later time t_2, the initial length L(1) will have evolved to length L'(2), i.e., $L'(2) = |x_2 - y_2|$, where $z_2 = x_{j+1} = (x(t_{j+1}), x(t_{j+1-T}), . . . , x(t_j + 1 - (m-1)T))$.
4. We now look for a new data point, y_2, that satisfies two criteria reasonably well: its separation, $L(2) = |x_2 - y_2|$, from the evolved reference point, x_2, is small, and the angular separation between the

evolved and replacement elements is small, that is, between the line segment x_2y_2 and x_2z_2. If an adequate replacement point cannot be found, we retain the points that were being used.
5. Repeat steps 3–4 until the data sequence is exhausted. Then compute the first Lyapunov exponent as

$$\lambda = 1/M \sum_{k=1}^{M} \log 2L'(k)/L(k-1) \qquad [9.4]$$

where M is the total number of replacement steps.

If the Lyapunov exponent is nonpositive, slightly separated trajectories converge and the attractor is either fixed point or periodic. If the Lyapunov exponent is positive, nearby trajectories diverge; the attractor is sensitive to initial conditions, and therefore chaotic or random. The magnitude of a positive Lyapunov exponent will also determine the speed of divergence of two paths. For example, if $\lambda = 0.693$, the separation between two paths will double on each iteration.

Correlation Dimension

A second basic numerical measure of chaos is the *correlation dimension*. It is a measure of spatial correlation of scatter points or particles in d-dimensional space. When a time series is chaotic, the geometric shape of the trajectories in the phase plot is known as a strange attractor (illustrated for the logistic map in Figure 9.9) to distinguish it from simpler attractors, such as fixed points (see Figure 9.5) and limit cycles (see Figure 9.7). An attractor is a set of points in the phase space trajectories that represents the possible states that a time series tends to take over time. The correlation dimension indicates the attractor's dimension. We know, for example, that a point has a dimension of zero, a line has a dimension of one, a plane has a dimension of two, and a cube has a dimension of three. At issue here is whether an attractor in a seemingly random time series is of low-dimensional chaos or high to infinite-dimensional randomness.

It was shown in Figure 9.12 that a two-dimensional phase plot of a time series of uniformly distributed random numbers fills the square. If these random numbers are plotted against each other in three-dimensional space, $\{x_t, x_{t-T}, x_{t-2T}\}$, they will fill the cube. If we continue with spaces of higher dimensions, in the limit random numbers are infinite-dimensional. As Jayanthi and Sinha (1998) note, a major difference between a chaotic process and a truly random process is that—while they both appear random to the naked eye and to standard linear-time series methods—the truly random process will have high to infinite dimension, whereas the chaotic process will have low dimension. Brock, Hsieh, and LeBaron state "when we speak of 'low-dimensional chaos,' we usually think of their correlation dimensions to be substantially lower than 10, perhaps 5 or 6" (1991, p. 17). Hence, the identification of chaotic behavior involves testing whether or not a seemingly random process exhibits low-dimensional structure.

Grassberger and Procaccia (1983) developed an effective algorithm for extracting the correlation dimension from a time series of a single variable (say $x(t_i)$, $i=1, 2, \ldots, N$). The algorithm consists of four steps.

1. Embed the time series

$$\mathbf{X_{d,k}} = (x(t_k), x(t_{k-T}), \ldots, x(t_{k-(m-1)T}),$$

    where $\mathbf{X_{d,k}}$ is a point in m-dimensional space, m is the embedding dimension, and T is the embedding lag.
2. Calculate the correlation integral

$$C_d(L) = \frac{1}{N^2} \sum_{\substack{i \neq j}}^{N} H\left(L - \left|x_{d,i} - x_{d,j}\right|\right) \qquad [9.5]$$

    where $|\,.\,|$ defines a Euclidean length of a vector, $H(y)$ is the Heaviside function ($H(y)=1$ if $y \geq 0$ and $H(y)=0$ if $y<0$), and $\mathbf{X_{d,i}} = (x(t_i), x(t_{i-T}), \ldots, x(t_i-(d-1)T))$. Correlation integral measures the fraction of the total number of pairs $(\mathbf{X_{d,i}}, \mathbf{X_{d,j}})$ such that the distance between $X_{d,i}$ and $X_{d,j}$ is no more than L.
3. Plot $\log C_d(L)$ versus $\log(L)$ for a range of L sufficient to cover the maximum separation of any two data points.
4. Calculate the slope, v_d, of the plot of $\log C_d(L)$ versus $\log(L)$ for small values of L, by utilizing the traditional regression model yields,

$$\log C_d(L) = d + v_d \log(L) \qquad [9.6]$$

The v_d is the correlation dimension in embedding dimension d. Generalized least-squares regression is used to fit the above linear models. In fact, the correlation dimension itself is defined by the limit of v_d as d goes to infinity. Several computer programs now exist for calculating the correlation dimension.

The foregoing steps for calculating the correlation dimension are based on the straight-line portion of the log-log plots of the correlation integral, $C_d(L)$, versus L, for each embedding dimension (2 to 10). The slope, v_d, of this selected linear region of each embedding dimension is calculated by fitting a linear regression. Here v_d is the correlation dimension in the embedding dimension d. Difficulty and ambiguity arise when defining the "linear region." Kaplan and Glass (1995) give some rough guidelines; one should be aware, however, that this is a major source of possible error in one's analysis.

If a time series is truly random, the slope, v_d, of $\log C_d(L)$ versus $\log(L)$ will increase indefinitely as d is increased. If the time series is low dimensional (either chaotic or periodic), the slope, v_d, of $\log C_d(L)$ versus $\log(L)$ increases at a rate slower than d (Scheinkman & LeBaron, 1989); the specific value v_d^* where v_d stabilizes is then an estimate of the correlation dimension. Therefore, if convergence does not occur, we accept the null hypothesis that the time series is random. If convergence occurs, we need to run further tests that will control for a type I error or a false alarm. Examples regarding interpretation of the correlation integral plot will be shown later.

DEVELOPMENTAL MODELS AND ETSNDA

The four different dynamical models—periodicity,[5] chaos, colored noise, and white noise—each imply a different type of underlying generative mechanism, and hence, a different process theory. Table 9.1 categorizes the observed dynamical patterns into a 2×2 matrix, where the "cell" is defined by considering the *dimension* of the causal system and the nature of *interaction* between causal factors. Low-dimensional causal systems yield periodic and chaotic dynamics, while high-dimensional causal systems yield white and colored noise dynamics. Periodic and white noise dynamics stem from systems where causal factors act independently, or in a linear fashion, while chaotic and colored noise systems stem from systems where causal factors act interdependently, in a nonlinear fashion. In analyzing a time series, one might find that multiple dynamical signatures are present. For example, an ARMA model that captures 50% of the observed variation in the data ($r^2 = 0.50$) implies that half the variation in the data can be explained by periodic behavior and half by white noise behavior. Therefore, multiple organizational stories may be appropriate for explaining observed behavior.

White noise corresponds to high dimensionality in the observed state

---

5. Note that for the purposes of our model, there is no explicit need to differentiate a periodic pattern (limit cycle attractor) from a stable equilibrium (fixed point attractor). Obviously, periodic and fixed point attractors create different paths and patterns; however, both are generated from low-dimensional causal systems where causal factors behave independently. Thus, the label "periodic" here is meant to cover the case of a fixed point attractor. Theoretically, a fixed point attractor is periodic with a natural frequency of zero (Pandit & Wu, 1983).

Table 9.1 Characteristics of the Causal System and Oberved Dynamics

		DIMENSIONALITY OF CAUSAL SYSTEM	
		LOW DIMENSIONAL	HIGH DIMENSIONAL
Nature of Interaction Between Causal Factors	No interaction, Linear Interaction	Periodic	White noise
	Nonlinear Interaction	Chaotic	Pink Noise

(Peitgen et al., 1992). In an earlier section we showed that dimensionality is related to the geometric complexity of the space required to graph a time series of events. In mathematical terms, dimensionality relates to the number of different independent variables affecting the output of a system (Gell-Mann, 1994). If a time series of data is high dimensional, it implies that many variables are affecting output variation; if data is low dimensional, it implies that few variables are affecting output variation. In fact, the correlation dimension (Grassberger & Procaccia, 1983) of a time series is equal to the number of variables required to completely define the dynamical behavior of the system (Peitgen et al., 1992). Thus, if a time series has a correlation dimension of 5.6, then six variables, coupled together in a set of nonlinear differential (difference) equations, could define the observed dynamics. In practice, current statistical methods for modeling time series data restrict us from being able to determine dimensionality of much more than five or six (Brock et al., 1991). So, in essence, dimensionality is considered low if the actual dimensionality is less than five or six, and high if it is greater than five or six. Theoretically, white noise has infinite dimensionality. White noise also implies that the "many variables" affecting the observed state are doing so in an independent fashion (from the law of errors; see Ruhla, 1992).

If the observed white noise behavior stems from an organizational process, this would imply that the process was under the influence of a wide range of organizational factors. If the observed behavior corresponds to collective action stemming from the human system, this would imply that individuals' behaviors were independent—namely, that people were acting in an uncoordinated, uncontrolled fashion. Furthermore, white noise is path independent; the time series progresses with no memory of past behavior. This implies that the system in question is not using any cognizance of its current state in order to determine future action; or, in the case of a human system, such information is being interpreted uniquely by each individual, leading to independent actions.

Colored noise shares many of the same statistical characteristics as white noise; therefore, it will have a generative model form similar to that described for white noise. Colored noise is high dimensional, so it also implies that a large number of variables are affecting the observed state, or in the case of a human system, that a large number of individuals are contributing to the observed collective action. Unlike white noise, colored noise implies a sort of "constrained randomness," whereby interactions between the factors or individuals constrain the system away from pure white noise (Schroeder, 1991).

These interactions between factors may stem from the presence of feedback loops and/or constraints within the organization. It is important to distinguish, however, that these constraints and/or feedback loops are likely to be local (or micro) rather than global (or macro) in nature; the presence of global feedback and/or constraint would tend to greatly reduce the dimensionality of the system and would therefore not generate pink noise. For example, consider a time series of inventory levels. We might expect that data generated by a Kanban system, which constrains behavior between adjacent (local) workstations, might generate pink noise; while data from a centralized inventory control system, operating on global information, may be more likely to generate data with low dimensionality (e.g., periodic or chaotic). Likewise, consider a time series corresponding to action events in a supply chain. We might expect pink noise to be present if the data corresponded to actions throughout a single chain (where each supplier-customer coupling represented a local constraint), whereas we might expect lower-dimensional behavior if viewing data corresponding to institutional actions by the large and powerful organization doing final assembly.

The discovery of chaos implies low dimensionality in an observed time series, since current methods of detecting chaos do not work effectively with dimensions much above five or six (Brock et al., 1991). Chaos also depends on the necessary although not sufficient condition that nonlinear interactions exist between the factors or variables responsible for driving behavior. How is it possible to obtain low-dimensional behavior in an organizational system that by nature tends to be high dimensional—especially in the context of human behavior, where individuals have free will, unique interpretive schema and behavioral rules, unique goals, and unique access to relevant information? There are two possibilities. First, the observed behavior could correspond to quite a limited portion of the organization. For example, time series data corresponding to the quality level generated by a single machine or workstation may well be low dimensional, behaving in a

Pareto-sense where a few factors influence the observed behavior. Similarly, the observed data may correspond to actions being executed by only one (or a few) individuals within the system.

Second, it is possible that some other type of mechanism is being enacted that reduces the dimensionality of the causal system. In general, if the system in question is large in scope, then dimensionality is being reduced by the presence of global feedback and/or constraints. In the case of an organizational process, this would imply the presence of a global control mechanism. For example, in monitoring financial expenditures within the organization, the discovery of low-dimensional behavior may imply that a centralized budget or an authorization entity tightly controls local expenditures. In the case of actions stemming from a human system, low-dimensional behavior implies a reduction in the freedom and autonomy of individuals—a mechanism that ensures that interpretive schema and behavioral rules are common, and that provides unified access to relevant information. These mechanisms can be thought of as representing either control of individuals and/or cooperation between individuals. Control and cooperation may be managerial, adaptive, institutional, or self-induced.[6]

Interactions between causal factors must be nonlinear in order for chaos to be induced. Because of issues of bounded rationality, it is highly unlikely that the control and/or cooperation alluded to above stems from a planned, "rational" response (March, 1994). Humans tend not to develop organizational controls that are nonlinear in their nature, because they are difficult to design, operate successfully, and understand. In addition, humans typically do not consciously (adaptively) respond in a nonlinear fashion (unless to do so for strategic, competitive reasons)—their reactions tend to be linear in nature, where response is proportional to desired change

---

6. The presence of chaos in observed organizational states is characteristic of an organizational system where, either through control and/or cooperation, independence and autonomy between individuals has been lost. This would appear to be in direct contrast to the common, vernacular use of the word "chaos." Managers and organizational writers commonly use the word chaos to mean "a state of extreme confusion and disorder" (Webster's Revised Unabridged Dictionary, 1913). From a common language standpoint, their use of the word is correct. From a mathematical standpoint, in fact, the opposite is true. Chaos, in its correct mathematical form, implies *a state of high order and lack of confusion.* The high order is produced either through control and/or cooperation, which reduces the system's large number of degrees of freedom to some very small number. This reduction from complexity to simplicity could not occur without control and/or cooperating mechanisms being responsible. There is a lack of confusion in that future action is in large part deterministically generated based on current state (although in reality the individuals within the system may not be cognitively aware that such a deterministic mapping is taking place or what the exact nature of the mapping is).

(March, 1994). Therefore, in a chaotic system, the nature of control and/or adaptation is likely such that it exists beyond the full cognizance of organizational members.

Periodic behavior also arises from systems that are low dimensional, and so the comments made above concerning how a causal system with reduced dimensionality might occur (small scope, or the presence of cooperation and/or control mechanisms) apply. The key difference between periodic and chaotic behavior is that in a periodic system, causal factors interact either not at all, or in a simple linear fashion. While such a system could arise naturally, it is also possible that interactions are linear (or absent) because the system was designed to be so. For example, consider situations where behavior is calendar-driven, such as daily, weekly, monthly, or annual phenomena. The temporal regularity of required organizational action will be mirrored in the observed dynamics of the organization.

One should note that in many nonlinear systems (e.g., the logistic map), it is possible to obtain periodic or chaotic behavior simply by adjusting "order parameters." This implies that from an organizational context, chaos and randomness are not akin; rather, chaos and periodicity can potentially point toward the same generative mechanism. The fact that in a periodic system causal factors interact either not at all, or in a simple linear fashion, has huge implications. Simple interaction patterns among causal factors lead to a lack of sensitivity to small changes (unlike chaos, where there is hypersensitivity), and to some level of predictability in outcome. One should not be "fooled" however by these implications—just because chaotic dynamics and periodic dynamics are far away from each other in terms of "implications" does not mean they are far away from one another in terms of causal theories or implied organizational stories. In fact, the "butterfly effect" metaphor may be useful here: even though the causal mechanisms generating chaotic and periodic behavior may be nearly identical (small difference in initial conditions), this small difference (the nature of interactions between causal factors) leads to huge differences in observed output (the implications of chaos versus periodicity, in terms of predictability and sensitivity).

In terms of the developmental models presented in chapter 3, some general relationships can be hypothesized. In terms of dimensionality, it is likely that a teleological process will be low dimensional, meaning it will be affected by few variables, as the process single-mindedly moves toward its end goal. Evolutionary processes may tend to be high dimensional, as different variables become more or less "important" along the developmental path.

Life cycle and dialectic processes may either be low or high dimensional. For example, the "many voices" contributing to the dialectic may result in high dimensionality; the two-dimensional clash between thesis and antithesis may tend to "mobilize" the many degrees of freedom in the system around these two themes, and thus the system would behave in a low-dimensional manner. In terms of interaction between causal variables, it might be reasonable to assume that (for better or worse) a teleological process would tend to treat causes in an independent manner, simply because it is easier for humans to do so. Dialectical and evolutionary processes are likely to be driven by complex interactions between causal factors, as contingencies drive both the way the world is framed and change process itself. Life cycle models may incorporate both independent and interdependent behavior between causal factors.

Putting these propositions together, we obtain:

- The dynamics associated with a life cycle model may be any one of the four dynamical patterns.
- The dynamics associated with a dialectical model may tend to be either chaotic or colored noise.
- The dynamics associated with a teleological model may tend to be periodic.
- The dynamics associated with an evolutionary model may tend to be colored noise.

For example, ETSRA and ETSNDA results from the CIP study indicate that actions at the beginning of the innovation journey were chaotic, and actions at the ending of the innovation journey were periodic. This would imply that either a life cycle model (which posited phases of development) or a dialectical model (competing dominant designs) would be appropriate for explaining the initial journey. A life cycle or teleological model (desire to launch design into production and market) would be appropriate for explaining the ending portion of the journey.

DATA TRANSFORMATION FOR ETSNDA

The statements made in the last chapter regarding the collection of event data and the transformation of it into quantitative time series for ETSRA also remain true for ETSNDA. Because of the computational complexity of ETSNDA, however, some additional comments are warranted. The CIP study is a good example of two basic problems common to event time series data of organizational change processes: (1) restricted number of data points, and (2) measurement error. These two problems are the "Achilles heel" of many other social scientific studies of dynamic organizational processes.

Restricted Number of Data Points in a Time Series

Typical applications of the diagnostic methods used here have been on very large datasets, having thousands of time series observations. Event time series on organizational change processes often consist of one hundred data points or less. Social processes, such as an organizational change or innovation development, are temporally finite, and we must live with the limits of few data points in this research. The development of CIP lasted 12 years (1977–1989), which is long in comparison with most innovations (Freeman, 1986).

While events in the development of the innovation occurred at different times during these 12 years, most methods for the analysis of time series require that the data be in a fixed temporal interval (e.g., weekly, monthly, or yearly data). As discussed in chapter 8, the procedure for aggregating data into fixed temporal intervals is to count the number of occurrences of a coded event in each time period. The question is what temporal interval should be chosen—week, month, quarter, or year? The answer, of course, is that the temporal interval for aggregating coded events should reflect the substantive change process being studied. For example, the CIP data are monthly counts of the occurrences of action and outcome events. Garud and Van de Ven (1992) indicate that a month was a natural temporal interval for aggregating coded events, given the fact that many activities, meetings, and reporting procedures fit or revolved around a monthly clock.

One might argue that in order to obtain more observations, we should use shorter temporal intervals, such as weekly or daily event frequency counts. However, artificial dependencies are introduced when the temporal interval chosen is shorter than the duration of the substantive behavior being examined. These artificial dependencies may produce spurious evidence of nonlinear dynamics. Hsieh (1991) recommends that researchers increase the sampling interval in order to average out these artificial dependencies. However, at some higher level of temporal aggregation, a finite number of observed events in a time series will produce no evidence of chaos, even if it exists at a less-aggregated level. To obtain more observations, the researcher must look for longer histories of the social process being investigated. Any social process lasts only so long before it stops or shifts into another regime. As one extends a data set further and further back in time, nonstationarity (e.g., an unpredictable regime change) becomes increasingly likely. Thus, as Hsieh discusses, the requirements of long sampling intervals (to avoid artificial dependencies) and short histories (to avoid nonstationarity) impose severe trade-offs in data analysis.

MEASUREMENT ERROR

The existence of measurement error in the data creates a problem because a relatively low level of measurement error is required to empirically distinguish whether a time series is random or chaotic. Specifically, a low signal to noise ratio decreases the likelihood of finding chaos and increases the likelihood of concluding that a time series is random. If chaos is found, then it *must* be at a distinct level from true noise (Ben-Mizrachi & Procaccia, 1984). If chaos is not found, it may be either that it is not there or that it is masked by noise (Koput, 1992). Thus, the presence of measurement error decreases the likelihood of finding evidence of a chaotic pattern in time series data.

NONLINEAR STATISTICAL ANALYSIS OF TIME SERIES PATTERNS

Let us start by summarizing the steps involved in diagnosing the pattern embedded in the observed time series. The techniques dealing with periodic (linear) patterns were discussed in the previous chapter; the techniques dealing with chaotic and random patterns will be discussed throughout the rest of this chapter. Figure 9.16 illustrates the decision tree.

First, summary statistics, a time series plot, and a phase plot are generated for visual inspection. Other diagnostic statistics such as the autocorrelation, partial autocorrelation, and sample power spectrum are found. The modeler determines if an ARMA model is present, or if the data needs to be detrended. If so, a periodic pattern exists. Analysis can continue to seek nonlinear patterns, either by using the residual series or adjusting the series via determination of an embedding lag. If no periodic pattern exists, analysis continues with the raw data. A positive Lyapunov exponent and a saturated correlation dimension indicate possible chaotic dynamics; surrogate testing generates a significance level for the result. If statistically significant, one can conclude a chaotic pattern exists. If not, analysis continues to seek out a distribution and dynamical power law. This further classifies random patterns into colored noise or purely random white noise.

A common starting point in distinguishing between random, chaotic, or periodic patterns in a time series is to construct and visually examine phase

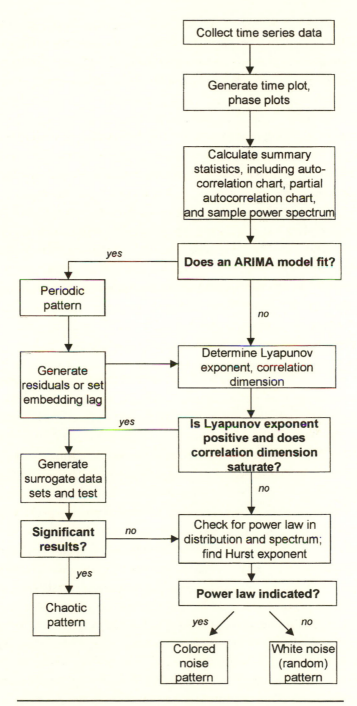

Figure 9.16 Methodology for pattern diagnosis

plots from the time series by the method of time-delay. The resulting geometric pattern is then compared with the patterns produced by systems with known properties, such as the fixed, periodic, and chaotic patterns of the quadratic maps in Figures 9.5, 9.7, and 9.9, or a uniform cloud of points in a phase portrait of a random series as in Figure 9.12. Such visual inspections of phase portraits are useful for distinguishing geometric patterns in time series data with numerous (thousands) of data points. Brock, Hsieh, and LeBaron (1991) point out that geometrical patterns are often difficult, if not impossible, to visualize when they are based on time series data with measurement error and with relatively few (less than one hundred) data points, as is typical of event time series data on organizational change processes. As a result, we must often rely on numerical measures that can detect patterns in noisy and short time series in ways that are more robust than our visual imaginations of geometrical shapes in phase portraits.

We have discussed two numerical diagnostics that are useful for triangulating on periodic, chaotic, and random patterns in time series data—the Lyapunov exponent, indicating sensitivity to initial conditions, and the correlation dimension, measuring the presence of a strange attractor in a low-dimensional phase space. Before applying these diagnostics, we must deal with any linear dependencies in the event time series data. Linear dependence in the raw time series data may positively bias finding a chaotic pattern in a time series with relatively few data points. As Morrison (1991) discusses, autocorrelated randomness can look a lot like chaos. Therefore, we must remove any linear dependence, such as autocorrelation, from the raw event time series before performing any of the three diagnostics. There are two approaches used. The common approach in econometrics is to filter the raw data using an autoregressive, integrated moving-average model (ARIMA). Brock and colleagues describe a variety of autoregressive models that are customarily considered to remove linear dependencies from a time series (1991, p. 133). The residuals (instead of the raw data) from the filtered time series are then used for the diagnostics described below. A concern with this approach is such filtering itself can actually produce artificial dynamics (Theiler & Eubank, 1993). A second approach is to identify the proper "embedding lag" and adjust accordingly. This is usually taken as the lag where the sample autocorrelation function diminishes to zero (Kaplan & Glass, 1995). By adjusting the embedding vector by the appropriate embedding lag, one effectively "jumps over" the linearly dependent portion of the time series. Our recommendation is to use both approaches as both may yield useful results.

SURROGATE TESTING

The presence of a positive Lyapunov exponent and a finite correlation dimension have historically been taken as indicative of chaos. However, there is no control over type I error, which has increased the likelihood of researchers to discover "chaotic" patterns. To control for type I error, Cheng and Van de Ven (1996) used the BDS statistic (Brock et al., 1991), which is one common way to test the formal null hypothesis of a random time series. However, the BDS statistic has fallen out of favor; the method of surrogate testing proposed by Theiler, Eubank, Longtin, Galdrikian, and Farmer (1992) is emerging as the preferred approach (to the BDS statistic) for controlling type I errors. Surrogate testing is preferred over the BDS statistic because the method of surrogate testing is more powerful and does not rely on distributional assumptions (i.e., it is nonparametric, which makes it more robust across a diversity of situations).

The basic premise of surrogate testing is that one develops a number of additional time series, each one with similar properties as compared to the original, and then compares the correlation dimension (or some other statistic of interest) of these additional surrogate time series to the correlation dimension of the original time series. The properties that one chooses to select to equate the original and surrogate time series define the null hypothesis that will be tested.

In order to test the null hypothesis that the time series is random, one develops surrogates by taking the original time series and completely (randomly) shuffling the sequence of the data. In this way the surrogates will have the same statistical (distributional) characteristics as the original time series, but all dynamics will be "erased" by the shuffling (in fact, this is often called the "shuffle test"; see Theiler et al., 1992). Suppose one has developed 20 shuffled time series and only one had lower estimated correlation dimension than the original time series. The (nonparametric) level of statistical significance of our results would then be $1/20$, or $p=0.05$. Thus, the null hypothesis of randomness could be rejected at a 95% confidence level.

Even though linear dependencies in the time series were addressed by either selection of an appropriate embedding lag or ARIMA filtering, they still may be the "cause" of a low correlation dimension. In order to test the null hypothesis that the data are linear periodic, we need to develop surrogate time series which are not only identical distributionally, but also in terms of their linear dynamics. This is accomplished through phase randomization (Kaplan & Glass, 1995). The sample spectrum of the original time series is actually composed of a magnitude and phase estimate at each frequency. If one maintains magnitude but randomizes phase, one will essentially develop a time series that has similar linear dynamics to the original but dissimilar nonlinear dynamics. Kaplan and Glass (1995) define a method to develop phase randomized surrogates.

Even if the null hypothesis of linear periodicity can be rejected by phase randomized surrogates, one must use caution in interpreting the results as "chaotic." Other behavior may induce the "look of chaos," including non-stationarity, non-Gaussian inputs, nonlinearity in the measurement process, and nonlinearities that do not involve chaos (Kaplan & Glass, 1995). If the time series under investigation is judged to reflect a chaotic pattern, then analysis stops and a search for a substantive explanation of the process can begin using the nonlinear dynamical system.

TESTS FOR COLORED NOISE

If the time series is determined to be random, three additional diagnostics can be performed on event time series data in order to test whether the noise is purely random (white noise), persistent and mean drifting (brown and black noise), or antipersistent and mean reverting (pink noise): (1) plot the logged data to determine if it is distributionally fractal, (2) calculate the power spectrum, and (3) calculate the Hurst exponent. These diagnostics are conducted as follows.

First, as discussed in the introductory section on the self-organized critical state of colored noise, an event sequence time series will be log-normally distributed if the system is distributionally fractal. This can be visually confirmed via a histogram of the data. The data used in this analysis are the same as that used to test for periodicity or chaos. One can also take the logarithm of the raw data and plot the transformed data on normal probability paper. Normal probability paper is scaled so that when the data are plotted as rank versus cumulative percentage, normally distributed data will plot as a straight line. Therefore, log-normal data, after being logged, should also plot out as a straight line.

Second, if the system is dynamically fractal, then it should have a power spectrum whose magnitude decreases as a function of $1/f^\alpha$. Chapter 8 described how to interpret the sample power spectrum. When looking at periodic systems, we look for characteristic peaks in the spectrum to indicate dominant frequencies. A random time series, however, will not shown such characteristic peaks. Rather, it will show a tendency either to be flat or to have a negative slope. If one estimates the slope by the estimate $-\alpha$ (simple linear regression techniques can be used), then the estimated value of α will define the type of "colored noise" the system is generating (Peters, 1994):

if $\alpha = 0$, then it is white noise (random)

if $0 < \alpha < 2$, then it is pink noise (self-organized criticality; antipersistent)

if $\alpha = 2$, then it is brown noise (random walk)

if $2 < \alpha < 4$, then it is black noise (persistent systems which are known to collapse spontaneously).

Finally, calculating the Hurst exponent provides a third diagnostic of colored noise. The Hurst exponent (H) can be thought of as a measure of autocorrelation; it can measure, however, nonlinear and long-term "persistence," unlike the sample autocorrelation function that only measures linear dependencies. Black noise is related to long-term memory effects (H < 0.50), while pink noise is related to antipersistence (H < 0.50). An H-value of 0.50 corresponds to Brownian motion. For values of α between 1 and 2, there is a direct correspondence between H and α: $\alpha = 2H + 1$. Note that since both the power spectrum and the Hurst exponent can both be used to yield an estimate of α, the two estimates should give roughly the same results (e.g., within 10% of one another). This duality is just another way in which the analyst can remain objective and double-check one's work.

The Hurst exponent essentially derives from the fact that the range of a dataset will increase by the square root of its size, if the data set represents Brownian motion (Peters, 1994). This power-law relationship stills holds for non-Brownian motion (but yet still colored noise) sequences, although the exponent is no longer 0.5. A "rescaled" range (dividing the range by the standard deviation) normalizes the statistic appropriately. Peters (1994) gives equations for calculating the Hurst exponent:

1. Break the time series up into equally sized subseries. Start with a subseries size (M) of 10 (subseries of shorter length do not yield reliable information about the range of the data, in general), and increment M until the time series is broken up into two equal halves. For example, a time series of length 100 (n=100) would first be broken into 10 subseries of length 10, then 9 subseries of length 11, 8 subseries of length 12, etc., up to two subseries of length 50.
2. For each value of subseries of size M, and for each subseries, calculate the range and sample standard deviation of the subseries.
3. For each subseries of size M, calculate the rescaled range $(R/S)_M$ as the average of the sample ratios between the sample range and stan-

dard deviation in each subseries. For example, if the time series had been broken into 3 equal subseries of size M=50, and the range for each subseries was {40.2, 50.1, 45.8}, and the standard deviation for each subseries was {22.0, 15.6, 18.5}, then the rescaled ranges would be {40.2/22.0, 50.1/15.6, 45.8/18.5}, or {1.83, 3.21, 2.48}, and $(R/S)_{50}$ would be equal to the average of those 3, or 2.51.

4. Perform ordinary least squares regression between log(M) and log $(R/S)_M$ (the log-log analysis is necessary because the relationship in its raw form is a power law); the slope of the equation estimates the Hurst exponent H.

In summary, if the time series is determined to be random by rejecting hypotheses of peridocity and chaos, then the data has arisen from a system at self-organized criticality (i.e., pink noise) when the following conditions are met: (a) the logged data plots as a straight line on normal probability paper, (b) the power spectrum follows a $1/f^\alpha$ relationship, where $0 < \alpha < 2$, and (c) the Hurst exponent is between 0 and 0.50.

EXAMPLE ANALYSIS OF CIP DATA

We will now provide an example of the application of the methods for diagnosing chaos and self-organizing criticality using the CIP event sequence time series data. The example will illustrate what kinds of results might be obtained when applying the diagnostic tests to an event sequence file, suggest some ways to present results in tables for research reports, and provide some conventions for reading and interpreting the diagnostic results.

The example expands upon the initial analysis by Cheng and Van de Ven (1996), which was undertaken to determine if the developmental process of two biomedical innovations followed either (a) an orderly periodic progression of stages or phases, (b) a random sequence of chance "blind" events, or (c) a seemingly random process of chaotic events. To illustrate the application of the diagnostic methods, we will focus on only one of the biomedical innovations that Cheng and Van de Ven considered, the cochlear implant innovation. The data consisted of three event sequence time series dealing with the monthly number of continuing or changing courses of action undertaken by the CIP innovation unit, the positive or negative outcomes they experienced, and environmental context events that occurred during the innovation development process. Recall that the developmental period of the cochlear implant program (CIP) innovation lasted 106 months (1978–1986), of which 59 months occurred in the beginning premarket development period (beginning), and 47 occurred in the ending

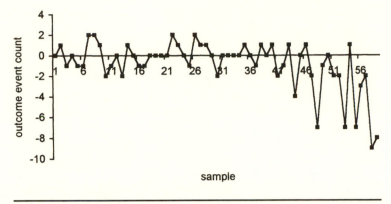

Figure 9.17 Beginning outcomes time series—time plot

market-entry period (ending). Subsequent analysis will divide the overall time series into two segments, as was done in chapter 8. Figures 8.18 and 8.22 showed the monthly event counts for beginning and ending actions. To complete the picture, Figures 9.17–9.20 show the monthly event counts for outcomes and context for beginning and ending periods.

PHASE PLOT RESULTS

Following the method of time delay, three-dimensional phase plots are constructed on the residuals for action, outcome, and context events for the beginning and ending development periods of the CIP innovation. Figures 9.21 and 9.22 show the phase plots for the actions in CIP.

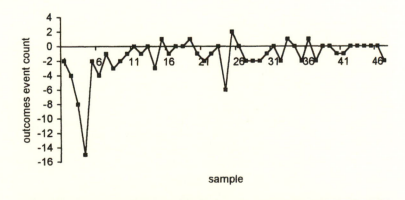

Figure 9.18 Ending outcomes time series—time plot

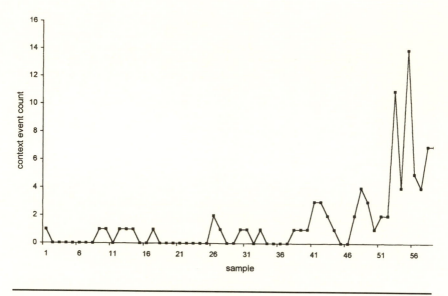

Figure 9.19 Beginning context time series—time plot

Since the number of data points in the time series is relatively small and possibly masked by measurement error, the interpretation of the phase portraits requires a great deal of visual imagination. However, it is worthwhile articulating this visual imagination so that the reader knows what we are looking for in the geometric shapes of the phase portraits.

During the beginning period of development, the attractor for actions in Figure 9.21 shows a light pattern of stretching and folding, and the center of the overall state-phases appear to resemble a self-similar structure that is triangular in shape. In the ending period of CIP's development, Figure 9.22

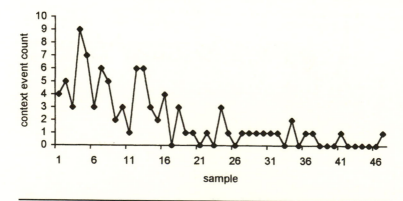

Figure 9.20 Ending context time series—time plot

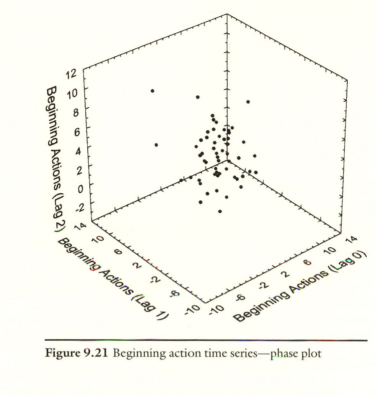

Figure 9.21 Beginning action time series—phase plot

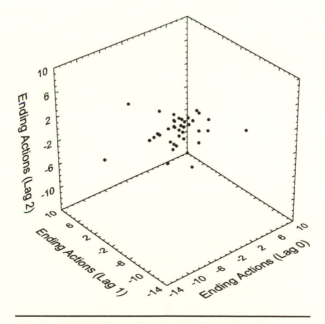

Figure 9.22 Ending action time series—phase plot

shows the appearance of an attractor for actions consisting of some finite number of points connected in closed loops. Both attractors imply a periodic system. These interpretations of the phase portraits admittedly require too much visual imagination to warrant publication. The geometric patterns of random, chaotic, or periodic behavior are not clear cut because the time series data are noisy and have few data points. As a result, we must rely on numerical measures to distinguish the noise more reliably than our intuitive vision.

LYAPUNOV EXPONENT RESULTS

Table 9.2 shows the calculated Lyapunov exponents for the actions event time series. Because prior research found qualitatively different patterns in the beginning and ending periods of CIP's development, each coded event time series was divided into two segments, beginning and ending developmental periods, and separate Lyapunov exponents were calculated for each segment. Two approaches for treating the data are shown in Table 9.2. As discussed in chapter 8, there are two ways to account for linear dependencies in time series data: (a) via selection of an appropriate embedding lag for Lyapunov exponents that are calculated on the original time series data, shown in the first two rows of Table 9.2, or (b) by calculating the Lyapunov exponents on the residuals of filtered time series data. The residuals were calculated using both ARIMA models and Granger causality models and are shown in the bottom two rows of Table 9.2. The Chaos Data Analyzer program (Sprott & Rowlands, 1995) was used to estimate the values given in the table.

If the Lyapunov exponent is positive, it indicates the time series could be either chaotic or random; if the Lyapunov exponent is negative or zero, it indicates the time series is periodic (linear). The exponent is calculated across different values for the embedding dimension (m) in order to see

Table 9.2   Lyapunov Exponents for CIP Actions Data

	EMBEDDING DIMENSION (M)			
TIME SERIES	3	4	5	6
Actions-Beginning	0.04	0.03	0.02	0.02
Actions-End	−0.04	0.01	0.03	−0.01
Actions-ARIMA Residuals-End	−0.01	0.06	0.04	0.00
Actions-Granger Residuals-End	−0.01	−0.04	−0.01	0.00

how stable the estimate is across different dimensional spaces. If results are not consistent across different embedding dimensions, the time series is typically diagnosed as random. The embedding lag T is chosen as the lag at which the sample autocorrelation function first approaches zero or becomes negative. For actions-beginning, T was chosen as 2 since the sample auto-correlation at lag 2 was negative (and the value at lag 1 was not; see Figure 8.19); for actions-ending, T was chosen as 1 since the sample autocorrelation at lag 1 was negative. For the Granger and ARIMA residuals, T was chosen as 1 since the residual series should be uncorrelated.

The time series corresponding to actions-beginning has a positive Lyapunov exponent across embedding dimensions 3 to 6, indicating the time series is either random (white or other colored noise) or chaotic. The other three time series have inconsistent results across different embedding dimensions, and thus should be considered random.

Note that the time series corresponding to actions-ending was previously found to be periodic (see chapter 8), and yet the Lyapunov exponent for the time series was not consistently negative, as would be expected for a periodic time series. Unfortunately, this shows the lack of consistency that is exhibited by the Lyapunov exponent, and is one of the key reasons why we use surrogate testing (see subsequent section) to ensure that our diagnostic results have some validity.

CORRELATION DIMENSION RESULTS

Rosenstein et al.'s (1993) version of the Grassberger and Procaccia (1983) algorithm was used. Table 9.3 shows the results of the estimated correlation dimension, v_d, for each embedding dimension (3 to 7), for the same four time series analyzed previously. The embedding lag T, chosen in the same manner as discussed above, is shown in the second column.

The correlation dimension estimate represents the (fractal) dimension of the time series' attractor as it is plotted into higher and higher dimensional space (larger values of m, the embedding dimension). As shown in Figure 9.12, a random system will display no visual pattern as it is plotted into higher and higher dimensional space—it simply fills the space into which it is plotted. Thus, for a random time series, the correlation dimension of the attractor at different values of the embedding dimension will be slightly less than or equal to the dimension of the embedding space. A perfectly random time series would have a correlation dimension exactly equal to the embedding dimension.

Conversely, a low-dimensional periodic system, or a chaotic system, will

Table 9.3   Correlation Dimensions for CIP Data

TIME SERIES	EMBEDDING LAG (T)	EMBEDDING DIMENSION m = 3	m = 4	m = 5	m = 6	m = 7
Actions-Beginning	2	2.65	3.42	3.83	3.93	4.05
Actions-End	1	2.96	3.22	4.71	5.29	7.00
Actions-ARIMA Residuals-End	1	2.12	2.84	3.86	6.00	7.00
Actions-Granger Residuals-End	1	3.06	4.00	5.00	6.00	7.00

yield a time series whose attractor has a dimension that is finite. If the time series is embedded in a dimension less than its true dimension, it will appear random and thus have a correlation dimension that is near the embedding dimension. If the time series is embedded in a dimension equal to or greater than its true dimension, it will have a correlation dimension that is near or equal to its true dimensionality. Thus, a system with a dimension 4.5 would have a correlation dimension of 3 and 4 when plotted in an embedding dimension of 3 and 4, respectively; and it would have a correlation dimension of 4.5 when plotted in an embedding dimension of 5 or greater.

The embedding dimension is varied from 3 to 7. From experience, time series will rarely have a correlation dimension less than 3; also from experience, a low-dimensional, chaotic time series will have a correlation dimension of less than 7, and thus correlation dimension estimates should stabilize by that point. Systems with correlation dimensions much above 6 or 7 are typically best treated as simply random.

It is easy to see that the only dimensional estimates which appear "bounded" are the ones for action-beginning time series; as values appear to stabilize around 4, we could tentatively conclude that this time series (coupled with the results showing it to have a positive Lyapunov exponent) is chaotic with a dimension 4. All the other series must be taken as either random or periodic.

SURROGATE TESTING RESULTS

The validity of concluding that actions at the beginning of the CIP project were chaotic needs to be checked via surrogate testing. A total of 10 phase randomized surrogates sets were generated—this means that a sample of $n = 10$ is available to calculate a nonparametric level of statistical significance. The null hypothesis being tested by phase randomized surrogates is that the time series is linear (periodic). Rejection of the null hypothesis allows one to claim that the time series is nonlinear (although not necessarily chaotic).

The results for correlation estimates are shown in Table 9.4. The bottom row shows the results for the actual data set, as reported in Table 9.3. Phase-randomized surrogates were created using the program by Rosenstein et al. (1993). A phase-randomized surrogate time series has a length, distribution, and linear dynamical structure that is equivalent to the original time series. The only thing altered between the original and surrogate is the nonlinear structure of the data. Thus, if a time series has a low correlation dimension because it is periodic in nature, then the surrogates will also have a low correlation dimension, because linear structure between the original and surrogate time series is unaltered. If, however, the time series has low correlation dimension because of nonlinear (and potentially chaotic) dynamics, then the surrogate time series will have high correlation dimension, since the phase randomization hides the low-dimensional, nonlinear structure.

The embedding lag used for the original time series ($T=2$) is also used for the surrogates. As one can see, only one of the surrogates (#4) has a lower correlation dimension (3.98) than the original time series (4.05). Since one of the 10 surrogates displays a lower correlation dimension than the original, a significance value of $p=1/10=0.10$ is achieved. This leads us to conclude that the action event time series during the beginning period

Table 9.4 Correlation Dimension Estimates for Surrogate Tests, Actions-Beginning

SURROGATE	m = 3	m = 4	m = 5	m = 6	m = 7
1	1.61	2.36	3.69	4.84	6.12
2	2.54	3.18	4.30	4.61	5.07
3	2.16	3.30	4.28	6.18	5.67
4	2.05	2.86	3.26	3.44	3.98
5	1.66	2.36	3.08	3.87	4.72
6	1.52	2.45	3.18	4.00	5.80
7	1.48	2.26	3.13	4.34	5.69
8	2.88	3.39	4.03	4.93	5.24
9	2.69	3.92	4.05	4.90	5.27
10	2.90	3.95	4.94	4.79	7.45
Actual Data Set	**2.65**	**3.42**	**3.83**	**3.93**	**4.05**

of CIP's development is nonlinear, with a significance level of p=0.10. Note that if none of the surrogates had a lower correlation dimension, then our conclusion would be that the significance level p was less than 0.10; we would have to run more surrogates to estimate it with more precision.

Thus far, we have presented the results of three basic diagnostics for determining if event time series in our CIP example reflect random, chaotic, or periodic patterns: (1) the Lyapunov exponent indicating sensitivity to initial conditions, (2) the correlation dimension measuring the presence of a strange attractor in a low-dimensional phase space, and (3) surrogate testing to determine the level of statistical significance in (1) and (2). No single diagnostic test provides conclusive evidence of a temporal pattern when the tests are conducted on event time series with relatively few (a hundred) data points. Most previous applications of these tests have been on time series with thousands of observations. Given the reality that most organizational change processes consist of relatively short time series, we caution against relying on only one diagnostic test. Instead, we recommend that researchers use several different diagnostics to triangulate on the empirical pattern in event time series. This reduces the likelihood that false conclusions are drawn when all diagnostic tests converge to produce the same conclusion.

One useful way to gather the evidence from numerous diagnostic tests is to combine the test results in a single table. Table 9.5, for example, summarizes the results of various tests on the CIP example, and combines them with the model-fitting procedures discussed in chapter 8. For purposes of illustration all relevant time series are shown. Based on the preponderance of the evidence from numerous tests, one can draw substantiated research conclusions. For example, from the results summarized in Table 9.5 we

Table 9.5   Summary of Diagnostic Tests

TIME SERIES	LYAPUNOV EXPONENT > 0?	CORRELATION DIMENSION SATURATE?	SURROGATE TESTING SHOWS $p < 0.20$?	WHAT WAS BEST FIT ARIMA MODEL?	FINAL DIAGNOSIS
Actions-Beginning	yes	yes	yes	none	chaotic
Actions-End	no	no		AR(8)	linear periodic
Outcomes-Beginning	yes	no		none	random
Outcomes-End	no	no		none	random
Context-Beginning	yes	no		none	random
Context-End	no	no		none	random

conclude that the actions taken by entrepreneurs during the CIP innovation journey began in chaos and ended in periodic order, while outcomes and exogenous context events occurred randomly during both beginning and ending periods of CIP's development.

Providing explanations of such conclusions, of course, requires disciplined knowledge of the data and other studies. For example, one could rely on measurement procedures to explain that contextual events were found to be random because they capture the host of uncontrollable exogenous influences that influence innovation development; it would be extremely surprising to find them anything but random.

The fact that outcome event time series were also found to be random throughout CIP's development presents a more challenging explanation, because they appear contrary to findings in chapter 8 and contradict findings reported by Cheng and Van de Ven (1996). The modeling results in chapter 8 found actions and outcomes to be coupled during the ending development period. It may therefore seem surprising that outcomes during CIP's ending period were not periodic. To find that outcome events are related to actions does not exclude the possibility that outcomes are influenced by many other factors. The test results in this chapter motivate a reexamination of the sample autocorrelation function for outcomes-ending. While the values indicate that outcomes are weakly periodic, the strength of the periodicity is too weak to be seen clearly over the noise. These results suggest that a more tentative and qualified conclusion should be taken about the outcome event sequence.

Such a tentative conclusion is supported by the contradictory findings reported by Cheng and Van de Ven (1996). Using the same algorithms (Wolf's for the Lyapunov exponent, and Grassberger and Procaccia's for the correlation dimension) as used here, they found the outcome event time series to be chaotic in the beginning period and periodic during the ending developmental period; our analysis here indicates that both time series are random. The difference in findings can be traced to differences in methodology. The data analysis in Cheng and Van de Ven (a) did not identify the most appropriate linear (ARIMA) model, and so linearities were still present in the data, and (b) an embedding lag of $T=1$ was used throughout the analysis (an embedding lag of $T=2$ or $T=3$ would have been more appropriate), once again potentially highlighting rather than removing the effect of linear dynamics in the data.

Finally, all the diagnostic tests reported here and in Cheng and Van de Ven corroborate the finding that CIP's actions were chaotic in the beginning and periodic during the ending periods of development. How might these consistent findings be explained? Consider the periodic behavior first. The context of this behavior is that actions were primarily confined to a single decision-making team, unlike earlier in the process. The sample spectrum indicated the cyclical period was just over two months. This means that expanding events dominated in one month and contracting events dominated in the next, and this oscillation was regular. In addition, actions and outcomes were strongly positively correlated during the ending period. This alternating pattern of expanding and contracting actions, which was influenced by outcomes, indicates a process of trial-and-error learning was occurring.

The chaotic behavior of actions in the beginning of CIP's development is more intriguing. Because actions are completely under the control of the "actors" in the system, it is not surprising to find that such a sequence of actions would be low dimensional—the bounded rationality of decision makers would necessarily reduce the "degrees of freedom" inherent in any action path. Low dimensionality does not imply chaos alone, however. A chaotic series of actions indicates a complex search strategy—such a strategy, alternating in complex ways between exploration (divergence) and exploitation (convergence), would be optimal if the "landscape" being searched is complex. Complex landscapes have many local optima, and only a chaotic or random search strategy (such as via simulated annealing or genetic mutation) will avoid entrainment to a suboptimal answer (in this case, the "answer" is a conceptual design for cochlear implants). Thus, at the construct level, a chaotic action series provides a novel way for understanding organizational learning processes.

In order to empirically ground and further explore the plausibility of this kind of explanation, we can rely on another set of diagnostic tests of the *action* event time series to determine if it provides evidence of a process of self-organizing criticality (Bak, Tang, & Wiesenfeld, 1988).

Colored Noise Results

If the time series is determined to be random, then three different diagnostics can be applied to determine if the time series is purely random (white noise), or whether there are long-term persistencies (black and brown noise) or antipersistencies (pink noise): (1) plot the logged data to determine if it is distributionally fractal, (2) calculate the power spectrum, and (3) calculate the Hurst exponent.

In order to demonstrate that different operational definitions can lead to different diagnoses, recall how the monthly count is derived for actions: the value of the time series in any given month is the number of expansion and/or continuation actions in that month, minus the number of contractions and/or change actions in that month. Using such an operational definition, we found that the actions-beginning time series was chaotic, and the action-ending time series was periodic. Let us alter the operational definition and instead calculate the value of the time series in any given month as the number of expansion and/or continuation actions in that month, *plus* the number of contractions and/or change actions in that month. Thus, the time series now represents not the collective direction of actions in a given month, but rather the level of activity. The two new time series shall be called actions-total-beginning and actions-total-ending.

ARIMA and chaos-based data analysis on actions-total-beginning and actions-total-ending time series indicates a random time series: the switch from a minus to a plus sign changes the nature of the dynamics observed! This is not disturbing, however, since the two different numbers really correspond to two different concepts. For illustrative purposes, we shall present the subsequent colored noise test results performed on the actions-total-beginning time series.

The first diagnostic test is to plot the event time series data on log paper to determine if it is distributionally fractal. Before doing this, we prepared a simple histogram of the total number of action events undertaken by the CIP innovation unit during the beginning period of CIP development. The x-axis shows the number of total *action* events in a given month, and the y-axis shows the frequency with which that many events is observed. The histogram (Figure 9.23) shows that the total number of actions taken in any given month reflects a log-normal distribution—it is single peaked, skewed to the right.

Next, the data were logged and plotted on a normal probability plot, as shown in Figure 9.24. The figure shows (rank-ordered) frequency counts of the log number of action events on the x-axis, the y-axis shows the cumulative probability (scaled linearly for normally distributed data), and the diagonal line shows the expected probability of action event frequencies if they are normally distributed. This figure illustrates that the logged CIP action-total events are approximately normal. If logged-data are normal, then the unlogged-data can be taken as log-normal. As discussed previously, log-normal data tends to arise in systems where an event takes place due to a sequence of multiple, interdependent causes. Thus, we can conclude that actions taken during the initial development of CIP arose from a system of

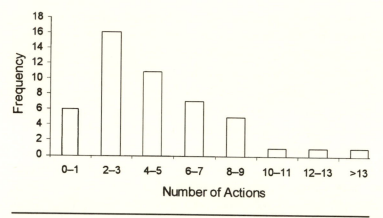

Figure 9.23 Histogram of total number of actions in beginning of CIP

multiple, interdependent causes—beginning actions are distributionally fractal.

The second diagnostic test for colored noise is to calculate the power spectrum of the time series. This is done by methods described in chapter 8. Figure 9.25 shows the power spectrum of the action-total-beginning time series (on a log-log scale). The figure is the same as described in chapter 8, only each axis has been plotted in a logarithmic scale. The downward

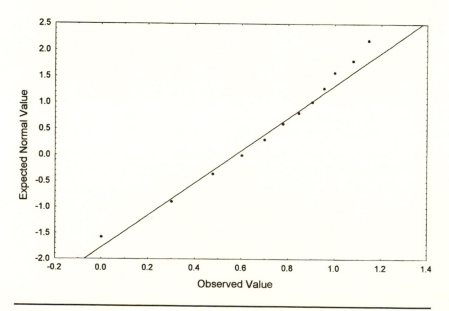

Figure 9.24 Normal probability plot of (logged) actions in beginning of CIP

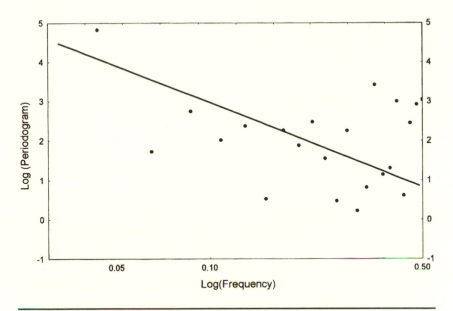

Figure 9.25 Power spectrum (log-log) of actions in beginning of CIP

sloping diagonal line in the figure shows the plot of an inverse power law, and the dots plot the log-log of CIP action events along this power curve.

The conclusion we draw from Figure 9.25 is that the action-total events time series during CIP's initial development period is dynamically fractal, as indicated by its power spectrum following a $1/f^{\alpha}$ inverse power law. The value of (, and/or the Hurst exponent H, can be used to classify the type of colored noise which is present (see Table 9.6). Simple regression (using standard least squares) between the logged frequency and logged peri-odogram values were used to estimate the (negatively valued) slope of the line, and $\alpha = 1.15$ was obtained, which corresponds to the regime of pink noise.

Table 9.6 Diagnosis of Colored Noise

TYPE OF COLORED NOISE	α	H
white	0	0
pink	0–2	0–0.5
brown	2	0.5
black	2–4	0.5–1.0

Since the Hurst exponent H and power law exponent α are related by $\alpha = 2H + 1$, a value of H can be back calculated as 0.075. As a final check, the actual Hurst exponent was estimated using the rescaled-range algorithm (Peters, 1994) as implemented in the Chaos Data Analyzer program (Sprott & Rowlands, 1995), and a value of H=0.16 was obtained. Since this calculated value of H also corresponds to a diagnosis of pink noise, it is reasonable to conclude that we have confirmation of the pink noise hypothesis.

The results of the diagnostic tests of self-organized criticality can now be discussed as they apply to the CIP innovation example. The significance of being able to confirm that the behavior found in actions is due to pink noise is that it allows one to postulate a model of behavior concerning how such dynamics arise. For example, we might posit two explanations. The first explanation is based on the randomly time-varying mean discussed in the introduction that does not depend on the concept of self-organized criticality. The second explanation is based on the "sandpile" analogy that does depend on self-organized criticality. The commonality between the two models rests on two points. First, they both assume that the system is composed of multiple innovators whose actions and outcomes are being monitored. Second, they both assume that the innovators are loosely coupled so that one innovator's actions and outcomes may trigger another to take actions that influence subsequent outcomes.

Participants in an innovation venture may undertake actions in a random fashion at any given time; however, they are biased toward either expanding or contracting their actions, depending on what the "prevailing winds" are. At a random time, some information comes along (outcome, context, or otherwise) that changes the perceptions of the innovators and their proclivity to alter their behavior patterns, for example, if they were generally taking expanding actions, they switch to contracting actions, and vice versa. Such a random process, where values are biased in one direction or another and then change bias at randomly distributed intervals of time, will give rise to pink noise.

Assume that each innovator decides to take action when a certain critical threshold of information is reached; such a threshold model of decision making has strong support in psychological theory (e.g., Kiesler & Sproull, 1982). These thresholds can be different for each innovator. Further assume that information comes from two places: external to the innovation network (context), and internal to the innovation network (outcomes and other innovators' actions). These randomly arising pieces of information would usually trigger no action, but sometimes an individual innovator's threshold would be met and an action would occur. Such an action may or may not cause another innovator's threshold to be met, and ad infinitum. In cases when the amount of information triggered action, it would usually involve a moderate amount of activity, but occasionally a piece of information would cause a tremendous number of actions (e.g., FDA's statement that the single-channel device was not the most attractive technology). The latter cases represent the avalanches in the sandpile model. The subsequent aggregate behavior of the system will be pink noise, and hence as observed, the potential for chaotic dynamics. The decision-making thresholds serve as relaxation processes, where an innovator moves from one state to another (no action, action) after a random interval of time. The multiplicity of innovators, and their corresponding coupling, led to parallel relaxation processes and thus the pink noise behavior.

CONCLUSION

It is evident that an elaborate process is involved when applying these diagnostics to make empirical distinctions between random, chaotic, or stable patterns in time series with relatively few data points. Most previous applications of the diagnostics used here have been on very large data sets, often having thousands of time series observations. The event time series in our applications consist of less than a hundred data points. Ramsey and Yuan (1989) examine the bias and error bars associated with correlation dimension estimation (Grassberger and Procaccia's algorithm) and show that the slope of the graph of $\log C_d(L)$ versus $\log(L)$ is biased downward in small data sets. In addition, Brock (1986) indicated that Lyapunov exponent estimation algorithms may generate spuriously positive values for a small data set. These biases may lead to conclusions of a chaotic pattern, even if none is present.

The fact remains that social processes, such as innovation development, are temporally finite, and we must live with the limits of few data points in this research. The development of CIP lasted 152 months (1977–1989)—which is long in comparison with most innovations (Freeman, 1986). The problem of few data points is the "Achilles heel" of this and many other social scientific studies of dynamic organizational processes. This issue can in part be addressed by being extremely thorough in one's analysis and extremely conservative in one's analysis. Consistency of evidence using the different diagnostics increases confidence in the findings from a study. In our case, the presence of chaotic dynamics in the beginning-actions time series was not only verified by two diagnostics and subsequent surrogate testing, but because the data was also found to be pink noise, we could hypothesize an actual generative model of how the chaotic dynamics arose. This model had intuitive appeal and was generally supported in other theoretical findings. Of course, studies of other organizational innovations are necessary to generalize the findings.

There are important substantive implications of finding a chaotic pattern in event time series data. For one thing, they call into question the two most common explanations for the progression of events in which an organizational change unfolds. The most common explanation is that organizational innovations emerge in an orderly periodic progression of stages or phases of development. The alternative common explanation is that innovations originate in a random sequence of chance or "blind" events. These two common explanations are not plausible when chaos is found.

Chaos tells us that the process consists of a nonlinear dynamical system, which is neither stable nor predictable nor stochastic and random. This research reduces and sharpens the range of plausible explanations by identifying when and what dimensions of the innovation process are orderly, random, and chaotic. Once we know this, then we have a better idea of what models to apply to understand the dynamics. As Morrison (1991) discusses, (1) use stochastic models and statistics to explain random processes; (2) use linear deterministic models to explain periodic cycles or stable equilibria; and (3) use nonlinear dynamic modeling to explain chaotic processes.

Empirical evidence of chaos provides important clues for determining the form of a dynamic model that may explain the observed process of organizational change. We know that a low-dimensional chaotic pattern has a hidden order that typically consists of a relatively simple nonlinear dynamic system of only a few variables. The number of variables approximates the number of dimensions at which the correlation dimension is found to saturate (Brock et al., 1991). For example, the findings discussed in this chapter suggest that the complexity of the nonlinear dynamic system is bounded within no more than four or five dimensions or variables. Brock and his colleagues point out that this finding of low-dimensional chaos is important because from a practical viewpoint, there is no way to distinguish between high-dimensional chaos and randomness in data sets with only finite length on real-world processes.

In a chaotic system, we also know that the temporal development of variables is dynamic, nonlinear, and sensitive to initial conditions. Dynamic means that the values a variable takes on at a given time are a function (at least in part) of the values of that same variable at an earlier time. Nonlinearity implies that the dynamic feedback loops vary in strength (loose or tight coupling) and direction (positive or negative) over time. Sensitivity to initial conditions means that small initial differences or fluctuations in variables may grow over time into large differences. As Eubank and Farmer (1990) discuss, since only a few variables are sufficient to generate chaos, we may be able to model short-term (but not long-term) behavior with some accuracy, and thereby make predictions that are superior to those from a stochastic model based on random processes. However, we must humbly admit that the specification of a nonlinear dynamical model based on observed time series data is a complex and difficult undertaking. New modeling techniques, such as systems dynamics and cellular automata, may lead us to discover some basic archetypal models, thus facilitating the analytical process.

10 Conclusion ≣

> *A study of human affairs in movement is*
> *certainly more fruitful, because more*
> *realistic, than any attempt to study them*
> *in an imaginary condition of rest.*
>
> *Arnold Toynbee*

THE STUDY OF ORGANIZATIONAL CHANGE is concerned with two kinds of questions:

- What are the antecedents or consequences of changes in an organizational entity? and
- How does an organizational entity change over time?

While the vast majority of research to date has focused on the first question, recently there has been a growing interest in the second question, which is concerned with the temporal sequence of events that unfold as an organizational entity changes over time. Process studies are fundamental to understanding the dynamics of organizational life and to the development and testing of theories of organizational creation, innovation, adaptation, and termination. However, a dearth of systematic and codified research methods for studying question 2, relative to the abundance of methods for studying question 1, has impeded many scholars in their attempts to conduct process studies. We wrote this book to address this problem by presenting a theoretical framework and a family of research methods for studying processes of organizational change.

We began in Part I with an argument that a different type of theory and research approach is needed to explore the intricacies of organizational processes. We articulated process theory, which incorporates narrative explanation, as the best route to understanding development and change. To flesh out the abstractions of process theory, we advanced four basic models of change and development: teleology, life cycle, dialectics, and evolution. Each of these four models incorporates a distinctive narrative cycle as a generative mechanism. Considered alone, any single model is relatively simplistic, but more complex theories of organizational change and development can be composed by combining two or more of these basic models. One benefit of viewing theories in terms of the four models is that there are fairly clear guidelines for determining whether one or more of the models holds in a given case.

Part II of the book presented a variety of methods for developing and testing narrative explanations. Process research methods utilize many operations similar to those in standard, variance-based statistical analysis, but the manner in which these operations are employed and the claims they support are quite different. The differences stem from the need for systematic analysis of the complex, layered histories that are the best way to capture the detailed movement of development and change processes. Traditionally, such histories have been the subject of qualitative analysis, but our aim was to detail an alternative methodology based on clear-cut decision rules and statistical reasoning. This approach is meant to complement, rather than to replace qualitative analysis. Ideally, process research methods should achieve a good balance between contextual sensitivity and systematic procedure. Achieving such a balance requires special approaches to collecting data and innovative analytical techniques.

The collection of process research data typically requires researchers to untangle and bracket an observed stream of actions and occurrences into an event sequence. This event sequence—which may portray history at the individual, group, organizational, interorganizational, or societal level—comprises the basic data for process analyses. Event sequences are not self-evident; they must be constructed through painstaking effort and evaluated in terms of measurement reliability and validity. Once the event sequence has been constructed, the second step in data preparation involves coding events into conceptual categories (typologies) that reflect underlying dimensions relevant to a given hypothesis or model. For some analytical methods a third step is necessary, which involves further transformation of the coded data into fixed temporal intervals (e.g., weekly or monthly counts) to yield continuous variables. In both of these last two steps, it is also necessary to assess the reliability and validity of coding procedures before analysis begins to examine substantive questions or hypotheses. We argued that the analysis of process research data entails one or more of five basic tasks:

- Event identification
- Characterizing event sequences and their properties
- Specifying necessary linkages and enchainment of events
- Evaluating hypotheses of formal and final causality
- Recognizing the coherent pattern that integrates the narrative

These analyses provide the evidence necessary to specify the nature of a development or change process and its generative mechanism. We introduced four classes of methods in Part II—stochastic modeling, phasic analysis, event time series analysis, and nonlinear modeling. Each of these methods can be applied to all four tasks, and each generates a specific type of evidence regarding event sequences, connections among events, causality, and narrative pattern. Because they differ in the types of evidence they produce and in the hypotheses they address, the four methods are not equally appropriate for all situations. The strengths of one method tend to compensate for the weaknesses of another method. While no single method can exhaust the field of process-related questions, together the four methods cover the lion's share of possible questions.

In this concluding chapter, we will first recapitulate the key attributes of the process research approach. Then we will discuss what methods are appropriate to the researcher's needs. Finally, we will consider the future of process research, its needs and its prospects.

THE PROCESS APPROACH

The move from variance to process assumptions requires a shift in how we think about explanation and about research methods. Socialized and trained as we are to variance-based, variable-centered approaches, it is often difficult to recognize how distinctive process theory and research is compared to most traditional social scientific approaches. In chapter 2 we discussed the following distinguishing features of the process approach:

- The goal of process research is to use systematic observational and analytical methods to identify and test generative motors underlying narratives. The process approach goes beyond humanistic, interpretive understanding of narratives in its quest for explanation.
- Data in process research reflect qualitative understandings of events and event sequences, rather than simply recording the values of variables over time. When variables are used in process research, they serve as indicators of patterns or dynamics in an event sequence, not as the primary objects of interest. Process theories are not about variables; they are about the course of change and development.
- Narrative explanations feature final, formal, and efficient causation. They presume that development and change are shaped primarily by formative causation due to final causes and formal patterns. Efficient causal forces, the focus of variance approaches, serve a secondary role in that they "bump" the entity from point to point in the sequence and introduce unique variations into the process.
- Narrative explanations take path-dependence into account: they assume that events later in a sequence are conditioned by earlier ones.

Such influence may be incorporated into models of change and development in two ways. First, the meaning of later events may be influenced by earlier events. Second, deeper or more distal causal influences may be posited, such that an event or critical incident in the past continues to exert influence over the subsequent direction of development and change after it has occurred.

- The generalizability of narrative explanations hinges on their versatility, which refers to their ability to help researchers discern a common narrative in a broad range of cases, despite the appearance of differences in event sequences. Versatile narratives can be applied across cases with different paces of change, variations in event duration, and particular, "local" causal factors that introduce unique turns into each sequence. Hence, the measure of generalizability of a process theory is its sensitivity to the pattern that enforms change, not its ability to apply uniformly across cases.

- Process theories do not regard unique variation in cases as "error"; once the basic narrative explanation has been identified, it can be used as a frame for understanding each specific case and how factors particular to this case came into play. This contrasts with the variance approach, which focuses on the average or modal case and regards departures as a function of a distribution of error around the average point.

These attributes of process theories present unique challenges for researchers. They involve an explanatory pattern that straddles humanism and traditional social science. However, process explanations are clearly different from typical thoughtways of quantitative social science, particularly the tendency to assume that variables are central and that relationships among variables are sufficient to explain the process. The process approach emphasizes that satisfactory explanations of organizational change and development are based in narratives. Investigating and establishing narrative models requires different patterns of reasoning and evidence than does variable-based research. Despite its challenges, the process approach is uniquely suited to explain questions about how change unfolds with all its twists and turns over time.

Process Theory vis-à-vis Variance Theory

While process theory was explicitly contrasted with variance theory in order to highlight its unique characteristics, we view variance and process theory as complementary. The two theories deal with different domains of knowledge, and each approach can inform the other. Any development and change process will leave "footprints" that can be studied with variance methods, such as the shape of a developmental curve. Such analyses do not get at the process directly, but they may be used to test particular assumptions of process theories. In the same vein, process approaches can be used to explore and evaluate the stories that underlie variance theories.

The event sequence data used in process research can be transformed into a form suitable for variance analyses, so it is relatively simple to utilize variance methods as an adjunct to a process study. However, the reverse is not always the case: many variance datasets do not have the information required to reconstruct an event sequence. As a result, a study designed with the variance approach in mind often will not yield data to support a process analysis. The relative paucity of information in variance-based datasets compared to process datasets highlights the importance of qualitative methods in process research.

QUALITATIVE FOUNDATIONS OF THE PROCESS APPROACH

Qualitative analysis is an important part of process research, much more so than in the variance approach. Qualitative case studies help to flesh out narrative explanations, uncovering aspects of narratives that may be missed in systematic analysis. They also provide important information to facilitate the process analysis. For example, qualitative information can supplement stochastic modeling by identifying critical points at which the process might shift from one stochastic structure to another; this would enable researchers to fit separate Markov models to different segments of the event sequence, avoiding problems of nonstationarity. In the same vein, these critical incidents may signal inflection points in developmental curves and provide clues important to fitting an appropriate event time series model. Qualitative information is also helpful in interpreting what is occurring during phases that show up as "mixed" in a phasic analysis. These are just a few examples of how information generated through qualitative analyses can help researchers address puzzles that arise in the application of systematic process methods.

Process research methods can reciprocate the contributions of qualitative analyses by providing structured, systematic evaluation of qualitative insights. Phasic analysis could be used, for example, to determine whether an activity cycle discovered in a few cases was common across a larger set. Stochastic modeling could uncover variations on a learning sequence identified in a case study; regression analysis of transition probabilities could also be used to ascertain how often and under what conditions the learning sequence occurred. Event time series analysis can be used to test the degree to which causal factors posited in a qualitative study could account for the ebb and flow of variables such as commitment.

Rather than being antithetical, the process research methods described in this book and qualitative analyses are synergistic. Each reveals important aspects of organizational processes, and the findings from one type of analysis can trigger insights by the other, which in turn illuminate the original findings. To the extent that they can be interwoven, the contributions of the two methods offer a fuller picture of development and change than either alone could provide. Process research methods can best contribute to qualitative understanding, if the appropriate methods are selected for the case and questions at hand. It is to this that we now turn.

SELECTING THE APPROPRIATE METHOD

We have covered a wide array of process research methods, and it is useful to pull together some criteria that might be considered in selecting among them. We hope that the guidelines detailed in this section can offer some rough guidance.

NATURE OF THE TASK AT HAND

In chapter 4 we presented an overview of how the different methods could be used to address the five process research tasks and to test assumptions of the four process models. Chapters 6 through 9 considered the types of problems and questions each of the methods was suited for. Table 10.1 presents a summary view of how the different methods can be used in process research. This synoptic table cannot provide the level of detail presented in previous chapters, but it does pull together the various applications in a single view.

As the table shows, each of the four methods can be used to tackle most of the process research tasks. The notable exception is determining the nature of the central subject. While evidence for a coherent narrative implies an integral subject, the exact nature of this subject must be established with an independent qualitative analysis, using evidence that goes beyond the event sequence.

Table 10.1 also suggests that some methods are more appropriate for certain tasks than others. Overall, stochastic modeling and phasic analysis are strongest in tasks that involve defining events and characterization of

Table 10.1 Applications of the Four Types of Methods to Process Research Issues

	STOCHASTIC MODELING	PHASIC ANALYSIS	EVENT TIME SERIES ANALYSIS	NONLINEAR MODELING
Event Identification	Higher-order events can be identified that are comprised of interacts, double interacts, or short chains of events, up to the order of the transition matrix.	Higher-order events can be identified that are comprised of phase types. Cycles or short sequences of phases can also be used to identify higher-order events.	Events that signal critical change points or transitions in the process in the process can be identified.	Events at transition points between different types of order can be identified.
Characterizing Event Sequences: (1) Event Types	Different types of event processes can be defined based on different stochastic structures. For example, one Markov matrix might indicate a learning process, while another indicates routinization with little learning or change. The first might hold for 75% of a case, while the second takes over for the remaining 25% of the case. The events occurring during learning would be one type, while those during routinization would be another. Differences between types can be derived using matrix comparison procedures to obtain matrix correlation values between pairs of Markov matrices. These can be used to cluster sequences in order to derive types empirically.	Higer-order event types can be defined based on phase orders of subsequences. For example, a particular series of phases might indicate learning, while a second series indicates negotiation, and a third indicates routinization. Event types could be assigned to those segments of the event sequence that exhibit these series of phases. Optimal matching and clustering procedures canbe used to derive types empirically.	Event types corresponding to change points or inflection points in the time series can be identified. Event types corresponding to distinct portions of the times series can be identified. For example, in CIP the first 2/3 of the sequence corresponded to an initiation period, while the remaining 1/3 corresponded to a contraction period.	Different types of order may indicate different types of events.

Characterizing Event Sequences: (2) Event Variables	Short sequences can be used to identify event variables: e.g., the interact expand-expand could serve as an indicator of growth.	Phases can serve as indicators of event types or event variables; e.g., an idea development phase could serve as in indicator of a growth event.	Event variables can be defined based on characteristics of the time series; e.g., when the slope of the series trends up, events might be classified as growth events, while those on the downslope as shrinkage events.	Event variables could be defined based on different types of order.
Characterizing Event Sequences: (3) Overall Sequence Properties	The transition matrix provides a summary of microlevel linkages. Specific transition probabilities can serve as indicators of sequence properties; e.g., the relative magnitude of the expand-expand probability can be used to indicate the amount of emphasis placed on growth by an innovation team.	Several summary properties of a phase sequence can be derived including (1) similarity to target (hypothesized) sequence; (2) number of cycles in a sequence; (3) relative amount of time devoted to different activities(indicated by phases); (4) proportion of "null" periods; (5) complexity of developmental path.	The structure of the time series model can be used to identify several characteristics of overall temporal patterns including (1) cycles; (2) trends; (3) degree of order in the series; (4) shape of the developmental curve; (5) relationshipof two or more variables in the time series. Analysis of Tuckerized curves described later in this chapter, can be used to cluster time series to derive types	Sequences can be characterized based on the type of noise they exhibit, e.g., brown, pink, etc., which may indicate (1) the number of independent variables influencing the sequence; (2) the degree to which the system has a "memory" (i.e., the degree to which prior events have an influence over later ones); (3) presence and type of feedback governing the process.
Characterizing Event Sequences: (4) Subsequences	Subsequences comprised of interacts, double interacts, triple interacts, etc. can be identified. Stochastic modeling provides statistical evidence that the subsequences occur in the series above a minimal level of frequency.	Short series of phases may identify macrolevel subsequences. Composite phases indicating subsequences could be identified from more microlevel phases and and included in the overall phase sequence.	Segments of the time series with particular properties can be identified. Change and inflection points may enable identification of key subsequences. Once this has been done, all properties of the box above can be characterized for the subsequence.	—

continued

Table 10.1 Continued

	STOCHASTIC MODELING	PHASIC ANALYSIS	EVENT TIME SERIES ANALYSIS	NONLINEAR MODELING
Identification of Temporal Dependencies	Stochastic structure of transition matrix indicates temporal dependencies among 2-event, 3-event, etc. sequences up to the order of the model.	Phase sequence can indicate dependencies among macrolevel units, such as phases ot higer-order events; the degree to which they are dependencies turns on whether prior phases can be shown to cause or lead to subsequent phases.	The structure and properties of the time series model (e.g., ARMA) indicate the nature of the temporal dependencies in the event sequence.	The different types of noise indicate different types of temporal dependencies in the time series.
	Lag sequential analysis can describe specific chains of temporal dependency.		Granger causality can be used to determine dependencies between different event variables.	The dimensionality of the time series gives an indication of how many causal factors may influence the event sequence.
Assessing Formal and Final Causality	Insofar as the causal mechanism implies recurrent patterns among events, a Markov model can be used to identify the degree to which such pattern is present.	Formal and final causal explanations often imply macrolevel temporal patterns among events that can be detected with phasic analysis.	To the extent that formal and final causes imply a definite shape of the developmental curve or change points, time series analysis can be utilized to test for these.	Different nonlinear models are consistent with different types of formal and final causes. E.g., a chaotic pattern is not consistent with a life cycle model, but may be consistent woth a teleological model.
Testing Alternative Motors: (1) Unitary Sequence?	The unitary sequence model implies a particular series of phases. The existence of consecutive pairs of phases can be tested with a first-order Markov model, 3-phase sequences with a second-order model, and so on. The Markov model would be fit to macrolevel phase data, smoothed using procedures detailed in Ch. 7.	Existence of a set, unitary sequence of stages can be evaluated with phasic analysis methods. Optimal matching can be used to determine the degree to which observed sequences differ from a hypothesized unitary sequence.	The unitary sequence model implies qualitatively different behavior in each successive stage, which should be reflected in change points.	Finding a chaotic pattern in the time series indicates that a unitary sequence is not likely.

Testing Alternative Motors: (2) Patterning Sequence?	A microlevel patterning device would exhibit regular behavior that would allow the fitting of a Markov model. Markov analysis could be used to induce the presence of a patterning device or to test a hypothesis about a patterning device.	As with stochastic modeling, regularities due to a patterning device could be detected or tested with phasic analysis.	A patterning device that caused trends, cycles, or discontinuities in the time series could be detected with time series methods.	Low dimensionality of the time series may indicate the operation of an external patterning device.
Testing Alternative Motors: (3) Is There a Goal-Setting Process?	The goal-setting cycle of the teleological motor could be detected using lag sequential analysis or by fitting a Markov model.	The goal-setting cycle of the teleological motor implies a particular sequence of phases.	Once a goal has been set, the system tends toward first-order change to achieve the goal; this would yield a simple time series with low order.	Periodic time series may indicate a teleological model with goal setting.
Testing Alternative Motors: (4) Is There a Central Subject?	—	—	—	—
Testing Alternative Motors: (5) Are Individual Cases Unpredictable; Population Level Prediction Instead?	If this assumptiuon is tenable, then a stationary model will not be found for individual cases, but a model can be fit for the cases aggregated into a single process. The Markov model will have to be adopted to allow for the aggregate data. For example, rather than using the event series of a single case to estimate transitions of experiment to adopt, the number of cases making this transition at a given point in time would be used to estimate the probability.	If a phase strucure could be found for aggregates of cases, but not for individual cases, a population-level analysis would be indicated.	This would be supported if a time series model could not be fit for cases, but could for aggregates of cases.	This would be indicated if the aggregate data had low dimensionality and relatively simple interactions among causal factors, but the individual cases did not.

continued

Table 10.1 Continued

	STOCHASTIC MODELING	PHASIC ANALYSIS	EVENT TIME SERIES ANALYSIS	NONLINEAR MODELING
Testing Alternative Motors: (6) Do Conflict or Contradiction Occur?	Microlevel sequences involved in conflict and contradiction can be identified with Markov or lag sequential analysis.	The existence of phases of conflict and patterns of conflict management can be identified with phasic analysis.	The time series should show increased variation (as the conflict escalates) followed by a sharp decrease in variance (as the conflict is resolved). Modeling the standard deviation of the event counts could be used to test for this pattern.	Either chaotic or colored noise systems are consistent with the existence of a dialectical conflict.

event sequences. Event time series analysis and nonlinear modeling come into their own on research tasks that require representation of the overall series and its properties.

NATURE OF THE AVAILABLE DATA

In principle, research design should be driven by the researcher's theory and research questions. In the real world, however, exigencies of the research situation dictate that only certain types of designs are feasible. Limitations in time, money, and personnel, difficulties in gaining access to research sites, constraints imposed by sources of data and information, and accidents of history may restrict the data available to the researcher. For this reason it is useful to consider how analytical methods match up with different types of data. There are suitable methods for almost any conceivable type of data, and knowing the options may help the researcher make adjustments within his or her constraints that tailor the data to the best available method.

Chapter 5 classified the method-data match based on the number of cases available in the dataset and the number of temporal observations within cases. In typical process datasets, the number of temporal observations per case will be quite large, since event streams often entail several hundred events. Hence, the main influence of interest is the number of cases. As Table 5.2 indicated, a researcher with only a few cases can draw powerful conclusions about those cases using phasic analysis, event time series regression analysis, and stochastic modeling, supplemented by qualitative case studies. These analyses provide sufficient evidence to determine the nature of change and development in the case and the generative mechanism that drives it.

As the number of cases available for analysis increases, researchers have more flexibility and can draw more general conclusions. With many cases, they can derive typologies of developmental paths based on phasic analysis or of microlevel patterns based on Markov analysis. They can use methods such as regression and analysis of variance to determine factors that influence the transition probabilities in Markov models. They can employ time series methods to determine causal influences on developmental trends. The major disadvantage to conducting studies with many cases is that they cannot be analyzed with the painstaking detail of smaller samples. To gain the advantages of both types of analysis, researchers might follow a two-step strategy, conducting statistical analyses on many cases, and then sampling a smaller number of cases for in-depth temporal analysis.

A second consideration in selecting process analysis methods is the degree to which the researcher desires to maintain the original form of the event data. Two of the four analytical methods—stochastic modeling and phasic analysis—utilize the codings of event data directly. Event time series analysis and nonlinear modeling, as well as some subsidiary analysis of stochastic models and phasic sequences, require the coded data to be transformed into fixed temporal intervals of count data and continuous variables. Moving one transformation away from the original qualitative data glosses over some significant aspects of the qualitative data, and two transformations may result in the loss of even more significant detail. Transformations have the advantages of centering the analysis clearly on a few factors and of rendering the data suitable for statistical analysis, but this comes at the cost of eliding significant features. Hence, an important consideration for researchers is the degree to which they find this information loss acceptable.

DEDUCTION VERSUS RETRODUCTION

In chapter 5 we introduced the traditional distinction between designs based on deduction, which posit logically derived theories and hypotheses, and designs based on retroduction (often called induction), which build a theory or hypothesis by drawing inferences from data. Retroduction leans primarily on methods capable of discerning structure in data; once a tentative hypothesis has been developed, it also utilizes hypothesis-testing methods. Deduction, on the other hand, depends primarily on hypothesis-testing. While descriptive analysis can be used to evaluate some aspects of hypotheses, in general, it is less central to the deductive approach.

All four methods can be used for descriptive purposes: Markov models describe the local structure of events; phasic models generate descriptions of phase sequences and their properties; event time series analysis describes trends in development and change along significant dimensions; and nonlinear modeling methods can be used to draw conclusions about the degree of order in event time series. For larger samples, typologies of developmental sequences can be derived from phasic analysis and typologies of sequential structures can be created using stochastic modeling. This involves calculating a measure of similarity between cases (we discussed the use of optimal matching for phase data and quadratic assignment for Markov transition matrices); the similarity data is then subjected to factor analysis, cluster analysis, or MDS to group cases as the basis for the typology. Methods are also available for clustering cases based on the shape of longitudinal curves (Brossart, Patton, & Wood, 1998; Tucker, 1966). Such analysis of growth curves enables typologies to be derived based on event time series.

Hypothesis-testing is the second stage of retroduction and the primary activity in deduction. Stochastic analysis can be used to test hypotheses about the nature of the microlevel process underlying an event sequence and about the factors that influence the magnitude of event-to-event relationships, among other things. Some of the hypotheses phasic analyses can test include those concerning the degree to which a sample of phase sequences are similar, the degree to which they resemble a hypothesized sequence, and the number and nature of cycles in the sequences. Event time series analyses can test hypotheses regarding the impact of external events on development and relationships between two developmental dimensions, among other things. Finally, nonlinear modeling can be used to test hypotheses of disorder and order in time series.

While all four methods may be used for both retroductive and deductive purposes, they differ in the "reach" they provide researchers. Stochastic analysis focuses attention on microlevel connections. Though it provides an overall summary description, this description is a summary of microlevel connections over the entire process. Phasic analysis focuses on intermediate level units, phases comprised of individual events. Overall, summary descriptions of sequence types can be generated, but they are based on lower-level phase structures. Time series and nonlinear methods, in contrast, analyze the entire sequence of events as a whole. Hence, different methods will be appropriate for different temporal scales in the retroductive or deductive process.

These Guidelines Are Open-Ended

Applying the research methods is a matter of improvisation to address the research question and the particular needs of the situation. We cannot possibly envision all the exigencies that might confront researchers. No doubt others will find applications for these methods in novel situations that we have not foreseen. Hence, our guidelines are intended to provide some basic directions and suggestions that can be further developed and supplemented as process research is elaborated.

FUTURE DIRECTIONS FOR PROCESS RESEARCH

The process research methods discussed in this book have emerged through the efforts of many scholars in a wide array of disciplines. Researchers confronted the problem of how to study development and change with underdeveloped research models and methods. Faced with a need to improvise, they adapted and modified existing methods for the immediate needs at hand. More formal development has followed those methods that are used repeatedly and adopted by other researchers.

Development of process research methods generally seems to follow a common path. First, there is a period of adaptation of traditional methods; researchers struggle to address new problems with existing methods. To the extent this is possible, traditional methods are refit to apply to the new approach. Several of the methods discussed in this book, including stochastic modeling and event time series analysis, are currently at this stage of development. At a certain point, it becomes evident that existing methods cannot cope with all of the issues that arise in the new approach, and researchers attempt to derive their own methods to address particular problems. At first this is done ad hoc, in a manner not founded on any firm methodology. In some instances, methodologies developed in other areas, such as statistics or operations research, are applied to new problems. Some of the methods used in phasic analysis and nonlinear modeling are presently at this stage. As time passes, the new methods should become more formalized, until methodologists finally work out their formal foundations and develop a theory of the new methods.

One way to promote the evolution of process research is to expose key limitations in current approaches. So we will conclude by suggesting four issues that require attention.

THE NEED FOR MORE EXPLICIT PROCESS THEORIES

In chapter 2 we reviewed three general process theories, those of Mohr, Abell, and Abbott. These theories differ from the majority of organizational change and development theories in that they explicitly attempt to address the nature of narrative explanations. While almost every theory of change and development elaborates a narrative that explains the process, very few consciously attempt to theorize about the constitution of the narrative itself. Mohr offers a mechanistic, stochastic view of narratives, depicting them as chains of occurrences. Abell attempts to develop a model of narratives based on a particular conception of human action. Abbott focuses on narratives at different levels of analysis and the relations among them. These three views, while suggestive, certainly do not exhaust the possibilities underlying narratives and their explanation. Underlying most theories of organizational change and development are assumptions regarding the general form of narrative explanations, and it would be useful to analyze these theories with the aim of developing a more diverse repertoire of narrative formats.

The quest for generic narrative models is fundamental to process research. Articulating generic models has the potential to illuminate the connections between seemingly disparate theories of change and development. Generic models can also support theory development by carefully examining the key components of process theories. While scholars have made much progress in understanding the nature of narrative explanation, many facets of this approach remain to be uncovered.

THE NEED FOR MORE SOPHISTICATED CODING

Coding is an important operation in process research. However, as usually practiced, coding and content analysis are among the least sophisticated methodologies in the social sciences. Coding is often regarded as a thankless bookkeeping task that involves classifying acts into categories devised for the immediate purposes of a study. The coding process, which involves painstaking classification of events or acts by researchers, is time-consuming and expensive. It is difficult to maintain reliability during extended periods of coding. And commonly the validity of coding systems is not assessed; often it is incorrectly equated with logical consistency and reliability. It is little wonder that many researchers are reluctant to undertake systematic coding.

The adoption of several practices could place coding methodologies on a stronger base. First, many coding tasks can be automated, thus reducing the effort required and lessening errors of human judgment and fatigue (see appendix for some exemplary computer programs). Several packages to facilitate coding and content analysis are now generally available. Programs are available to assist researchers in the transcription of interviews and the derivation of qualitative event sequences. Programs are also available to support the development and application of coding systems. Other programs parse linguistic content and assign it to categories in a first pass that can then be checked by coders. Language recognition software is becoming increasingly sophisticated, and we can look forward to a time in the near future where verbal accounts can be transcribed, parsed, and coded electronically. Of course, this will not eliminate the need for human judgment and systematic attention to details; researchers are still in the best position to understand the significance of events. Hence, we must carefully consider automated classifications, for they are inherently less sensitive to meaning than what the researcher can personally infer.

A second constructive practice involves decomposing the entire coding process into workable steps. Rogers and Farace's Relational Control Coding System (1975) provides an excellent example of how to break the

coding process into steps that enhance the precision and consistency of classification. Their system first codes the type of speech act of a statement (e.g.,
question, assertion), and then in a second step assigns a control code to each
act (one up, one down, one across). The benefits of dividing the coding
process into self-contained steps stem not only from enhanced control over
coding, but also from the enhanced understanding of events and actions
that develops as the interpretive process is systematically refined.

THE NEED FOR MORE ARROWS IN OUR QUIVER

The methods discussed in this book by no means exhaust the repertoire of
methods that could be applied in process research. Several techniques seem
to be promising candidates for further consideration. Factor analysis has
been used successfully in human development research to track changes in
larger sets of variables. Basically, this technique involves conducting factor
analyses at discrete points in time and comparing the factor structures
(Cunningham, 1991; Horn, 1991). Changes in factor structure can signal
changes in latent variables. This technique may be a useful supplement to
time series analysis.

Cliff (1991) discusses the use of ordinal statistics in assessing change.
One advantage of such statistics is that they are distribution-free, so there is
no need to assure normality, as would be the case for most inferential statistics designed for interval and ratio level data. Ordinal methods seem particularly useful for process research, because data derived from event sequences are often ordinal due to the nature of the phenomena being
examined and imprecision introduced by transforming qualitative data into
quantitative variables. One other appealing characteristic of ordinal analyses is their simplicity relative to methods such as factor analysis and the
analysis of time series.

In chapter 6 we briefly mentioned time series models for nominal data.
One promising avenue involves the analysis of multivariate binary time series data with logistic regression (Liang & Zeger, 1989). This method enables assessments of associations between qualitative variables at a single
time and also identifications of lead-lag relationships among variables. This
method could be employed to analyze the categorical codes contained in
the bitmaps directly, eliminating the need to transform nominal data into
continuous variables.

Another promising mode of analysis is the multivariate point process
model (Amburgey, 1986). The purpose of this family of models is to study
the rate of occurrence of multiple and repeatable events. They enable re-

searchers to model the time intervals between occurrences of events, the number of times an event repeats within a given period, and the instantaneous probabilities of events. Multivariate point process models can handle event structures of greater complexity than do traditional event history analyses.

THE NEED TO MODEL DEVELOPMENT AND CHANGE

Two vexing problems face those who study development and change processes. First, empirical studies of development and change often suffer either from limitations in number of cases or number of temporal events observed. Unfortunately, researchers are finite beings (with families and other interests, even), and their ability to follow many cases of a change process over long periods of time has its bounds. Problems of access may also limit the amount of data that can be gathered. And even those organizations that are willing to provide the researchers with everything they need may run out of patience in the face of the demands of process research. A second problem stems from the "messy" nature of development and change theories and their application to data. As noted in chapter 3, many theories of development and change are comprised of several interacting generative mechanisms or models, and this makes it difficult to sort out the explanatory factors.

Simulation modeling offers one means to address these problems. Simulations are typically derived from theory supplemented by empirical results. One way in which simulation can be used in process research is to construct a model of a hypothesized developmental motor for a given organizational context and use it to generate trajectories of key variables. For example, Van de Ven and Polley (1992) posited a learning-based model of organizational innovation that included five variables derived from the event sequence of a technological innovation: external shocks, resource controller intervention, stability of action, goal, and feedback. They fit this model to their data with time series regression analysis and reported a good degree of fit. To further explore this process model, a simulation could be built that incorporated the variables and relationships in Van de Ven and Polley's statistical model. The model could then be run for substantial periods of time over hundreds of replications for a range of starting values, exogenous variable structures, and parameter values. The simulation results could be compared to the trajectories of values for the actual data of this and other technological innovations to assess the fidelity of the model to actual innovation processes. The results of the simulation could also be subjected to sensitivity analyses to determine which variables account for the model's behavior over changing conditions; these critical factors can then be the focus of future empirical research.

Modeling allows researchers to construct much larger samples than they could feasibly collect in empirical studies. Moreover, the sample can be constructed to vary systematically on key factors, enabling researchers to consider the impacts of a range of possible conditions that would be difficult to find in the empirical world. Models can also be run over many iterations, ensuring a sufficient observational period to understand the course of the process. Models instantiating competing models—or adding motors to the present model—can also be constructed and compared, enabling researchers to assess their relative plausibility.

However, because models are constructions, they necessarily simplify the empirical world. While such simplification is often very useful for clarification, it may also distort things. For a model to be helpful, it is important that it be based on clear theoretical assumptions and as many sound empirical findings as possible. Starting values and values of exogenous variables should be based on empirical data regarding their range and variability.

POSTSCRIPT

This book attempts to offer a map for those setting forth on the demanding but rewarding quest to understand organizational processes. At present, our map is rather like those beautiful old figures that guided voyagers in the Age of Exploration. Some parts are clear, but others must be marked "terra incognita." And though monsters may lurk around the edges of known territory, we are confident they can be tamed by careful theoretical and methodological development. The progress of the past twenty years gives us every reason to believe that existing tools for charting development and change will be improved and that new ones will emerge.

We should also remember that "the map is not the territory." We have presented one framework for the construction of understandings about organizational processes, but we are confident that it is not "the one true way." Other approaches and frameworks will certainly provide different types of insight into development and change. We welcome fellow explorers on this journey.

Appendix

To help readers undertake process research, this appendix details how to obtain relevant software. Most companies listed here can be contacted through the World Wide Web.

CODING SYSTEM DEVELOPMENT AND CODING

In recent years a number of systems for managing the development of coding systems have been developed. These include MacShapa® (for the Macintosh), developed at the University of Illinois and available from CSERIAC at Wright-Patterson Air Force Base (937–255–4842); the Observer®, available from Exeter Software (on the World Wide Web); and ATLAS.ti®, NUD*IST®, and Code-A-Text®, all available from Scolari, a part of Sage Publications.

MARKOV ANALYSIS

Most general statistical packages, such as SPSS® and SAS®, support the types of loglinear analyses required to fit a Markov model, as described in chapter 6.

LAG SEQUENTIAL ANALYSIS

MacShapa® and the Observer®, described above, both have the capability to do lag sequential analysis. Bakeman's program ELAG®, though it still runs in MS-DOS, is still a reliable means for conducting lag sequential analysis. Bakeman is at Georgia Tech University in Atlanta.

PHASIC ANALYSIS

A general purpose program for phasic analysis, WINPHASER®, has been developed by Michael Holmes. It can be obtained by writing him at the University of Utah.

Matrix correlation procedures developed by Hubert and colleagues are available in the UCINET IV® network analysis package. It can be obtained from Analytic Technologies in Columbia, South Carolina.

TIME SERIES ANALYSIS

Most general statistical packages, such as SPSS® and SAS®, support time series analysis. Another useful package is RATS®, Regression Analysis of Time Series, available from Estima Software, Evanston, Illinois. Also useful is the time series application for the Mathematica® software package by Y. He, Mathematica Applications Library: Time Series Pack®. This is available from Wolfram Research in Champaign, Illinois.

A copy of the SELAGGR program can be obtained from Andrew Van de Ven by writing him at the University of Minnesota.

ANALYSIS OF NONLINEAR DATA

The Chaos Data Analyzer® by J. C. Sprott and G. Rowlands supports the calculation of many of the statistics needed in nonlinear modeling. It can be obtained from the American Institute of Physics in New York.

References

Abbott, A. (1984). Event sequence and event duration: Colligation and measurement. *Historical Methods, 17,* 192–204.

Abbott, A. (1988). Transcending general linear reality. *Sociological Theory, 6,* 169–186.

Abbott, A. (1990). Conceptions of time and events in social science methods: Causal and narrative approaches. *Historical Methods, 23,* 140–150.

Abbott, A. (1991). The order of professionalization. *Work and Occupations, 18,* 355–384.

Abbott, A. (1992). From causes to events: Notes on narrative positivism. *Sociological Methods and Research, 20,* 428–455.

Abbott, A. (1993). Measure for measure: Abell's narrative methods. *Journal of Mathematical Sociology, 18,* 203–214.

Abbott, A. (1995). Sequence analysis: New methods for old ideas. *Annual Review of Sociology, 21,* 93–113.

Abbott, A., & Forrest, J. (1986). Optimal matching methods for historical sequences. *Journal of Interdisciplinary History, 16,* 471–494.

Abbott, A., & Hrycak, A. (1990). Measuring resemblance in sequence data: An optimal matching analysis of musician's careers. *American Journal of Sociology, 96,* 144–185.

Abell, P. (1987). *The syntax of social life: The theory and method of comparative narratives.* Oxford: Clarendon Press.

Abell, P. (1993). Some aspects of narrative method. *Journal of Mathematical Sociology, 18,* 93–134.

Abernathy, W. J., & Clark, K. B. (1985). Innovation: Mapping the winds of creative destruction. *Research Policy, 14,* 3–22.

Abraham, F. D., Abraham, R. H., & Shaw, C. D. (1990). *A visual introduction to dynamical systems theory for psychology.* Santa Cruz, CA: Aerial Press.

Aldrich, H. (1979). *Organizations and environments.* Englewood Cliffs, NJ: Prentice Hall.

Allison, P. D. (1984). *Event history analysis: Regression for longitudinal event data.* Beverly Hills, CA: Sage.

Allison, P. D., & Liker, J. K. (1982). Analyzing sequential categorical data on dyadic interaction: A comment on Gottman. *Psychological Bulletin, 91,* 393–403.

Amburgey, T. L. (1986). Multivariate point process models in social research. *Social Science Research, 15,* 190–207.

Anderson, P. A. (1983). Decision-making by objection and the Cuban missile crisis. *Administrative Science Quarterly, 28,* 201–222.

Anderson, T. W. (1971). *The statistical analysis of time series.* New York: Wiley.

Anderson, T. W., & Goodman, L. A. (1957). Statistical inference about Markov chains. *Annals of Mathematical Statistics, 28,* 89–110.

Anscombe, G. E. M. (1957). *Intention.* Oxford: Blackwell.

Argyris, C. (1968). Some unintended consequences of rigorous research. *Psychological Bulletin, 70,* 185–197.

Argyris, C. (1985). *Strategy, change, and defensive routines.* Marshfield, MA: Pitman.

Aristotle (1941). *The basic works of Aristotle* (ed. R. McKeon). New York: Random House.

Arnold, A. J., & Fristrup, K. (1982). The theory of evolution by natural selection: A hierarchical expansion. *Paleobiology, 8,* 113–129.

Arthur, W. B. (1989). The economy and complexity. In D. L. Stein (Ed.), *Lectures in the sciences of complexity* (pp. 713–140). Redwood City, CA: Addison-Wesley.

Arundale, R. (1980). Studying change over time: Criteria for sampling from continuous variables. *Communication Research, 7(2),* 227–263.

Astley, W. G. (1985). The two ecologies: Population and community perspectives on organizational evolution. *Administrative Science Quarterly, 30,* 224–241.

Baer, T. (1997). Strategy, structure, detail, function: Four parameters for the appraisal of business records. In J. M. O'Toole (Ed.), *The record of American business* (pp. 75–130). Chicago, IL: Society of American Archivists.

Bak, P. (1996). *How nature works.* New York:Springer-Verlag.

Bak, P., Tang, C., & Wiesenfeld, K. (1988). Self-organized criticality. *Physical Review A, 38,* 364–373.

Bakeman, R., & Gottman, J. M. (1986). *Observing interaction: An introduction to sequential analysis.* Cambridge: Cambridge University Press.

Bales, R. F. (1950). *Interaction process analysis.* Chicago: University of Chicago Press.

Bales, R. F., & Strodtbeck, F. L. (1951). Phases in group problem-solving. *Journal of Abnormal and Social Psychology, 46,* 485–495.

Baltes, P. B., Dittman-Kohli, F., & Dixon, R. A. (1986). Multidisciplinary propositions on the development of intelligence during adulthood and old age. In A. B. Sorensen, F. E. Weinert, and L. R. Sherrod (Eds.), *Human development and the life course: Multidisciplinary perspectives* (pp. 467–507). Hillsdale, NJ: Lawrence Erlbaum.

Baron, R. M, & Kenny, D. A. (1986). The moderator-mediator variable distinction in social psychological research: Conceptual, strategic, and statistical considerations. *Journal of Personality and Social Psychology, 51,* 1173–1182.

Barton, S. (1994). Chaos, self-organization, and psychology. *American Psychologist, 49,* 5–14.

Ben-Mizrachi, A., & Procaccia, I. (1984). Characterization of experimental (noisy) strange attractors. *Physical Review A, 29,* 975–977.

Benson, J. K. (1977). Organizations: A dialectical view. *Administrative Science Quarterly, 22,* 1–21.

Berger, P. L. & Lucknann, T. (1966). *The social construction of reality.* Garden City, NY: Doubleday.

Bishop, Y., Fienberg, S. & Holland, P. (1975). *Discrete multivariate analysis: Theory and practice.* Cambridge, MA: MIT Press.

Blalock, H. M. (1960). *Social statistics.* New York: McGraw-Hill.

Blau, P. M., & Schoenherr, R. (1971). *The structure of organizations.* New York: Basic Books.

Borgatti, S., Everett, J., & Freeman, L. (1992). *UCINET IV, Version 1.0.* Columbia, SC: Analytic Technologies.

Box, G., & Jenkins, G. (1976). *Time series analysis: Forecasting and control.* San Francisco: Holden-Day.

Box, G., & Tiao, G. (1975). Intervention analysis with applications to economic and environmental problems. *Journal of the American Statistical Association, 70,* 70–79.

Boyd, R., & Richerson, P. J. (1985). *Culture and the evolutionary process.* Chicago: University of Chicago Press.

Brock, W. A. (1986). Distinguishing random and deterministic systems. *Journal of Economic Theory, 40,* 168–195.

Brock, W. A., Hsieh, D. A., & LeBaron, B. (1991). *Nonlinear dynamics, chaos, and instability: Statistical theory and economic evidence.* Cambridge: The MIT Press.

Brossert, D. F., Patton, M. J., & Wood, P. K. (1998). Assessing group process: An illustration using tuckevized growth curves. *Group Dynamics: Theory, Research, and Practice, 2,* 3–17.

Bruner, J. (1986). *Actual minds, possible worlds.* Cambridge, MA: Harvard University Press.

Brunsson, N. (1982). The irrationality of action and action rationality: Decisions, ideologies, and organizational actions. *Journal of Management Studies, 19,* 29–34.

Bryson, J. M., and Roering, W. D. (1989). Mobilizing innovation efforts: The case of government strategic planning. In A. H. Van de Ven, H. L. Angle, and M. S. Poole (Eds.), *Research on the management of innovation: The Minnesota studies* (pp. 583–610). New York: Ballinger / Harper & Row.

Bunderson, J. S., Dirks, K. T., Garud, R., & Van de Ven, A. H. (1995). *Spinning a web of relationships between organizations.* Discussion paper #212. Strategic Management Research Center, University of Minnesota, Minneapolis.

Burgelman, R. A. (1991). Intraorganizational ecology of strategy making and organizational adaptation: Theory and field research. *Organization Science, 2,* 239–262.

Burgelman, R. A., & Sayles, L. R. (1986). *Inside corporate innovation: Strategy, structure, and managerial skills.* New York: Free Press.

Burke, K. (1969). *A grammar of motives.* Berkeley, CA: University of California Press.

Cameron, K., & Whetten, D. (1983). Models of the organizational life cycle: Applications to higher education. *Review of Higher Education, 6,* 269–299.

Campbell, D. (1989). Introduction to nonlinear phenomena. In D. L. Stein (Ed.), *Lectures in the sciences of complexity, Vol. 1* (pp. 3–105). Redwood City, CA: Addison-Wesley.

Campbell, D. T. (1969). Variation and selective retention in socio-cultural evolution. *General Systems, 16,* 69–85.

Campbell, D. T. (1974). Evolutionary epistemology. In P. A. Schilpp (Ed.), *The philosphy of Karl Popper* (pp. 413–463). LaSalle, IL: Open Court Press.

Campbell, D. T., & Stanley, J. C. (1963). *Experimental and quasi-experimental designs for research.* Dallas: Houghton-Mifflin.

Carroll, G., & Hannan, M. T. (1989). Density delay in the evolution of organizational populations: A model and five empirical tests. *Administrative Science Quarterly, 34,* 411–430.

Chakravarthy, B. S., & Lorange, P. (1991). *Managing the strategy process.* Englewood Cliffs, NJ: Prentice Hall.

Cheng, Y. & Van de Ven, A. H. (1996). Learning the innovation journey: Order out of chaos? *Organization Science, 7,* 593–614.

Clark, K. B. (1985). The interaction of design hierarchies and market concepts in technological evolution. *Research Policy, 14,* 235–251.

Cliff, N. (1991). Ordinal methods in the assessment of change. In L. M. Collins and J. L. Horn (Eds.), *Best methods for the analysis of change: Recent advances, unanswered questions, future directions* (pp. 34–46). Washington, DC: American Psychological Association.

Cohen, J. (1960). A coefficient of agreement for nominal scales. *Educational and Psychological Measurement, 20,* 37–46.

Cohen, J. (1968). Weighted kappa: Nominal scale agreement with provision for scaled disagreement or partial credit. *Psychological Bulletin, 70,* 213–220.

Cohen, M. D., March, J. G., & Olsen, J. (1972). A garbage can model of organizational choice. *Administrative Science Quarterly, 17,* 1–25.

Coleman, J. S. (1964). *Introduction to mathematical sociology.* New York: Free Press.

Commons, J. R. (1950). *The economics of collective action.* Madison, WI: University of Wisconsin Press.

Cook, T. & Campbell, D. T. (1979). *Quasi-experimentation.* Boston: Houghton-Mifflin.

Coombs, C. H., & Smith, J. E. K. (1973). The detection of the structure of attitudes and developmental processes. *Psychological Review, 80,* 337–350.

Cottrell, T. J., (1993, August). *Nonlinear dynamics in the emergence of new industries.* Paper presented at Academy of Management Conference, Miami.

Crocker, L., & Algina, J. (1986). *Introduction to classical & modern test theory.* New York: Holt Rinehart and Winston.

Cronbach, L. J. (1990). *Essentials of psychological testing* (5th ed.). New York: HarperCollins.

Cunningham, W. R. (1991). Issues in factorial invariance. In L. M. Collins and J. L. Horn (Eds.), *Best methods for the analysis of change: Recent advances, unanswered questions, future directions* (pp. 106–113). Washington, DC: American Psychological Association.

Darwin, C. (1936). *The origin of species.* New York: Modern Library.

Davison, M. L., King, P. M., Kitchener, K. S., & Parker, C. A. (1980). The stage sequence concept in cognitive and social development. *Developmental Psychology, 16,* 121–131.

Davison, M. L., Robbins, S., & Swanson, D. B. (1978). Stage structure in objective moral judgments. *Developmental Psychology, 14,* 137–146.

DeRosnay, J. (1970). Evolution and time. *Main Currents, 27,* 35–47.

Delbecq, A., Gustafson, D., & Van de Ven, A. H. (1975). *Group techniques for program planning: A guide to nominal group and delphi processes.* Glenview, IL: Scott Foresman.

Delbecq, A., & Van de Ven, A. H. (1971). A group process model for problem identification and program planning. *Journal of Applied Behavioral Science, 7,* 486–492.

Dendrinos, D., & Sonis, M. (1990). *Chaos and socio-spatial dynamics.* New York: Springer-Verlag.

Diesing, P. (1991). *How does social science work?: Reflections on practice.* Pittsburgh, PA: University of Pittsburgh Press.

Dooley, K. (1997). A complex adaptive systems model of organizational change. *Nonlinear Dynamics, Psychology, and the Life Sciences, 1,* 69–97.

Dooley, K. & Kapoor, S. (1990). An enhanced quality evaluation system for continuous manufacturing processes: theory. *ASME Journal of Engineering for Industry, 112,* 57–62.

Dooley, K., Johnson, T., & Bush, D. (1995). TQM, chaos, and complexity. *Human Systems Management, 14,* 1–16.

Elder, G. H., Pavalko, E. K., & Clipp, E. C. (1993). *Working with archival data: Studying lives.* Newbury Park, CA: Sage.

Etzioni, A. (1963). The epigenesis of political communities at the international level. *American Journal of Sociology, 68,* 407–421.

Eubank, S., & Farmer, D. (1990). An introduction to chaos and randomness. In E. Jen (Ed.), *1989 Lectures in complex systems* (pp. 75–190). Redwood City, CA: Addison-Wesley.

Falconer, K. (1990). *Fractal geometry: Mathematical foundations and applications.* Chichester: John Wiley and Sons.

Featherman, D. L. (1986). Biography, society, and history: Individual development as a population process. In A. B. Sorensen, F. E. Weinert, and L. R. Sherrod (Eds.), *Human development and the life course: Multidisciplinary perspectives* (pp. 99–149). Hillsdale, NJ: Lawrence Erlbaum.

Feigenbaum, M. J. (1979). Universal metric properties of non-linear transformation. *Journal of Statistical Physics, 21,* 669–706.

Fienberg, S. E. (1980). *The analysis of cross-classified categorical data* (2nd ed.). Cambridge: MIT Press.

Flavell, J. H. (1972). An analysis of cognitive-developmental sequences. *Genetic Psychology Monographs, 86,* 279–350.

Flavell, J. H. (1982). Structures, stages, and sequences in cognitive development. In W. A. Collins (Ed.), *The concept of development: The Minnesota symposia on child psychology* (pp. 1–28). Hillsdale, NJ: Lawrence Erlbaum.

Folger, J. P., Hewes, D. E., & Poole, M. S. (1984). Coding social interaction. In B. Dervin and M. Voight (Eds.), *Progress in communication sciences, Vol. 4* (pp. 115–161). New York: Ablex.

Forgas, J. P. (1975). *Social episodes: The study of interaction routines.* London: Academic Press.

Freeman, C. (1986). *The economics of industrial innovation.* Cambridge, MA: MIT Press.

Freeman, W. (1991, February). The physiology of perception. *Scientific American, 264,* 78–85.

Frey, P. W. (1986, November). A bit-mapped classifier. *BYTE,* 161–172.

Galtung, J. (1967). *Theory and methods of social research.* New York: Columbia University Press.

Garud, R., & Van de Ven, A. H. (1989). Technological innovation and industry emergence: The case of cochlear implants. In A. H. Van de Ven, H. L. Angle, and M. S. Poole (Eds.), *Research on the management of innovation: The Minnesota studies* (pp. 489–532). New York: Ballinger/Harper & Row.

Garud, R., & Van de Ven, A. H. (1992). An empirical evaluation of the internal corporate venturing process. *Strategic Management Journal, 13,* 93–109.

Gell-Mann, M. (1994). *The quark and the jaguar.* New York: Freeman.

Gersick, C. J. (1991). Revolutionary change theories: A multilevel exploration of the punctuated equilibrium paradigm. *Academy of Management Review, 16,* 10–36.

Gibson, E. J. (1988). Exploratory behavior in the development of perceiving, acting, and the acquiring of knowledge. *Annual Review of Psychology, 39,* 1–41.

Ginsberg, R. (1971). Semi-Markov processes and social mobility. *Journal of Mathematical Sociology, 1,* 233–263.

Gioia, D. A., & Pitre, E. (1990). Multiparadigm perspectives in theory building. *Academy of Management Review, 15,* 584–602.

Gleick, J. (1987). *Chaos: Making a new science.* New York: Penguin.

Gluck, F. W., Kaufman, S. P. & Walleck, A. S. (1980). Strategic management for competitive advantage. *Harvard Business Review, 58,* 154–161.

Goldstein, J. (1994). *The unshackled organization.* Portland: Productivity Press.

Gordon, T. J., & Greenspan, D. (1988). Chaos and fractals: New tools for technological social forecasting. *Technological Forecasting and Social Change, 34* (August): 1–25.

Gould, S. J. (1989). Punctuated equilibrium in fact and theory. *Journal of Social and Biological Structures, 12,* 117–136.

Gould, S. J., & Eldridge, N. (1977). Punctuated equilibria: The tempo and model of evolution reconsidered. *Paleobiology, 3,* 115–151.

Granger, C. (1969). Investigating causal relations by econometric models and cross-spectral methods. *Econometrica, 37,* 424–438.

Granger, C. W., & Newbold, P. (1986). *Forecasting economic time series.* New York: Academic Press.

Grassberger, P., & Procaccia, I. (1983). Measuring the strangeness of strange attractors. *Physica, 9D,* 189–208.

Grebogi, C., Ott, E., Pelikan, S., & Yorke, J. (1984). Strange attractors that are not chaotic. *Physica, 13D,* 261–268.

Greiner, L. (1972). Evolution and revolution as organizations grow. *Harvard Business Review,* July-August, 165–174.

Greybill, F. A. (1983). *Matrices with applications in statistics* (2nd ed.). Belmont, CA: Wadsworth.

Griffin, L. J. (1993). Narrative, event-structure analysis, and causal interpretation in historical sociology. *American Journal of Sociology, 98,* 1094–1133.

Gross, A. J. & Clark, V. A. (1975). *Survival distributions: Reliability applications in the biomedical sciences.* New York: Holt, Rinehart & Winston.

Guastello, S. (1995). *Chaos, catastrophe, and human affairs.* Mahwah NJ: Erlbaum.

Guo, Y., & Dooley, K. (1995). Distinguishing between mean, variance, and auto-correlation changes in statistical quality control. *International Journal of Production Research, 33(2),* 497–510.

Hannan, M. T., & Freeman, F. (1977). The population ecology of organizations. *American Journal of Sociology, 82,* 929–964.

Hannan, M., & Freeman, J. (1989). *Organizational ecology.* Cambridge, MA: Harvard University Press.

Harre, R., & Madden, E. A. (1975). *Causal powers.* Totowa, NJ: Littlefield Adams.

He, Y. (1995). *Mathematica applications library: Time series pack.* Champaign, IL: Wolfram Research.

Heise, D. (1989). Modeling event structures. *Journal of Mathematical Sociology, 14,* 139–169.

Hernes, G. (1976). Structural change in social processes. *American Journal of Sociology, 82,* 513–545.

Hewes, D. E. (1980). Stochastic modeling of communication processes. In P. Monge (Ed.) *Multivariate techniques in human communication research* (pp. 393–427). New York: Academic Press.

Hewes, D. E., Planalp, S., & Streibel, M. (1980). Analyzing social interaction: Some excruciating models and exhilirating results. In D. I. Nimmo (Ed.) *Communication Yearbook* IV (pp. 123–141). New Brunswick, NJ: Transaction Books.

Hibbert, B., & Wilkinson, I. F. (1994). Chaos theory and the dynamics of marketing systems. *Journal of the Academy of Marketing Science, 22,* 218–233.

Hill, M. R. (1993). *Archival strategies and techniques.* Newbury Park, CA: Sage.

Holmes, M. E. (1992). Phase structures in negotiation. In L. L. Putnam and M. E. Roloff (Eds.), *Communication and negotiation* (pp. 83–108). Newbury Park, CA: Sage.

Holmes, M. E. (1997a). Processes and patterns in hostage negotiations. In R. G. Rogan and M. R. Hammer (Eds.), *Dynamic processes of hostage negotiations: Theory, research, and practice* (pp. 77–93). Westwood, CT: Praeger.

Holmes, M. E. (1997b). Optimal matching analysis of negotiation phase sequences in simulated and authentic hostage negotiations. *Communication Reports, 10,* 1–9.

Holmes, M. E. & Poole, M. S. (1991). Longitudinal analysis. In B. Montgomery &

S. Duck (Eds.), *Studying interpersonal interaction* (pp. 286–302). New York: Guilford.

Horn, J. L. (1991). Comments on "issues in factorial invariance." In L. M. Collins and J. L. Horn (Eds.), *Best methods for the analysis of change: Recent advances, unanswered questions, future directions* (pp. 114–125). Washington, DC: American Psychological Association.

Howard, R. (1971). *Dynamic probabilistic systems,* vol. 2. New York: Wiley.

Hsieh, D. A. (1991). Chaos and nonlinear dynamics: Applications to financial markets. *The Journal of Finance, 41,* 1839–1877.

Hubert, L. J., & Levin, J. R. (1976). Evaluating object set partitions: Free-sort analysis and some generalizations. *Journal of Verbal Learning and Verbal Behavior, 15,* 459–470.

Hubert, L. J., & Schutte, J. (1976). Quadratic assignment as a general data analysis strategy. *British Journal of Mathematical and Statistical Psychology, 29,* 190–241.

Hull, D. L. (1975). Central subjects and historical narratives. *History and Theory, 14,* 253–274.

Isaac, J., & Griffin, J. (1989). Ahistoricism in time series analyses of historical process: Critique, redirection, and illustrations from U.S. labor movement. *American Sociological Review, 54,* 873–890.

James, L. R., & Brett, J. M. (1984). Mediators, moderators, and test for mediation. *Journal of Applied Psychology, 69,* 307–321.

James, B., James, K. & Siegmund, D. (1987). Tests for a change point. *Biometrika, 74,* 71–83.

Jayanthi, S., & Sinha, K. K. (1998). Innovation implementation in high technology manufacturing: Chaos-theoretic empirical analysis. *Journal of Operations Management, 16,* 471–494.

Kalbfleisch, J. D., & Prentice, R. L. (1980). *The statistical analysis of failure time data.* New York: Wiley.

Kaplan, A. (1964). *The conduct of inquiry: Methodology for behavioral science.* New York: Chandler.

Kaplan, D., & Glass, L. (1995). *Understanding nonlinear dynamics,* New York: Springer-Verlag.

Kellerman, K. (1988, May). *The limits of lag sequential analysis in the description of patterns of dependence.* Paper presented at the annual conference of the International Communication Association.

Kiel, L. D. (1994). *Managing chaos and complexity in government.* San Francisco: Jossey-Bass.

Kiesler, S., & Sproull, L. (1982). Management response to changing environments: Perspectives on problem solving from social cognition. *Administrative Science Quarterly, 27,* 548–570.

Kimberly, J. (1980). The life cycle analogy and the study of organizations: Introduction. In J. Kimberly & R. Miles (Eds.), *The organizational life cycle* (pp. 1–14). San Francisco: Jossey-Bass.

Kimberly, J., & Miles, R. (1980). *The organizational life cycle.* San Francisco: Jossey-Bass.

Knudson, M. K., & Ruttan, V. W. (1989). The management of research and development of a biological innovation. In A. H. Van de Ven, H. L. Angle, and M. S. Poole (Eds.), *Research on the management of innovation: The Minnesota studies* (pp. 465–488). New York: Ballinger/Harper & Row.

Kohlberg, L. (1969). Stage and sequence: The cognitive-developmental approach to socialization. In D. A. Goslin (Ed.), *Handbook of socialization theory and research* (pp. 347–480). San Francisco: Rand McNally.

Koput, K. (1992). *Dynamics of innovative idea generation in organizations: Randomness and chaos in the development of a new medical device.* Unpublished doctoral dissertation, University of California at Berkeley.

Kugelmass, S., & Breznitz, S. (1967). The Guttman scale as a means of testing Piaget's theory of development. *Journal of Genetic Psychology, 111,* 169–170.

Kullback, S., Kupperman, M., & Ku, H. (1962). Tests for contingency tables and Markov chains. *Technometrics, 4,* 573–608.

Leik, R. K., & Matthews, M. (1968). A scale for developmental processes. *American Sociological Review, 33,* 62–75.

Leik, R. K., & Meeker, B. F. (1975). *Mathematical sociology.* Englewood Cliffs, NJ: Prentice Hall.

Leonard-Barton, D. (1990). A dual methodology for case studies: Synergistic use of a longitudinal single site with multiple replicated sites. *Organization Science, 1,* 248–266.

Levinson, D. J. (1978). *The seasons of a man's life.* New York: Knopf.

Lewin, K. (1945). The research center for group dynamics at Massachusetts Institute of Technology. *Sociometry, 8,* 126–135.

Liang, K-L, & Zeger, S. L. (1989). A class of logistic regression models for multivariate binary time series. *Journal of the American Statistical Association, 84,* 447–451.

Lin, T. (1989). *SELAGGR: A selection and aggregation program for bit-map data.* (Tech. Rep.). Minneapolis, MN: University of Minnesota, Strategic Management Research Center.

Lindblom, C. E. (1965). *The intelligence of democracy.* New York: Free Press.

Lorange, P. (1980). *Corporate planning: An executive viewpoint.* Englewood Cliffs, N.J.: Prentice Hall.

Lord, F. M., and M. R. Novick, (1968). *Statistical theories of mental test scores.* Reading, MA.: Addison-Wesley.

Maier, N. R. F. (1970). *Problem solving and creativity in individuals and groups.* Monterey, CA: Brooks/Cole.

March, J. G. (1981). Footnotes to organizational change. *Administrative Science Quarterly, 26,* 563–577.

March, J. G. (1991). Exploration and exploitation in organizational learning. *Organization Science, 2,* 71–87.

March, J. G. (1994). *A primer on decision making.* New York: Free Press.

March, J. G., & Olsen, J. P. (1976). *Ambiguity and choice in organizations.* Bergen: Universitetsforlaget.

March, J. G., & Simon, H. A. (1958). *Organizations.* New York: Wiley.

Masuch, M. (1985). Vicious cycles in organizations. *Administrative Science Quarterly, 30,* 14–33.

May, R. M. (1976). Simple mathematical models with very complicated dynamics. *Nature, 261,* 459–467.

Mayer, K. U. & Tuma, N. B. (1990). *Event history analysis in life course research.* Madison: University of Wisconsin Press.

McDowall, D., McCleary, R., Meidinger, E., & Hay, R. (1980). *Interrupted time series analysis.* Newbury Park, CA: Sage.

McGrath, J. E. (1988). *The social psychology of time.* New York: Guilford.

McGrath, J. E., & Kelly, J. R. (1986) (Eds.) *Time and human interaction.* Newbury Park: Sage.

McKelvey, B. (1982). *Organizational systematics: Taxonomy, evolution, classification.* Berkeley, CA: University of California Press.

Merton, R. (1968). *Social theory and social structure.* New York: Free Press.

Messinger, S. L. (1955). Organizational transformation: Case study of a declining social movement. *American Sociological Review, 20,* 3–10.

Meyer, A. D., Goes, J. B., & Brooks, G. R. (1993). Organizations reacting to hyperturbulence. In G. P. Huber and W. H. Glick (Eds.), *Organizational change and redesign* (pp. 66–111). New York: Oxford University Press.

Meyer, J. W., & Rowan, B. (1977). Institutional organizations: Formal structure as myth and ceremony. *American Journal of Sociology, 83,* 340–363.

Miles, M. B., and Huberman, A. M. (1984). *Qualitative data analysis: A sourcebook of new methods.* Beverly Hills, CA: Sage.

Miles, M. B., and Huberman, A. M. (1994). *Qualitative data analysis: A sourcebook of new methods* (2nd ed.). Thousand Oaks, CA: Sage.

Miller, D., & Freisen, P. H. (1982). The longitudinal analysis of organizations: A methodological perspective. *Management Science, 28,* 1013–1034.

Mintzberg, H., Raisinghani, D., and Theoret, A. (1976). The structure of "unstructured" decision processes. *Administrative Science Quarterly, 21,* 246–275.

Mitroff, I., and Emshoff, J. (1979). On strategic assumption making: A dialectical approach to policy and planning. *Academy of Management Review, 4,* 1–12

Mohr, L. (1982). *Explaining organizational behavior.* San Francisco: Jossey-Bass.

Montgomery, D. (1996). *Statistical methods for quality control.* New York: John Wiley and Sons.

Moon, F. C. (1987). *Chaotic vibrations.* New York: Wiley.

Morrison, F. (1991). *The art of modeling dynamic systems.* New York: Wiley.

Neal, M. A.,& Northcraft, G. B. (1991). Behavioral negotiation theory: A framework for conceptualizing dyadic bargaining. In L. Cummings and B. Staw (Eds.), *Research in organizational behavior, 13,* 147–190. Greenwich, CT: JAI Press.

Nelson, R. R., & Winter, S. G. (1982). *An evolutionary theory of economic change.* Cambridge, MA: Harvard University Press.

Newell, A. (1973). Production systems: Models of control structures. In W. G. Chase (Ed.), *Visual information processing* (pp. 463–562). New York: Academic Press.

Nisbet, R. A. (1970). Developmentalism: A critical analysis. In J. McKinney and E. Tiryakin (Eds.), *Theoretical sociology: Perspectives and developments* (pp. 167–213). New York: Meredith.

Norman, D. A. (1993). *Things that make us smart: Defending human attributes in the age of the machine*. Reading, MA: Addison-Wesley.

Nutt, P. C. (1984a). Types of organizational decision processes. *Administrative Science Quarterly, 29,* 414–450.

Nutt, P. C. (1984b). Planning process archetypes and their effectiveness. *Decision Sciences, 15,* 221–238.

Nutt, P. C. (1993). The formulation processes and tactics used in organizational decision making. *Organization Science, 4,* 226–251.

O'Toole, J. M. (Ed.) (1997). *The records of American business*. Chicago, IL: Society of American Archivists.

Pandit, S. (1991). *Modal and spectrum analysis: Data dependent systems in state space*. New York: Wiley.

Pandit, S. & Wu, S. (1983). *Time series and system analysis with applications*. New York: Wiley.

Parsons, T. (1951). *The social system*. New York: Free Press.

Peirce, C. S. (1955). *Philosophical writings of Peirce* (J. Buchler, ed.). New York: Dover.

Peitgen, H-O., Jurgens, H., & Saupe, D. (1992). *Chaos and fractals: New frontiers of science*. New York: Springer-Verlag.

Pelz, D. C. (1985). Innovation complexity and the sequence of innovating stages. *Knowledge: Creation, Diffusion, Utilization, 6,* 261–291.

Peters, E. (1994). *Fractal market analysis*. New York: John Wiley & Sons.

Pettigrew, A. M. (1985). *The awakening giant: Continuity and change in ICI*. Oxford: Basil Blackwell.

Pettigrew, A. M. (1990). Longitudinal field research on change: Theory and practice. *Organization Science, 1,* 267–292.

Pfeffer, J. (1982). *Organizations and organization theory*. Boston: Pitman.

Piaget, J. (1975). *The child's conception of the world*. Totowa: Littlefied, Adams.

Planalp, S. & Tracy, K. (1980). "Not to change the topic but . . . ": A cognitive approach to the management of conversation. In D. Nimmo (Ed.) *Communication yearbook* III (pp. 237–258). New Brunswick, NJ: ICA-Transaction Press.

Poggie, G. (1965). A main theme of contemporary social analysis: Its achievements and limitations. *British Journal of Sociology, 16,* 283–294.

Polkinghorne, D. E. (1988). *Narrative knowing and the human sciences*. Albany, NY: SUNY Press.

Polley, D. (1993, August). *Chaos as metaphor and science: Applications and risks*. Paper presented at Academy of Management Conference, Miami, FL.

Polley, D., & Van de Ven, A. H. (1989). Therapeutic apheresis program joint-venture case. In A. H. Van de Ven, H. L. Angle, and M. S. Poole (Eds.), *Research on the management of innovation: The Minnesota studies* (pp. 261–276). New York: Ballinger/Harper & Row.

Pondy, L., & Mitroff, I. I. (1979). Beyond open systems models of organization. In L. L. Cummings and B. M. Staw (Eds.), *Research in organizational behavior* (Vol. 1, pp. 3–39). Greenwich, CT: JAI Press.

Poole, M. S. (1981). Decision development in small groups I: A test of two models. *Communication Monographs, 48,* 1–24.

Poole, M. S. (1983a). Decision development in small groups II: A study of multiple sequences in decision making. *Communication Monographs, 50,* 206–232.

Poole, M. S., (1983b). Decision development in small groups, III: A multiple sequence model of group decision development. *Communication Monographs, 50,* 321–341.

Poole, M. S. (1985). Tasks and interaction sequences: A theory of coherence in group decision-making. In R. Street and J. N. Cappella (Eds.), *Sequence and pattern in communicative behavior* (pp. 206–224). London: Edward Arnold.

Poole, M. S., & Doelger, J. A. (1986). Developmental processes in group decision making. In R. Y. Hirokawa and M. S. Poole (Eds.), *Communication and group decision-making* (pp. 35–62). Beverly Hills, CA: Sage.

Poole, M. S., & Holmes, M. E. (1995). Decision development in computer-assisted group decision making. *Human Communication Research, 22,* 90–127.

Poole, M. S., & Roth, J. (1989a). Decision development in small groups IV: A typology of decision paths. *Human Communication Research, 15,* 323–356.

Poole, M. S., & Roth, J. (1989b). Decision development in small groups V: Test of a contingency model. *Human Communication Research, 15,* 549–589.

Poole, M. S., & Van de Ven, A. H. (1989). Toward a general theory of innovation. In A. Van de Ven, H. Angle, and M. S. Poole (Eds.), *Research on the management of innovation* (pp. 637–662). New York: Ballinger/Harper & Row.

Poole, M. S., Folger, J. P., & Hewes, D. E. (1987). Analyzing interpersonal interaction. In M. E. Roloff and G. R. Miller (Eds.), *Interpersonal processes* (pp. 220–256). Newbury Park, CA: Sage.

Popping, R. (1988). On agreement indices for nominal data. In W. E. Saris & I. N. Galhofer (Ed.) *Sociometric research, Vol. 1: Data collection and scaling* (pp. 90–105). New York: St. Martin's Press.

Priesmeyer, H. R. (1992). *Organizations and chaos.* Westport, CT: Quorum Books.

Prigogine, I. & Stengers, S. (1984). *Order out of chaos.* New York: Heinemann.

Quinn, J. B. (1980). *Strategies for change: Logical incrementalism.* Homewood, IL: Irwin.

Ramsey, J. B., & Yuan, H. (1989). Bias and error bars in dimension calculations and their evaluation in some simple models. *Physics Letter A, 134,* 287–297.

Ramsey, F. L. & Schafer, D. W. (1997). *The statistical sleuth: A course in methods of data analysis.* Belmont, CA:

Randall, J. H., Jr. (1960). *Aristotle.* New York: Columbia University Press.

Riegel, K. F. (1975). From traits and equilibrium toward developmental dialectics. In J. Cole and W. S. Arnold (Eds.), *Nebraska symposium on motivation* (pp. 349–407). Lincoln, NE: University of Nebraska Press.

Riegel, K. F. (1976). The dialectics of human development. *American Psychologist, 30(10),* 689–700.

Ring, P. & Rands, G. (1989). Transaction processes in 3M-NASA relations. In A. Van de Ven, H. Angle, and M. S. Poole (Eds.), *Research on the management of innovation* (pp. 337–366). New York: Ballinger/Harper & Row.

Ring, P. S., & Van de Ven, A. H. (1994). Developmental processes of cooperative interorganizational relationships. *Academy of Management Review, 19,* 90–118.

Roberts, N. C., & King, P. J. (1989). The process of public policy innovation. In A. H. Van de Ven, H. L. Angle, and M. S. Poole (Eds.), *Research on the management of innovation: The Minnesota studies* (pp. 303–336). New York: Ballinger/Harper & Row.

Rogers, E. (1995). *Diffusion of innovations* (5th ed.). New York: Free Press.

Rogers, L. E., & Farace, R. V. (1975). Analysis of relational communication in dyads: New measurement procedures. *Human Communication Research, 1,* 222–239.

Romanelli, E., & Tushman, M. (1994). Organizational transformation as punctuated equilibrium: An empirical test. *Academy of Management Journal, 37,* 1141–1166.

Rosenstein, M., Collins, J., & De Luca, C. (1993). A practical method for calculating largest Lyapunov exponents from small data sets. *Physica D, 65,* 117–134.

Ross, D. (1964). *Aristotle.* London: Methuen.

Ruelle, D., & Takens, F. (1971). On the nature of turbulence. *Communications in Mathematical Physics, 20,* 167–192, *23,* 343–344.

Ruhla, C. (1992). *The physics of chance.* Oxford: Oxford University Press.

Saberwhal, R., & Robey, D. (1993). An empirical taxonomy of implementation processes based on sequences of events in information system development. *Organization Science, 4,* 548–576.

Sackett, G. P. (1979). The lag sequential analysis of contingency and cyclicity in behavioral interaction research. In J. D. Osofsky (Ed.) *Handbook of infant development* (pp. 623–649). New York: Wiley.

Sackett, G. P. (1980). Lag sequential analysis as a data reduction technique in social interaction research. In D. Sawin (Ed.) *Psychosocial risks in infant-environment transactions* (pp. 300–340). New York: Brunner/Mazel.

Sackett, M., Holm, R., Crowley, C., & Henkins, A. (1979). A FORTRAN program for lag sequential analysis of contingency and cyclicity in behavioral interaction data. *Behavior research methods and instrumentation, 11,* 366–378.

Sambamurthy, V., & Poole, M. S. (1992). The effects of variations in capabilities of GDSS designs on management of cognitive conflict in groups. *Information Systems Research, 3,* 224–251.

Sankoff, D., & Kruskal, J. B. (Eds.). (1983). *Time warps, string edits, and macromolecules: The theory and practice of sequence comparison.* Reading, MA: Addison-Wesley.

Schaffer, W. M., & Kot, M. (1986). Differential systems in ecology and epidemiology. In A. V. Holden (Ed.), *Chaos* (pp. 158–178). Princeton: Princeton University Press.

Schaie, K. W. (1965). A general model for the study of developmental problems. *Psychological Bulletin, 64,* 92–107.

Schaie, K. W. (1973). An extension of developmental models that separate onto-genetic changes and cohort differences. *Psychological Bulletin, 80,* 466–479.

Scheidel, T. M., & Crowell, L. (1964). Idea development in small groups. *Quarterly Journal of Speech, 50,* 140–145.

Scheinkman, J. A., & LeBaron, B. (1989). Nonlinear dynamics and stock returns. *Journal of Business, 62,* 311–337.

Schroeder, M. (1991). *Fractals, chaos, power laws.* New York: Freeman.

Schroeder, R., Van de Ven, A. Scudder, G., & Polley, D. (1986). Managing innovation and change processes: Findings from the Minnesota innovation research program. *Agribusiness, 2,* 501–523.

Schumpeter, J. A. (1942). *Capitalism, socialism, and democracy.* New York: Harper & Row.

Schuster, H. G. (1989). Extraction of models from complex data. In N. B. Abraham, A. M. Albano, A. Passamante, and P. E. Rapp (Eds.), *Measures of complexity and chaos* (pp. 349–358). New York: Plenum Press.

Scott, B. R. (1971). *Stages of corporate development.* Unpublished manuscript, Harvard Business School at Boston, Massachusetts.

Scott, W. R., & Meyer, J. W. (Eds.). (1994). *Institutional environments and organizations: Structural complexity and individualism.* Thousand Oaks, CA: Sage.

Simon, H. A. (Ed.) . (1979). *Models of thought.* New Haven: Yale University Press.

Singer, B., & Spilerman, S. (1979). Mathematical representations of development theories. In J. R. Nesselroade & P. B. Baltes (Eds.) *Longitudinal research in the study of behavior and development* (pp. 155–177). New York: Academic Press.

Singh, J. V., & Lumsden, C. J. (1990). Theory and research in organizational ecology. *Annual Review of Sociology, 16,* 161–95.

Spilerman, S. (1972). The analysis of mobility processes by the introduction of independent variables into a Markov chain. *American Sociological Review, 37,* 277–294.

Sprott, J. C., & Rowlands, G. (1995). *Chaos data analyzer.* New York: American Institute of Physics.

Stacey, R. (1992). *Managing the unknowable.* San Francisco: Jossey-Bass.

Stanley, M., Amaral, L., Buldyrev, S., Havlin, S., Leschorn, H., Maass, P., Salinger, M., & Stanley, H. (1996). Scaling behaviour in the growth of companies. *Nature, 379,* 804–807.

Stinchcombe, A. (1972). *Constructing social theories.* New York: Harcourt, Brace and World.

Stutzer, M. (1980). Chaotic dynamics and bifurcations in a macro model. *Journal of Economic Dynamics and Control, 2,* 353–376.

Suppes, P., & Atkinson, R. C. (1960). *Markov learning models for multiperson interactions.* Stanford, CA: Stanford University Press.

Takens, F. (1981). Detecting strange attractors in turbulence. In D. A. Rand and L. S. Young (Eds.), *Lecture Notes In Mathematics, 898* (pp. 366–381). Berlin-Heidelberg-New York: Springer-Verlag.

Theiler, J., & Eubank, S. (1993). Don't bleach chaotic data. *Chaos, 3,* 771–782.

Theiler, J., Eubank, S., Longtin, A., Galdrikian, B., & Farmer, J. D. (1992). Testing for nonlinearity in time series: The method of surrogate data. *Physica D, 58,* 77–94.

Thietart, R. A., & Forgues, B. (1995). Chaos theory and organization. *Organization Science, 6,* 19–31.

Tornatsky, L. G., Eveland, J. D., Boylan, M. G., Hetzner, W. A., Johnson, E. C., Roltman, D., & Schneider, J. (1983). *The process of technological innovation: Reviewing the literature.* Washington, D. C.: National Science Foundation.

Tong, H. (1990). *Nonlinear time series.* Oxford: Oxford University Press.

Tsoukas, H. (1989). The validity of idiographic research explanations. *Academy of Management Review, 14,* 551–561.

Tucker, L. R. (1966). Learning theory and multivariate experiment: Illustration by determination of generalized learning curves. In R. B. Cattell (Ed.), *Handbook of multivariate experimental psychology* (pp. 476–501). Chicago: Rand-McNally.

Tuma, N. B., & Hannan, M. T. (1984). *Social dynamics: Models and methods.* San Diego, CA: Academic Press.

Tushman, M. L., & Anderson, A. (1986). Technological discontinuities and organizational environment. *Administrative Science Quarterly, 31,* 436–465.

Tushman, M. L., & Romanelli, E. (1985). Organizational evolution: A metamorphosis model of convergence and reorientation. In B. Staw and L. Cummings (Eds.), *Research in organizational behavior, 7,* 171–222. Greenwich, CT: JAI Press.

Utterback, J. M., & Abernathy, W. J. (1975). A dynamic model of process and product innovation. *Omega, 3,* 639–656.

Valente, T. (1995). *Network models of the diffusion of innovations.* Creskill, NJ: Hampton Press.

Van de Ven, A. H. (1980a). Early planning, implementation, and performance of new organizations. In J. R. Kimberly and R. H. Miles (Eds.), *The organizational life cycle: Issues in the creation, transformation, and decline of organizations* (pp. 83–134). San Francisco: Jossey-Bass.

Van de Ven, A. H. (1980b). Problem solving, planning and innovation: Part I, Test of the program planning model. *Human Relations, 33,* 711–740.

Van de Ven, A. H. (1980c). Problem solving, planning and innovation: Part II, Speculations for theory and practice. *Human Relations, 33,* 757–779.

Van de Ven, A. H. (1986). Central problems in the management of innovation. *Management Science, 32,* 590–607.

Van de Ven, A. H. (1992). Suggestions for studying strategy process: A research note. *Strategic Management Journal, 13,* 169–188.

Van de Ven, A. H., & Angle, H. L. (1989). An introduction to the Minnesota innovation research program. In A. Van de Ven, H. Angle, and M. S. Poole (Eds.), *Research on the management of innovation* (pp. 3–30). New York: Ballinger/Harper & Row.

Van de Ven, A. H., Angle, H. L., & Poole, M. S. (Eds.). (1989). *Research on the management of innovation,* New York: Ballinger/Harper & Row.

Van de Ven, A. H., & Chu, Y. (1989). A psychometric assessment of the Minnesota innovation survey. In A. H. Van de Ven, H. L. Angle, and M. S. Poole (Eds.),

Research on the management of innovation: The Minnesota studies (pp. 55–104). New York: Ballinger/Harper & Row.

Van de Ven, A. H., & Ferry, D. L. (1980). *Measuring and assessing organizations.* New York: Wiley.

Van de Ven, A. H., & Garud, R. (1993). Innovation and industry development: The case of cochlear implants. In R. Rosenbloom (Ed.), *Research on technological innovation, management and policy* (Vol. 5, pp. 1–46). Greenwich, CT: JAI Press.

Van de Ven, A. H., & Huber, G. P. (1990). Longitudinal field research methods for studying processes of organizational change. *Organization Science, 1,* 213–219.

Van de Ven, A. H. & Polley, D. (1992). Learning while innovating. *Organization Science, 3,* 92–116.

Van de Ven, A. H., & Poole, M. S. (1988). Paradoxical requirements for a theory of organizational change. In R. Quinn and K. Cameron (Eds.), *Paradox and transformation: Toward a theory of change in organization and management* (pp. 19–80). New York: Ballinger/HarperCollins.

Van de Ven, A. H., & Poole, M. S. (1995). Explaining development and change in organizations. *Academy of Management Review, 20,* 510–540.

Van de Ven, A. H. & Walker, G. (1984). The dynamics of interorganizational relationships. *Administrative Science Quarterly, 29,* 598–621

Van de Ven, A. H., Walker, G., & Liston, J. (1979). Coordination patterns within an interorganizational network. *Human Relations, 32,* 19–36.

Van den Daele, L. D. (1969). Qualitative models in developmental analysis. *Developmental Psychology, 1,* 303–331.

Van den Daele, L. D. (1974). Infrastructure and transition in developmental analysis. *Human Development, 17,* 1–23.

Venkataraman, S., & Van de Ven, A. H. (1989). Qnetics new business creation case. In A. H. Van de Ven, H. L. Angle, and M. S. Poole (Eds.), *Research on the management of innovation: The Minnesota studies* (pp. 228–243). New York: Ballinger/Harper & Row.

Venkatraman, N., & Prescott, J. E. (1990). Environment-strategy coalignment: An empirical test of its performance implications. *Strategic Management Journal, 11,* 1–23.

Von Wright, G. H. (1971). *Explanation and understanding.* Ithaca, NY: Cornell University Press.

Walsh, W. H. (1967). *Philosophy of history: An introduction.* New York: Harper.

Walster, G. W. and Cleary, T. A. (1970). Statistical significance as a decision rule. In E. Borgatta and Bohrnsteadt (Eds.), *Sociological methodology* (pp. 246–254). San Francisco: Jossey-Bass.

Watzlawick, P., Weakland J. H., & Fisch, R. (1974). *Change: Principles of problem formation and problem resolution.* New York: Norton.

Weber, M. (1949). *The methodology of the social sciences* (E. Shils & H. A. Finch, Trans.). Glencoe, IL: The Free Press.

Weick, K. E. (1979). *The social psychology of organizing* (2nd ed.) . Reading, MA: Addison-Wesley.

Weisberg, S. (1985). *Applied linear regression* (2nd ed.). New York: Wiley.

Weitzman, E. A., & Miles, M. A. (1995). *Computer programs for qualitative data analysis.* Thousand Oaks, CA: Sage.

West, B., & Deering, B. (1995). *The lure of modern science.* Singapore: World Scientific.

Whitney, H. (1936). Differentiable manifolds. *Annals of Mathematics, 37,* 645–680.

Willet, J. B., & Singer, J. D. (1991). How long did it take? Using survival analysis in educational and psychological research. In L. M. Collins and J. L. Horn (Eds.), *Best methods for the analysis of change* (pp. 310–328). Washington, D.C.: American Psychological Association.

Wohlwill, J. (1973). *The study of behavior development.* New York: Academic Press.

Wolf, A. (1986). Quantifying chaos with Lyapunov exponents. In A. V. Holden (Ed.), *Chaos* (pp. 273–290). Princeton: Princeton University Press.

Wolf, A., Swift, J. B., Swinney, H. L., & Vastano, J. A. (1985). Determining Lyapunov exponents from a time series. *Physica, 16D,* 285–317.

Wolfram, S. (1988). *Mathematica.* Redwood City, CA: Addison-Wesley.

Yin, R. K. (1984). *Case study research: Design and methods.* Beverly Hills: Sage.

Zeeman, E. C. (1976). Catastrophe theory. *Scientific American, 234,* 65–83.

Acknowledgments

The quotation on page 28 is reprinted from J. Kimberly and R. Miles, *The Organizational Life Cycle* by permission of Jossey-Bass Inc., Publishers. Copyright © 1980 by Jossey-Bass Inc., Publishers.

The quotation on page 33 is reprinted from L. Mohr, *Explaining Organizational Behavior* by permission of Jossey-Bass Inc., Publishers. Copyright © 1982 by Jossey-Bass Inc., Publishers.

The quotation on page 40 is reprinted from *History and Theory, 14,* 256. Copyright © 1975 by Blackwell Publishers.

The quotations on pages 40 and 45 are reprinted from *Historical Methods, 23,* 140–150, 1990. Reprinted with permission of the Helen Dwight Reid Educational Foundation. Published by Heldref Publications 1319 Eighteenth St., N.W., Washington, D.C. 20036-1802. Copyright © 1990.

The quotation on page 55 is reprinted from *Actual Minds, Possible Worlds* by Jerome Bruner. Copyright © 1986 by the President and Fellows of Harvard College. Reprinted by permission of Harvard University Press.

Chapter 3 is adapted from A. Van de Ven and M. S. Poole published in *Academy of Management Review, 20,* 510–540. Copyright © 1995 by the Academy of Management.

The quotation on page 76 is reprinted from A. Van de Ven, Suggestions for Studying the Strategy Process: A Research Note, *Strategic Management Journal, 13,* 169–188. Copyright © John Wiley and Sons Limited. Reproduced with permission.

The quotation on page 78 is reprinted from the *Nebraska Symposium on Motivation* by permission of the University of Nebraska Press. Copyright © 1976 by the University of Nebraska Press.

The quotation on page 112 is reprinted from D. Miller and P. H. Friesen, *Management Science, 28,* 1013–1034. Reprinted by permission of INFORMS.

The quotation on page 132 is reprinted from A. Abbott *Sociological Methods and Research, 20(3),* p. 439, copyrightr © 1992 by Sage Publications, Inc. Reprinted by permission of Sage Publications, Inc.

Table 7.1 is based on Cook, Thomas and Campbell, Donald, *Quasi-Experimentation: Design and Analysis Issues for Field Settings.* Copyright © 1979 by Houghton Mifflin Company. Adapted with permission.

Figures 7.4 and 7.5 are adapted from P. C. Nutt, The Formulation Processes and Tactics Used in Organizational Decision Making, *Organization Science, 4,* 226–251. Reprinted by permission, The Institute of Management Science (currently INFORMS), 901 Elkridge Landing Road, Suite 400, Linthicum, Maryland 21090-2909 USA.

Figures 9.10 and 9.11 are adapted from Daniel Stein, *Lectures in the Sciences of Complexity.* Copyright © 1989, Perseus Books. Reprinted by permission of Perseus Books Publishers, a member of Perseus Books, L.L.C.

Index

age effects: 120
agency: 26, 50–51
  and stochastic models: 179
archival data: 118, 136
  advantages and disadvantages of: 137–138
  quality of: 138
attributes: 32, 35, 47
autocorrelation: 293, 296–299

biases, measurement: 9
biogenesis: 58
biology: 29
bitmap: 150, 152, 168–170
blueprints: 96

case studies: 4, 112
categories
  as indicators: 140–141
  event categories
    action (activity): 102, 106, 107, 110
    context: 102, 106, 110, 130, 147, 344
    course of action: 107, 110, 212–227, 344
    feedback: 213
    idea: 106, 110, 130, 147
    interorganizational relations: 255
    outcome: 102, 107, 111, 130, 147, 213, 344
    people: 107, 110, 130, 147
    topic: 212
    transaction: 107, 130, 147

mapping to constructs: 141–142
systems (see also coding systems): 129
causal relationships: 6, 23, 33
  distal causation: 35, 46
  efficient cause: 33, 41, 43, 47
  final cause: 41, 45, 54, 94
  formal cause: 41, 45, 54, 94
  Granger causality: 301–303
  immediate causation: 35, 46
  inferences about: 9, 10
  material causation: 42
  necessary conditions: 32, 41
  pull-type causation: 33, 41
  push-type causation: 33
  sufficient conditions: 32
central subjects: 39, 97
change
  competence-destroying: 70
  competence-enhancing: 70
  components of: 120–121
  constructive: 68
  first-order: 68, 70
  incremental: 70
  modeling: 378–379
  prescribed: 68
  qualitative: 32
  quantitative: 32
  radical: 70
  second-order: 68, 69, 70
chaos: 310, 328, 333
  theory: 3
chronicles: 149–151
cluster analysis: 254